The Complete Handbook of CONDITIONING FOR SOCCER

CONDITIONING FOR SOCCER

Dr. RAYMOND VERHEIJEN (Ed.)

WITH ASSISTANCE FROM:

Dr. GERARD VAN DER POEL
FOPPE DE HAAN
Dr. LUC VAN AGT
FRANS HOEK
BERT VAN LINGEN
VERA PAUW
Dr. HAN INKLAAR
Dr. FRITS KESSEL
ROB OUDERLAND

INTERVIEWS WITH:

RUUD GULLIT
HANS WESTERHOF
HUUB STEVENS
FRANK RIJKAARD
DANNY BLIND
RONALD KOEMAN
DICK ADVOCAAT
RONALD DE BOER
EDWIN VAN DER SAR
RINUS MICHELS
YVONNE VAN DER POL
LEO BEENHAKKER
CEES-REIN V.D. HOOGENBAND
MARC OVERMARS

WITH A FOREWORD BY   JAN REKER

PHOTOS: PAUL VAN DEN BOOGERT

For Rinus and Thea.

Published by:
REEDSWAIN VIDEOS AND BOOKS
88 Wells Road • Spring City, PA 19475 • 1-800-331-5191
www.reedswain.com

Library of Congress Cataloging - in - Publication Data

Verheijen, Dr. Raymond
The Complete Handbook of Conditioning for Soccer/Dr. Raymond Verheijen

ISBN No. 9781591642558

COPYRIGHT© 1998

This book was originally published by Uitgeverij Eisma bv, P.O. Box 340, 8901 BC Leeuwarden, The Netherlands.

All rights reserved. Except for use in a review. The reproduction or utilization of this book in any form or by any electronic, mechanical, or other means, now known or here after invented, including xerography, photocopying, and recoding, and in any information storage and retrieval system, is forbidden without written permission of the publisher.

REEDSWAIN books are available at special discounts for bulk purchase. For details contact REEDSWAIN at -1-800-331-5191.

Layout and Design: Kimberly N. Bender

Photos: Paul van den Boogert   Jan de Koning
            Ger Stolk   Hans van Tilburg
            De Voetbaltrainer

With thanks
to the subjects of the photos: **to the subjects of the photos:**
Tjalling van der Berg   Marco Boogers
Jan Derks   John van de Brom
Henk Heising   Patrick van de Gullik
Ruud Kaiser   Sergei Pemrukov
Rob Kramer   Stefan Postma
Harold van Krevelen   Richard Ruiter
Henk Mariman   Nicky Scheepens
Ricardo de Sanders   Stefan Verheijen
Michael Vlaarkamp

for the facilities: ALB Gym (Marcel Thonhauser)
                          Frans Hoek Sport (Eugene, Michel and Nancy)
                          SC Heerenveen
                          Medical Section of the KNVB (Dutch Soccer Association)
                          SC Neerlandia/SLTO
                          PSV

and also: Wytse Goud, Jaap de Groot, Chris Jansen, KNVB (Dutch Soccer Association), Hugo Maarleveld (De Tijdstroom), Auke Post.

TABLE OF CONTENTS

FOREWORD xii

INTRODUCTION 2

LEGEND 5

CHAPTER 1 • THE PHYSICAL LOAD ON SOCCER PLAYERS 6

1.1 • Introduction 6

1.2 • The Physical Load on Outfield Players 7
1.2.1 Position in the Team 8
1.2.2 The Level of Play 9
1.2.3 Style of Play 12
1.2.4 Fatigue 14

1.3 • The Physical Load on Youth Players 15
1.3.1 The Total Running Work of Youth Soccer Players 15
1.3.2 Sprinting Work of Youth Soccer Players 16
1.3.3 The Soccer Specific Work of Youth Soccer Players 16

1.4 • The Physical Load on Goalkeepers 16

1.5 • The Physical Properties Needed to Perform Soccer Work 17
1.5.1 Total Running Work: Endurance 17
1.5.2 Sprinting Work: Speed 18
1.5.3 Soccer Specific Work 20
1.5.4 Coordination 20
1.5.5 Flexibility 20

1.6 • Conclusion: The Physical Nature of Soccer is Complex 21

Summary 22

Five Practical Questions 23

Interview with Jan Wouters 24

Literature 27

CHAPTER 2 • SOCCER AND PHYSIOLOGY 28

2.1 • Introduction 28

2.2	• **The Nervous System**	29
2.2.1	The Central and Peripheral Nervous System	29
2.2.2	The Role of the Nervous System in Soccer	30
2.2.3	The Conscious and Unconscious Components	33
2.2.4	Conclusion	33

2.3	• **The Oxygen Transport System**	34
2.3.1	The Heart	34
2.3.2	Respiration	35
2.3.3	Blood	35

2.4	• **The Energy Systems**	36
2.4.1	The Oxygen System	36
2.4.2	The Phosphate System	39
2.4.3	The Lactic Acid System	40
2.4.4	Interaction Between the Energy Systems	42

2.5	• **The Muscular System**	42
2.5.1	Muscle Structure	42
2.5.2	The Various Types of Muscle Fibre	43
2.5.3	The Composition of the Muscles of Soccer Players	45

2.6	• **Conclusion**	45

Summary	46
Five Practical Questions	49
Interview with Hans Westerhof	50
Literature	53

CHAPTER 3 • THE SCIENCE OF CONDITIONING	54

3.1	• **Introduction**	54

3.2	• **The Basic Motor Properties**	54

3.3	• **Flexibility**	55
3.3.1	The Role of Flexibility in Soccer:	55
3.3.2	The Various Types of Stretching	57
3.3.3	Stretching • Fact and Fable	58
3.3.4	Flexibility Exercises for Soccer Players	60

3.4	• **Conditioning Laws**	61
3.4.1	The Overload Principle	61
3.4.2	Durability	64
3.4.3	Specificity of Conditioning	65

3.5	• **Conditioning Principles**	65
3.5.1	The Principles of the Systematic Approach	65
3.5.2	Age and Experience as the Basis for a Conditioning Program	65
3.5.3	The Principles of Intensivation	66
3.5.4	Principles of Variety	66
3.5.5	Technique as a Basis for Soccer Specific Overload Training	67
3.5.6	The Individuality Principle	67
3.6	• **Conditioning Methods**	67
3.6.1	Endurance	67
3.6.2	Speed	68
3.6.3	Strength	68
3.7	• **Forms of Training**	68
3.8	• **Structure of a Training Session**	69
3.8.1	Warming-up	69
3.8.2	Core Aspects of a Training Session	70
3.8.3	Warming-down	71
3.8.4	Variation as a Basis for Each Training Session	71
3.9	• **Conclusion**	73
Summary		74
Five Practical Questions		75
Interview with Huub Stevens		76
Literature		80
CHAPTER 4 • CONDITIONING FOR SOCCER STRENGTH		81
4.1	• **Introduction**	81
4.2	• **The Properties of Muscle Strength**	81
4.2.1	General and Specific Muscle Strength	81
4.2.2	Types of Muscle Work	82
4.3	• **The Effect of Strength Conditioning**	83
4.3.1	Improved Muscle Coordination by the Nervous System	83
4.3.2	Changes in the Muscle Itself	84
4.3.3	Strength Conditioning Effects in Beginners	84
4.3.4	Loss of Muscle Strength Through Inactivity	85
4.4	• **Soccer Strength**	85
4.4.1	Basic Strength	85
4.4.2	Kicking Strength	85

4.4.3	Jumping Strength	85
4.4.4	Strength in the Challenge	86
4.4.5	Starting Strength	86

4.5 • Muscle Work During Soccer Actions ... 86
4.5.1	Dynamic Soccer Strength	86
4.5.2	Static Soccer Strength	88
4.5.3	Explosive Strength and Fast Strength	88

4.6 • Conditioning for Soccer Strength ... 90
4.6.1	How Should Conditioning for Soccer be Carried Out	90
4.6.2	Basic Strength Conditioning	90
4.6.3	Conditioning for Kicking Strength	93
4.6.4	Conditioning for Jumping Strength	94
4.6.5	Conditioning for Strength in the Challenge	96
4.6.6	Conditioning for Starting Strength	98
4.6.7	Conditioning for Eccentric Soccer Strength	100
4.6.8	Integrating Strength Conditioning	101
4.6.9	Dosing Soccer Related Strength Conditioning	101
4.6.10	Position Specific Strength Conditioning	101

4.7 • General Strength Conditioning for Soccer Players ... 102

4.8 • Drawing-up a Strength Conditioning Program ... 103
4.8.1	Step-by-Step Plan	103
4.8.2	The Maximal Test	104

4.9 • Methods of Conditioning for General Strength ... 104

4.10 • Organization of General Strength Conditioning ... 105
4.10.1	Station Drills	105
4.10.2	Small Pyramid Drill	105
4.10.3	Broad Pyramid Drill	106
4.10.4	Contrast Method	106
4.10.5	Circuit Training	107

4.11 • Drills for General Strength Conditioning ... 107

Summary ... 114

Five Practical Questions ... 115

Interview with Frank Rijkaard ... 116

Literature ... 116

CHAPTER 5 • SPRINT AND COORDINATION CONDITIONING FOR SOCCER PLAYERS ... 119

5.1 • Introduction ... 119

5.2 • General Soccer Related Sprint Conditioning ... 120
5.2.1 Start Speed ... 120
5.2.2 Acceleration ... 120
5.2.3 Speed Endurance ... 122
5.2.4 Repeated Short Sprint Capacity ... 123
5.2.5 Planning Sprint Conditioning ... 124
5.2.6 Position-Specific Sprint Conditioning ... 124

5.3 • Coordination Conditioning ... 125
5.3.1 The Ideal Sprinting Technique ... 125
5.3.2 Coordination Conditioning to Improve Speed ... 125
5.3.3 Integrated Coordination Conditioning ... 127

5.4 • General Coordination Conditioning ... 127
5.4.1 Soccer Action Can Never Be Viewed In Isolation ... 128
5.4.2 It is Never too Soon to Learn ... 129
5.4.3 The Growth Spurt ... 130
5.4.4 When Should Coordination Conditioning be Carried Out ... 130

Summary ... 131

Five Practical Questions ... 132

Interview with Danny Blind ... 133

Literature ... 135

CHAPTER 6 • CONDITIONING FOR SOCCER FITNESS ... 136

6.1 • Introduction ... 136

6.2 • Soccer Fitness ... 136
6.2.1 The Utility of Good Soccer Fitness ... 136
6.2.2 How Should Soccer Fitness be Conditioned ... 137

6.3 • Endurance ... 138
6.3.1 Conditioning for Acyclic Aerobic Endurance ... 138
6.3.2 Conditioning for Acyclic Anaerobic Endurance ... 141

6.4 • Soccer Related Sprint Conditioning ... 143
6.4.1 Reaction Speed and Starting Speed ... 143
6.4.2 Acceleration ... 143

| 6.4.3 | Speed Endurance | 144 |
| 6.4.4 | Repeated Short Sprint Capacity | 144 |

6.5 • Periodization 145
6.5.1	Conditioning Plan	145
6.5.2	The Extent and Intensity of Training Sessions	146
6.5.3	General and Specific Training	146

Summary 149

Five Practical Questions 150

Interview with Ronald Koeman 151

Literature 154

Training Situations 155

CHAPTER 7 • PREPARATION FOR A NEW SEASON 175

7.1 • Introduction 175

7.2 • The Purpose of the Preparation 175
7.2.1	The Vacation Break	175
7.2.2	Building-up Match Fitness	176
7.2.3	Changes in the Squad and/or the Style of Play	176

7.3 • A Fit Start Saves Time 176

7.4 • Structure of the Preparation Program 177
7.4.1	From General to Specific Conditioning	177
7.4.2	From Extent to Intensity	178
7.4.3	The Work-to-Rest Ratio	178
7.4.4	Building-up Acyclic Aerobic Endurance	179
7.4.5	Building-up Acyclic Anaerobic Endurance	180
7.4.6	Building-up Soccer Strength	180
7.4.7	Building-up Speed	181
7.4.8	Integrated Conditioning	182
7.4.9	Linking Soccer Conditioning to Soccer Objectives: Specific Soccer Related Conditioning	182

7.5 • General Guidelines for Pre-season Preparation in Relation to the Standard of Play 182
7.5.1	Professionals	183
7.5.2	Top Amateurs	183
7.5.3	Competitive Players	183
7.5.4	Recreational Players	184

7.6	• Strength Training Sessions and Matches: A Possible Conflict	184
7.7	• The Winter Break	184

Summary 185

Five Practical Questions 187

Interview with Dick Advocaat 188

Literature 192

CHAPTER 8 • TESTING SOCCER PLAYERS' FITNESS 193

8.1	• Introduction	193
8.2	• The Utility of Fitness Tests	193
8.3	• What Physical Parameters Should be Tested?	194
8.4	• Soccer-Specific Fitness Tests	194
8.4.1	Speed off the Mark: the 10 meter sprint test	195
8.4.2	Acceleration: the 30 meter sprint test	195
8.4.3	Speed Endurance: the shuttle sprint test	195
8.4.4	Repeated Short Sprint Capacity: the interval sprint test	196
8.4.5	Acyclic Aerobic Endurance: the shuttle run test	197
8.4.6	Acyclic Anaerobic Endurance: the shuttle tempo test	198
8.5	• When Must All of These Various Tests Be Carried Out?	198
8.6	• Standardization	199
8.7	• Test Standards	200
8.8	• Post Mortem	200

Summary 201

Five Practical Questions 202

Interview with Ronald de Boer 203

Literature 205

CHAPTER 9 • THE PHYSICAL ASPECTS OF GOALKEEPING 206

9.1	• Introduction	206

9.2	• What Does a Goalkeeper do During a Game?	206
9.3	• The Frans Hoek Philosophy	207
9.3.1	The Task and Function of the Goalkeeper in the Team	207
9.3.2	Possession	208
9.3.3	Opposition in Possession	209
9.3.4	The Moment When Possession is Lost to the Opposition	210
9.3.5	The Moment When Possession is Won from the Opposition	211
9.3.6	Technique, Insight, Communication	212
9.3.7	The Match Ingredients from a Goalkeeper's Point of View	212
9.3.8	Conclusion	213
9.4	• The "Frans Hoek Method"	212
9.5	• The Framework Conditions	214
9.5.1	The Coaching Staff: composition and cooperation	214
9.5.2	Training Resources	214
9.6	• The Goalkeeper's Soccer Fitness	215
9.6.1	Speed	215
9.6.2	Endurance	216
9.6.3	Strength	217
9.6.4	Flexibility	217
9.6.5	Coordination	217
9.7	• Conditioning Goalkeeping Fitness	218
9.7.1	Speed	219
9.7.2	Acyclic Aerobic Endurance	223
9.7.3	Strength	225
9.7.4	Flexibility and Coordination	231
9.8	• The Structure of the Season for Goalkeepers	232
9.8.1	The Structure of the Season in Terms of Time	232
9.8.2	Content of the Soccer Season	232
9.8.3	Take the Goalkeeper's Phase of Development into Account	234
9.9	• Physical Conditioning of Young Goalkeepers	234
9.10	• How Young Goalkeepers Should Look After Themselves	236
9.10.1	How to Handle Injuries	236
9.10.2	Personal Hygiene	236
9.10.3	Good Equipment Prevents Injuries	236
Summary		239
Five Practical Questions		241

Interview with Edwin Van Der Sar 242

Literature 244

CHAPTER 10 • CONDITIONING FOR YOUNG SOCCER PLAYERS 245

10.1 • Introduction 245

10.2 • What are the Important Aspects of Youth Soccer? 245

10.3 • Who are Young Soccer Players? 247

10.4 • You Learn to Play Soccer by Playing Soccer 249

10.5 • Better Soccer, More Pleasure: '4 against 4' 251
10.5.1 '4 against 4' 251
10.5.2 The Rules of '4 against 4' 252

10.6 • Soccer Training is Conditioning;
Conditioning is Soccer Training 253

10.7 • Youth Soccer, Soccer for Boys and Girls 254
10.7.1 Mixed Soccer 254
10.7.2 Difference Between Boys and Girls 256
10.7.3 The Future of Women's Soccer 256

Summary 259

Five Practical Questions 261

Interview with Rinus Michels 262

Literature 265

CHAPTER 11 • NUTRITION AND SOCCER 266

11.1 • Introduction 266

11.2 • General Nutritional Principles 266
11.2.1 Carbohydrates 267
11.2.2 Fat 268
11.2.3 Proteins 269
11.2.4 What Fuel is Used When? 270
11.2.5 Water 271

11.3 • Nutrition in Relation to Soccer Performance 272
11.3.1 Glycogen: the 'soccer fuel' 272

| 11.3.2 | The Influence of Glycogen on Soccer Performance | 273 |

11.4 • Nutritional Guidelines for Soccer Players 273
11.4.1	The Daily Diet	273
11.4.2	Carbohydrate Intake Before a Match	275
11.4.3	Carbohydrate Intake During a Match	276
11.4.4	Carbohydrate Intake After a Match	277
11.4.5	Carbohydrate Intake Before, During and After Training Sessions	277
11.4.6	The Importance of Fluid for Soccer Players	278

11.5 • The Energy Balance 279
11.5.1	The Ideal Body Weight on the Basis of Height	280
11.5.2	The Quetelet Index	280
11.5.3	The Percentage of Body Fat	282

11.6 • Nutrition in Relation to Health 283
11.6.1	Vitamins	286
11.6.2	Minerals	288
11.6.3	Trace Elements	289
11.6.4	Conclusion	289

Summary 291

Five Practical Questions 293

Interview with Yvonne Van Der Pol 294

Literature 297

CHAPTER 12 • INJURIES AT VARIOUS LEVELS 298

12.1 • Introduction 298

12.2 • The Seriousness and Extent of Soccer Injuries 299
12.2.1	What is a Soccer Injury?	299
12.2.2	The Extent of Soccer Injuries	299
12.2.3	The Seriousness of Soccer Injuries	300

12.3 • The Causes of Soccer Injuries 300
| 12.3.1 | External Risk Factors | 301 |
| 12.3.2 | Personal Risk factor | 303 |

12.4 • The Problem of Injuries in Practice 304
| 12.4.1 | Selection: the creation of various playing levels | 304 |
| 12.4.2 | At Which Standard of Play is the Risk Greatest? | 305 |

12.5 • Research Results 306
| 12.5.1 | Differences Between Playing Levels | 306 |

| 12.5.2 The Type and Location of Soccer Injuries | 306 |

Summary 309

Five Practical Questions 310

Interview with Leo Beenhakker 312

Literature 315

CHAPTER 13 • THE EMERGENCY TREATMENT OF SOCCER INJURIES 316

13.1 • Introduction 316

13.2 • First-Aid on the Soccer Pitch 316

13.3 • Treatment and Prevention of Soccer Injuries 317
13.3.1 Nosebleed 317
13.3.2 Scrapes 317
13.3.3 Blisters 318
13.3.4 Cuts 319
13.3.5 Bruises 319
13.3.6 Sprains 319
13.3.7 Dislocations 320
13.3.8 Bursal Damage 322
13.3.9 Muscle Cramp 322
13.3.10 Torn Muscles 323
13.3.11 Tendinitis 324
13.3.12 Fractures 324
13.3.13 Cartilage Injuries 325
13.3.14 Meniscus Injuries 325
13.3.15 Various Injuries 326

13.4 • The Task of a Doctor in the Locker Room and on the Pitch 326

Summary 328

Five Practical Questions 329

Interview with Dr. Cees-Rein Van de Hoogenband 330

LIterature 334

CHAPTER 14 • PHYSIOTHERAPY IN SOCCER 335

14.1	Introduction 335

14.2 • Tasks of the Physiotherapist Before, During and After Matches and Sessions 336
14.2.1 Specific Tasks Before Matches and Training Sessions 336
14.2.2 Specific Tasks During Matches and Training Sessions 337
14.2.3 Specific Tasks After Matches and Training Sessions 337

14.3 • The Role The Physiotherapist During the Rehabilitation Process 337
14.3.1 Anamnesis 338
14.3.2 The Examination 339
14.3.3 Examination of Physical Function 341
14.3.4 Making a Diagnosis 341

14.4 • Various Phases of Connective Tissue Recovery 341
14.4.1 The Inflammation Phase 342
14.4.2 The Proliferation Phase (3 days to 3 weeks) 342
14.4.3 The Remodeling Phase (3 weeks to 3 months) 343
14.4.4 The Functional Phase 344
14.4.5 Central Points of Attention During the Recovery Process 345

Summary 361

Interview with Marc Overmars 363

Literature 366

The Authors 367

FOREWORD

REQUIRED READING

Modern soccer is evolving at the speed of an express train. Ever increasing technical, tactical, mental and - especially in recent years - physical demands are made on the players. In the Netherlands we are so sure of ourselves that we put the emphasis on technical and tactical problems. In the modern game, however, these problems can only be solved if you also have the necessary physical qualities. You cannot make it at the top without strength, speed and agility.

"Just getting by" is no longer an option. Coaches who take their job seriously have to keep up with the latest developments. That should not be too difficult in the field of conditioning, thanks to the publication of this book. As I read it, I realized with growing admiration that author Raymond Verheijen has succeeded in incorporating all of the new approaches, while still retaining all that was and remains of value.

One frequent disadvantage of manuals is that they are highly theoretical. From his scientific articles in the Dutch magazine "The Soccer Coach," we know that Verheijen is capable of making the connection to actual practice. He has brilliantly succeeded in doing so again in this book. To do this, he has called on a large number of specialists, whose contributions give an added dimension to the whole work.

As the director of the CBV (the Dutch Professional Coaches Association), I travel to a lot of countries. Everywhere I go, I find that Dutch soccer is greatly respected. Soccer is well organized in the Netherlands. Our coaching courses, for example, are of such a high standard that other countries look at us with envy.

The publication of this book about conditioning, which I regard as required reading for every coaching course, can only serve to increase the admiration for Dutch soccer.

Jan Reker

Director, Dutch Professional Soccer Coaches Association

INTRODUCTION

For many years there has been too much emphasis on the physical side of soccer, with players being subjected to hours of general fitness training. However, attitudes have recently started to change. There has been a growing appreciation that, in soccer, physical fitness is simply a means towards achieving soccer objectives, and should never be an objective in itself. The basis of good soccer conditioning is not just correct training but also a healthy body. There have also been a lot of changes in the medical support and supervision of soccer players in recent years. More attention is being paid to diet and nutrition, fitness tests, injury prevention and rehabilitation, and physiotherapy. Soccer is a complex sport, however, and a host of factors can affect the final result. As a consequence there is no single ideal way of conditioning soccer players or providing proper (medical) support and supervision. This handbook contains a whole range of contemporary soccer concepts. They are all based on situations that are encountered during play. Conditioning training must always incorporate characteristic elements of the actual game. Drills and exercises that are typical of, and specific to, soccer can therefore best be used.

1. **General soccer-related conditioning training:** this type of training does not involve playing soccer but approximates soccer situations as closely as possible. Sprinting exercises, for example, contain soccer ingredients such as turning and changing direction, stopping and accelerating. During endurance training the interval principle must be applied. This type of training is suitable for establishing the conditional basis needed to play soccer at a certain level.

2. **Specific soccer-related conditioning training:** this involves conditioning players to deal with soccer situations on the basis of what is required in a given match situation. During a game, players always sprint and jump for a purpose, such as to keep the ball in play or to head a cross towards the goal. The purpose of the training situations referred to here is therefore related to specific soccer situations. This type of conditioning is intended to develop a player's basic fitness a stage further and to make him "match fit."

This handbook consists of three parts. First of all a coach must know exactly what happens during the game if he is to improve the conditioning of his players. Chapter 1 contains facts and figures concerning the loads that soccer players have to cope with. In Chapter 2 the physiological systems at the basis of the work done while playing soccer are examined in more detail. The nervous system occupies a central place in the treatment of this topic. The first part of the book closes with Chapter 3, which looks at the laws and principles of conditioning that can be applied to improve the various physiological processes. In addition Gerard van der Poel throws fresh light on the debate concerning the benefits of stretching exercises.

Chapter 4 is the first real "conditioning chapter." The key point made in this chapter is that strength conditioning is not so much concerned with developing bigger and stronger muscles but rather with improving the technique and coordination of various soccer movements. Speed is perhaps the most important physical attribute required by a modern soccer player. Chapter 5 is therefore devoted to general soccer-related sprint conditioning. A player needs more than just pure speed, however; he also needs to time his start to perfection, and to take up good positions. This can only be learned by playing a lot of soccer; general soccer-related sprint conditioning is not sufficient on its own. Chapter 6 therefore deals with specific soccer-related sprint conditioning. The same chapter also explains how to improve endurance. Long-distance runs fell out of favor with coaches long ago, and Foppe de Haan draws on his many years of experience to explain what types of soccer drills are suitable for conditioning soccer players' endurance. A successful soccer season depends on a well balanced period of pre-season preparation. In Chapter 7 Luc van Agt describes how soccer fitness can be built up gradually. A central aspect is the transition from general to specific soccer-related conditioning.

A real match is always the best test of a player's condition. However, a coach sometimes needs more information. The physical condition of the players is always the starting point for drawing up a training program. Chapter 8 is a good guide for anyone who wants to test soccer players' physical fitness.

Physical fitness is just as important for goalkeepers as for the other players in the team. There are, however, differences in the approach to aspects such as strength and speed. In Chapter 9 Frans Hoek explains how the various elements of conditioning for goalkeepers can best be dealt with during training. In doing so he uses only conditioning exercises based on genuine match situations.

Anyone who watches a game of soccer between two youth teams can see that moves do not break down because of lack of strength or stamina. In Chapter 10 Bert van Lingen points out that young players are often let down by their lack of technical skills and insight. In the same chapter Vera Pouw emphasizes that both boys and girls can play youth soccer. Incidentally, we have used only the "he" form in this handbook for reasons of convenience, but this is a soccer book and is therefore intended for both sexes.

The final four chapters of the book are devoted to the (medical) supervision of soccer players. First of all the role of nutrition is discussed in Chapter 11. Carbohydrates in particular have a significant influence on soccer performance.

Han Inklaar has written a thesis on the problem of injuries at various playing levels. In Chapter 12 he demonstrates that more injuries occur at the higher playing levels, despite the better medical support and supervision that is available. Such support and supervision cannot compensate for the higher levels of aggression during matches. There is much room for improvement in the field of injury prevention.

If a player is injured it is very important that first-aid is directly available and correctly applied. In Chapter 13 Frits Kessel specifies the guidelines that should be followed when dealing with the most common soccer injuries. Correctly applied first-aid can sometimes shorten the length of the rehabilitation period considerably.

The physiotherapist is now an indispensable part of the medical staff. We therefore include a chapter on physiotherapy in soccer. Rob Ouderland sketches the steps that a physiotherapist has to take during a player's period of rehabilitation from a hamstring injury. This is intended as guidance for physiotherapists who need to treat this, the most prevalent and troublesome of soccer injuries.

As a means of ensuring the handbook's practical relevance, a survey was carried out among 50 Dutch soccer coaches who are active at various levels. The coaches were asked whether they had any questions about the book's content. All of the questions received have been dealt with in the various chapters. Moreover the five most frequently asked questions on each topic have been answered by the author of the relevant chapter. Each chapter closes with an interview. A coach or player from the professional soccer world states his views on some of the subjects dealt with in the relevant chapter. Huub Stevens explains the differences in the training methods of German and Dutch soccer clubs; Frank Rijkaard reveals that skill rather than pure strength is required to win the ball; Ronald de Boer relates how he felt when he was first confronted with fitness tests; and Marc Overmars sketches a picture of the rehabilitation process he went through with the Dutch Soccer Association's medical section in Zeist.

All in all, I hope that this handbook will make a contribution toward improving the quality of soccer training and that it will stimulate discussion of soccer conditioning. The most important message that I would like to give all coaches is that they should never blindly follow the lessons of this book. The handbook assumes an ideal situation, but a coach should always give due consideration to what his players can and cannot do, and the conditions under which they have to train. If you have any questions while you are reading this handbook, or while you are trying to put its lessons into practice, you are welcome to contact the author. He will be glad to consider any comments or suggestions that can result in improvements.

Finally, I would like to thank the co-authors who helped to create this handbook. It took two years of hard work, but I hope that you found it just as satisfying as I did. Thank you for your endurance.

Raymond Verheijen
Amsterdam, October 1997

Legend

△	Attacker
○	Defender
Ⓚ	Goalkeeper
⊗	Coach/neutral player
△ (circled)	Neutral player
→	Path of the ball
----→	Path of player without the ball
wwww→	Line dribbled by player with ball
⇒	Goalscoring attempt
①,②,③ etc.	Players' numbers
1 , 2 , 3	Sequence of drills
△ (cone)	Cone
●	Ball
▭	Full-size goal
▭	Goal measuring 16' x 6'
▭	Small goal (6' x 6')

CHAPTER 1

THE PHYSICAL LOAD ON SOCCER PLAYERS

Dr. Raymond Verheijen

1.1 INTRODUCTION

Training for sport is always concerned with the balance between load and loading capacity. In this context load is the resistance that the body has to overcome when engaging in sporting activity, and loading capacity is the maximum resistance that the body can cope with. During training, loads are imposed on players with the aim of increasing their loading capacity. If the load persistently exceeds the loading capacity, however, overstrain may occur. The game of soccer is becoming faster and faster, and the intensity of the play is increasing. In addition more games are being played, especially at the professional level, and the intervals between games are more irregular. In other words, the load on the players is steadily increasing. Modern soccer requires players to have more strength and endurance. Players who are in physically good condition (and therefore have a high loading capacity) are still able to perform at a high level of efficiency during the final phase of a match, and this can make all the difference between winning and losing. The aim of this chapter is to explain the relationship between load and loading capacity in soccer by sketching the physical load that soccer players have to cope with. It shows that soccer players not only have to do a lot of running but also carry out all sorts of other strength-sapping activities during a match. Chapter 2 looks at the loading capacity of soccer players. The players are not all exposed to the same load, and load also varies with circumstances. Factors such as a player's position in the team, the level and style of play, and fatigue all influence the ways in which a player expends effort on the field of play. The influence of all these factors on the total amount of work (running, sprinting, soccer-specific tasks) he performs is explained and backed up with facts and figures. It is important, however, to focus on the message behind the figures rather than the figures themselves. This information can be used as an aid to determining the physical parameters that are of most significance for soccer players. A coach can gear his training sessions more effectively to an upcoming match if he has accurate match data. This sort of data can also be of use to physiotherapists and rehabilitation trainers, who have to make a player match fit again after a long-term injury.

1.2 THE PHYSICAL LOAD ON OUTFIELD PLAYERS

The physical load on soccer players is the work they have to perform while running and carrying out soccer-specific tasks. Their running work can be broken down into a number of categories, expressed as distance covered (see Fig. 1.1). For reasons of clarity, only the total distance covered and the distances walked, jogged, run and sprinted are given. The distances covered during other activities are virtually negligible. The distance covered, however, does not give a complete picture of the physical load on soccer players. A detailed analysis of a game of soccer shows that the players also engage in activities such as jumping, shooting and tackling. All of these activities cost strength and increase the physical load on soccer players. Players who compete at various levels of Dutch soccer have been filmed for the purpose of obtaining an indication of the physical load with which they have to cope. The five levels involved were:

- the Dutch professional league
- top class Dutch Soccer Association league
- second class Dutch Soccer Association league
- fifth class Dutch Soccer Association league
- top division of the Under 18 youth league

Activity	Description
Walking	Moving forward, always with at least one foot on the ground
Jogging	Running slowly
Running	Running fast and purposefully, but not flat out
Sprinting	Running flat out
Walking Sideways	Every movement in a sideways direction
Walking Backwards	Moving backwards, always with at least on foot on the ground
Jogging Backwards	Every movement in a backward direction except walking
Movement in possession	Every movement carried out when in possession of the ball

Figure 1.1:
Description of the various activities that make up the running work of a soccer player.

The physical load on soccer players can be determined by filming matches and carrying out computer analysis.

The work carried out by three defenders, three midfielders and three attackers at each of these levels was analyzed. This chapter also refers to the results of an earlier study of the work performed by English professionals.

	Walking	Jogging	Running	Sprinting	Total
Defenders					
Professional league	3.2 km	2.0 km	1.4 km	1.4 km	8.4 km
Top class amateurs	3.2 km	1.8 km	0.8 km	0.7 km	7.2 km
2nd class amateurs	4.2 km	1.7 km	0.7 km	0.5 km	7.6 km
5th class amateurs	5.0 km	1.2 km	0.4 km	0.3 km	7.5 km
Under 18 juniors	3.0 km	2.5 km	1.2 km	0.9 km	8.0 km
Midfielders					
Professional league	2.6 km	5.2 km	1.8 km	1.1 km	10.9 km
Top class amateurs	2.5 km	4.0 km	1.3 km	0.7 km	9.1 km
2nd class amateurs	3.1 km	3.3 km	1.0 km	0.6 km	9.0 km
5th class amateurs	4.5 km	2.0 km	0.6 km	0.3 km	8.4 km
Under 18 juniors	1.9 km	5.9 km	1.2 km	0.8 km	10.7 km
Attackers					
Professional league	3.4 km	2.0 km	1.6 km	1.8 km	9.8 km
Top class amateurs	3.2 km	1.9 km	0.8 km	1.2 km	7.8 km
2nd class amateurs	4.0 km	1.4 km	1.0 km	0.9 km	7.6 km
5th class amateurs	5.5 km	1.1 km	0.6 km	0.5 km	8.0 km
Under 18 juniors	4.6 km	2.2 km	1.0 km	1.3 km	9.3 km

Figure 1.2: *Running work carried out by Dutch soccer players in different positions and at different playing levels.*

1.2.1
Position in the team

Although modern players have to be able to play in various positions, it remains true that each position in the team is associated with a number of specific tasks. To what extent does this influence the amount of work that a player performs?

Total running work per position

It is generally recognized that midfielders cover the greatest distance, and defenders the least, during a match. The total amount of running work therefore depends on player's position. This is true at all levels of play (see Fig. 1.2).
Midfielders have to cover the greatest distance owing to their role in the team. They have to operate in the zone between defense and

Player A	as defender:	9.3 km and 9.4 km
	as midfielder:	11.9 km
Player B	as defender:	12.5 km and 12.7 km
	as attacker:	10.5 km
Player C	as attacker:	10.2 km, 10.4 km and 10.4 km
	as midfielder:	12.2 km

Figure 1.3: *Positional dependency of the running work carried out by three soccer players.*

attack. When their team is in possession of the ball they have to support their attackers by bringing the ball forward, linking up with the attackers and being available to receive passes. When the opposition has possession the midfielders have to assist their defenders by defending as far away from their own goal as possible, and by covering behind the defenders when necessary. The difference in the total distance covered is attributable to the amount of walking and jogging carried out by the midfielders. Midfielders frequently have to jog, whereas defenders can make do with walking when their team is in possession, and the same applies to attackers when the opposing team has possession. Midfielders are almost constantly in action. A soccer player does roughly the same amount of running in each game, provided he plays in the same position. If he changes position then the amount of running also changes. The amount of running done by a defender who has to play in midfield is closer to that of a midfielder (see Fig. 1.3).

There are also differences between players in the same line of the team (see Fig. 1.4). This is because a group of attackers (or defenders or midfielders) is not homogeneous and cannot therefore be looked at as such. Attackers may be wingers, advanced strikers (center forwards) or withdrawn strikers who play slightly deeper than their center forward. The wingers themselves may also differ in style, with the one functioning as a "genuine" outside forward while the other tends to play much deeper. The coach will expect these different types of winger to carry out different tasks.

Figure 1.4: *The running work carried out by six English professionals who play in the same team. There are considerable differences in the type and amount of running work within the various lines of the team.*

	Walking	Jogging	Running	Sprinting	Total
Central defender	4.2 km	2.7 km	0.5 km	0.2 km	8.4 km
Full-back	2.8 km	4.2 km	1.3 km	0.3 km	9.8 km
Defensive Midfielders	2.4 km	9.4 km	0.6 km	0.1 km	14.3 km
Offensive Midfielders	2.2 km	6.8 km	2.6 km	0.4 km	12.8 km
Withdrawn striker	2.2 km	5.0 km	0.6 km	0.4 km	10.6 km
Central striker	4.4 km	2.1 km	1.3 km	0.9 km	9.8 km

Sprinting work per position

Figure 1.5 shows the sprinting work carried out by soccer players, again expressed in terms of the distance covered. At every level of play, attackers sprint more than defenders and midfielders. This difference is attributable to the number of short forward sprints (1 - 5 yards and 5-10 yards) attackers carry out. This comes about because attackers are usually closely marked, and therefore need to make short sprints to get away from their direct opponent. Midfielders have to make more long sprints (30 - 40 yards and more) as a consequence of their linking role between defense and attack. When possession of the ball changes, a midfielder often has to sprint half the length of the field to assist in defense or link up with his attackers.

Soccer-specific work per position

The soccer-specific work carried out by the players also differs from position to position (see Fig. 1.6). Defenders and attackers jump to head the ball most often. The logical explanation for this is that heading opportunities frequently occur in and around the penalty area, when corners or free kicks are taken or the goalkeeper kicks the ball upfield. Soccer is a physical sport, in which a certain degree of bodily contact is allowed. Players compete for possession of the ball during the whole 90 minutes of the game. During these challenges the players brace themselves so that an opponent cannot get to the ball. Midfielders are most frequently involved in such challenges. Coaches often claim that a game is won or lost in midfield. They regard the ability to win the ball as one of the most important keys to success. Midfielders have the most shots at goal, and defenders make the most sliding tackles.

	Total Sprinting Distance	Total Number of Sprints	1-5 yards	5-10 yards	10-20 yards	20-30 yards	30-40 yards	40+ yards	Maximum Distance
Defenders									
Professional league	1.4 km	162	83	47	18	8	4	2	56 yds
Top class amateurs	0.7 km	111	71	22	10	4	3	1	49 yds
2nd class amateurs	0.5 km	62	33	14	8	3	2	2	62 yds
5th class amateurs	0.3 km	48	28	11	5	3	1	0	36 yds
Under 18 juniors	0.9 km	101	54	24	12	6	3	3	54 yds
Midfielders									
Professional league	1.1 km	127	70	31	11	6	6	3	63 yds
Top class amateurs	0.7 km	92	59	12	9	5	4	3	56 yds
2nd class amateurs	0.6 km	69	44	11	5	3	4	2	66 yds
5th class amateurs	0.3 km	51	35	6	4	4	1	1	48 yds
Under 18 juniors	0.8 km	94	57	14	11	6	4	2	66 yds
Attackers									
Professional league	1.8 km	183	76	59	28	14	4	2	53 yds
Top class amateurs	1.2 km	127	67	32	16	7	3	2	56 yds
2nd class amateurs	0.9 km	99	52	26	13	4	2	2	55 yds
5th class amateurs	0.5 km	66	41	12	10	3	0	1	49 yds
Under 18 juniors	1.4 km	134	54	21	21	8	3	1	51 yds

Figure 1.5: *Overview of the sprinting work carried out by soccer players over various distances.*

	Sliding Tackles	Jumping	Shooting	Challenges	Total
Defenders					
Professional league	9x	15x	24x	34x	82
Top class amateurs	11x	17x	27x	42x	97
2nd class amateurs	19x	23x	19x	37x	98
5th class amateurs	16x	15x	37x	51x	119
Under 18 juniors	18x	21x	27x	39x	117
Midfielders					
Professional league	6x	11x	37x	56x	110
Top class amateurs	6x	11x	32x	38x	87
2nd class amateurs	19x	9x	32x	42x	102
5th class amateurs	16x	14x	41x	29x	100
Under 18 juniors	8x	12x	37x	51x	108
Attackers					
Professional league	6x	17x	32x	36x	91
Top class amateurs	4x	24x	26x	28x	82
2nd class amateurs	7x	22x	19x	24x	72
5th class amateurs	14x	16x	18x	29x	77
Under 18 juniors	10x	10x	30x	43x	93

Figure 1.6: *Soccer-specific work carried out by Dutch soccer players in various positions and at various playing levels.*

1.2.2 The level of play

Every soccer fan knows that more physical effort is involved in playing professional soccer than amateur soccer. But how much more? The only way to answer this is to analyze and compare the work performed at each level of play.

Total running work per playing level

Soccer players at lower levels do less running, and they tend to walk and jog more. The amount of running and sprinting decreases with the level of play. There is a shift from more intensive to less intensive work. This demonstrates that the total distance covered does not give the full picture. The ways in which the distance is covered are more important. The higher the playing level, the higher the proportion of running and sprinting. A midfielder in a fifth class team and a defender in a Dutch professional league team both cover an average of 8.4 kilometers (5.25 miles) per game. At first sight this seems remarkable, but closer analysis reveals that the professional defender runs and sprints 2.5 kilometers (1.6 miles), whereas the equivalent figure for the amateur midfielder is "only" 0.9 kilometers (0.5 miles). These figures succinctly reflect the difference between professional and amateur soccer. More specific, intensive work has to be performed at the higher level. A comparison of the various levels of play in the Netherlands confirms that, in absolute terms, the load on the players decreases in direct relationship to the level at which they play. Of course, it should not be forgotten that the level of physical fitness of players in the fifth class is generally not high (i.e. they have a lower loading capacity). This means that 7 kilometers (4.4 miles) are just as strenuous for a midfielder in this class as 9 kilometers (5.5 miles) for a midfielder in the highest amateur league.

Good soccer players are not just fast; they also time their runs perfectly.

Every team needs piano removers and piano players.

Jan Boskamp

Sprinting work per playing level

Soccer players in the lower leagues sprint less. This is true of all three types of players. Closer analysis reveals that the main difference is in the number of short sprints. Professional soccer players make many more sprints than players in the top amateur league, and this trend continues through the lower playing levels. This indicates the importance of speed over the first few yards in professional soccer. In soccer, however, quality is more important than quantity when it comes to sprinting. This is another factor that marks the difference between the various playing levels. The better players are not just faster but are also more likely to choose the right moment to start a sprint.

Soccer-specific work per playing level

There are big differences between the various playing levels in terms of soccer-specific work. The increase in the number of sliding tackles and challenges for the ball during matches in the fifth class is very noticeable. This is an indication that the game is more physical at this level. The players are more inclined to look for physical solutions to soccer problems in order to compensate for their technical and tactical shortcomings.

Another consequence of the lower level of ability is the slower pace of the game. The players' speed of action is slower, so that their opponents have more chance of getting closer to them. This increases the chance of physical contact occurring.

1.2.3 Style of play

Modern soccer is characterized by the large number of tasks that coaches expect their players to fulfill. Many teams play to a tactical concept, in which each player in each position has specific responsibilities. Moreover different countries have different traditional styles of play and ideas of how the game should be played. There is the Brazilian "samba" soccer, for example, or English "kick and rush," and Dutch "total" soccer. Differences in style of play can result in differences in the way in which players move about the field.

Total running work per style of play

Some soccer players rely on their running ability, others rely on stopping their opponents from running.

Han Fennema

If the data collected in England and the Netherlands are compared, it can be seen that Dutch professional soccer players cover less ground during a game than their English counterparts (see Fig. 1.7). Dutch teams let the ball do more of the work, whereas it is well known that English players keep running for the whole 90 minutes. Figure 1.8 shows a comparison of the total number of runs made by English and Dutch professionals

	Walking	Jogging	Running	Sprinting	Total
Defenders					
Netherlands	3.2 km	2.0 km	1.4 km	1.4 km	8.4 km
England	2.2 km	4.6 km	0.6 km	0.1 km	9.0 km
Midfielders					
Netherlands	2.6 km	5.2 km	1.8 km	1.1 km	10.9 km
England	2.8 km	7.0 km	0.8 km	0.2 km	12.1 km
Attackers					
Netherlands	3.4 km	2.0 km	1.6 km	1.8 km	9.8 km
England	3.5 km	4.0 km	1.2 km	0.4 km	10.4 km

	Sliding Tackles	Jumping	Shooting	Challenges	Total
Defenders					
Netherlands	3.2 km	2.0 km	1.4 km	1.4 km	8.4 km
England	2.2 km	4.6 km	0.6 km	0.1 km	9.0 km
Midfielders					
Netherlands	2.6 km	5.2 km	1.8 km	1.1 km	10.9 km
England	2.8 km	7.0 km	0.8 km	0.2 km	12.1 km
Attackers					
Netherlands	3.4 km	2.0 km	1.6 km	1.8 km	9.8 km
England	3.5 km	4.0 km	1.2 km	0.4 km	10.4 km

Figure 1.7: *The running work and the soccer-specific work carried out by Dutch and English professionals.*

	Total number of runs
Defenders	
Netherlands	1557
England	1313
Midfielders	
Netherlands	1570
England	1257
Attackers	
Netherlands	1473
England	1297

Figure 1.8: *The difference in the number of runs made by Dutch and English Professionals.*

during the course of a soccer match. The number of runs is higher in the Netherlands because the pace of the game is constantly changing, whereas in England the same high pace tends to be maintained all the time. In the Netherlands, periods of rapid end-to-end play are interspersed with intervals of slower play, so that games in the Netherlands seem to proceed in phases.

Sprinting work per playing style

There is an enormous difference in the sprinting work carried out by Dutch and English professionals. This is because Dutch teams frequently operate a "man against man" system. Every player has a direct opponent, and players are therefore paired in all parts of the pitch. A player will frequently make a short sprint as a means of escaping from his opponent. Many teams in England use a 4-4-2 system with a zonal defense. This means that a player has no direct marker but is covered by whichever opponent is responsible for the zone in which he is located at any given moment. The players therefore have more room to operate

Soccer players make lots of short sprints to escape their markers.

in, and do not need to sprint away from their markers so frequently. Dutch teams tend to play along the ground, whereas English players make frequent use of the long high ball. The Dutch positional type of play means that all the units of the team may be involved in attack, with defenders joining in the buildup and midfielders playing a crucial role. In the English "kick and rush" style the midfielders are often simply bypassed. In the Netherlands the midfielders have the task of transporting the ball from the defenders to the attackers. They make short sprints to win space and take up position to receive a pass from their defenders. In this way the ball is circulated rapidly through the team. An essential aspect of this style of play is that the attackers must drop back towards the ball to allow it to be played long. When a team is in possession, the opposition's half of the pitch is often crowded. Attackers therefore have difficulty in finding space. Many of the sprints they make bring them no personal advantage, but may create space that a colleague can run into to receive a through pass.

Soccer-specific work per style
The comparison of the soccer-specific work carried out by English and Dutch professionals clearly shows that English players challenge for the ball more often, jump to head the ball more frequently, and make more sliding tackles. This, together with the fact that English players do more running, leads to the conclusion that English soccer is more physical than Dutch soccer. If we remember that English professionals play a lot more games per season than their Dutch colleagues, it is clear that their bodies are subjected to a greater physical load than those of their Dutch counterparts. German and Scandinavian soccer is also known to be very physical. By contrast, the soccer philosophy of the French, Spanish and Italians has more in common with that of the Dutch. Soccer in these countries is characterized by technical and tactical aspects.

1.2.4 Fatigue
During a long period of exertion it is inevitable that fatigue will set in. Soccer players also have to deal with this phenomenon during a match. It is interesting to know the extent to which they are confronted with fatigue.

Fatigue in relation to total running work
From Figure 9 it can be seen that, irrespective of the playing level, the total amount of running work performed in the second half of a match is lower than in the first. When the difference between the first and second half is calculated for each level, it is found that it is smallest in the professional game. This seems logical in view of the considerable amount of time devoted to training at this level. The difference steadily increases as the level becomes lower. A slight difference can also be detected between playing positions. The decrease in the amount of running done by defenders and attackers in the second half is less marked than for midfielders. This may be because midfielders carry out more work in the first half and therefore tire more quickly. Another possible cause is discussed in Chapter 11, page 250 ("Nutrition and Soccer").

Fatigue in relation to sprinting work
Figure 10 shows the sprinting work carried out during each half of the game by players in all positions and at all playing levels. At every level there is a clear decrease in sprinting work during the second half. This applies to all three positions, and the decrease is again greatest for midfielders. Once more the difference is smallest at the top level and largest

at the bottom. It is worth emphasizing again that good soccer players must have good sprinting ability. The decrease in sprinting work is again expressed in terms of distance covered. This information is certainly interesting, but of course it gives no indication of whether the players sprint with the same speed and explosive power in the second half. The answer to this question is as yet unknown.

1.3 THE PHYSICAL LOAD ON YOUTH PLAYERS

The players in the first division of the "A" youth league are usually 17 or 18 years old. Some of them will move up into the world of adult professional soccer at the end of the season. Soccer at this level imposes a considerable load. The difference in load between professional youth soccer and professional soccer at the adult level can be determined for the purpose of assessing whether youth players are ready to take this step.

1.3.1 The total running work of youth soccer players

The most surprising result of the analysis of the total running work done by Under 18 juniors is that the young players cover almost as much ground as professionals. The decrease during the second half is more marked than in the professional game but is not as great as at the adult amateur soccer level (see Fig. 1.9). The body of a 17 or 18 year-old youth player is not as strong as that of an adult soccer player, which makes it even more remarkable that youth players do more work during a match than adult amateur players. This is an indication that youth soccer players at the highest level must be in good physical condition. However, youth players should not start doing physical training at too early an age. The message of Chapter 10 ("Training youth soccer players") is that young players should first learn how to play soccer. Physical condition is secondary in the context of soccer, and should be dealt with at a later stage (usually from the age of 16).

	Distance in 1st half	Distance in 2nd half	Total Distance	Decrease in 2nd half
Defenders				
Professional league	4406 m	3970 m	8376 m	436 m (5.2%)
Top class amateurs	3984 m	3259 m	7243 m	725 m (10.0%)
2nd class amateurs	4201 m	3375 m	7576 m	826 m (10.9%)
5th class amateurs	4166 m	3286 m	7452 m	880 m (11.8%)
Under 18 juniors	4268 m	3762 m	8030 m	506 m (6.3%)
Midfielders				
Professional league	5934 m	4954 m	10888 m	980 m (9.0%)
Top class amateurs	5148 m	3988 m	9136 m	1160 m (12.7%)
2nd class amateurs	5170 m	3807 m	8977 m	1363 m (15.2%)
5th class amateurs	4874 m	3476 m	8350 m	1398 m (16.7%)
Under 18 juniors	5867 m	4816 m	10683 m	1051 m (9.8%)
Attackers				
Professional league	5253 m	4581 m	9834 m	672 m (6.8%)
Top class amateurs	4300 m	3504 m	7804 m	796 m (10.2%)
2nd class amateurs	4338 m	3306 m	7644 m	1032 m (13.5%)
5th class amateurs	4597 m	3433 m	8030 m	1164 m (14.5%)
Under 18 juniors	5045 m	4272 m	9317 m	773 m (8.3%)

Figure 1.9: *Running work in the first half and second half, by position and playing level, in games of soccer in the Netherlands.*

1.3.2 Sprinting work of youth soccer players

In contrast to total running work, there is a clear difference between youth and professional players when it comes to sprinting work. Youth players sprint appreciably less often. This is true of both long and short sprints. Moreover the decrease in sprinting work in the second half is more marked (see Fig. 1.10). This again indicates that sprinting work, not total running work, makes the difference between the various levels of play. These figures suggest that talented 18 year-olds who make the transition to professional soccer are faced with a considerable increase in sprinting work.

1.3.3 The soccer-specific work of youth soccer players

It is noticeable that the Under 18 players carry out a lot of soccer-specific work. In broad terms they score better than adult amateurs and professionals in this respect. In particular there are lots of challenges for the ball. This is a sign that the highest youth league in the Netherlands is extremely competitive. It may also be a sign of the uninhibited approach to soccer of many youngsters, but it must be remembered that these players are fighting to show that they are worthy of being offered a professional contract.

1.4 THE PHYSICAL LOAD ON GOALKEEPERS

More and more coaches are realizing that, although the role of a goalkeeper differs from that of an outfield player, the goalkeeper is an integral part of the team. For example, a goalkeeper who can gage exactly the right moment to bring the ball into play can be of crucial value. The conditioning of goalkeepers is dealt with in Chapter 9, so the work they carry out during a match is only dealt with briefly at this point. Very little research has been carried out into the physical load on goalkeepers. It is only known that a goalkeeper covers an average of 4 kilometers (2.5 miles) during a match (see Fig. 1.11). This is more

	Distance in 1st half	Distance in 2nd half	Total Distance	Decrease in 2nd half
Defenders				
Professional league	735 m	621 m	1356 m	114 m (8.4%)
Top class amateurs	428 m	305 m	733 m	123 m (16.8%)
2nd class amateurs	317 m	222 m	539 m	95 m (17.6%)
5th class amateurs	198 m	124 m	322 m	74 m (23.0%)
Under 18 juniors	504 m	374 m	878 m	130 m (14.8%)
Midfielders				
Professional league	621 m	496 m	1117 m	125 m (11.2%)
Top class amateurs	437 m	303 m	740 m	134 m (18.1%)
2nd class amateurs	356 m	209 m	565 m	117 m (24.2%)
5th class amateurs	249 m	100 m	349 m	109 m (31.2%)
Under 18 juniors	445 m	334 m	779 m	111 m (14.2%)
Attackers				
Professional league	957 m	795 m	1752 m	162 m (9.2%)
Top class amateurs	675 m	475 m	1150 m	200 m (17.4%)
2nd class amateurs	515 m	347 m	862 m	168 m (19.5%)
5th class amateurs	300 m	175 m	475 m	125 m (26.3%)
Under 18 juniors	726 m	534 m	1260 m	192 m (15.2%)

Figure 1.10: *Sprinting work in the first half and second half, by position and playing level, in games of soccer in the Netherlands.*

than would be expected. It is no surprise that most of this distance (60%) is covered at walking pace. A goalkeeper walks a total distance of 1 kilometer (0.6 miles) backwards, runs an average of 0.5 kilometers (0.3 miles), and sprints 0.2 kilometers (0.1 miles). The sprints vary in length from 1 to 25 yards. One reason why goalkeepers have to cover 4 kilometers during a game is that they are increasingly being forced to join in the outfield aspects of the game. Moreover, goalkeepers need to keep moving as an aid to retaining concentration and sharpness. If it is cold, goalkeepers also keep moving to stay warm. However, a goalkeeper does more than walk back and forth during a match. He has to jump to intercept crosses, or dive to make saves, and he often has to kick or throw the ball out. Unfortunately no data are yet available about these activities, but it can be assumed that all of this jumping, diving, kicking and throwing, together with the necessary sprinting work, add up to a considerable physical load.

	Walking Forward	Walking Backward	Jogging	Running	Sprinting	Total
Goalkeepers	1.6 km	1.0 km	0.7 km	0.5 km	0.2 km	4.0 km

Figure 1.11: *Average running work by goalkeepers.*

1.5 THE PHYSICAL PROPERTIES NEEDED TO PERFORM SOCCER WORK

It is clear that a soccer player covers a lot of ground during a match, makes a lot of sprints and performs soccer-specific work. What physical properties does he need to enable him to carry out all of this work?

1.5.1 Total running work: endurance

Soccer players run between 9 and 12 kilometers (5.6 and 7.5 miles) in 90 minutes. This is equivalent to an average speed of 6 to 8 kilometers (3.7 to 5 miles) per hour. Players must have good powers of endurance to maintain this speed over one and a half hours. In this context, the term "endurance" is used in preference to stamina, which tends to be associated with athletes such as marathon runners, who run for long periods at virtually one speed. Marathon running can be regarded as a cyclic sport. By contrast the intensity of a soccer match varies considerably. Soccer is therefore said to be acyclic, being characterized by lots of intervals of different activity. Figure 1.12 shows that professional soccer players make between 1400 and 1600 runs during a match. On average, this means that a player switches over to another run every 3.5 to 4 seconds. This is a good reflection of the interval-type character of soccer. Soccer players must have endurance to enable them to run for a long time in a widely fluctuating tempo **(acyclic aerobic and anaerobic endurance)**. Chapter 6 deals with the conditioning of soccer players for this type of endurance. The terms aerobic and anaerobic are dealt with in the next chapter.

> *As a soccer player you shouldn't have to do a lot of running if you take up the right position. Nowadays I see too many long-distance runners and too few soccer players.*
>
> **Allen Hansen**

	Total number of "runs"	Walking	Jogging	Running	Sprinting	Sideways	Walking backwards	Jogging backwards	In Possession
Defenders									
Professional league	735 m	662	335	83	162	110	158	19	28
Top class amateurs	428 m	581	311	50	111	93	124	21	32
2nd class amateurs	317 m	512	320	41	62	63	103	17	33
5th class amateurs	198 m	474	289	21	84	56	71	13	21
Under 18 juniors	504 m	686	347	72	101	82	120	18	32
Midfielders									
Professional league	621 m	539	503	117	127	91	139	17	37
Top class amateurs	437 m	520	410	83	92	79	106	22	33
2nd class amateurs	356 m	519	352	54	69	69	86	20	26
5th class amateurs	249 m	502	312	37	51	48	54	15	17
Under 18 juniors	445 m	517	466	88	94	76	100	21	31
Attackers									
Professional league	957 m	500	397	90	183	121	144	23	15
Top class amateurs	675 m	449	386	56	127	84	116	17	17
2nd class amateurs	515 m	461	365	60	99	60	91	17	11
5th class amateurs	300 m	492	329	39	66	57	70	11	12
Under 18 juniors	726 m	537	403	72	134	102	116	19	16

Figure 1.12: *Total number of "runs" made by soccer players during a game.*

1.5.2 Sprinting work: speed

Soccer players have to make a lot of sprints. Speed is the basis of this work, but speed is a complex concept. It is a collective term for a number of (speed) components. In a soccer context, speed refers first of all to speed of reaction, i.e. the ability to react quickly to constantly changing situations on the pitch. This component cannot be viewed in isolation but must always be seen in combination with other speed components. A fast reaction has to be followed up by fast action.

Perhaps the most remarkable aspect of the data mentioned above is the enormous number of short sprints (1 to 10 yards) made by soccer players in the Netherlands. Professional players make 100 to 120, and even fifth classers make 40 to 50. The most important reason for making a short sprint is to gain space by getting away from a marker. The most essential speed component of such sprints is starting speed.

Sometimes a short sprint becomes a long sprint, and in a game of soccer such sprints can vary from 10 to 40 yards. Longer sprints occur less frequently than short ones, but they account for a large proportion of the sprinting work carried out by soccer players. During a sprint over a distance of, say, 30 yards it is essential to reach maximum speed in a relatively short time, and acceleration is the most important speed component required to achieve this.

Sprints of more than 40 yards only occur if a player has to cover the whole length of the field, for example during a counterattack. It is then important to be able to maintain maximum speed for a longer time, and for this a player needs another speed component, i.e. **speed endurance**.

Professional soccer players make 150 sprints during a game, and amateurs 50. Players in the first group therefore make an average of 2 sprints per minute, and those in the second 0.5. If these are average values it follows that players may need to make 3 to 5 sprints per minute during intensive periods of play. They therefore need another speed component, i.e. a good **repeated short sprint capacity**. This capacity enables players to make a number of sprints in quick sequence without becoming too fatigued.

In soccer, therefore, speed is made up of a number of components (see Fig. 1.13). It is important to understand that speed also has an acyclic character. Soccer players only rarely sprint in a straight line, but often have to turn or reverse direction in reaction to a change in the direction of the ball or opponent. Speed conditioning is described in Chapters 5 and 6.

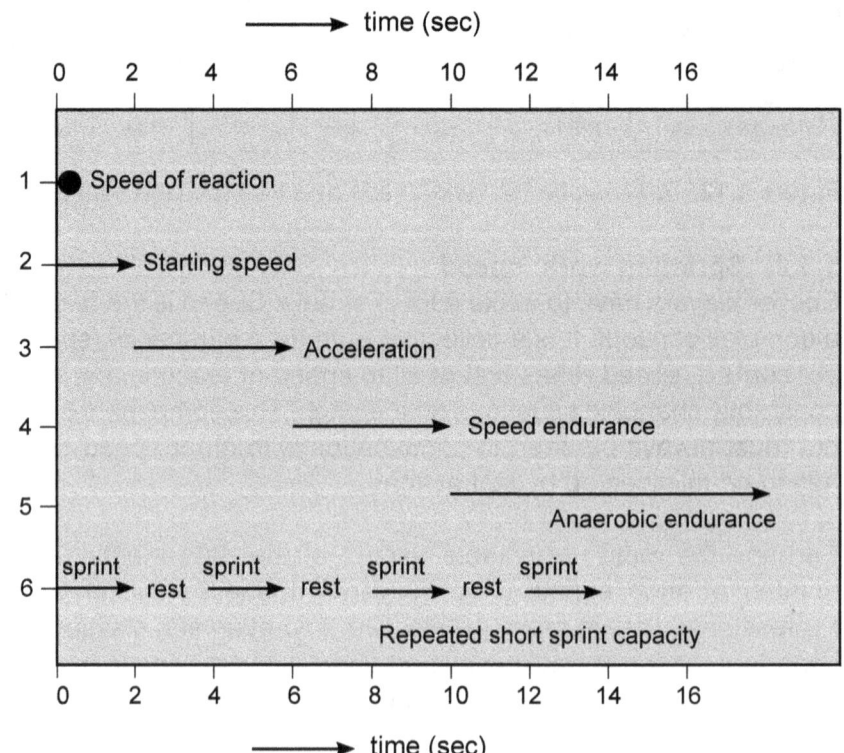

Figure 1.13: *The various components that make up the concept of speed.*

soccer conditioning

1.5.3 Soccer-specific work

Soccer players carry out not only running work but also work that is soccer-specific, such as sliding tackles, challenges for the ball, jumping to head the ball, and shooting. To carry out this soccer-specific work a player needs muscle strength in his upper body (challenges for the ball) or lower body (shooting, jumping, sliding tackles). Strength is also a part of soccer conditioning. Chapter 4 makes clear, however, that conditioning for soccer strength is concerned more with improving technique than improving various soccer actions. A player learns to kick with his left foot by improving his kicking technique rather than by increasing the strength of his left leg. A player who learns to coordinate the kicking movement better can apply more of the strength that is already present in his left leg. Of course, he must have a good basic level of general bodily strength. Looked at from this point of view, soccer strength consists of **basic strength, kicking strength, jumping strength, tackling strength and starting strength**. For all of these components it is important to make the best possible use of the general basic strength. This subject is dealt with in more detail in Chapter 4.

1.5.4 Coordination

Technique is the most important factor in playing soccer. The ball must be brought under control so that an opponent cannot gain possession of it. All kinds of actions must then be performed with the objective of getting the ball into the opposing team's goal. Physical coordination is at the heart of all of these actions. Physical coordination is also an important aspect of sliding tackles and challenges for the ball. The success or otherwise of such an action often depends on timing. If an action is made a fraction too late or too early, it will usually fail in its purpose. Timing is an important aspect of coordination. Another example of this is jumping. Good timing can compensate for lack of inches in a heading duel. Scarcely any of the actions carried out on a soccer field require just a single muscle to be active. If an action is to proceed smoothly it is necessary to activate the various muscles at just the right moment. The harmonization of muscle activity is termed coordination, and is carried out under the control of the nervous system. This is dealt with in more detail in Chapter 2. The following chapters explain how coordination plays an important role in strength conditioning, speed conditioning and endurance conditioning.

> *The English think that soccer players have to race non-stop around the pitch to play soccer. I have a different outlook.*
>
> **Glen Hoddle**

1.5.5 Flexibility

Soccer players constantly have to turn and change direction to get away from or follow an opponent. Players sometimes make the most unnatural movements in an attempt to control the ball. Flexibility is required for all of these actions. This subject is treated in Chapter 3, where it is explained that flexibility is not essential to good performance but is also far from unimportant.

1.6 CONCLUSION: THE PHYSICAL NATURE OF SOCCER IS COMPLEX

A lot of figures are provided in this chapter, although these figures only serve to give an impression of the whole picture. Taken in isolation they are not particularly significant, but are more a means of illustrating certain facts. It is therefore necessary to look at the message embodied in the figures rather than the figures themselves. It has been shown that the players in a soccer team do not all have to cope with the same load. A player's load depends on his position and on his team's style of play. The coach's philosophy must therefore be the starting point for conditioning. Players should make the same runs during training that they make during a game. A soccer player must build up his condition on the basis of his function and task. The physical nature of soccer is complex. A soccer player must have strength, speed, endurance, coordination and flexibility. What do all of these factors mean in terms of a player's physical makeup? What physiological processes take place in his body when he is playing soccer? The degree of development of the various physiological systems determines how much soccer work a player can perform. It is a measure of the player's loading capacity. The following chapter attempts to shed more light on this.

SUMMARY

- The work performed by soccer players consists of running work and soccer-specific work (jumping, shooting, challenging for the ball, sliding tackles).

- At every level of play midfielders do the most running and defenders the least.

- A soccer player performs almost the same amount of running work in each game, provided he always plays in the same position. When a player changes his position, the amount of running work he performs also changes.

- At every level of play, attackers sprint more than defenders and midfielders. This difference is especially marked in the number of short sprints (1 to 10 yards). Midfielders make the most long sprints (30 to 40 and 40+ yards).

- Analysis of soccer-specific work shows that defenders and attackers jump more for the ball than midfielders, midfielders make the most challenges for the ball, and defenders make the most sliding tackles.

- At lower levels of play there is less running and sprinting and more walking and jogging. There is a shift from more intensive to less intensive work.

- At lower levels of play there are more sliding tackles and more challenges for the ball. This is an indication that soccer at this level is more physical, possibly as a form of compensation for the players' technical and tactical shortcomings.

- Dutch professionals do less running during a match than their English counterparts. Dutch players let the ball do more work. Dutch players make more runs. The game therefore has a more marked "interval" character. English players run more at high speed.

- Dutch professionals make more sprints than English professionals.

- In comparison with Dutch professional soccer, more soccer-specific work is performed in England. The English game is more physical.

- Irrespective of position and playing level, soccer players cover less ground in the second half than in the first. The difference is widest for midfielders. The higher the level of play, the narrower the difference between the two halves.

- Players also sprint less in the second half. Again the difference is greatest for midfielders, and again it is smallest at the top level and increases as the level becomes lower.

FIVE PRACTICAL QUESTIONS

1. How long does it take to recover physically and mentally from a strenuous training session or match?

A period of 36 to 48 hours of rest is usually necessary after intensive work. This is the time that the body needs to repair all kinds of damage to the muscles and connective tissue. The energy systems also need time to recover.

2. If a team plays a match on Sunday and trains on Tuesday and Thursday, is it more sensible to use the Thursday rather than the Tuesday for the most strenuous training session?

At the level of amateur soccer it is not advisable to alternate very intensive and light training sessions. It is better to spread the necessary intensive work equally over the two sessions. Every training session must reflect the situation in a real match.

3. Are two training sessions per week enough for an amateur soccer player?

There are various levels of amateur soccer. In this handbook we refer to three groups: top amateurs (the top class, 1st class and 2nd class Dutch Soccer Association leagues), competitive amateurs (3rd to 5th class Dutch Soccer Association leagues), and recreational amateurs (6th class Dutch Soccer Association leagues and lower). Three training sessions per week are advisable for the first group, 2 for the second and a minimum of 1 for the third.

4. What effect does going out on the town, consuming alcohol and getting to bed late have on the physical capacity of soccer players if they have to play a match the following day?

Alcohol has a relaxing effect on the human body. This is not very good for soccer players who have to play the following day, because muscular tension is essential to competitive performance. A late night out on the town can of course result in tiredness the next day. One of the characteristics of a tired body is reduced coordination. There is a danger that a tired player will make uncontrolled movements during a match, and this can endanger the player himself as well as his teammates and opponents.

5. Must a coach take his players' everyday jobs into account? One player may work in an office while another has to carry heavy loads all day.

All that a coach can do is make sure that he knows what his players do, and keep an eye on potential problem cases during training. He can also encourage the players to speak up if they need to take things easier or, conversely, want to train harder. Communication is the important thing here. A coach must give his players the confidence to be able to approach him about such problems without any fear of losing their place in the team.

INTERVIEW WITH JAN WOUTERS
(Assistant Coach at Ajax Amsterdam)

You were known as a player who did a lot of the hard work in midfield, covering for others. Did you yourself realize that you carried out so much work?
I was not aware that I did a lot of running, because it just happened naturally. Later, when I saw recordings of games, or heard people talking about them, I realized that I was constantly in motion and always in the vicinity of the ball. I often noticed that I was tired in the second half. The difference was not so great, but my strength definitely diminished. The reason was that I always played flat out from the start, without any thought for the consequences. Initially this was because I was inexperienced, and later I wanted to be wherever the ball was. I only started to use my strength more sparingly when I became older. Even so, I have never consciously taken things easy during a game.

Besides all that running, you also had to carry out other exhausting actions. What did your soccer-specific work consist of?
As a central midfielder, it was my task to exert pressure on the man in possession. Because of this, I was involved in a lot of challenges for the ball. Although tackling makes playing soccer especially difficult, winning the ball is not a matter of pure strength. You can compare it with shooting. If you have a good technique, you can shoot very hard. But if you just try to kick the ball with all your strength, you cannot impart much speed to it. The same applies to tackling. You do need strength, of course, but you have to know how to use it properly. Probably the most important aspects are dexterity and positioning. If an opponent comes from the left, you have to ensure that your weight is on your left foot. You lean towards your opponent. In this way you can block the ball. If you lean forward with your weight on the right foot, you will simply be pushed over. These are things you can only learn by playing a lot of soccer. Weight training is of no help.

When you were transferred from Utrecht to Ajax, did the physical stresses increase as a result of the higher playing standard?
At Ajax it was not so much a matter of becoming used to a higher level of physical stress during the game, but rather to the fact that we trained more frequently. Utrecht played a battling style of game, so the workload was high. When you play for Ajax, you can often make use of the higher level of soccer skill to avoid physical challenges. Moreover you have a lot of possession, so the opposing players have to do a lot of chasing after the ball. This means that you are not expending your strength as quickly as your opponents, and in the second half you are usually a lot fitter than them. I felt a lot stronger in my Ajax period. Some people also thought that I looked stronger. This might have been a consequence of the greater number of hours on the training pitch.

German soccer is known to be very physical. Did you find this when you played for Bayern Munich?

German soccer is harder, because there is more man-to-man marking. The strength factor is more important. Soccer there is less tactical. My teammates often ran blindly forward, so that I found myself without a teammate who was closer than 40 meters away. If the team loses possession you then have to cover a distance of 40 meters before you can put pressure on the man with the ball. That was very strenuous. Although the physical resistance in the Germany league was greater, fitness conditioning was less advanced than I was used to in the Netherlands. Training sessions were often simply occupational therapy. And when there was a session of intensive conditioning, it was not approached properly. Sprint drills, for instance, simply consisted of individual sprints. We never had to do a series of short sprints, with turns and changes of direction. Most of my teammates had very good powers of endurance, but this was not the result of specific conditioning. It was more a consequence of the enormous competitive effort that was put into each game. The competitive mentality was fantastic. The players ran their hearts out from start to finish. In this way you are bound to build up good endurance.

How good was the medical support at Bayern Munich?

Bayern Munich has a good medical team headed by Dr. Wohlfart. They were able to make a diagnosis very quickly when an injury occurred. The interval between an injury and the necessary operation was therefore very short. The support was perfect. The period after the operation was less well organized. In the Netherlands you are used to being treated by a physiotherapist, for example, to promote the mobility of the knee joint after a knee operation. At Bayern the period after an operation simply consisted of rest, without any treatment. When you were able to run again you were given massages.

Do you think that today's soccer players have to cope with more physical stress than those of ten or twenty years ago?

If you look at games from 1974, for example, you see that the playing area was very large and the players had more time and space. But just as in athletics and skating, conditioning methods in soccer have steadily improved, so everyone has become faster and you have less time to react. There is now more chance that you will be just too late with a tackle. That means that players are on the receiving end of more kicks and pushes. You also have to turn and change direction faster, so there is a greater chance of twisting your knee. There are many more injuries as a consequence of the increased pace of the game. It is silly to say that the present-day injury problem is caused by harder play. Soccer players in years gone by were just as tough and mean as now, or maybe even more so. Today's injuries result from the increased physical stress. Not only do the players have to do more work but there is more physical contact. This is reflected in an increased number of injuries to ligaments and joints. Determining the level of stress that the body can take is a big problem, because you cannot measure the load that the knee and angle ligaments and joints can withstand. You only notice that something is wrong when it is too late.

As second-team coach of Ajax, can you say anything about the problems of moving up from the youth level into the second team?

A lot of factors play a role when a young player moves up from the youth team into the world of professional soccer. I have never noticed much difference in sprint work between the top youth teams and professional players. But when I look at the figures, I can imagine that this plays a role. The big problem for Ajax's youth players is that they are not used to the resistance they suddenly meet in the second team. At the youth level they often win by a large margin. They have problems in switching over when a change of possession occurs. They have never had to switch over quickly. We therefore use special drills to practice this during training sessions.

In your opinion, how much does a coach need to know about the physical stresses on soccer players and the general principles of exercise physiology?

I think that a coach should be well informed about the basic principles of coaching theory. I often rely on my instinct, because I know from experience how difficult certain drills are. You also have to watch the players' body language. When a drill becomes bogged down because the players are too fatigued to escape from their markers or to switch over when there is a change of possession, you have to stop. Nevertheless, I would like to know more, because there is always a risk that you will let players go too far. As a coach you have a responsibility for your players' health. My first priority is to learn all I can about the technical and tactical aspects of coaching. Then it will be the turn of the physical aspects.

LITERATURE

1. Work-rate and Time-motion analysis of soccer players.
R. Verheijen.
Faculteir der Bewegingswetenschappen, Vrije
Universiteit Amsterdam, 1995.

2. Wedstrijdspecifieke conditietraining voor voetballers.
R. Verheijen.
De Voetbaltrainer 55.
Richting/Sportgericht 50 (1995) 1.

3. Soccer: changes in the work-rate of midfield players during a match.
N. Rijvers.
Faculteit der Bewegingswetenschappen, Vrije Universiteit Amsterdam, 1996.

4. Handbook of Sports Medicine and Science - Football 'Soccer'.
B. Ekblom.
ISBN: 0-632-0332802.
Blackwell Scientific Publications Ltd.

5. Science and Football.
T. Reilly, A Lees, K. Davids and W.J. Murphy.
ISBN: 0-419-14360-2.
E & Fn Spon, London.

6. Science and Football II.
T Reilly, J. Clarijs and A. Stibbe.
ISBN: 0-419-17850-3.
E & FN Spon, London.

CHAPTER 2

SOCCER AND PHYSIOLOGY

Dr. Raymond Verheijen

2.1 INTRODUCTION

An insight into the loading capacity of soccer players can best be gained by learning how the body functions during a game of soccer. When the factors that determine the loading capacity are known, progress can be made in deciding how this capacity can be better aligned to the loads encountered while playing soccer. Despite all the attention focused on the various physiological and anatomical components of the human body, it must not be forgotten that "human motor function" is more than just "muscle contractions". Muscle contraction is only one part of motor function. In terms of physiology, the activities involved in playing soccer depend on the nervous system. It does not matter how strong or fast the muscles are, if they are not properly triggered by the nervous system then it is not possible to carry out soccer actions correctly. The subject of the nervous system therefore recurs constantly during this chapter. The nervous system is a control system, in which decisions are taken. It is where the commands to the muscles originate. Muscles are under the direct control of the nervous system. However, the muscles need energy to be able to carry out the commands they receive. There are three systems in the body that produce this energy. These systems have to be supplied with oxygen and/or nutrients. This is the task of the circulatory system (heart and blood supply) and the respiratory system (lungs and breathing), which together are referred to as the circulo-respiratory system. Basically, the better these physiological systems function, the greater is the loading capacity. After dealing with the nervous system, therefore, this chapter also looks at the circulo-respiratory system, the body's energy systems, and the muscular system. It should always be remembered, however, that the activity of the latter three systems depends on the nervous system.

In a game of soccer, the muscles are just an aid to solving soccer problems.

2.2 THE NERVOUS SYSTEM

Every human movement depends on the nervous system. Every soccer action is controlled by the nervous system. It is true that these activities could not be carried out without muscles, but muscles are just an aid, with which the nervous system realizes certain soccer objectives. Playing soccer can be regarded as using the brain to solve soccer problems, with the muscles simply serving as a means of putting the solution into practice. The human body is in a state of constant interaction with its environment. Humans perceive things and they act on the basis of these perceptions. Players must recognize situations on the field of play so that they know what to do, i.e. how to carry out the correct soccer actions, when their team or the opposition is in possession of the ball or when possession changes from one team to the other. To understand how this process occurs, it is necessary to understand how the nervous system functions.

2.2.1 The Central and Peripheral Nervous Systems

The nervous system is made up of two parts: the central nervous system and the peripheral nervous system (see Fig. 2.1). The central nervous system (CNS) consists of the brain and the spinal cord. The peripheral nervous system (PNS) is made up of the nerve fibers that connect the sensory receptors and muscles with the CNS. The body has all sorts of sensory receptors, which are responsible for touch, taste, smell, vision, hearing, balance, etc. These sensory receptors are present in the skin, the muscles, the tendons and the organs, and they transmit information about their environment through the nerve fibers to the spinal cord. This information is then transmitted to a specific part of the brain. The brain consists of all sorts of nerve centers, where stimuli acquire significance (enter consciousness) and can be translated into executive commands to the muscles (see Fig. 2.2). The brain can send information back to the muscles through the spinal cord and the nerve fibers if an activity needs to be carried out in reaction to a certain situation (stimulus). When the signal from the brain reaches the muscle, the muscle contracts and an action is executed.

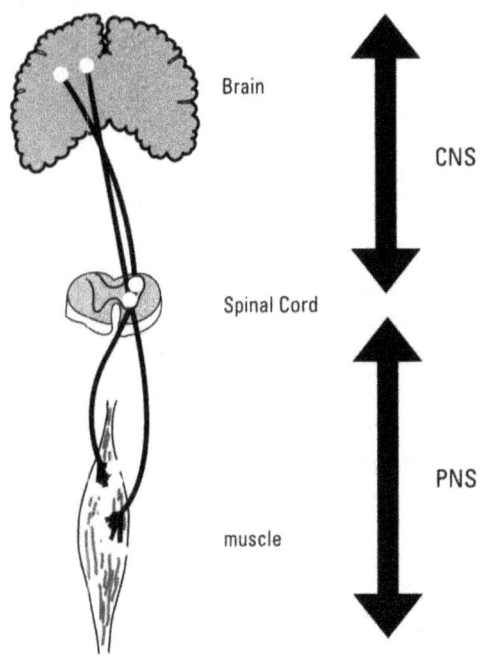

Figure 2.1: *The nervous system consists of two parts: the central nervous system (CNS), to which belong the brain and the spinal cord, and the peripheral nervous system (PNS), containing nerve fibers that connect sensors and muscles with the spinal cord.*

Sometimes there is a reaction to a stimulus from the environment without the brain having been involved. This is referred to as a reflex. It is an action that is performed under impulse from the spinal cord. The fact that the brain is not involved explains why reflexes occur unconsciously. Normally the brain produces signals (impulses) that determine which muscles contract when, for how long, how strongly, and in what combinations. The muscular system can be compared with a piano. The keys of a piano, just like the muscles, are insignificant on their own; they only acquire significance when they are played well. The muscles are "played" by the nervous system, and this process is termed coordination. The muscles are therefore, in effect, the slaves of the nervous system.

2.2.2 The Role of the Nervous System in Soccer

The nervous system is a stimulus-processing (sensory) and stimulus-generating (motoric) organ. All movements are coordinated by means of motoric and sensory processes.

Sensory processes: perception of soccer situations

Soccer players are confronted with numerous situations during a game. Before a player can make the right decision he must first recognize such a situation. Perception is central to this. The eyes are naturally the most important aid to perception. Visual information tells a player most about a situation. Perception is more than sight, however. We have many more sources of information than our eyes. The ears also play an important role. A teammate who is out of sight can make it clear that he is unmarked or is making a forward run by using his voice.

Sensors in the skin send signals to the brain indicating that, for example, a player is about to challenge from behind.

Hearing is therefore a crucial channel for acquiring information. The skin contains tactile sensors, which are responsible for our sense of touch and are activated by bodily contact. This sense tells a player when, for example, an opponent is close behind him. The muscles contain kinesthetic sensors, which provide information connected with our sense of movement. Think of the suppleness with which a feint is carried out, for example. By carrying out a specific movement in a number of different ways, a player can "feel" which way suits him best. Finally there is our sense of balance. This is crucial for soccer players. It provides information about the body's center of gravity. This changes constantly as a player twists and turns. Soccer players must be able to retain their balance in such situations. Otherwise they will be outplayed or lose a challenge for the ball. There are therefore a whole lot of sensors that provide a soccer player with information about his own movements and the constantly changing situation around him on the pitch.

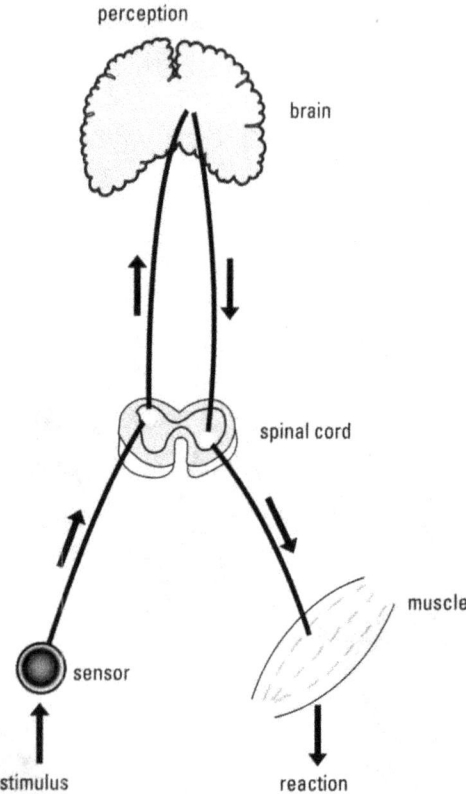

Figure 2.2: *Example of a stimulus from the environment, which is picked up by a sensor and transmitted to the brain. In the brain the stimulus is translated into a conscious perception. If necessary, a signal is sent to the muscles to trigger a reaction to the stimulus.*

Sensory information can be divided into two categories, i.e. exafferent and reafferent. **Exafferent** information is provided by signals from outside the body. Think of, for example, the course of the game, the positions of opponents and teammates, instructions from the coach, and the condition of the pitch. Such information helps to form the basis for a soccer player's actions. Meaningful exafferent information that precedes a soccer player's action is sometimes also termed "feedforward" information. Movement always has sensory consequences. Any action during a game also yields information. A soccer player can see and feel the result of his action (KR = knowledge of result) and how the movement is carried out (KP = knowledge of performance). This **reafferent** information is also termed "feedback" information. The difference between exafferent and reafferent information can best be explained with the help of an example. If two people sit in a car, information about how the car is being driven is reafferent for the driver and exafferent for the passenger. Exafferent and reafferent information is sent from the sensors to the brain. The brain uses these signals to form a picture of the game situation. A decision then has to taken: what soccer action is best suited to the prevailing game situation? A search is carried out in the brain to determine whether a solution is stored there. If the search is successful, the player recognizes the situation and immediately knows what to do, because he has been confronted with the situation several times before. If a solution is not immediately found in the brain, the player chooses to carry out the action that suits him best. If this proves successful it will be stored in his brain. If it is unsuccessful he will also remember this the next time. Children who play a lot of soccer are confronted with lots of soccer problems, which they have to solve. The solutions are then stored in their brains and are called up when a certain situation occurs again.

> *Scoring goals is just like breathing, you never forget how to do it.*
>
> **Peter Houtman**

Motoric Processes: Carrying out Soccer Actions

After the brain has created a picture of the game situation and the player has decided which action is most suitable, this action then has to be carried out. At that moment the motoric part of the nervous system becomes active. The brain sends signals to the muscles that have to carry out the soccer action(s). These are often very complex signals. They contain information about which muscle has to contract at what time, for how long and with what force. The complexity becomes even greater if it is remembered that a soccer action often involves between five and ten muscles. A number of muscles execute the action, while other muscles hold the body in balance during the execution. A soccer action must therefore be viewed as an interaction of various muscles, with each muscle performing its own specific function. At each moment of a soccer action, a specific combination of muscle actions is employed. In this context the whole is greater than the sum of its parts. The entire process is coordinated by the nervous system. The conditioning of this coordination is the central theme of Chapter 5 ("Sprinting and coordination training for soccer players"). The objective of coordination conditioning is to refine and harmonize the interplay of the muscles. Soccer actions will then be carried out more flexibly and efficiently, so that they cost less strength. Figure 2.3A shows, as an example, the activity of six muscles during the execution of a soccer action. Initially the action looks very wooden. Frequent practice, however, improves flexibility. Figure 2.3B shows that this is because muscle 1 relaxes now and then, muscle 4 contracts less strongly, and muscle 6 is not used at all any more. A "natural" movement is made possible when no cramped movements occur (muscles 1, 4 and 6).

Undesirable muscle actions must be curbed. An important objective of the learning process is the reduction of unnecessary muscle actions. The nervous system develops optimal control of the various muscles so that the efficiency of a movement increases. To summarize, it can be said that, in physiological terms, a soccer player is a

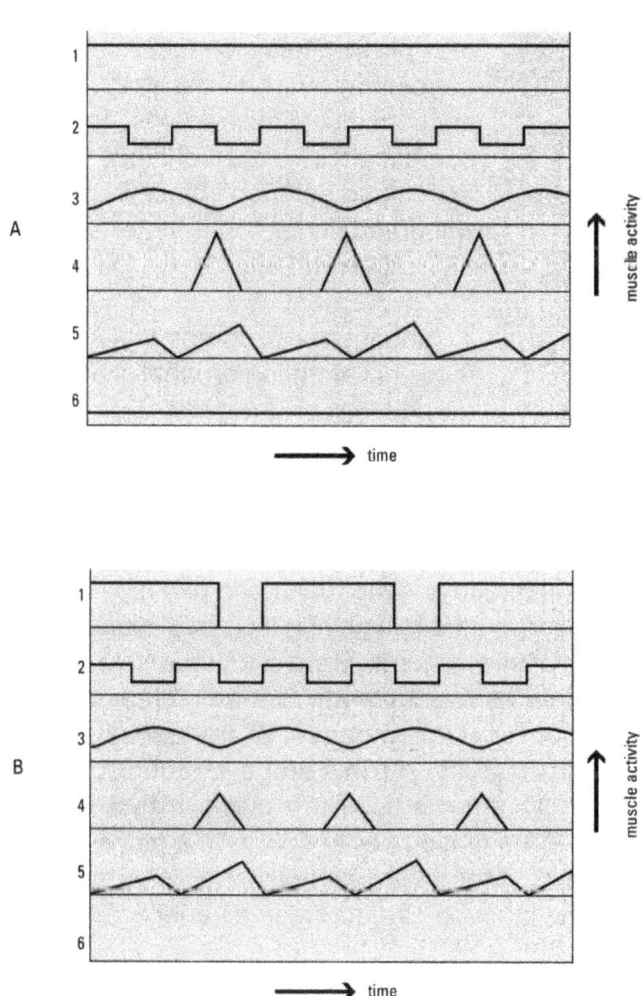

Figure 2.3: *An overview of the activity of six different muscles during the execution of a soccer action (A). During conditioning the player learns to carry out the action more flexibly, and this is reflected in better harmonization of the activity of the six muscles (B).*

complex "control system," which continuously registers information and processes and uses it to execute soccer actions.

2.2.3 The Conscious and Unconscious Components

As has already been mentioned, human beings are aware of certain information and unaware of other information. The functioning of the central nervous system can therefore be divided into two components. The conscious component includes all bodily processes that require thought. The unconscious component includes all processes that occur unconsciously in the body (e.g. the beating of the heart, the flow of blood in the internal organs, reflex actions). In soccer there are numerous examples of how a conscious movement ultimately becomes an unconscious (automatic) movement. A good example is seen in the process of learning to carry out a feint. Initially the player has to focus all of his concentration on carrying out the sequence of movements (conscious component). As his technique, speed of action and self-confidence increase, he will gradually become better and faster and will eventually be able to carry out the movement without thinking about it (unconscious component). He can focus his attention on what is happening around him on the pitch. This is similar to learning to drive a car. Initially a lot of attention has to be focussed on releasing the clutch at the right time when the car starts, and on changing gear.

As players' techniques improve, there is more time to focus on what is happening around them.

After a while these actions become automatic and the driver can pay more attention to the road. In practice, improved coordination is paralleled by an increase in unconscious processing of information and execution of movements. As a movement is gradually mastered, ever less attention is focussed on its execution. In fact an increasingly large part of the coordination is left to the "unconscious" component of the nervous system. The objective is ultimately to achieve "ultrastability." At this stage a technique can be carried out well under any circumstances. What is the point of a player mastering a feint under circumstances of zero resistance? This situation never occurs in a game of soccer - there is always some degree of resistance. Moreover this resistance can take widely different forms. For this reason conditioning must be carried out in a variety of situations.

2.2.4 Conclusion

A soccer player depends on his nervous system in everything that he does. The nervous system - and not the various physiological systems - is therefore correctly viewed as the most important facilitating factor in the context of playing soccer. Characteristics such as maximum oxygen uptake and speed, however, are genetically determined to a large extent, and the nervous system cannot overcome this barrier of genetic inheritance. Physiological systems can therefore be a limiting factor with regard to soccer capacity.

2.3 THE OXYGEN TRANSPORT SYSTEM

The oxygen transport system consists of the heart, respiration and blood. As the name suggests, the most important task of this system is to carry oxygen from the air to the muscles in the body. The blood also carries nutrients to the muscles. The oxygen transport system is essential during exercise, because without oxygen (and nutrients) the muscles would be (almost) incapable of performing work. The following paragraphs are therefore devoted to the various components of the system.

2.3.1 The Heart

The heart is the engine that drives the oxygen transport system. The blood from all parts of the body repeatedly collects in the right side of the heart. From there it is sent to the lungs, where it is provided with fresh oxygen. The blood then passes back into the left side of the heart (see Fig. 2.4). The heart then pumps the oxygen-rich blood to the various parts of the body.

Heart Rate

The blood is driven around the body by the regular contractions of the heart. These contractions are triggered by an electrical stimulus that is generated in the heart itself. The blood is literally squeezed through blood vessels to another location. Hormones dictate how often the stimulus is generated and therefore how high a person's heart rate is.

Blood Circulation

The job of the heart is to pump the blood around the entire body. The cardiac output is the total volume of blood that the heart pumps in one minute. The volume that is pumped by one heartbeat is termed the stroke volume. The heart rate is the number of heartbeats in one minute. The relationship between these three variables is as follows:

Cardiac output = Heart rate x Stroke volume

When the body is in a state of rest, the heart pumps out some 80 milliliters of blood per heartbeat, i.e. the stroke volume is 80 milliliters. The cardiac output of an average person in a state of rest is therefore about 4.8 liters (60 x 0.08). The cardiac output increases during exercise as a reaction to the increased oxygen demand of the active muscles. An increase in cardiac output from 5 liters per minute at rest to 25 liters per minute during exercise is not unusual.

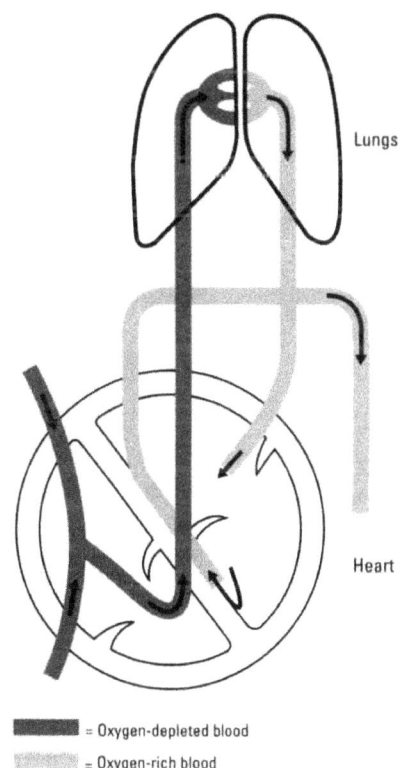

Figure 2.4: *Blood from all parts of the body is carried back to the heart. Much of the oxygen in the blood is removed during its journey round the body, and it is therefore low in oxygen when it arrives back at the heart. Before it is pumped round the body again it is sent to the lungs, where it replenishes its oxygen content.*

2.3.2 Respiration

Inspired air contains about 21 % oxygen. Some of this oxygen is absorbed by the blood in the lungs. The blood returns to the heart (see Fig. 2.5), from where it is distributed to all parts of the body. The oxygen that is not absorbed into the blood is expired. If the amount of oxygen in the inspired and expired air is measured and compared, this gives a picture of how much oxygen is absorbed by the muscles. The volume of air inspired or expired in one minute is referred to as the minute ventilation. In a state of rest this is about 5 liters. During exercise the muscles need more oxygen and the respiration rate increases. The respiration rate of an unconditioned person can rise to 100 liters per minute during intense exercise, while that of a conditioned person can exceed 200.

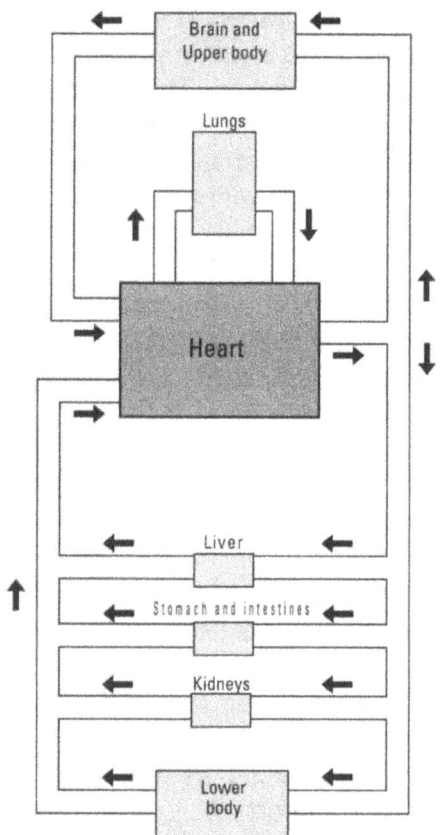

Figure 2.5: *Overview of the body's major blood circulation routes.*

2.3.3 Blood

The body of an adult contains about 5 liters of blood. About 40-45% of blood consists of red blood cells, and the remainder is made up of white blood cells and a liquid called blood plasma.

Figure 2.6: *Overview of the exchange of oxygen and carbon dioxide at various places in the body.*

The red color of blood is attributable to the protein hemoglobin, which is present in red blood cells. As the blood passes through the lungs, the hemoglobin combines with oxygen. When the blood arrives at a muscle that needs oxygen, the hemoglobin releases it again. The muscle takes more than just oxygen from the blood. Nutrients such as carbohydrates, fats and proteins get to the muscles through the blood. Blood plasma is responsible for the transport of such nutrients to the muscles. Inside the muscle the nutrients are converted into energy. One of the waste products of this process is carbon dioxide (CO_2), which, when it leaves the muscle, is carried in the blood plasma to the lungs, where it is expelled from the body during respiration. Figure 2.6 gives a picture of the exchange of oxygen and carbon dioxide in the body of a soccer player. During exercise the blood plays another important role. It carries the heat generated by the active muscles to the skin, where it is dissipated into the ambient air. The passage of larger amounts of blood to the skin during exercise can prevent the body from becoming overheated.

2.4 THE ENERGY SYSTEMS

Chapter 1 contains a detailed description of the work carried out by soccer players during a game. A lot of energy is needed for this (muscular) work. However, the body has only a small store of energy available for this purpose. The body therefore needs to take in nutrients from which to replenish its supply of energy (see Chapter 11). Carbohydrates, fats and proteins cannot be used directly to carry out work. The body first has to convert them into energy-rich ATP (adenosine triphosphate). ATP is the source of the energy that fuels all activities that take place in the body see Fig. 2.7). The body has three energy systems with which it converts nutrients into ATP:

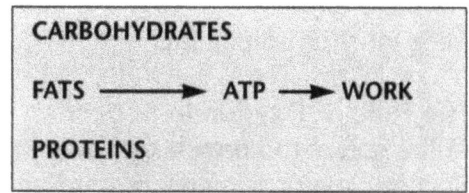

Figure 2.7: *The body has to convert nutrients to ATP before their energy can be used to perform work.*

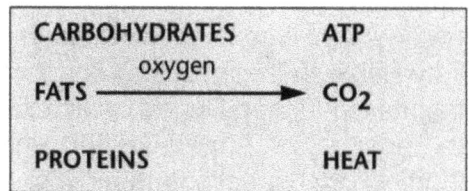

Figure 2.8: *The energy process that occurs in the oxygen system.*

- the oxygen system;
- the phosphate system;
- the lactic acid system.

2.4.1 The Oxygen System

The most favorable way for the body to produce ATP is with the help of oxygen (aerobically). The oxygen system converts carbohydrates, fats and (to a lesser degree) proteins into ATP in the muscles (see Fig. 2.8). Carbon dioxide and heat are generated during this process, and are transported away by the blood.

You score the best goals when you have no time to think. It happens in an instant. You have to have a feeling for it, and that can't be taught.

Ties Kruize

Maximum Oxygen Uptake

The amount of oxygen that the body uses per minute is referred to as the oxygen uptake (VO2). In a state of rest this amounts to about 0.3 liters per minute. During exercise the muscles need more ATP. They therefore take more oxygen from the blood to produce the extra energy needed. Oxygen consumption therefore increases. The increased demand for oxygen in the muscles can only be met if they are supplied with a larger volume of blood. The heart therefore has to pump more blood per unit of time. This is reflected in an increased heart rate and stroke volume. The capacity of the body to absorb oxygen is, however, limited. When the heart rate reaches its maximum value (220 heartbeats per minute on average), the body has reached its maximum rate of oxygen delivery to the muscles. At that moment the body has no more resources with which to send oxygen to the muscles. The maximum amount of oxygen that can be absorbed by the body in one minute is termed the maximum oxygen consumption (VO2max). An individual's maximum oxygen consumption is largely genetically determined, and in healthy persons it varies from 2 to 7 liters per minute.

Conditioning can achieve an improvement of 10-20% at the most. The heart rate of a soccer player during a game is about 170 beats per minute. Because there are intervals of strongly fluctuating activity, the heart rate also varies considerably, so that minima and maxima of, respectively, 100-110 and 190-200 beats per minute may be registered. It is therefore important to vary the intensity of training sessions. The whole range of heart rates must be stimulated.

The Role of Oxygen in Soccer

At the end of the previous chapter we touched on cyclic and acyclic aerobic endurance. Soccer players primarily require acyclic endurance. This can be explained very clearly from a physiological point of view. Cyclic endurance enables an athlete to maintain a form of movement for a long time (long-distance running, cycling, skating). The intensity remains virtually constant, so the heart rate and the flow of blood through the muscles remain steady. All of the energy needed during this type of exercise is produced with the help of oxygen. An increase in cyclic aerobic endurance means that more oxygen is available to the muscles, which can produce more energy. Exertion can therefore be maintained longer. During cyclic exercise the slow (red) muscle fibers are the ones that are most active. Acyclic aerobic endurance enables an athlete to carry out all sorts of short, explosive actions (sprinting, jumping, shooting) in sequence over a long period of time. The intensity varies constantly, so the heart rate and flow of blood through the muscles also fluctuate. Exercise is clearly phased, and this makes completely different demands on the body than cyclic exercise. Short, explosive actions make use of the energy stored in the body (ATP and phosphocreatine; see section 2.4.2). This energy does not therefore need to be initially produced with the help of oxygen. Nor is there time to do so. During an explosive sprint, energy must be immediately available. After the sprint the reserves of ATP and phosphocreatine are (partly) exhausted. The phosphocreatine is replenished without oxygen. Oxygen is, however, needed to replenish the reserve of ATP. Oxygen is therefore more of an indirect fuel in relation to acyclic aerobic endurance. The oxygen system plays a very important role in the recuperation process of soccer players in the period between peak loads.

The Effects of Aerobic Soccer Conditioning

Conditioning for acyclic aerobic endurance can best be achieved with the help of extensive and intensive endurance training, extensive interval training and Fartlek training. In Chapter 6 there is a long and detailed description of how this can best be done in practice. The following is a short summary of the most important effects of aerobic soccer conditioning. One of the changes that takes place in the body as a consequence of aerobic conditioning is an increase in the cardiac output (see Fig. 2.9A). This is the result of an increase in stroke volume (see Fig. 2.9B). This means that more oxygen-rich blood flows to the muscles per unit of time. Because the capacity of the muscles to extract oxygen from the blood also increases, there is an improvement in endurance. More oxygen in the muscles results in more ATP, which enables work to be carried out longer or more intensively and shortens the period of recovery after intensive work. Aerobic conditioning also results in a lower heart rate for a given amount of exercise, indicating that less effort is needed for the exercise (see Fig. 2.9C). Another conditioning effect that can occur is an increase in the capacity of the muscles to store carbohydrates. This means that carbohydrate reserves will be exhausted less quickly. This is important, because exhaustion of these reserves can also result in tiredness (see Chapter 11).

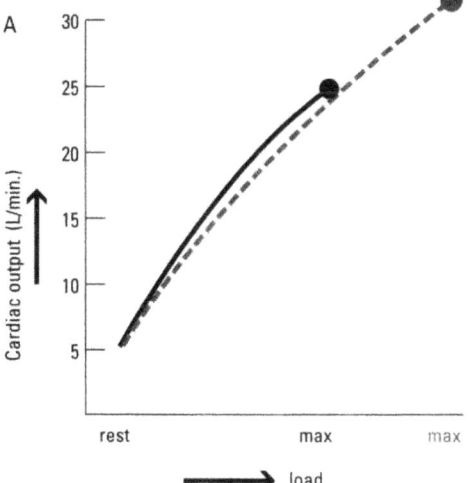
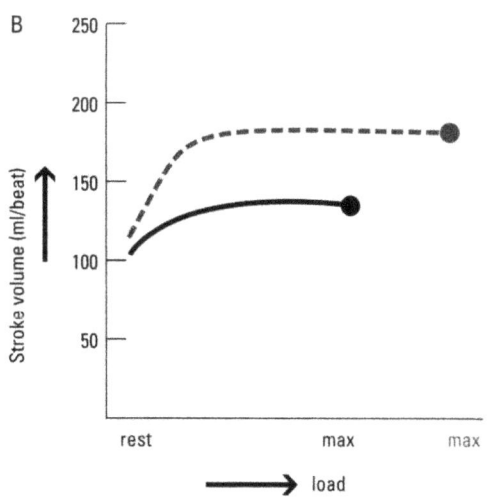
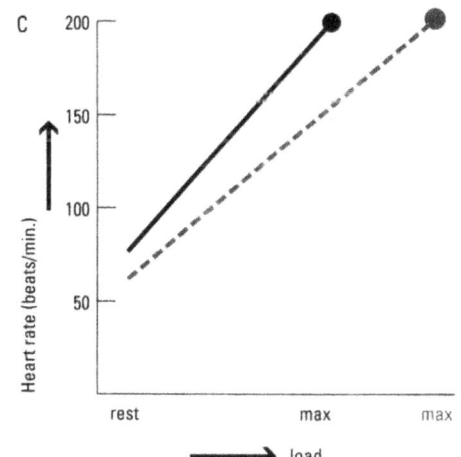

Figure 2.9: *One of the effects of anaerobic conditioning is that the cardiac output increases (A). This increase is due to an increase in the stroke volume (B) as a consequence of the heart's increase in size and strength. The heart rate becomes more efficient (C). This means that the heart performs less work when the body has to cope with a given load.*

Oxygen Deficit

At moments of peak exertion the muscles suddenly need more energy. However, the oxygen system is not able to produce this "extra" energy fast enough (see Fig. 2.10). Factors such as respiration rate and heart rate cannot be steeply increased from one moment to the other. Everyone knows from experience that this can only be done gradually. The oxygen system is too slow to provide the energy needed for short sprints of only a few seconds. As a consequence of this "adjustment problem" there is a so-called oxygen deficit when the body is called upon to make a sudden effort or to suddenly increase its level of exertion. Given that soccer players change from one form of activity to another every 5 seconds, the logical conclusion is that soccer players are regularly confronted with an oxygen deficit.

Conclusion

Soccer players are almost constantly in motion during a game. The oxygen system is therefore of considerable importance. It is responsible for producing most of the energy consumed. However, during peak moments of exertion it cannot cope with the demand

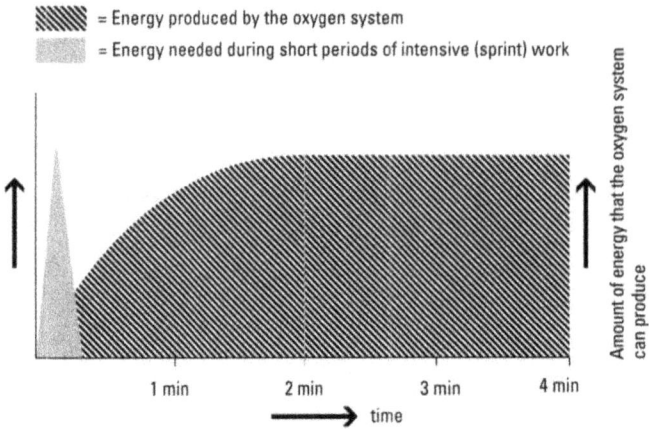

Figure 2.10: *During short periods of intensive exercise, more energy is suddenly required. The oxygen system cannot respond quickly enough to the abrupt increase in demand for energy. There is too little oxygen (oxygen deficit) to produce the necessary energy.*

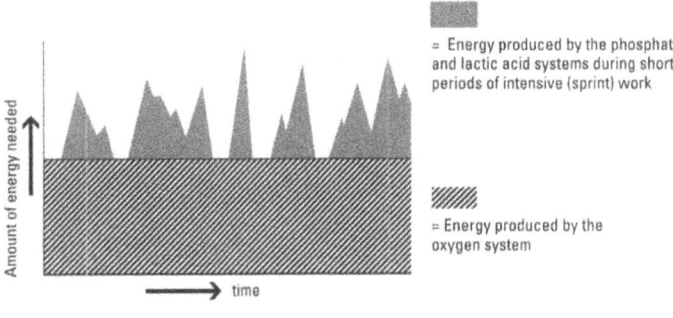

Figure 2.11: *Most of the energy expended by a soccer player during a game is supplied by the oxygen system. During short periods of intensive exertion, however, he has to rely on the phosphate system and, sometimes, the lactic acid system.*

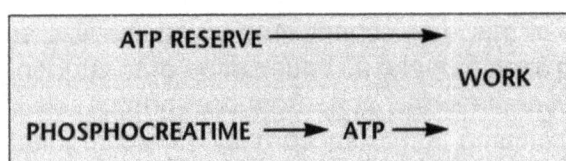

Figure 2.12: *Energy production by the phosphate system.*

for additional energy, e.g. to make sudden sprints, etc. (see Fig. 2.11). This shortcoming is compensated for by the body's two other energy systems, which produce ATP without any need for oxygen. These are the phosphate system and the lactic acid system.

2.4.2 The Phosphate System

The phosphate system is one of the body's two anaerobic systems. The term anaerobic indicates that the system does not need any oxygen to enable it to supply the muscles with ATP (see Fig. 2.12). This is the fastest option for the body to produce ATP when there is an oxygen deficit. The phosphate system contains a small amount of stored ATP, sufficient for a maximum of 1 or 2 seconds of work. The system also has a reserve of phosphocreatine (PC), which can be converted quickly to ATP. This again is sufficient for only a few seconds of work. When the phosphate system is completely exhausted, some 60-90 seconds are needed to replenish the reserves of ATP and PC. This usually occurs while soccer players are standing still, walking or jogging.

The Role of the Phosphate System in Soccer

In Chapter 1 it was stated that soccer players make 100 to 200 sprints, most of them over a distance of 5 to 10 meters, during a game. The sprints last 1 to 2 seconds on average, and thus draw mainly on the ATP reserve. The extent of this reserve is one of the factors that determines a player's starting speed. Longer sprints draw on the phosphocreatine reserve, from which it can be concluded that the size of this reserve influences a player's acceleration, speed endurance and repeated short sprint capacity. After an intensive effort it is necessary to recuperate as soon as possible. The more efficient the recuperation, the smaller the chance that fatigue will set in. The ATP and PC reserves must be repeatedly replenished. Oxygen is needed to make ATP. During peak exertion the oxygen system cannot supply sufficient energy (there is an oxygen deficit). It therefore "borrows" ATP from the phosphate system. When the peak effort has been concluded, the oxygen system pays back this debt to the phosphate system. With the help of oxygen the ATP reserve is replenished. Because of the necessity of paying off this "oxygen debt", the respiration rate and the heart rate remain high for some time after an intensive soccer action. The better the oxygen system is conditioned, the faster the "oxygen debt" can be repaid, and the sooner the phosphate system recovers. A soccer player is out of breath for a shorter period after an action. This has a positive effect on all the components that make up the player's speed. It also explains why soccer players should not be made to carry out long-distance runs. During such runs the players are not confronted with "oxygen debt," and the body cannot learn how to restore the phosphate system quickly. Only interval training is suitable for this purpose. That is endurance training with lots of changes in speed.

> *A sportsman can have all the money in the world, but if he has no heart, no soul, no emotion, then he can never really enjoy his sport.*
>
> **Joel Despaigne**

Improving the Phosphate System

The training methods for conditioning the phosphate system are explained in detail in Chapters 5 and 6. The following is a summary of the effects of this (sprint) training. The main effect is that the phosphate system becomes faster. This means that more energy is liberated per unit of time (increased power). This improves a player's speed off the mark and, to a lesser extent, his acceleration. The phosphate reserve stored in the muscles becomes bigger. It is therefore depleted less quickly and intensive (sprint) work can be maintained for a longer period (increased capacity). This results in improved acceleration, speed endurance and repeated short sprint capacity.

2.4.3 The Lactic Acid System

Sometimes soccer players have to put in an intensive effort for more than 10 consecutive seconds. Even the phosphate system cannot cope with this, and the body's second anaerobic energy system comes into action. This is the lactic acid system. An example is shown in Figure 2.13. In this example a soccer player has to put in an intensive effort for more than 30 consecutive seconds. In such a situation the lactic acid system comes to the aid of the phosphate system. The player's acyclic anaerobic endurance is called upon. This is the ability to perform anaerobic work for a longer period of time. The principle of the system is that carbohydrates (glycogens) are converted to ATP in the absence

Time (sec)	Activity
7	Jogging
4	Running
2	Sprinting Jumping
3	Sprinting Turning
6	Running
3	Jogging Shooting
3	Sprinting Turning
3	Sprinting
4	Jogging
7	Running
7	Jogging
31	Walking

Figure 2.13: *A fragment from a game, in which a player had to perform intensive work for more than 30 consecutive seconds. After 10 seconds the lactic acid system takes over from the phosphate system as the main supplier of energy. Lactic acid is then formed as a waste product.*

of oxygen (see Fig. 2.14). The disadvantage is that lactic acid is formed as a waste product of this process. This accumulates in the muscles, causing fatigue. The phosphate system (which does not involve the formation of lactic acid) is sometimes termed alactic in contrast to the lactic acid system, which is termed lactic. These terms are used to distinguish between two systems that are both anaerobic.

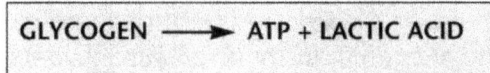

Figure 2.14: *Energy production by the lactic acid system.*

The Role of Lactic Acid in Soccer

Scientific research has shown that soccer players are not subject to considerable build up of acid. These results can be interpreted as indicating that the lactic acid system may not be of major importance for soccer players. Such a conclusion, however, overlooks the fact that lactic acid buildup was usually measured after the end of the first or second half, and not during play. The measurements therefore provide no information about the fluctuation in lactic acid content during a game. More measurements were therefore taken recently during the course of a match. These indicate that soccer players do not experience a considerable build-up of lactic acid, but the lactic acid system is nevertheless more active during play than the earlier research results indicated (see Fig. 2.15).

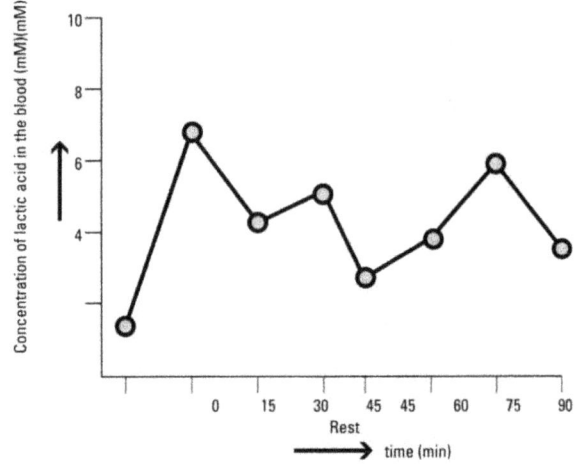

Figure 2.15: *Soccer players produce considerable amounts of lactic acid during a game. However, severe acidification never occurs.*

Acyclic anaerobic endurance should therefore be taken into account during training sessions (see Chapter 6).

The Effects of "Acidifying" Soccer Conditioning

Anaerobic lactic conditioning makes the body more resistant to the negative effects of lactic acid. Lactic acid has the annoying property of disrupting all types of processes in and around the muscles. As a consequence fatigue sets in sooner than usual. During training for anaerobic conditioning the load must be as large as possible. The players should be mentally and physically exhausted afterwards. Block training and interval sprinting training can be used for this purpose. The training must also be soccer-specific. This means that the period of work must not be too long. A high lactic acid level is worthless for soccer players. It also impairs their aerobic endurance. Lactic acid is also aggressive and breaks down the walls of the cells. Holes therefore form in the walls and all kinds of enzymes, which play an important role in endurance, escape from the cells. "Acidifying" soccer conditioning brings about an increase in lactic acid tolerance. The body acquires resistance against lactic acid.

2.4.4 Interaction Between the Energy Systems

Although the three energy systems have been treated separately, no bodily activities take place during which the necessary energy is produced by only one of the energy systems. All three systems play a role during any activity, whatever it may be. It is true, however, that one system may be of greater importance than another during any given activity. Figure 2.16 indicates how the systems overlap. The phosphate system is the most active of the three during the first 10 seconds of exertion, then the lactic acid system takes over for 2 to 3 minutes. Subsequently most of the energy needed is supplied by the oxygen system. However, all three systems are active to a greater or lesser degree during each of these phases. During a game a soccer player also makes use of each system. From the above it can be concluded that soccer players carry out a lot of activities during a game that make use of the phosphate system in particular. Very few of a soccer player's actions last for more than 10 seconds.

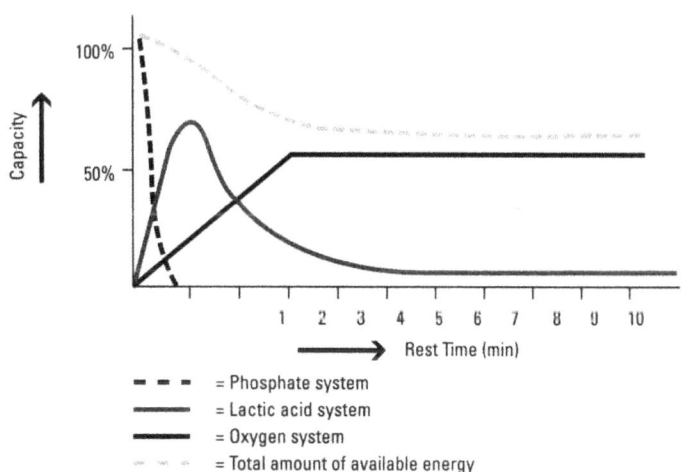

Figure 2.16: *The activity of the three energy producing systems as a function of time.*

2.5 THE MUSCULAR SYSTEM

The body has a great many large and small muscles, all of which are controlled by the nervous system. Under the control of the nervous system, the muscles and the skeleton enable us to move. This paragraph deals with the most important basic principles of the structure and functions of the muscles, and focuses especially on the relationship between nerves and muscles.

2.5.1 Muscle Structure

A muscle consists of bundles made up of muscle fibers (see Fig. 2.17). Muscle fibers are surrounded by small blood vessels and nerves. The blood vessels provide the muscle fibers with fuels, building materials and oxygen, and they remove the waste products of muscular activity. The nerves ensure that signals from the brain reach the muscles, and vice versa. Muscle fibers in their turn are built up of light and dark zones that alternate over the whole length of the fiber (see Fig. 2.18). These zones consist of protein chains, which are thick in the dark zones and thin in the light ones. Together they form the sarcomeres. Sarcomeres are the building blocks of the muscles. Figure 2.19A shows a sarcomere. The thick protein chains do not lie against each other but float in the fluid of the muscle fiber. This also applies to the thin protein chains, which lie alongside the thick chains. They partially overlap each other. This structure is geometrical (see Fig. 2.20). Each thick protein chain is surrounded by six thin protein chains. When the muscle contracts the light zones of the muscle fiber become narrower, because the thin protein chains are drawn towards the thick ones (see Figs. 2.19B and C). The muscle becomes shorter, and in doing so exerts force on the bones via the tendons. This whole mechanism is triggered by a stimulus from the nervous system. Each muscle fiber is connected with a nerve fiber.

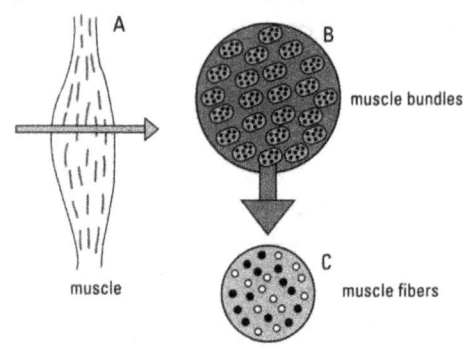

Figure 2.17: *A cross-section (B) of muscle (A) shows that it is made up of bundles, which in turn are made up of muscle fibers (C).*

Figure 2.18: *A muscle is made up of muscle fibers. Closer analysis of a muscle fiber shows that it consists of light and dark zones, which alternate along its whole length.*

2.5.2 The Various Types of Muscle Fiber

A muscle does not consist of just one type of muscle fiber. There are two main groups, which both have specific characteristics. They are referred to as slow and fast muscle fibers.

Slow Muscle Fibers

Slow muscle fibers are found in muscles that have to perform the same work for long periods of time, such as the muscles that keep the body balanced. The leg muscles of long-distance athletes (marathon runners, cyclists) also contain lots of slow muscle fibers (see Fig. 2.21 A). This type of muscle fiber is usually active for long periods, but cannot exert a very powerful force. Long-term work is carried out by slow muscle fibers. The oxygen system is therefore emphatically present in this type of fiber. After all, this system is essential to endurance. Because the slow fibers need a lot of

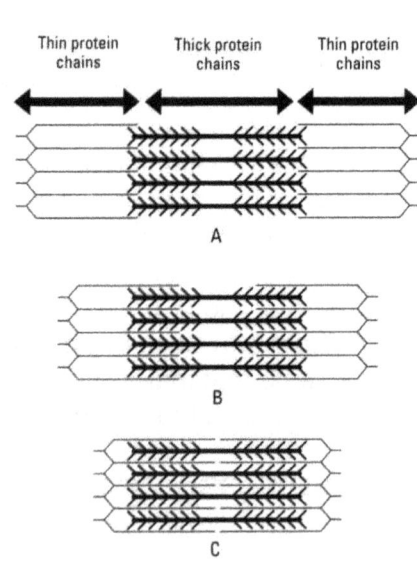

Figure 2.18: *A muscle fiber consists of sarcomeres (A), which are arranged in sequence. When a muscle contracts, the sarcomeres cluster up closer together, so that the muscle as a whole becomes shorter (B and C).*

oxygen they are rich in blood vessels. And because muscles are permanently under tension during long-term exercise, the blood vessels are regularly squeezed. This makes even higher demands on the blood flow. Slow muscle fibers are red in color. This is attributable to their many blood vessels and the presence of myoglobin. Myoglobin is a protein that binds oxygen to itself, just like hemoglobin. If, despite the large number of blood vessels in the slow muscle fibers, an oxygen deficit occurs, the oxygen reserve of myoglobin can be tapped. Myoglobin therefore acts as a sort of oxygen battery.

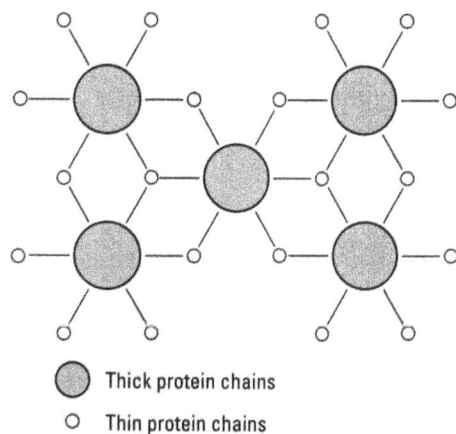

Figure 2.20: *Each thick protein chain is surrounded by six thin protein chains. The resulting structure is geometrical.*

Fast Muscle Fibers

Fast muscle fibers make it possible to perform intensive work for short periods. Sprinters in particular have muscles with large numbers of fast muscle fibers (see Figure 2.21b). The phosphate system is essential to explosive work. This system is therefore present in the fast muscle fibers. Because the energy in the fast muscle fibers is mainly produced anaerobically, these fibers have little myoglobin and few blood vessels. The color of the fast muscle fibers is therefore white.

Conditioning Slow and Fast Muscle Fibers

Muscles consist of slow and fast muscle fibers. It appears that the relationship between these two types of muscle fiber is genetically determined. Marathon runners have lots of slow fibers in their leg muscles, and sprinters have lots of fast fibers. If a sprinter wanted more fast muscle fibers, he might want to carry out training exercises that would convert his slow fibers to fast ones. Research has shown that this is practically impossible. The only gain that can be achieved in this area is to make the fast fibers stronger, and intensive conditioning can bring about an improvement of 15 to 20% at most. In contrast, a lot of one-sided endurance work (long-distance running, for example) can make the fast muscle fibers slow. Although this "conditioning effect" can only occur to a limited degree, it is very unfavorable for sportsmen who rely on their explosive pace. Some of this is lost if a lot of endurance training is carried out.

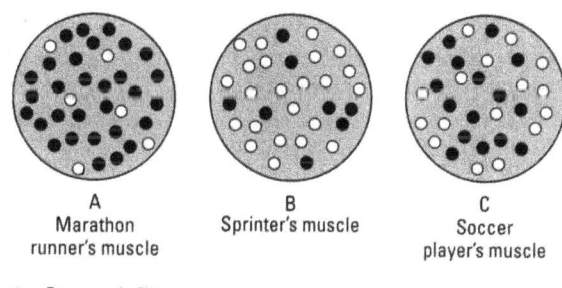

Figure 2.21: *A muscle is built up of slow and fast muscle fibers. The leg muscles of a marathon runner contain mainly slow muscle fibers (A). A sprinter has leg muscles that largely consist of fast muscle fibers (B). A soccer player's leg muscles contain both types (C). Speed and endurance are both of importance for a soccer player.*

2.5.3 The Composition of the Muscles of Soccer Players

Explosive muscle work is essential to most soccer actions. Soccer players must have muscles that can develop a lot of strength in a short time. Fast muscle fibers are most suitable for this. A player needs more than speed, however, to come through a game of 90 minutes duration. Soccer players have to walk and jog considerable distances during a game. Slow muscle fibers therefore also play a role in soccer (see Fig. 2.21 C). Research has shown that top soccer players have more fast muscle fibers than amateur players. This perhaps explains why top soccer players can carry out more sprints than amateurs.

> *When I attended the coaching course I heard a few difficult words. I didn 't write them down, other wise my fingers would have become tied in knots.*
> **Willem van Hanegem**

2.6 CONCLUSION

We know which of the body's physiological systems allow soccer work to be performed. The oxygen transport system ensures that oxygen and/or nutrients are delivered to the oxygen system, the phosphate system and the lactic acid system. These systems ensure that the muscles that carry out soccer work are supplied with energy. The whole process is under the control of the nervous system. By conditioning each of the above-mentioned systems in a soccer context, a player's loading capacity can be increased. All of this knowledge is an insufficient basis for starting on a program of soccer conditioning. A factor such a strength, for instance, cannot be conditioned by just one program of training exercises. All kinds of specific conditioning methods and principles are needed. Each of these methods has to be adapted to a soccer context, but also has its own specific principles. These are dealt with in the following chapter, in which the role of flexibility in soccer is also described.

SUMMARY

- The nervous system controls every human movement. Every soccer action is therefore controlled by the nervous system.

- The nervous system consists of two parts: the central nervous system (brain and spinal cord) and the peripheral nervous system (nerve fibers that connect sensors and muscles with the spinal cord).

- The nervous system is a stimulus-processing (sensory) and stimulus-generating (motoric) organ. All movements are coordinated by means of motoric and sensory processes.

- Sensory processes enable soccer players to perceive soccer situations. Motoric processes enable them to carry out soccer actions.

- The sensory information on which a soccer player's perceptions are based comes from his sense of sight, hearing, movement and balance. This information can be reafferent or exafferent.

- When the brain has formed a picture of the game situation and the player has decided on the best action to take, this action then has to be carried out.

- The brain sends signals to the muscles that will carry out the action. These signals are often very complex. They contain information about which muscle has to contract, and when, and how strongly. A soccer action is therefore brought about by the concerted efforts of various muscles under the direction of the nervous system.

- The job of the nervous system can be regarded as having a conscious and an unconscious component. The conscious component relates to all bodily processes that require a degree of conscious thought, and the unconscious component relates to all bodily processes that occur automatically (e.g. heart beat, blood pressure).

- Improved coordination results in a steady increase in the amount of information that is unconsciously processed during the execution of a soccer action; the soccer action is carried out more automatically. The soccer player can then pay more attention to what is happening around him on the pitch.

- The oxygen system consists of the heart, the respiration and blood. The system carries oxygen and nutrients to the muscles. It also removes the waste products of muscular activity.

- The body has to convert nutrients such as carbohydrates, fats and proteins into ATP before their energy can be used by the muscles.

- The body has three energy systems: the oxygen system, the phosphate system and the lactic acid system.

- The most efficient way for the body to produce ATP is with the help of oxygen (aerobically). The oxygen system makes use of oxygen to convert carbohydrates, fats and proteins to ATP.

- The oxygen system plays a major role in helping players to recover from periods of peak exertion.

- Aerobic conditioning makes the heart bigger and stronger. The muscles are also better able to absorb oxygen from the blood.

- The oxygen system is too slow to respond effectively to sudden demands for lots of energy (for example, to power a sprint). Factors such a respiration and heart beat need time to increase. There is therefore a shortage of oxygen during an increase in intensity.

- The phosphate system contains a small amount of stored ATP. This amount is only sufficient for about 2 seconds of maximum exertion. The system also has access to phosphocreatine, which can be quickly converted into ATP. This can fuel a few more seconds of intensive exertion.

- The ATP reserve is crucial to starting speed. Phosphocreatine plays a key role in acceleration capacity, speed endurance and repeated short sprint capacity.

- A soccer player sometimes has to put in an intensive effort for more than 30 consecutive seconds. In such a situation the phosphate system cannot fuel the final 10 seconds and the lactic acid system takes over as the main supplier of energy.

- The principle of this system is that glycogen is converted to ATP in the absence of oxygen. The disadvantage is that lactic acid is formed. Lactic acid disrupts all types of processes in and around the muscles and causes fatigue to set in sooner than usual.

- Soccer players do not experience severe acidification. However, the role of the lactic acid system in soccer should not be underestimated.

- "Acid" conditioning causes the body to become more resistant to the negative effects of lactic acid (lactic acid tolerance). Moreover the amount of energy produced increases in relation to the amount of lactic acid produced.

- During a soccer action all three energy systems are active. Depending on the type of action, one may be more active than another.

- A muscle consists of two types of fibers - slow and fast muscle fibers. A soccer player needs both types, with a slight preference for the fast muscle fibers.

FIVE PRACTICAL QUESTIONS

1. The physical load that we have to cope with in our everyday work is steadily decreasing as automation increases. Does this mean that our loading capacity is decreasing?

It does appear that we are less active than we were 20 or 30 years ago. Moreover our dietary habits have gradually become worse. This is reflected in a rise in so-called diseases of civilization. In general, therefore, loading capacity is decreasing. This has irreversible consequences for the quality of amateur soccer.

2. Each individual's body is different. No two persons are exactly the same. Must a coach take this into account, and how?

It is true each individual body is unique. One player may have good natural endurance, while the other may be naturally fast or strong. A coach can exploit this by letting a player with good natural endurance play in midfield, and by using fast players in attack or defense. He can only do this, however, if the players have the soccer skills that will allow them to function well in these positions.

3. What is the anaerobic threshold, and is this of relevance for soccer players?

During periods of intensive exertion the body produces lactic acid. At the same time the body consumes lactic acid in order to produce energy. For a long time these two processes remain in equilibrium. At a given moment the level of exertion is so great that lactic acid production exceeds lactic acid consumption, and a surplus of lactic acid builds up in the body. This point is referred to as the anaerobic threshold. For soccer players it is of little relevance. Soccer players do not experience considerable "acidification" during a game.

4. What is the physiological background of recovery training, and is this of any value in amateur soccer?

During recovery training the intensity of the work carried out is low. The blood circulation is increased, but no new waste substances are produced. The increased circulation accelerates the rate of supply of nutrients and other elements. The removal of wastes is also accelerated. In amateur soccer such training is not worthwhile. There is usually a minimum of two days between a game and the next training session. This is sufficient to enable the players to recover.

5. Is it worthwhile to occasionally use cardiometers during training sessions?

It is certainly worthwhile to use a cardiometer now and then as a monitoring aid. A coach can check whether the desired intensity is actually reached during a given training exercise. A cardiometer is also useful during a player's rehabilitation process. During rehabilitation it is important that players work gradually towards their complete recovery. The cardiometer is then a useful aid.

INTERVIEW WITH HANS WESTERHOF (Director of Youth Coaching at A.F.C. Ajax)

When did you become interested in physiology?
After I completed my education at the Academy for Physical Education I served in the army in Hooghalen. After my period of service was over I was asked to stay on as an instructor of "medical" subjects. My predecessor, Leen Pfrommer, had written a paper on modern training methods and it was my task to translate its content into practice. I started to collect a lot of literature and spoke to people who had a knowledge of physiology. At that time, however, not much information was available. Later, at the Dutch National Sports Training Institute in Heerenveen, I taught exercise physiology in combination with game sports. When I was appointed coach of F.C. Groningen there was a clash of interests with my work at the Institute, and I eventually stopped.

In your opinion, how important is a knowledge of physiology for coaches?
A coach has a moral obligation to know how the human body functions. After all, you are working with people, and mistaken training methods can cause them physical injury. If you are not familiar with the effects of intensive training methods, you should steer clear of them, otherwise you are putting your players' health at risk. A knowledge of physiology therefore improves your chances of success. You can train your players' more purposefully.

How do you exploit your physiological background during training sessions?
During the preseason preparation period you have to get your players match fit and make sure that they do not suffer injuries. Injuries can badly disrupt preseason preparations. Thanks to my knowledge of physiology I know how hard I can push my players. Players can suffer injury as a result of being asked to do too much too soon, and I can avoid this. A coach has to learn all kinds of laws and principles of training. He then has to see how they work in practice. Ultimately he will be in a position, on the basis of his experience and intuition, to improve the conditioning of a group of soccer players. But he can only do this on the basis of acquired knowledge.

Do you often measure your players' heart rates?
I check the heart rates of specific players now and again. Because I have done this for so many years I can recognize a player's condition within a few seconds. You can also detect differences between, for example, midfielders and attackers. Midfielders have a much fuller, more regular, heartbeat than attackers. Because they have to do a lot of running they develop a stronger heart with a more powerful heartbeat. This is a useful way of checking whether the objective of a training session is really being achieved.

Is the physiological aspect dealt with adequately during coaching courses?
I cannot say much about the current situation but I remember how it was when I took the course. I felt that there was too much attention paid to physiology. The participants were swamped with facts and figures, and as a result most of them found the course too difficult and gave up. Every coach must be familiar with general exercise physiology and be able to apply it. But if you go into it too deeply there is a risk of overkill. This is a mistake that is often made in sport. The problem is that outsiders are always brought in to explain about strength training, running training or psychology. One of our failings in the soccer world is that we have not been able to look at other fields, take on board the useful knowledge that is already present there, and translate this knowledge into a form that is suitable for our own purposes.

Do you agree that the muscles are the slave of the brain?
It is true that the nervous system is the starting point for playing soccer. The reason why we used to think in terms of muscles is that we were looking for factors that responded measurably to conditioning. Obviously it is not very easy to measure the activity of the nervous system. Conditioning of the nervous system is aimed at helping players to acquire secure technique. We work at making conscious technique so familiar that it becomes unconscious, freeing up attention for new techniques.

Should players not have some knowledge of physiology, so that they treat their bodies with more care?
I have always found that players are very interested in this. When I measure players' heart rates they often want to know what it means. The same applies to the results of tests. Players like to see how they have developed over a given period of time, and how their marks compare with those of their teammates. By talking about these things a lot, and by explaining them, players can be encouraged to change their outlook. They are better able to understand the objective of certain conditioning exercises. This is certainly true of players who follow a coaching course.

The merits of stretching are currently disputed. What is your view?
The Ajax youth players carry out a standard warming up routine, in which static stretching exercises no longer play a part. In the past I have seen players carry out short stretching exercises before starting on a training drill that focused on starting speed. Obviously this is wrong. After a training session or a game I have no problem with light stretching exercises. It also helps the players to relax.

Players in different positions have to do different amounts of running work. Do you, as a coach, exploit this fact?
When I was the coach of F.C. Groningen I held a test every six weeks. The minimum performance that I demanded from each player depended on his position and age. In regard to training drills I never took the differences in conditional demands associated with various positions into account. Each Thursday morning, however, the training session focused on the different lines in the team. Midfielders were used as such, and therefore automatically had to cope with a midfielder's load. The same applied to attackers and defenders. In addition the players received position-specific stimuli during the game.

No two bodies are physiologically identical. Players nevertheless take part in training sessions in groups. To what extent do you take account of the fact that players are all different?
In the first place natural selection plays a role. A player without good endurance will not want to play in midfield. He will probably play at the heart of the defense. This usually occurs of its own accord. Because conditioning training is usually based on a player's position, real problems do not often arise. I certainly took account of the players' ages. Everyone who was older than thirty only trained once each day.

No considerable amount of acidification occurs in soccer players' bodies during a match. Do you carry out "acidifying" training?
I have never made use of training drills that exhaust the players. However, it is not a bad thing to occasionally use a training drill that results in a degree of lactic acid formation. This type of training is very useful, for example, for players who have a low lactic acid tolerance. Making such players carry out "acidifying" exercises can raise their tolerance threshold. Some players run themselves into the ground during a game, while others do less than their share of the work. I sometimes make players who fall into the latter category perform "acidifying" exercise so that they can experience what they are doing to their teammates. But this is more a psychological trick.

Youth players from 6 to 18 years old are continuously developing. How can this be taken into account from a physiological point of view?
It is important to take the right decisions on how often young players should train, and how strenuously. The 8 to 12 year-olds train 3 times each week for a good hour. In addition they can train another two times if they want to. They can therefore play soccer each day. The 13 to 16 year-olds train four times per week. The 17 and 18 year-olds train six times per week, with two sessions on Tuesdays and Thursdays. The 13 to 18 year-olds also take part in soccer aerobics and additional strength training. If they experience growth problems, the training program is, of course, adjusted appropriately.

LITERATURE

1. Schema's Fysiologie.
B. van Cranenburg.
De Tijdstroom, Lochem. 1991.

2. Inleiding in de toegepaste neurowetenschappen.
B. van Cranenburg.
Lemma, Utrecht. 1993.

3. Neurale sturing van de motoriek.
B. van Cranenburgh.
Richting/Sportgericht 50 (1996) 3/5.

4. Textbook of Work Physiology.
P.O. Astrand and K. Rodahl.
ISBN: 0-07-100114-x.
McGraw-Hill.

5. Fysiologie van Lichamelijke Opvoeding and Sport.
E.L. Fox en D.K. Mathews.
ISBN: 90-352-1406-4.
De Tijdstroom.

6. Fysiologie van de mens.
J.A. Bernards and L.N. NBouman.
ISBN: 90-31130835-8.
Bohn, Scheltema en Holkema.

CHAPTER 3

THE SCIENCE OF CONDITIONING

Dr. Raymond Verheijen
Dr. Gerard van der Poel (section 3.3)

3.1 INTRODUCTION

Conditioning is the process of "getting fit" for a particular sport, and a soccer coach should have a thorough knowledge of its laws and methods. A conditioning stimulus must be given regularly, systematically, and above all variably. It is therefore important to choose the correct conditioning methods. This choice depends on what effect is required. Not all conditioning effects are produced by the same conditioning program. The conditioning effect achieved - whether it is endurance, sprinting or strength - is specific to the method used. All conditioning programs must be structured so that they improve specific physiological functions that are needed for certain skills in a particular sport. Soccer conditioning must also be systematic and variable. This chapter therefore explains the most important conditioning laws, principles and methods with the help of practical examples. The importance of special conditioning is also emphasized.

3.2 THE BASIC MOTOR PROPERTIES

The physical basis of a sportsman's performance comprises a number of fundamental motor properties: strength, speed and endurance. These three factors are interlinked (see Figure 3.1).

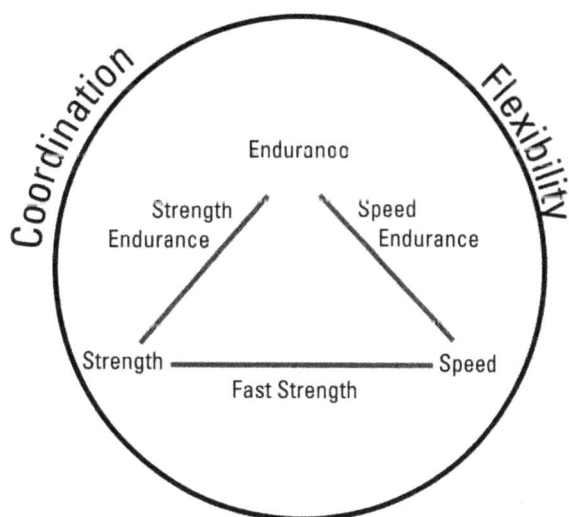

Figure 3.1: *The relationships between the various basic motor properties.*

The main requisite for a marathon runner is endurance, whereas a sprinter needs speed and a weight lifter needs strength. Soccer players make use of a combination of these three factors. This alone is an indication of the complexity of soccer conditioning.

Strength, Speed and Endurance
It has always been said that soccer players need strength, speed and endurance. This is, however, a somewhat oversimplified view. In soccer, work is performed on the basis of a combination of these fundamental motor properties. Soccer players need more than pure strength, speed and endurance; they also require speed endurance, strength endurance and speed strength. The fundamental motor properties are therefore sport- dependent. Perhaps it would be better to speak of sport-related motor properties. Besides the trinity of strength, speed and endurance there are also two other fundamental motor properties - flexibility and coordination. These too can be said to be sport-related. Soccer players do not need the extreme flexibility of gymnasts or the finely tuned coordination of figure-skaters. Nevertheless both properties are important for a soccer player. The role of coordination has been extensively described in Chapter 2 and will also be dealt with in Chapter 5. The following paragraph is dedicated to the function of flexibility in soccer.

3.3 FLEXIBILITY
There is considerable confusion about flexibility and flexibility conditioning in the soccer world. In a sport such as gymnastics, flexibility is one of the main factors that determine performance. An analysis of the range of movement required of the joints involved in actions such as shooting, changing direction, turning and jumping justifies the conclusion that soccer players' joints do not have to be as flexible as those of gymnasts. The fundamental property "flexibility" is of subordinate importance in soccer, but is certainly not unimportant.

3.3.1 The Role of Flexibility in Soccer Minimum
A soccer player must have a minimum of flexibility, especially in the hips. If a player in a sitting position tries to touch his knee with his nose but remains sitting virtually upright, he has very stiff hips. This can have a negative effect on important soccer actions such as starting, sprinting and turning. Specific flexibility conditioning can improve the flexibility of the hips, thereby also improving speed and agility. Limited movement in the hips, etc., is not often encountered. When it is, it must be eliminated by conditioning. The subsequent level of flexibility must then be maintained. This applies to every soccer player.

Short-long
In popular sports literature it is often suggested that muscles become "shorter" as a consequence of conditioning. This is an old wives' tale. It is simply not true that muscles become shorter "of their own accord" as a consequence of conditioning. The implication is that sportsman will become stiffer and stiffer if he does not carry out stretching exercises, and will finally only be able to lie in his bed like a sort of mummy. A muscle simply adapts its length to the length at which it is most often used. If a muscle is frequently stretched to the maximum then it will slowly adapt. It will become longer to enable it to function better in the "long" state. More sarcomeres come to lie behind each other (see Figure 3.2). If a muscle often has to carry out work in its "short" state, then in time it will become shorter. The number of sarcomeres decreases. Muscles do not therefore, by definition, become shorter as a consequence of conditioning. Muscle length is completely dependent on

how the muscle is used. Shortening of the muscle can best be prevented by making the players carry out all sorts of different movements. Vary the conditioning program rather than letting the players always carry out the same exercises.

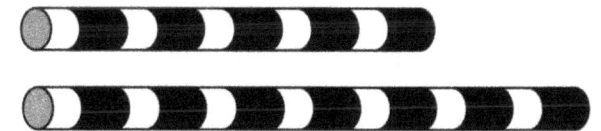

Figure 3.2: *If the muscle regularly has to carry out work in the extended state, the number of sarcomeres increases. The muscle then becomes longer.*

Specificity

Flexibility is a general physical property but is joint-specific. In any team, some of the players will be regarded as flexible and others as stiff. But if flexibility is put to the test it may be found that a "flexible" player has a good range of hip movement but only a modest degree of movement in his shoulders. On the other hand it may be true that a "stiff" player cannot bend forward very far, but that is not to say that his ankles are also stiff. Each joint has its own "cripples" and "champions." This is not so surprising if we remember that each movement is the outcome of many factors, including the structure and shape of the joint, the capsule and the ligaments, the joint lubrication, the length of the tendons and muscles, and the control exerted by the nervous system. Other factors that can considerably influence a joint's range of movement are age (as we get older the elasticity of the connective tissue slowly decreases), fatigue, time of day, ambient temperature and the temperature of the tissues. These factors differ from person to person and, in any given individual, from joint to joint. Each individual has his own maximum, and so does each joint.

Active Flexibility

Active flexibility means that a joint is moved by the muscles that "belong" to it and not by external force. A leg is lifted as high as possible without any help from the arms. Passive flexibility is the range of movement of a joint under the influence of external force. One example is the bending of the wrist by pushing the fingers back with the other hand. Dynamic flexibility exercises are the best way of training for active flexibility (see section 3.3.4). These are "loosening up" exercises. The accent, however, is less on gentle loosening up than on "big" movements. Naturally there must be a gradual build up from smaller to extensive movements.

Soccer players make use of active rather than passive flexibility.

3.3.2 The Various Types of Stretching

There are three ways of stretching. The first is the widely familiar "static stretching". The muscle is stretched and held in that position for a few seconds. This method is therefore familiar on account of the resulting statue-like pose. The "contract-relax" method is another stretching technique. The slightly stretched muscle is first contracted strongly, then immediately statically stretched. The muscles can be stretched either passively (by an external force) or actively (by contracting them). The third method is dynamic stretching.

Objective: Range of movement/flexibility conditioning

Conclusion 1: It is of no consequence what form of stretching is chosen (dynamic/static/contract-relax) for long-term (more than 3 months) stretching programs if the aim is to maintain or increase the (passive) range of movement.

Conclusion 2: Work specifically aimed at improving flexibility should be carried out at least 3 times each week in the form of more than 10 minutes of stretching exercises on each occasion. One session of more than 10 minutes each week is sufficient to maintain flexibility at a given level, allowing limited coaching time to be devoted to other topics.

Conclusion 3: A stretch phase of 10 to 15 seconds appears to be sufficient to affect the range of movement of a joint.

Conclusion 4: An increase in range of movement acquired through dynamic stretching is most rapidly lost when training is no longer carried out.

Objective: Prevention

Conclusion 5: It has not been proved that stretching prevents injuries.

Conclusion 6: A single session of 3 or 4 seconds static stretching is useful as a preventive check. You "listen" to your body to determine whether it is ready yet.

Conclusion 7: By stretching during warming up, you avoid reduced range of movement 24 hours after the training session.

Conclusion 8: Stretching has no clearly proven preventive effect on muscle pain.

Objective: Relaxation

Conclusion 9: During static stretching, muscle tone remains at a low level. Static stretching is useful for reducing an excessively high level of muscle tone.

Conclusion 10: The basic idea "the more relaxed, the more effect on the range of movement" is not correct.

Objective: What to do/avoid doing
Conclusion 11: If you want to extend a muscle, let it supply strength in the extended position.
Conclusion 12: If you have muscle pain, do not carry out stretching!
Conclusion 13: Do not do any more than light stretching during a training session.
Conclusion 14: The greater the tension, the greater the risk of damage. So stretch gently, not fiercely!

Objective: Strength/speed
Conclusion 15: The angular velocity of joint movements of untrained individuals can be increased by all forms of stretching.
Conclusion 16: Carrying out static stretching exercises shortly before taking part in a form of sport that requires explosive power impairs performance (slightly).
Conclusion 17: There is no sound basis of fact to justify the disfavor into which dynamic stretching has fallen.

Objective: Blood circulation
Conclusion 18: The blood circulation is not improved very much by stretching exercises. Active movement does improve it.

3.3.3 Stretching - Fact and Fable

In the late 1970s static stretching began to take over on Dutch sports fields and at the same time dynamic stretching fell out of favor. These trends were set in motion by the bestselling book "The Stretching Method" by the American Bob Anderson.

Around 1987, motivated partly by his own experience but largely by curiosity, the author of this section, Gerard van der Poel, started to question the view that "stretching is always good." He looked into the scientific justification for stretching. After 10 years of collecting research literature, and of study, discussion and experimentation, he has built up a considerable body of knowledge about stretching. The literature on the subject clearly indicates that a number of aspects are in clear contradiction to what is now frequently assumed in popular literature and in sports practice. Gerard van der Poel has written a series of three articles in the magazine "Richting/Sportgericht" (the "stretching file"). The conclusions are listed at the end of this article, but a few of the most important conclusions for soccer coaches are described in the following paragraphs.

Static is not Explosive
There are clear indications that static stretching causes a deterioration in the specific coordination of explosive movements. In view of the fact that there are a great many of these explosive movements during a game of soccer, it is not advisable to carry out a lot of static stretching before a training session or a game. A soccer player does not need relaxed muscles - he needs warm, fast, reasonably elastic muscles (see Conclusion 16).

A brief period of stretching relaxes the players. Stretching too powerfully might aggravate the muscle damage.

Prevention of Injuries

An analysis of how and when soccer injuries, such as pulled and torn muscles and other acute muscle lesions, occur shows that they are not caused by actions requiring a large range of movement. Injuries are only rarely caused by "too extreme" a range of movement. It is doubtful whether large ranges of movement are necessary, by definition, to prevent injuries. Nor is there any proof that stretching prevents injuries (Conclusion 5). An individual's loading capacity differs from day to day, so a "standard" warming-up routine will not always have the same effect. It is very important that a sportsman does not go "full out" until he is ready to do so. A short, calm spell of static stretching is an excellent way of "listening" to the muscles concerned. Is the muscle stiffer than usual? If so, or if it does not feel quite right, the player should continue with his warming up before he starts the training session or match.

Soccer players must have flexible hips if they are to be able to control a high ball with the foot.

3.3.4 Flexibility Exercises for Soccer Players

A dynamic flexibility exercise might involve, for example, raising the right knee while in a standing position, then describing ten small circles towards the outside with the knee. Ten larger circles can then be described, with the emphasis on the outward rotation of the hip. This can then be repeated with the other leg. The same exercise can be performed with the leg outstretched. This type of flexibility exercise can be combined with other exercises. In this case the

first exercise could be followed immediately by an exercise requiring a high ball to be brought down with the foot. Numerous other flexibility exercises can be carried out in this way.

The Back
Stand with the legs slightly apart, the knees slightly bent and the arms straight out to the front. Slowly rotate alternately to right and left. The aim is to rotate as far as possible. There is no need to hold the position of maximum rotation.

The Hips
With hands at sides and feet together, rotate the hips alternately to right and left, gradually increasing the degree of rotation; the speed of the rotations should not be too high.

Flexibility in the hips as an aid to stopping an opponent.

Flexible hips are the basis of a good passing and shooting technique.

3.4 CONDITIONING LAWS
3.4.1 The Overload Principle

If the aim of conditioning is to improve a player's "fitness," the overload principle must be applied. During training the body must be asked to do more than it is used to. This can be done by constantly varying the extent, the intensity, the number of repetitions and pauses, and by stepping up the level of difficulty. During a game of 11 against 11 on a full-sized pitch, the overload principle can be applied to acyclic aerobic endurance by asking the players to pair off. They must then follow each other over the entire pitch. They will have to run much further than usual, especially when there is a switch of possession. This overload can be stepped up by reducing the number of players without reducing the size of the pitch. A period of 10 against 10 can be succeeded

Top: Lift the right foot and turn it outward. Then swing the right leg forward and backward as far as possible. Keep the left knee slightly bent. This exercise requires good concentration, otherwise it is easy to lose your balance.

Bottom: The ankles. With the foot on the ground, rotate the ankle of the foot to the largest possible degree. Carry out this exercise with the right and left foot alternately.

by 8 against 8, with only 16 players having to cover the entire pitch. Another possibility is to work with zones. A team can only score when all of its players are in a specified zone. This will make greater demands on the running power of the players. Drills of this type are described in Chapter 6. The overload principle can also be employed in small sided games of 3 against 3 or 4 against 4, but the emphasis is then on strength in one against one situations rather than running capacity. If a lot of players are concentrated in a small area there will obviously be many more challenges for the ball. This promotes physical strength and agility. The smaller the field of play, the greater the degree of overload. The more players there are in a small area, the more complex the situation becomes. The players are confronted with increasingly difficult soccer problems. Their soccer capacities are overloaded. They are asked to find solutions for situations to which they are not (yet) accustomed. The nervous system has to deal with sensory information (through perception) about game situations that it has not yet encountered. It must learn to

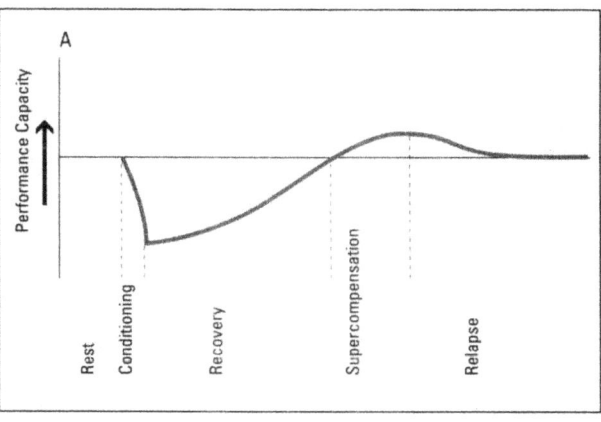

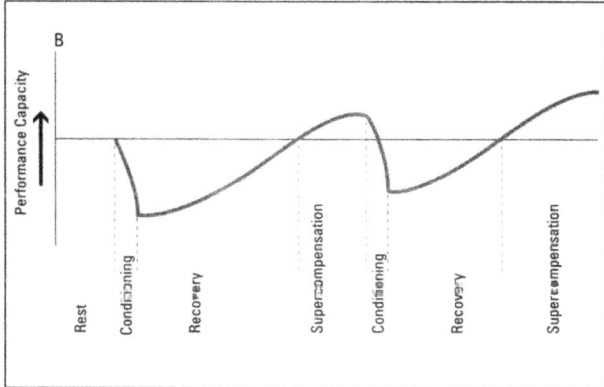

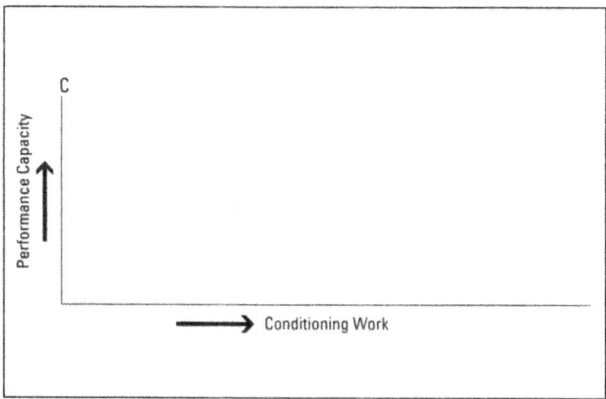

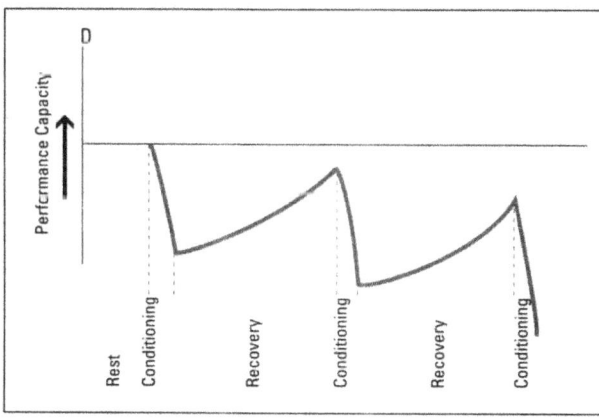

coordinate familiar soccer actions in a new (and more complex) situation. The term "overload" can therefore also be applied to the nervous system. If soccer players are not regularly confronted with an intensive workload during training, their bodies will adapt to the situation. In effect a negative conditioning effect will occur. The physical condition of the players will deteriorate as a result of this "underload."

Supercompensation

The body has the property of adapting to a strong stimulus (see Fig. 3.3A). This process of adaption is also referred to as conditioning effect or supercompensation. If the overload principle is consistently applied, a player's ability to perform will improve (see Fig. 3.3B). Improvement through supercompensation is not, however, an endless process. Further progress can only be achieved at the cost of an increasing amount of work during training (see Fig. 3.3C). Small improvements in performance require more and more time and energy. This is an example of the law of decreasing returns in action. It must be realized that the body needs a period of rest to recover from a powerful (conditioning) stimulus and to build up supercompensation. During overload situations the body is exposed to loads that are, in effect, beyond its present capabilities. One of the consequences is that muscle damage occurs. The body needs a period of rest after overload training to repair this damage. The "repaired" muscles are even a little stronger than before, so that they will be able to cope with an equally powerful conditioning stimulus in future. If, over a long period of time, the body is not allowed to recover sufficiently between successive overload stimuli, this can result in overstrain or overtraining. The body is forced to cope with overload stimuli during training, although the energy systems are tired and the body has not yet been able to repair all the (muscle) damage. As a consequence the player's performance capacity decreases (see Fig. 3.3D). More training therefore results in poorer performance (frustration curve). The work:rest ratio is therefore crucial for achieving supercompensation. Because the nervous system can also be overloaded, it can also undergo a conditioning effect - in this case supercompensation in the form of an increased capacity for solving complex soccer problems, and improved technique. This is a consequence of changes in the brain and in the control of the muscles by the brain. The conditioning laws and principles that apply to the muscles also apply to the nervous system.

The Work: Rest Ratio During the Soccer Season
A player usually has to give his utmost during a game of soccer. Playing a game of soccer can therefore be regarded as an overload stimulus. As a consequence it is not possible to train intensively on the days immediately before and after a game. If a team is to play on a Sunday, Friday and Saturday are dominated by the pre-match preparations, and Monday and Tuesday are set aside for the players to recover. This only leaves the Wednesday and Thursday for intensive training sessions. Amateur teams that play on Sundays should therefore train on Tuesdays and Thursdays, and amateurs who play on Saturdays are best advised to train on Mondays and Wednesdays. Most coaches do follow this pattern. Professional soccer is frequently played on Sundays. The Monday training session is then devoted to recovering from the game and Tuesday should be a day off. The Wednesday and Thursday would then be available for intensive training. In the Netherlands, however, Wednesday is traditionally a free day. Coaches would do well to change this. The second day after a game should be the day off because this is the day when the body recuperates most from the exertions of the previous game. In professional soccer, however, it is often necessary to play another game on the Wednesday.

Flexible hips are the basis of a good passing and shooting technique.

The logical conclusion is that there is not a single day that is suitable for intensive training. All that can be done is to ensure that the players' maintain their condition, and it can even be said that they are "underloaded." If this situation continues for a long period of time the players physical condition will deteriorate. Their bodies will adapt to the less strenuous workloads experienced during training. However, the exertion required during matches remains at the same (high) level. Soccer players therefore have a lower loading capacity but have to cope with an unchanged workload. This is clearly an example of a situation in which the balance between load and loading capacity is disturbed. Overstrain is the logical consequence.

Not only do the players have to take part in a large number of games but these games are held at irregular intervals. In principle the body can adapt to any situation that it regularly encounters. The Sunday-Wednesday-Sunday cycle is nothing new. Nowadays, however, it may be followed by a Wednesday-Saturday-Tuesday cycle. The body can adapt to any stimulus (or cycle) provided there is an element of regularity. An irregular fixture list does not allow the body to adapt and it therefore starts to protest. This may be one of the reasons why coaches are faced with so many injuries nowadays. Professional soccer coaches tend to give their players time off during quiet periods (e.g. when no fixtures have been arranged because the national team is playing), but this is precisely the time when overload conditioning can be carried out.

> *If the man in the street tried to imitate the methods of top athletes, he would soon come a cropper.*
> **Herman Kuiphof**

Sometimes there are pauses of seven to ten days in the fixture list. This means that there is sufficient time to recover from intensive training before the next game. Rest is important in periods when there are a lot of games. This also applies to amateur soccer, although the overstrain problem is less of a problem at this level.

3.4.2 Durability

An injury may force a soccer player to endure several months of enforced idleness on the sidelines. During this period of relative inactivity his physical condition deteriorates. The rate of decline depends on the makeup of his physical condition. Conditional elements that have been acquired as a consequence of long-term conditioning work will regress slowly, and elements that have been built up quickly will also disappear quickly. Gradual development of soccer conditioning yields clear benefits for the players. Just think of the rehabilitation process described in Chapter 14 ("Physiotherapy in soccer"). The more gradually a player's condition deteriorates after an operation, i.e. the more durable his condition is, the faster he can get back to his former level. The law of durability also plays an important part in preseason preparation. It is not necessary to start with heavy work in an attempt to get the players into top condition. A gradual buildup is more sensible. Players with minor injuries can regain contact with the group more quickly without first having to spend a lot of time working on their condition. This is important for a coach, because he must try to come through the preparations with as complete a group of players as possible. It is, of course, of great importance for the players to maintain their basic condition during the close season. If they do not, the preparation period will be too short to allow a gradual buildup and intensive conditioning will have to be carried out from the very start. This increases the probability of injuries occurring.

> *I am convinced that more talent is destroyed by too much training than by too little. The problem is that athletes become impatient when they are standing still.*
> **Harm Kuipers**

3.4.3 Specificity of Conditioning

Chapter 2 describes all kinds of systems that are present in the body and are of more or less significance for soccer players. Each of these systems can be improved through conditioning. A coach must be aware that conditioning effects are not equally important and/or desirable for soccer players. Soccer conditioning must be based on what happens in a real game. The important thing is to identify what sorts of conditioning soccer players need. Specificity of conditioning is based on two physiological background elements. First of all the energy systems that are used during a game play a major role in soccer- specific conditioning. Secondly, soccer-specific conditioning improves the brain's ability to control typical soccer activities. As a result, the movements the body needs to make during a game of soccer are coordinated more effectively. Finally there is the motivation factor. Soccer players do not want to spend their time doing things that bear no relationship to soccer. Their motivation can be maintained by incorporating soccer elements into every type of drill. This is one of the requisite conditions for achieving conditioning effects. The players see the sense of the drill and are then prepared to give their all. Only then can the objective of the drill be achieved.

3.5 CONDITIONING PRINCIPLES

A conditioning program must be correctly approached and organized if the above mentioned laws of conditioning are to be exploited to the best advantage. This can be done by applying a number of conditioning principles.

3.5.1 The Principle of the Systematic Approach

The content of a training session must always be viewed in relation to the next session. The starting point must always be the improvement of performance. A training session is one element in a long-term program. A coach whose aim is to teach his team how to play "fast circulation soccer" must work out a plan beforehand, in which he describes his objective and how to achieve it. This can best consist of a number of steps. The team should not immediately be confronted with tasks that are too demanding. Intermediate objectives should be defined. This is also advisable from the point of view of motivation. The coach himself must specify the ingredients that go to make up "fast circulation soccer" (for example, one-touch play, firm passes, escaping a marker and playing the ball out to the flank, etc.). On the basis of this information he must look for the most suitable drills for achieving the intermediate objectives and, ultimately, the final objective.

3.5.2 Age and Experience as the Basis for a Conditioning Program

A conditioning program is naturally dependent on the age level of the group. Children who have not yet reached puberty should not be asked to overcome excessive resistances. Their bodies are still developing, and the growth process may suffer if they are overtaxed. At this age, therefore, the only resistance they encounter should be from their own bodies and those of their contemporaries. During puberty hormones are released that make it possible to condition strength and endurance. The workloads that the youngsters have to cope with can then be increased. This must be done gradually, however, and under qualified supervision. Older players must realize that their loading capacity is not what it used to be. The aging process has obvious physical consequences. Such players must not overestimate their physical capacity. Another key factor in planning the conditioning buildup is the extent of a player's experience of soccer. A player with a lot of experience can step up the extent and intensity of conditioning more quickly than a player who has just become acquainted with the sport. A learner is unfamiliar with the sport and is so enthusiastic that he cannot see the dangers. On the other hand an experienced player may rely on his routine, and as a consequence his concentration may sometimes lapse.

3.5.3 The Principle of Intensivation

The training load must be gradually stepped up until ultimately the maximal or optimal level of performance is reached. The training load is the sum of all of the types of training work. The load can be increased smoothly or in small steps. In conditioning science this is termed the principle of progression. If a coach wants to improve his team's capacity for playing a pressing game, for example, he must start with simple drills. Gradually the drills can be transformed into complex situations that are encountered during a real match.

Pressing is physically exhausting. It is one of the few soccer situations where a lactic acid buildup can occur. If a coach tells his team to switch to a pressing game without any prior conditioning during training, this lactic acid will harm the players' bodies. Their performance will therefore suffer. It is better to select drills in which the intensity is gradually stepped up. This gives the body the opportunity to build up lactic acid tolerance. Drills focussed on pressing can be made more exhausting by increasing the number of passing options for the attacking team. This gradually increases the pressure on the defending team that is using the pressing tactics.

The overload principle demands technical ability.

3.5.4 Principle of Variety

When a soccer player has just started to train, variable loading should be chosen. All basic motor properties must be conditioned. It is important that learners should lay a good foundation for their subsequent soccer development. If the body is subjected to a continuously one-sided stimulus during training, it may fail to develop harmoniously. If a player always shoots or starts off with his right foot, the development of his right leg will differ from that of the left. This difference can result in an imbalance in the player's running pattern, which may possibly even result in injuries. A conditioning program must therefore always contain general drills. This ensures that groups of muscles that are worked only slightly or not at all during soccer movements are also conditioned. In this way unbalanced growth of the muscles, and of the supporting tissue in particular, is avoided. Another argument for introducing a lot of variety is that we are lazy by nature. After a player has carried out a drill a few times, he has usually found a way of performing it more easily. As a result this "simplified" drill is no longer suitable for achieving the conditioning objective. The use of constantly changing drills avoids this "familiarization" effect. Finally, variation serves to maintain motivation. The players must not get into a fixed and mind-numbing rhythm in which drills are gone through by rote. The players have to be stimulated each time they train. This can be achieved by pursuing the same conditioning objective with constantly changing drills. Players must enjoy what they are doing.

3.5.5 Technique as a Basis for Soccer-Specific Overload Training

When players first start training, they must focus on technical skills such as controlling the ball, passing, etc. These skills must become automatic under all circumstances. The overload principle can only be applied within a drill if the players are able to carry out the soccer actions properly. In practice this means that a positional game cannot be used to impart a physical stimulus if the ball always runs out of play due to the players' technical shortcomings. This is one of the direct limitations on soccer-specific conditioning. Performing soccer actions intensively and frequently gives soccer players the physical stimulus they need to be able to play a match. If they have not mastered the relevant soccer actions, the conditioning effect will never be achieved.

3.5.6 The Individuality Principle

Each conditioning method and each conditioning principle is aimed at the average sportsman. Each coach should ask himself how far these general guidelines are applicable to his own players. He must take the biological and socio-psychological development phase of his players into account. A coach must observe his players closely and listen to what they say. No two individuals are the same, and youth players in particular need very careful supervision. It is a long-established tradition in soccer that teams are coached as a group. This is also logical. Soccer is a team sport and both cohesion and team spirit are essential for success. Nevertheless a coach must have an eye for the individual differences between players. Every player is different and has his own specific shortcomings. This latter point is very important. The coach can devise individual training programs to work on these shortcomings. Not just the player but the whole team will benefit from this in the long run.

3.6 CONDITIONING METHODS

There are specific methods for conditioning motor properties. The following overview serves as an introduction, and more detailed descriptions can be found in the other chapters of this book.

3.6.1 Endurance

Endurance simply indicates how long a certain effort can be maintained. Chapter 6 explains how soccer players can be conditioned for endurance. As a consequence of the intermittent character of a game of soccer it is said that players need acyclic endurance. This applies in both the aerobic and anaerobic fields.

Acyclic Aerobic Endurance

In the context of conditioning for aerobic endurance there is always a field of tension between intensive and extensive factors. The more intensive the training, the sooner the players are fatigued, and therefore the less extensive the training can be. Because a game of soccer demands extensive work at a high intensity, it is necessary to condition the players for both factors. For this reason a number of training methods are used in soccer:
- extensive continuous training
- intensive continuous training
- extensive interval training
- Fartlek training

Acyclic Anaerobic Endurance

Soccer players sometimes have to make an intensive effort over a longer period of time, for example when the opposing team is being subjected to pressing. Intensive interval training must be used to condition the players for this type of effort. There are two sub-divisions of this training method:
- block training
- interval training

3.6.2 Speed

The term "speed" is very general and can be divided into a number of components. Because these components do not automatically influence each other during training, they have to be developed by means of specific conditioning methods. These are described in more detail in Chapters 5 and 6. The components of speed are:
- reaction speed/start speed,
- acceleration,
- speed endurance,
- repeated short sprint capacity.

3.6.3 Strength

Just like speed, "strength" is a general term. Strength is manifested in a number of ways, and each of them requires its own specific method of conditioning.
- dynamic concentric strength,
- dynamic eccentric strength,
- static strength.

3.7 FORMS OF TRAINING

All of the above mentioned training methods can be applied in three different forms. The first of these is general training. The aim of this form of training is to condition the whole body, with no reference to any particular sport. This is necessary to establish a broad basis for specialization (in this case conditioning for soccer). General training is also the basis for the work carried out at the start of the preparations for a new season (Chapter 7) and during rehabilitation (Chapter 14). The second form is special training, which is used to improve elements that are important for a particular sport, such as technique, tactics and speed. Finally there is specific (match-related) training. The aim of this final, complex form of training is to improve a player's entire performance capacity in a match situation, in which all types of soccer resistances are present. When individuals first start to play a sport, a lot of attention has to be devoted to general training. When players are more experienced the emphasis can be shifted towards specific and match training. However, all three forms of training must be part of the overall training program, irrespective of the level of the group of players. Naturally the level determines the relationship between the three forms of training.

3.8 STRUCTURE OF A TRAINING SESSION

The manner in which a training session is structured is largely dependent on the age and ability levels of the players and the stage of the soccer season at which the session takes place. Other relevant factors are the available facilities and the weather. However, the general outline is always as follows:

1. warming up/introduction,
2. core aspects,
3. warming down, conclusion.

3.8.1 Warming up

Warming up is firmly established in the world of soccer. Its purpose is not simply to prepare the body for the coming exertion; it is also a period of psychological preparation (familiarization with the facilities and the weather, getting into the right frame of mind). A warming-up session is a key part of the preparation for a training session or a game. All kinds of psychological and physiological processes have to be taken from rest level to performance level if a sportsman is to make the best use of his ability. Warming up also helps to reduce the risk of injury. The intensity of the exertion required is usually higher during a game than during a training session (see Fig. 3.4A). The intensity can also vary from session to session. The level of intensity of the training session determines the extent to which all the physiological systems have to be activated during warming up. The extent and intensity of a warming-up session are also dependent on factors such as age, fitness and ambient temperature. The colder the weather, for example, the more time will be needed to reach the required level of intensity (see Fig. 3.4B). A good warming-up session can be roughly divided into three phases.

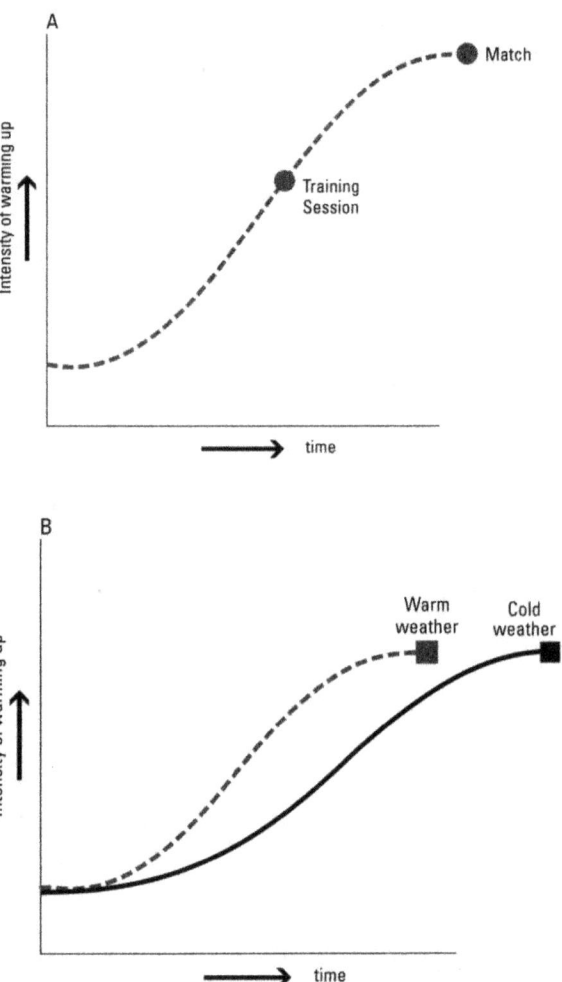

Figure 3.4: *The intensity of a warming-up session depends on the intensity with which the players will ultimately have to work. Warming up for a game is therefore usually more intensive than for a training session (A). The extent and intensity of a warming-up session also depends on a number of personal and circumstantial factors. One of these is the weather (B).*

Phase 1

For 5 to 10 minutes the muscles are warmed up by simple running exercises. Avoid sudden acceleration or changes of direction. Research has shown that the muscles perform better as they become warmer (see Fig. 3.5). Incidentally, the temperature of a working muscle rises faster than the body temperature (see Fig. 3.6). A higher temperature has a positive influence on the elasticity and viscosity of the muscle fibers and the smoothness of the articular surfaces. This reduces the internal resistance of the musculoskeletal system, thereby facilitating coordination. Heat also improves the conductivity of the nerves (signals are carried faster from the brain to the muscles), the distribution of the blood to the sites in the body where it is most needed, and the uptake of oxygen by the muscles from the blood.

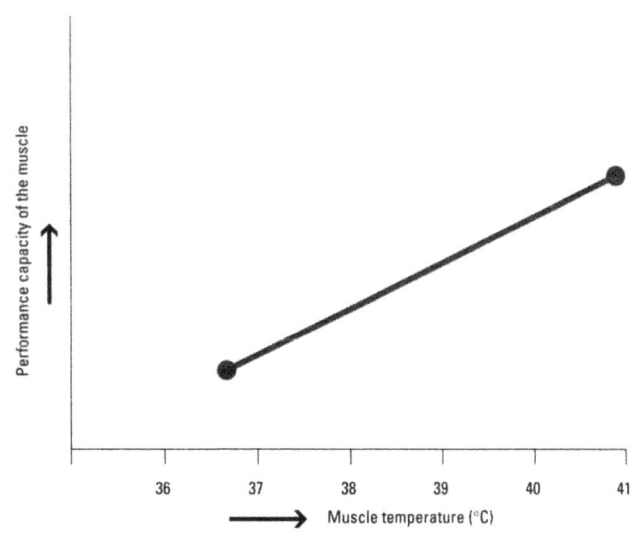

Figure 3.5: *The performance capacity of a muscle increases in direct relationship to its temperature. This is why warming up should be carried out before any training session or game.*

Phase 2

The purpose of this phase is to increase the freedom of movement of the joints and muscles that a soccer player uses during a training session or a game. The dynamic flexibility exercises referred to above can be used for this. During this phase of warming up the main emphasis is on "loosening up" the muscles. The range of the movements should not be too great. Short static stretches can be used to check whether the body is supple enough to start phase 3 (see Conclusion 6). It is essential that cooling down is avoided during the second phase (total duration: 5 to 10 minutes).

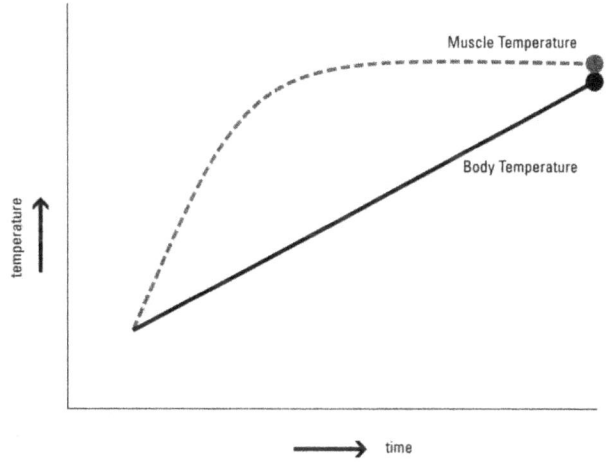

Figure 3.6: *The muscle temperature rises much faster than the body temperature during warming up.*

Phase 3

The final part of the warming-up session is used for the finishing touches. The core aspects of the session are achieved by means of all kinds of sport-specific actions. Movements that will recur during the training session or game are carried out keenly and intensively. This phase should last for 5 to 10 minutes.

3.8.2 Core Aspects of a Training Session

The first core aspect is learning basic technique and tactics. For instance, angles of running might be explained, or how to coordinate the offside trap. This type of training is methodically structured and includes specific movement drills. Learning is at the heart of these drills, therefore the intensity is not too high.

Second Core Aspect

The second core aspect is practicing the above mentioned basic technique and tactics in all kinds of different game situations. Just as with the first core aspect, use is made of practice drills that are clearly related to the game. These drills must be carried out with constant changes of speed, so that the players have a lot of ball contacts. All sorts of technical and tactical activities have to be carried out against a variety of resistances. It is important that the practice drills have a competitive element, so that the players train at high speed and under pressure.

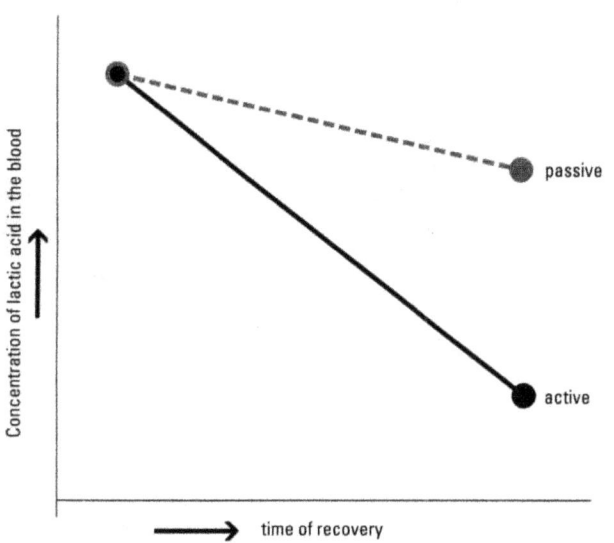

Figure 3.7: *Active recovery after intensive work ensures faster disposal of wasted substances such as lactic acid from the muscles. This accelerates the recovery process.*

3.8.3 Warming Down

In contrast to warming up, warming down is not a generally familiar concept. Only rarely does a team carry out gentle running exercises or relaxing drills after a game. The advantage of warming down is that the body's systems that have carried out the work during a game can be more gradually returned to the "at rest" state, which has a positive effect on the recovery of the body as a whole. The waste substances produced in the body during the game can be disposed of by carrying out gentle running exercises for 10 to 15 minutes. If players simply stop after a game, the disposal of these substances proceeds much more slowly (see Fig. 3.7). When the body is at rest, the blood circulation is much lower and less waste can be disposed of per unit of time. Any stretching exercises carried out after an (intensive) training session should be very light (see Conclusion 13).

3.8.4 Variation as a Basis for Each Training Session

The broad outlines of a training session are sketched out on the previous page. Within the general framework there is, however, room for variation. A coach has a wide range of available options for stimulating his players. It is important, for example, that warming-up sessions are never carried out in exactly the same way. Players should not come to look on warming up as an obligatory exercise, otherwise they may approach it with a lack of concentration. Do not always use the same (running) drills. Instead the body can be activated by practicing ball skills, playing tag, or playing team handball. Make sure that the competitive element does not take over in the last two cases, as the intensity may then be too high for a warming-up session. By varying the warming-up sessions, you can

During phase 1 of the warming-up session the muscles are warmed up with the help of simple running.

During phase 2 the emphasis is on loosening up and light static stretching.

Phase 3 involves hard and intensive work in preparation for the coming training session or game.

After each game and training session the players must gently warm down.

A warming-up session must be very varied. The body can be activated very well by carrying out exercises to practice technique.

keep your players mentally fresh. The same applies to the core aspects of the training session. A coach may always have the same aims, but he should approach them in a variety of ways. A coach who is always introducing new practice drills keeps his players guessing, and this helps to maintain their motivation and enthusiasm. A coach cannot be successful unless his players are well motivated.

3.9 CONCLUSION

After reading this chapter it should be clear that coaching requires a delicate touch. A coach has to take account of conditioning laws, principles, methods, forms and structure. Each of these factors has more or less influence on the final conditioning effect. This chapter on conditioning is the final chapter of the introductory part of this book. Until now the focus has been on the work that soccer players have to carry out, the processes that take place in their bodies while they are carrying out this work, and the laws and principles that have to be applied to increase their loading capacity. On the basis of this information, the following chapters explain how coaches can condition their players for soccer.

SUMMARY

- The basic motor properties: strength, speed, endurance, coordination and flexibility form the foundation for every sports performance.

- Soccer players carry out all sorts of work in the marginal areas between strength, speed and endurance: speed strength, speed endurance, and strength endurance.

- All soccer actions depend on coordination. Flexibility is of subordinate importance for soccer players. It is not crucial to performance, but neither is it totally irrelevant.

- Soccer players make use of active flexibility during a game. They should therefore carry out dynamic rather than static flexibility exercises during training sessions.

- If a coach wishes to improve his players' performance capacity, he must apply the overload principle. During training sessions the body is asked to do slightly more than it is accustomed to.

- The body is able to adapt to such a strong stimulus. This is referred to as a conditioning effect, or supercompensation.

- Improvements in performance capacity cost ever more time and energy. This is sometimes referred to as the law of diminishing returns. Other training laws that have to be applied relate to the continuity and specificity of conditioning.

- The applicable training principles are: the principle of systematic approach; age and experience as the basis for a training schedule; the principle of intensivation; the principle of variety; technique as the basis for soccer-specific overload conditioning; and the principle of individuality.

- Each (component of a) basic motor property has its own conditioning method.

- Each conditioning method can be divided into three different forms of training: general training, special (sport-related) training and specific (competition-related) training.

- In general each training session consists of a warming-up or introduction session, a number of core aspects, and a warming-down or concluding session. Coaches must provide as much variation as possible within this framework. Variation keeps players eager and alert.

FIVE PRACTICAL QUESTIONS

1. What are the most important changes in the science of conditioning in the field of soccer?

First of all the structure of the pre-season preparation is completely different. There used to be a buildup from stamina work and speed work to sprint work. Now endurance and speed are conditioned from the very start. During the season itself the emphasis is now much more on speed. It is generally recognized that this is one of the most important elements of soccer. Finally general practice drills are used less and less, and coaches look for soccer-specific conditioning situations in all areas.

2. In amateur soccer each training session is often a "100 percent" session. The players always have to give maximum effort. Is this sensible, or should these sessions be more varied in this respect?

In amateur soccer the time available for training sessions is limited. There is therefore a tendency for coaches to try to do too much in a short time, and as a result the work-to-rest ratio is distorted. In any training session, intensive drills must be directly succeeded by more gentle recovery drills. A coaching session should never be a continuous overload sequence.

3. What should be the maximum and minimum times between the last training session and a game?

It is not very sensible to train intensively on the last two days before a game. So if there is a game on Sunday, Thursday is the last possible day for a strenuous training session. A light training session can be carried out even on the day of the game, as long as the energy reserves are not depleted too severely and the players suffer no minor muscle damage, as occurs during intensive training.

4. From what age should flexibility conditioning be started?

Flexibility conditioning is first worthwhile at the age of 13 or 14. Most children are then going through puberty and their bodies are changing. Flexibility conditioning is advantageous at that age because the body is open to external stimuli.

5. How can a coach know if he is overloading his players during a training session?

In the first place a coach must work in a structured manner. There must be a logical structure in the drills. A coach sees that the players have problems during a certain drill, but in time they become accustomed to it and can carry it out without difficulty. That is the moment when he must make things more difficult, so that the players again have to struggle to do what is asked of them. It is important that the objective of a drill always remains within the players' reach.

INTERVIEW WITH HUBB STEVENS
(Coach of Schalke '04, Germany)

Germany is renowned for its sports science. To what extent have you been confronted with this since you went to Schalke'04?
Use is often made of infusions of vitamin preparations in German soccer. Because we are not familiar with this in the Netherlands, I initially found it strange. However, the players are in favor of this, so there is no reason to change it. In addition the medical support staff frequently measure lactate levels. All sorts of tests are carried out, during which the players' lactic acid production is measured. The cardiometer is also used regularly. During stamina training the players are told exactly what heart rate they should try to maintain. The cardiometer is also used during recuperation training sessions. This prevents the players' heart rates from exceeding a certain intensity, above which recuperation no longer takes place.

Does this scientific approach bring an extra dimension to soccer?
You must not forget that soccer is more strenuous in Germany than anywhere else. Soccer here is based more on stamina and strength than on technical ingenuity. Lack of creativity and technique is compensated by willpower and condition. The Bundesliga is a more difficult competition to play in than the Dutch league. You meet more resistance week by week, because the general playing standard is higher. In addition you have to travel further, there is more media interest, the interests of sponsors play a larger role, and you have more obligations to fulfill towards the fans. This is why all possible means are used to keep the players fit. As a coach I also have to adapt to this. In Germany you cannot play as you do in the Netherlands. It would not be sensible to throw everything overboard that has happened here in the past and try to introduce the Dutch school of soccer.

Do you still coach in the same way here?
In Germany there is a lot of emphasis on stamina. The players here have unbelievable endurance. That is also the case at Schalke. My predecessor came from the German school of coaching, and the players therefore had to do a lot of stamina work. Although this is necessary to establish a foundation, I think that you have to look more at the demands of the game. If you do that, you soon see that a player never has to run two and a half kilometers consecutively at the same speed. Then why should he have to do that during a training session? I am therefore gradually introducing more interval work.

How does this look in practice?
At Schalke the players were used to running for long periods at a low speed. Now I suddenly make them work very intensively, with more periods of rest in between. In addition I get them to practice passing and shooting within the context of soccer drills, instead of just running between cones. It took some time before the players became accustomed to these changes. They were worried that they would not be fit enough to last

a whole season. They were also tired after the interval training sessions. That is logical, because they suddenly had to cope with a completely different type of workload. I told the players that this was a phase they had to go through. It was also a difficult period for me, because I wanted to keep the players match-fit. Now they feel good. Even the older players, who have been used to doing stamina during their entire careers, admit that they are suddenly enjoying the training sessions. Incidentally, tests show that the endurance of the players is at the same level as in the period when they did lots of stamina work. Moreover we have fewer problems with muscle injuries.

What tests are used In Germany to measure endurance?
In Germany they frequently use one-kilometer runs, coupled with lactate measurements. I once made the players carry out the shuttle-run test, but even that needed a lot of familiarization. They have always been satisfied with their lactate test, so they see no need to change it. I now try to couple the shuttle-run test with the lactate test, so that endurance also acquires a more intermittent character in the area of condition tests.

How do you try to maintain the work-to-rest ratio during the season?
Naturally it becomes harder to train properly. The number of games is increasing and there are therefore more weeks when we have to play twice. It becomes more difficult to give players with minor injuries the time they need to recover. Another problem is that the players' endurance decreases as each half of the season progresses. You simply have too little time available to maintain their condition. During the winter break you can build up the players' condition again for the second half of the season. In addition a coach has to look at the match schedule to identify quieter periods that occur because, for example, the national team is playing. At Schalke we then often have ten days free. The players are usually given two days to recover. Then we have a number of training sessions aimed at bringing the players to peak condition. Then we gradually let up as the next game approaches. In this way you can maintain the players' basic condition between games.

Do you take individuals into account during training sessions?
In my opinion a coach must be flexible in this respect. In principle I have the program for each training session worked out well in advance. But if I see that certain players are lacking in enthusiasm, I must be able to adjust my program accordingly. Then there are times when a training session for the whole group can be a good idea because the players are going through a very busy period, but such a session will not be strenuous enough for the players who usually sit on the substitutes bench or for players who are on their way back to match-fitness after recovering from an injury. I have to give them an extra stimulus during such a training session. A coach must also look out for players who are close to their limits or are slightly injured. Sometimes it is better if they do not train. The same applies with regard to age. I sometimes let the older players train less intensively, because they do not recover as quickly as the younger players. You want to be sure that they will be fit for the next game.

Although it has been shown that sportsmen recover more quickly from exertion if it is followed by warming down, this has not yet caught on in soccer. What is the situation in Germany?
In Germany it is usual to warm down after a game. Players do this of their own accord. Sometimes this is difficult because you have to get away quickly after a game, but usually

warming down is carried out. I certainly think that this is very important when we have to play twice during a week. When I worked with Roda Kerkrade I also let the players warm down after a game. During busy periods of the season I felt that this gained us an extra day, because I did not need to hold a recuperation training session the next day. If you only have limited options for training, every day that you save gives you another option.

Besides vitamin preparations, is attention paid to other nutritional aspects in German soccer?
The Germans are very advanced in the field of nutrition. The players are closely supervised before, during and after the games. Personally I would like to take this further and control what the players eat and drink before and after training sessions. The problem is that during the week, due to the level of media interest, it can be very hectic at Schalke. The only place where the players can relax is at home, so I often let them go home between training sessions. As a result I have less control over what they eat and drink. Fortunately we go to a training camp before each game, so our club doctor can regulate the players diet very well during the run up to a game. During my time at Roda Kerkrade my experience with a nutritional specialist was very positive. We got her to talk to the group about the importance of nutrition for soccer players. This was a total success. Some players completely changed their eating habits and at the same time ate more than before. The result was that they lost weight, but performed better and suffered fewer injuries.

To what extent do you use training principles from other sports?
Naturally I can learn something from a volleyball coach when he talks about footwork and take-off power. At the same time, as a soccer coach you have the problem that your sport is unlike any other. It is so amazingly complex that you cannot just take over things blindly from other sports. You have to spend a lot of time and energy in analyzing how aspects of other sports will translate into practice in soccer. Soccer is a contact sport, a ball sport played with your feet, an intensive intermittent sport, and - which many people forget - almost everything that you do as a soccer player involves standing on one leg. In addition a soccer team often consists of all sorts of different types of players. Some have good stamina, some are fast, and some may be physically weaker than the others but technically and tactically superior. The team as a whole is therefore a mixture, and as a coach you have to take this into account during training sessions. You cannot make all of your players carry out the same drills. What might be too easy for one can be too strenuous for another. A coach has to be flexible in this respect.

Are psychological factors much more important than physical ones in soccer?
I do think that mentality is the most important factor. A good example is the situation that I was confronted with when I came to Schalke. The team was going through a difficult period. It was fighting against relegation and the players had lost their confidence. In such a situation a coach has to restore the players' enjoyment and confidence. A coach's starting point must always be that the players he works with must enjoy what they are doing. If they do not, there is no way that he can be successful. It is also important to keep the players mentally alert. They will then be sharper and the chance of them suffering injuries will be smaller. A player who is disappointed and unmotivated will not be sharp enough to dodge the crucial tackle. What I sometimes do at Schalke is to get all the players and their wives and children together. We then go, for example, on a bicycle tour

and have a meal together. These are simple things but they work. You create a sort of family feeling and you are occupying yourselves with something other than soccer.

LITERATURE

1. Elementaire trainingsleer en trainingsmethoden.
T. Kloosterboer.
ISBN: 90-6076-375-0.
De Vrieseborch, Haarlem.

2. Intervaltraining wetenschappelijk bekeken.
L.j. Klok.
Richting/Sportgerricht 50 (1996) 5.

3. Dossier Stretching.
G. van der Poel.
Richting/Sportgericht 50 (1996), 1-3.

4. Science of Flexibility.
J. Alter.
ISBN: 0-87322-977-0.
Human Kinetics.

5. Exercise: benefits, limits and adaptions.
D. Macleod, R. Maughan, M. Nimmo, T. Reilly and C. Williams.
ISBN: 0-419-14140-5.
E & FN Spon, London.

6. Intermittent High Intensity Exercise.
D. Macleod.
ISBN: 0-419-17860-0.
E & FN Spon, London.

CHAPTER 4

CONDITIONING FOR SOCCER STRENGTH

Dr. Raymond Verheijen

4.1 INTRODUCTION
In the context of soccer, strength is generally thought of as enabling players to shoot hard and jump high into the air. These are certainly attributes that a good player needs, but strength conditioning needs to be focussed on more than just the leg muscles. The whole body must be developed. This chapter describes a few general principles of strength conditioning, then examines the function of strength in soccer, and finally specifies how conditioning for soccer strength is put into practice. A central aspect of this chapter is that conditioning for soccer strength must be achieved with the help of soccer drills. In soccer we are not concerned with pure strength but with the translation of strength into soccer movements. Coordination is at the basis of this process. The best way of improving coordination is obviously to carry out the soccer movements themselves. General strength conditioning with weights is not entirely pointless, but is certainly of much less importance.

4.2 THE PROPERTIES OF MUSCLE STRENGTH
Before soccer strength can be conditioned we need a clear understanding of what strength is precisely and where it comes from. Strength is in fact a many-sided concept.

4.2.1 General and specific muscle strength
General muscle strength is the basic strength that is needed to take part in sport. General strength conditioning is not specifically related to soccer. The aim is to establish a platform to enable the player to handle soccer-specific workloads more effectively. No account is taken of soccer-specific movements during general strength conditioning. Usually this form of training is carried out with weights. Specific muscle strength is necessary for carrying out specific sport movements. These movements require more than just strength - timing also plays an important role. Muscle strength is therefore conditioned through sport-specific drills.

4.2.2 Types of muscle work
Muscle strength is the capacity of the muscles to deal with a load or resistance. However, muscles do not always supply strength in

the same way. There are two types of muscle work: dynamic and static. They are treated separately below, but many soccer movements require a combination of these two types of muscle work.

Dynamic muscle work

Each muscle has a specific length when it is at rest (see Fig. 4.1a). During dynamic muscle work a muscle applies force as it becomes shorter (concentric contraction) or longer (eccentric contraction) (see Figs. 4.1b and c). Dynamic muscle work can be subdivided into four components. The first of these is maximum strength, i.e. the greatest amount of strength that the muscle can exert. This is also referred to as basic strength. Too much emphasis on muscle strength, however, may have a price in terms of coordination and suppleness. Explosive strength is a muscle's capacity for overcoming a large resistance with the greatest possible speed. The body's weight is such a resistance. The leg muscles supply explosive strength at the moment when they take the body from a state of rest to a state of movement, e.g. at the start of a sprint or a jump. When explosive strength is exerted, acceleration is at a maximum. **Fast strength** is the capacity of the muscles to overcome a resistance quickly. The magnitude of the resistance is not always large, for instance when a sprint is continued after the initial explosive start. The feet push less powerfully off the ground but much faster. They are in contact with the ground for a shorter period. The speed with which strength is supplied is more important than the actual amount of strength. Finally strength endurance is the capacity of the muscles to continue supplying strength even when tired. In terms of soccer this means that soccer players must be able to produce the strength to shoot, sprint, jump and win challenges during the whole 90 minutes of the game.

Static muscle work

Static muscle work is the development of strength while the muscle length remains constant (see Fig. 4.1d). In this situation the muscles are active but the body is not in motion. Static muscle work is used to maintain the body or part of it in a given posture.

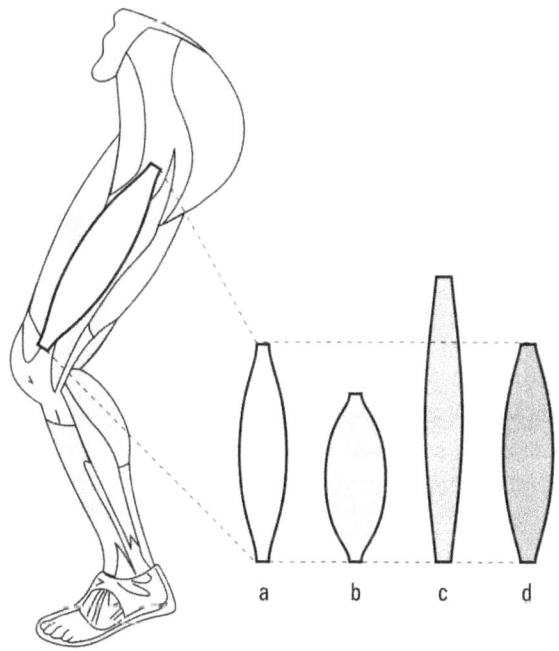

a = The muscle at rest. The muscle length is constant.
b = A concentric muscle contraction. The muscle becomes shorter.
c = An eccentric muscle contraction. The muscle is stretched.
d = An isometric contraction. The muscle remains the same.

Figure 4.1: *Each muscle has its own specific rest length (a). When a muscle works concentrically the muscle length decreases (b). When it works eccentrically its length increases (c). When a muscle works isometrically the muscle length does not change (d).*

4.3 THE EFFECT OF STRENGTH CONDITIONING

An increase in muscle strength is always attributed to the muscle becoming bigger and stronger. Although an increase in muscle size is indeed one of the consequences of strength conditioning, most of the improvement results from more efficient control of the muscle by the nervous system.

4.3.1 Improved muscle coordination by the nervous system

The amount of strength supplied by a muscle, and the type of work it carries out, depend on the way the nervous system controls it. Nerve paths run from the brain to the muscles. Stimuli from the brain or the spinal cord set the muscles working, which results in a movement or the maintenance of a posture. The nervous system can increase the force applied in two ways: by increasing either the stimulus strength or the stimulus frequency.

Stimulus strength

Each nerve that runs from the spinal cord to a muscle branches into a large number of nerve fibers just before it arrives at the muscle. Each nerve fiber then makes contact with a number of muscles fibers (see Fig. 4.2). The stronger the stimulus that a muscle receives from the brain, the larger the number of connected muscle fibers that are activated through the nerve fiber. As a result a larger part of the muscle contracts, and therefore more force is applied. One of the effects of strength conditioning is that the nerve system can stimulate the muscles more powerfully.

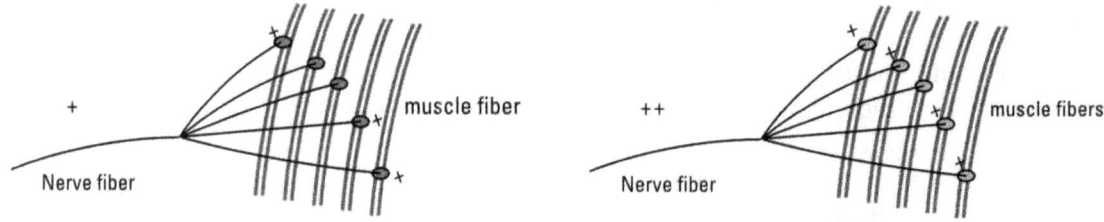

Figure 4.2: *Each nerve that comes from the spinal cord branches into smaller muscle fibers when it reaches the muscle. Each nerve fiber makes contact with a number of muscle fibers. The stronger the stimulus from the brain (++), the more muscle fibers are activated by the nerve fiber. A larger part of the muscle contracts, and the muscle therefore supplies more strength.*

Stimulus frequency

Muscle strength can also increase when the frequency of the stimulus increases. If the interval between stimuli decreases, the effect of the last stimulus has not ebbed before the following stimulus arrives. This causes the stimuli to have a cumulative effect (see Fig. 4.3). The muscle fibers experience a stronger stimulus and apply more force. The second effect of strength conditioning is that the nervous system is capable of stimulating the muscles at a higher frequency.

Strength conditioning and specific events

It is stated above that strength conditioning can lead to an increase in the stimulus strength and frequency. These are not conditioning effects in the usual sense. The capacity of the muscle fibers to impart a stimulus more strongly and more frequently only increases in relation to the movement that is practiced. If a larger stimulus capacity is required for other movements, these will also have to be practiced. Another reason why soccer strength has to be conditioned through soccer-related drills is that the success of many soccer actions depends on their timing. A player must be able to do more than just jump high in the air; he must also choose exactly the right moment to do this. The same applies to kicking the ball and challenging an opponent. A strong body alone is of no use to a soccer player. He must also have a feeling for the right moment to commit his body to the challenge. If this feeling is absent, a soccer player will look clumsy and commit a lot of fouls.

4.3.2 Changes in the muscle itself

Although strength conditioning effects are mainly a consequence of changes in the control of the muscles by the nervous system, some changes take place in the muscle itself. Initially the nervous system activates more muscle fibers, and in the course of time the muscle fibers become thicker (see Fig. 4.4). More sarcomeres come to be situated next to each other. Energy production in the cells also becomes more efficient. The phosphate system in particular becomes "stronger."

4.3.3 Strength conditioning effects in beginners

If an individual has never carried out strength conditioning before, he will initially make considerable progress. This first rapid increase in strength is almost completely the consequence of improved control of the muscle system. The execution of the practice drills themselves steadily improves. At a given moment, however, the rate of increase of muscle strength gradually slows down. More effort has to be put in to achieve a given conditioning effect (law of decreasing returns).

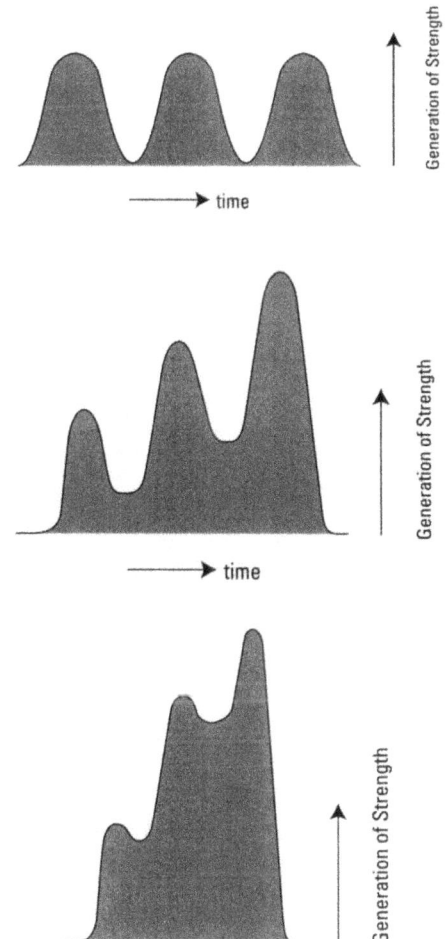

Figure 4.3: *When the stimulus frequency increases, the effect of the various stimuli is cumulative. More strength is gradually produced.*

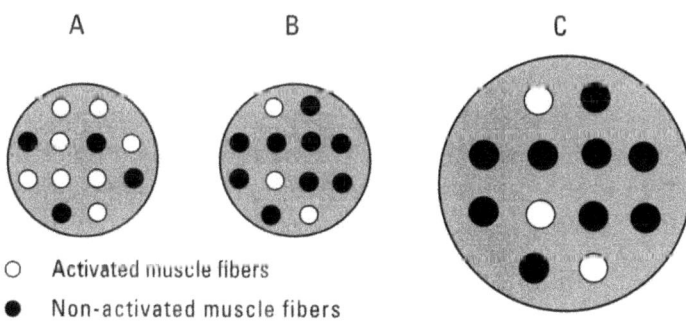

○ Activated muscle fibers
● Non-activated muscle fibers

Figure 4.4: *Through strength conditioning the nervous system learns to activate an increasing number of muscle fibers inside (A and B). Only then do muscle fibers become thicker and the muscles increase in weight (C).*

4.3.4 Loss of muscle strength through inactivity

If muscle strength is built up gradually, it will be lost only gradually during a period of inactivity. If it is built up quickly, it will soon be lost when strength conditioning is stopped. A slow, thorough build up ensures that players lose less strength if they are unable to be active for a long period, for instance after suffering a bad injury.

4.4. SOCCER STRENGTH

A soccer player needs strength for everything he does. He is always in motion. He runs about 10 kilometers during a match, and must constantly carry his body weight from one part of the pitch to another. The many sprints he makes are especially draining. It is pointed out in Chapter 1, however, that soccer players do much more than make runs. They perform all sorts of soccer actions such as jumping, shooting, making sliding tackles and challenging for the ball. This also costs strength. Soccer strength therefore consists of a number of elements.

Kicking strength is largely a matter of technique.

4.4.1 Basic strength

Every sport task requires a certain basic strength (see section 4.2.1). This also applies to soccer. Soccer is a contact sport. A great deal of physical contact occurs, in particular, during challenges for the ball. A well developed body is therefore essential. On the other hand, most soccer actions are carried out with the legs. The leg muscles must have sufficient basic strength to allow a player to shoot, jump or sprint. This basic strength is used to carry out the particular action.

4.4.2 Kicking strength

A soccer player naturally has to have kicking strength. Passing and shooting are the most essential part of soccer. The ball has to be directed over long and short distances. Kicking technique plays a crucial role in relation to kicking strength. The ball must not only be kicked far and firmly, but also accurately.

4.4.3 Jumping strength

Another "strong" aspect of soccer is jumping. Whether a player has to do a lot of jumping during a game depends on his position in the team. In a game of soccer a jump frequently has to be followed immediately by another action. This naturally has consequences for the choice of drills during a training session (see section 4.6.7).

4.4.4 Strength in the challenge

It is necessary to condition strength in the legs for all of the above elements. As was stated in the introduction to this chapter, however, it is important for a soccer player to develop his whole body. During a match, challenges are made for the ball over the length and breadth of the pitch. Coaches even regard winning these challenges as a prerequisite for success. Shielding the ball is also a basic skill in soccer. The body has to be braced so that the opponent cannot get to the ball. A soccer player therefore has to have a strong upper body and also be able to stand securely on his feet.

4.4.5 Starting strength

A soccer player repeatedly has to accelerate during a match: away from a marker, towards the ball, away from the ball, to make a challenge for the ball, to keep the ball in play. Starting strength is deliberately treated at the end of this series. Really it belongs in Chapter 5 (Sprint and coordination conditioning for soccer players). The reason for dealing with it here is that the conditioning of starting strength is concerned with improving the strength over the first 3 or 4 strides and therefore with strength conditioning.

4.5 MUSCLE WORK DURING SOCCER ACTIONS

Soccer strength consists of a number of elements. It is not the case, however, that the muscles are active in the same way during the above-mentioned actions. It has already been stated that in fact there are various forms of muscle work (see section 4.2.2).

4.5.1 Dynamic soccer strength

During dynamic actions such as sprinting, jumping and shooting, the muscles initially perform concentrical work. They therefore contract. In such soccer actions the muscle strength is used to develop speed. At the end of a sprint, jump or shot the speed of the body or the body part involved has to be braked. This is done with eccentric muscle work.

> *Gullit strides over the field with the dynamism of an unleashed horse, a sports animal that reveals previously unknown patterns of athletic power.*
>
> **Gianna Brera**

a.   Stopping after a sprint

During a sprint the body achieves a high horizontal speed. This is a frequent occurrence in a game of soccer. Such sprints are only rarely made in a straight line. Soccer players have to swerve and turn at full speed, sometimes through 180 degrees. In the latter case especially, the body has to absorb a sudden jolt. This is done with the muscles at the front of the upper leg (the quadriceps). They are tensed but are simultaneously stretched (see Fig. 4.5A). They work as a sort of elastic and ensure that the soccer player can quickly stop.

b.   Landing after a jump

During a jump the body develops speed in the vertical direction. This speed is initially directed upwards. After the highest point has been reached the body acquires speed in the downward direction. This speed must be absorbed by the body on landing, other-wise the player will fall, just as with stopping after a sprint, it is the quadriceps that absorb the jolt. The elasticity of these muscles (and tendons and connective tissue) ensures that the player's knees do not give way (see Fig. 4.5B).

c.   Braking the leg after a shot

When a player shoots he swings his leg forward. This occurs in two phases. First of all the upper leg moves forward, then the lower leg. The lower leg in particular is moving very quickly at the moment of contact with the ball. The lower leg must be stopped from following through after contact, otherwise it would overstretch the knee. This is done with the muscles at the back of the upper leg (the hamstrings). The hamstrings are tensed but are then stretched again like elastic (see Fig. 4.5C). If the hamstrings are not strong enough to cope with the speed of the lower leg, tears will occur in these muscles. The speed of the lower leg is largely dependent on the strength in the quadriceps. The strength of the hamstrings must be attuned to this (see section 4.7.1).

To summarize, it can be said that soccer players generally develop speed with the help of concentric muscle work, and that this speed is then braked by eccentric muscle work. Sometimes the order is reversed. Before a player jumps, he crouches slightly. This helps him to jump higher. What happens during the crouch is that the quadriceps are stretched like elastic. Just as when a piece of stretched elastic is released, this enables more strength to be developed during the jump, so the player can jump higher.

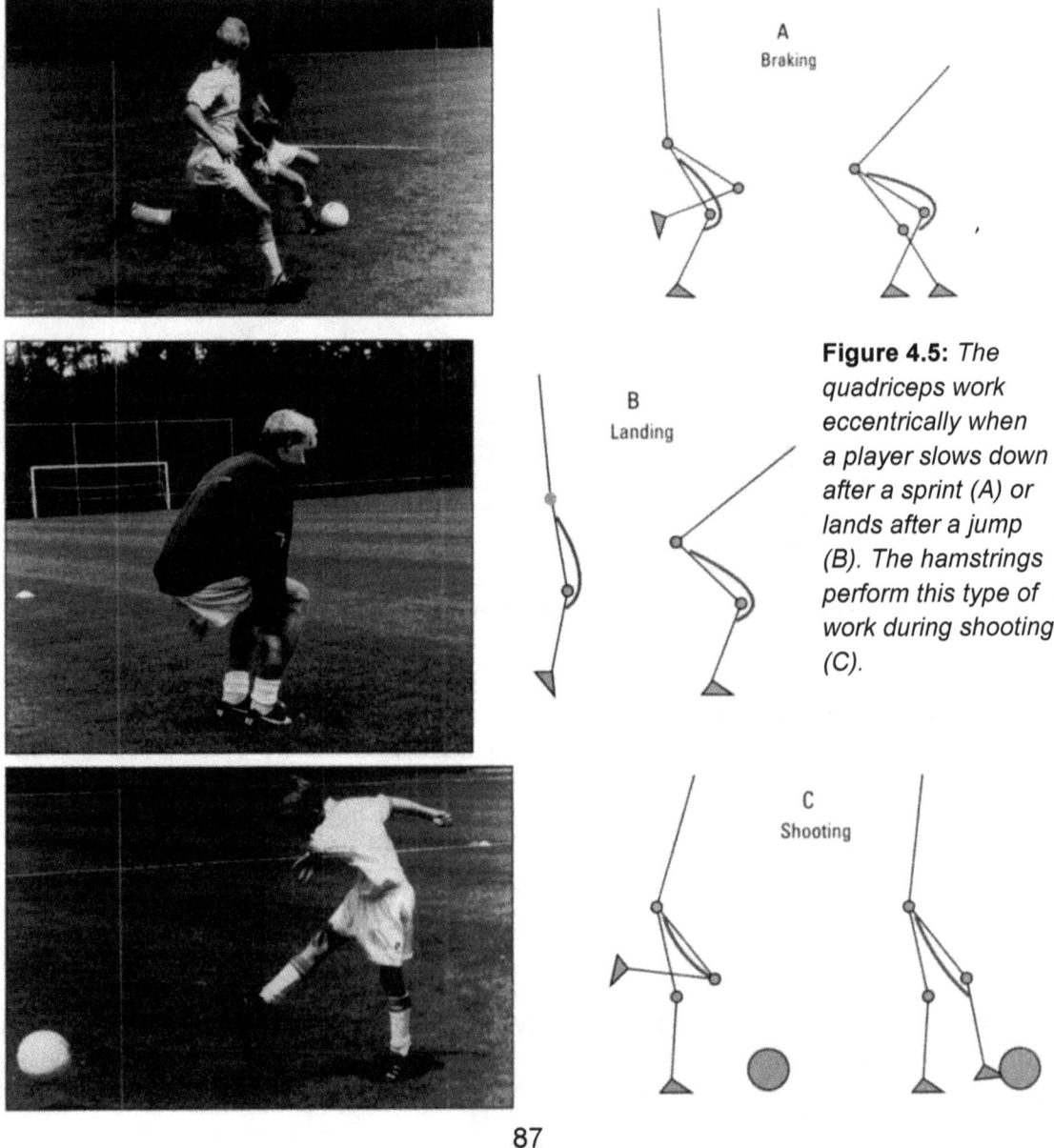

Figure 4.5: *The quadriceps work eccentrically when a player slows down after a sprint (A) or lands after a jump (B). The hamstrings perform this type of work during shooting (C).*

4.5.2 Static soccer strength

Sometimes a player has to brace all or part of his body. When this happens, muscles are tensed without any movement occurring. Instead of the muscles becoming shorter or longer, they change into "steel cables." This is the case, for example, when a player is **shielding the ball**. The ball is in front of the player at his feet, while an opponent is pushing him from behind. To resist this pressure from behind without losing the ball, the player tenses the muscles of his legs and upper body and attempts to maintain his posture. The same thing occurs in a **block tackle**. A player sets his foot in front of the ball at the moment when another player tries to kick it. The tackling player has to tense the muscles of his legs (statically) to resist the strength that the other player puts into his kick. Static muscle work may also be carried out when a **shoulder charge** occurs. The player has to tense his upper body. The stomach, back, shoulder, arm and chest muscles are all tensed so that together they form a block. Finally the muscles of the support leg perform static work when a player shoots. When a shot is executed properly the support leg is slightly bent. Static strength is needed to hold this posture. The whole weight of the body is supported by the one leg. If this leg moves, the shot or pass may not be as accurate as it should.

4.5.3 Explosive strength and fast strength

Section 4.2.2 describes the four components of dynamic muscle work. Two of these are explosive and fast muscle strength. Because soccer actions are generally explosive by nature, it is clear that these two components play a major role in soccer. The conditioning of explosive strength and the conditioning of fast strength are two very different aspects, especially with regard to coordination. The difference between explosive and fast strength is first explained here with the help of a number of soccer examples. Explosive strength is needed for actions that are carried out from a state of (relative) rest, in which the emphasis is mainly on strength. A good example is a sprint or a jump from a standing start. The body must be brought into horizontal or vertical motion through an explosion of strength. A **powerful push-off movement** is needed, involving as many muscle fibers as possible. The important aspect of fast strength is the speed at which strength is supplied. Fast strength plays a key role during actions when the body or part of the body is already in motion. An explosive start brings the body into motion. As the sprint is continued, the emphasis shifts gradually from explosive to fast strength. During acceleration a **fast push-off movement** gradually becomes more important than maximum push-off strength. The faster the push-off, the more steps per second the player can take. Because only the fastest muscle fibers can contract quickly enough, fast strength is supplied by only a limited number of muscle fibers. Because fewer muscle fibers means less strength, the important aspect of fast strength is clearly speed rather than absolute strength. Another good example of fast strength is jumping from a running start. Usually a number of sprint strides are made before taking off from one foot. The most important aspect here is to translate horizontal speed into vertical speed. Every soccer player knows from experience that such a jump requires less take-off strength than a two-footed jump from a standing start, and yet he can jump higher.

Explosive and fast strength are therefore two different components, each of which requires its own method of conditioning. The difference can be explained in terms of the nervous system. For explosive strength the nervous system needs to activate as many muscle fibers as possible in a short time. For fast speed the nervous system has to activate a limited number of muscle fibers as quickly as possible. Again everything depends on the brain's control of the muscles, and therefore on coordination.

Static soccer strength while shielding the ball, making a block tackle, making a shoulder charge, and shooting.

4.6 CONDITIONING FOR SOCCER STRENGTH

Resistances in soccer are becoming greater. As a result of tactical developments players have less space to play in. Players come into contact more frequently with their opponents. They therefore have to "lose" their markers more frequently, fight harder for the ball, run faster and jump higher than before. They have less time. Conditioning for soccer strength is therefore steadily gaining in importance.

4.6.1 How should strength conditioning for soccer be carried out?

Many people still regard training with weights (general weight training) as the best way of making the body stronger. This is a clear misunderstanding. Training with weights is focused on pure strength. Moreover only one group of muscles is exercised at any one time. This bears no relationship to the soccer situation. Firstly pure strength is not important for soccer players in the same way that it is for weight lifters. Soccer players must be able to translate their strength into soccer movements. An essential aspect of this is coordination - applying strength correctly. This can best be illustrated with an example. Right footed players usually shoot further and harder with the right foot than with the left. It might therefore be concluded that there is more strength in the right leg. But right-footed players usually take off on the left foot when they jump to head the ball. They can jump higher than when they take off on the right foot. This suggests that a right-footed player's left leg is stronger than the right. Both conclusions are wrong. Usually the right and left legs are equal in terms of their basic strength. This basic strength is applied better in the left leg when the player jumps, and the reverse is the case when he shoots. This is a matter of coordination and technique. Before conditioning is carried out for jumping strength, kicking strength or any other form of strength required for soccer actions, the technical execution of these actions must be good. This is where the most valuable gains are to be made.

Secondly, several muscles are used at the same time during a soccer movement. The nervous system must be able to coordinate the activity of the various muscles if such a movement is to be carried out in a smooth and supple manner. In soccer it is the combination of strength and coordination that is important. The only way of conditioning the two aspects at the same time is to make use of the soccer movements themselves. The coordination of a movement can only be conditioned by practicing the movement again and again. It is impossible to improve the coordination of one movement by practicing another. It is up to the coach to select the resistance so that strength conditioning actually takes place when the movement is carried out (overload principle).

In summary it can be said that sport-related conditioning takes precedence over general conditioning. Nevertheless, general strength conditioning is of value for soccer players in certain situations, e.g. at the start of the rehabilitation process after a long-term injury, or if a disequilibrium in the body's balance of strength is identified (see section 4.7.1).

4.6.2 Basic strength conditioning

Basic strength is the maximum strength that a person can apply with a certain muscle. All of the muscles that are of importance for a soccer player must have a certain level of basic strength. Basic strength can be maintained or brought up to the required level with the help of a number of general strength exercises on the field. During preseason preparations the players' basic strength has to be built up to the required level again. The players have been relatively inactive for a number of weeks or even months, during which it is only to be expected that the basic strength in the upper and lower body will decrease.

Arms/shoulders/chest/upper back

Drill 1: Push-ups
With two hands/one hand/clapping hands together/possibly on the knees.

Drill 2: Head-to-head challenge
Two players facing each other try to maintain the push-up position. Each player tries to pull one of the other's supporting arms away.

The lower back

Drill 3: Catch
Two players lie face down facing each other. They repeatedly throw the ball to each other. They have to keep their arms off the ground all the time. As an alternative they can repeatedly throw the ball to each other from a standing position.

Drill 4: Back extension
The player lies face down with arms and legs off the ground. He repeatedly tries to raise his arms and legs as far as possible, then lets them fall back again, but still keeping them off the ground.

The stomach
Drill 5: Sit-ups
The player lies on his back with knees bent and hands behind his neck and perform a series of sit-ups. Both the straight and the oblique stomach muscles can be exercised (nose to knees, or left elbow to right knee and vice versa).

The quadriceps
Drill 6: Squatting
With another player, preferably of the same weight, on his back, the player performs a series of knee bends. If the carried player is too heavy there is a danger of injuries occurring, but if he is too light the load is insufficient.

The hamstrings
Drill 7: Leg curls
The player lies face down and bends his leg back against resistance from a partner. This should be done with the right and the left leg.

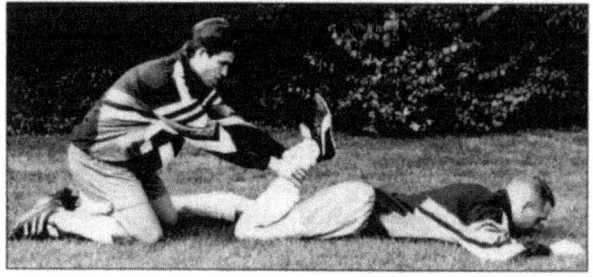

The calf muscles

Drill 8: Calf raise
With another player on his back, the player stands on the balls of the feet and stretches the feet upwards.

The ankles

Drill 9: Jumping

Drill 10: Hopping on the right and left legs (on the balls of the feet)

General strength endurance of the legs

Drill 11: Skipping with a rope

4.6.3 Conditioning for kicking strength

A soccer player should be able to kick the ball equally well with either foot, i.e. he should be "two-footed." Learning to kick with the "weaker" leg is proof that strength conditioning, especially during the initial phase, is primarily a matter of improving technique (see section 4.6.1). If a right-footed player practices kicking with his left foot, he will initially not be able to kick the ball very hard or very far. Although the basic strength of the left leg is normally the same as that of the right (see Fig. 4.6A), the kicking strength of the left leg appears to be less than that of the right (see Fig. 4.6B). With a lot of practice the kicking strength of

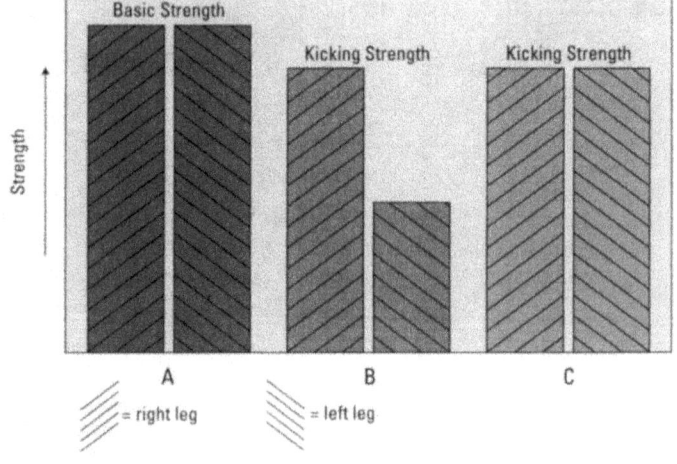

Figure 4.6: *Although both legs have the same general strength (A), the kicking strength of the left leg is much lower than that of the right (B). This is because the general strength that is present in the left leg is not optimally exploited. Lots of practice will improve the player's coordination of his left-footed kicking and the kicking strength of his left leg will ultimately match that of the right (C). The general strength in both legs remains the same.*

the left leg will gradually increase until the player is completely two-footed. The kicking power of the left leg is then equal to that of the right. The basic strength of both legs is the same as before. The kicking strength of the left leg has increased because the player is now able to apply most of the leg's basic strength when he kicks the ball (see Fig. 4.6C).

The brain's control of the muscles has been improved, so that it can now activate the muscles in the left leg at just the right moment when the player wants to kick the ball (see section 4.3.1). The result is increased kicking strength.

Passing and shooting must not be practiced in isolation. By playing a lot of soccer, a player automatically learns how to pass the ball over short and long distances. This is how children used to learn in the streets. Sidewalk edges, lampposts and trees ensured that children developed a wide arsenal of kicking techniques (left and right leg, inside and outside of the foot, instep). Practice games with more or less players per team are eminently suitable for learning to shoot and pass the ball. Special attention should be paid to shooting by letting the players carry out finishing drills now and then during training sessions. Coaches must look for good kicking technique and accuracy. During such finishing drills the ball often flies everywhere except into the goal. One of the reasons is that players often think they have to shoot as hard as they can. It is better to shoot in a relaxed and technically correct manner. A player can be given the task of simply shooting at goal. Then he can be asked to shoot into the bottom-left corner. When he can do this he can gradually shoot harder, but always on target. If a player shoots wide or over the goal, the coach can penalize the player, or he might even penalize the whole group after every third miss. Such a penalty could be 25 push-ups.

When they shoot at goal, many players focus more on shooting hard rather than accurately.

4.6.4 Conditioning for jumping strength

Jumping ability is also very dependent on good technique. Coordination is a crucial factor, especially when a player takes off on one foot. Coordination cannot be improved by making muscles stronger. It can only be learned by repeated practice. Timing also plays a role. Timing is the ability of the brain to select the right moment to activate certain muscles. This depends partly on information acquired during the game. The behavior of the ball, or of teammates and opponents, play a part in determining when a soccer player must jump to head the ball. This must therefore be practiced mainly in soccer-related situations. It has been found that jumping strength is partly dependent on a player's position in the team. The way a player jumps also differs from position to position. Attackers and defenders mainly have to jump for high crosses. Attackers are usually moving forward, whereas defenders are often stationary or moving backward. Midfielders, however, usually have to jump for high balls through the middle, e.g. from goal kicks or kicks into play. All of these different soccer situations require specific coordination. Jumping and heading as an attacker is completely different to jumping and heading as a defender. Conditioning for pure muscle strength in the legs is therefore not sufficient. Jumping strength has to be improved above all in the context of the above-mentioned soccer situations. Improvements in jumping technique enable more of the basic strength in the take-off leg to be applied. Better timing enables a player to take off at the correct moment. These two factors together ensure that a player can jump higher, and they increase the probability that the action will be successful.

General jumping strength

A number of drills are suitable for establishing basic jumping strength. Drill 12 in particular should be carried out carefully.

Drill 12: Plyometrics

Plyometric exercises involve jumping from a modest height. The landing is followed immediately by a jump.

It is possible to jump higher by bending the knees and squatting slightly before taking off. This stretches the quadriceps, and this elastic strength gives an added impulse to the jump and thus results in more jumping strength being applied. Eccentric muscle work is followed immediately by concentric muscle work. This effect can be increased by first jumping down from a slight height. In section 4.5.1 it is explained that the quadriceps absorb the downward speed by stretching. If a take-off is made immediately after landing, the stretched quadriceps supply additional strength. The jumping strength will be greater. It is important that the heels do not touch the ground during the landing and the subsequent take off. This form of muscle conditioning is also termed plyometrics. It is the most effective way of conditioning for general jumping strength. There is no other way of generating such considerable forces. The disadvantage of plyometrics is that, initially, it frequently results in muscle soreness. When the muscle is stretched, a large number of links between thick and thin protein filaments are broken. For this reason the height of the raised surface from which the player jumps should never be higher than 15 inches. This type of conditioning drill is not suitable for children, and should always be carried out with care.

Conditioning method
Intensity: 100%
Repetitions: 4-6
Sets: 3-5
Rest: 30 to 60 seconds between repetitions
             4 to 6 minutes between sets

Doubt in your own ability is more dangerous than any opponent, because just the thought of losing causes your strength to shrink.

Bjorn Borg

Drill 13: Series of jumps
The object of this drill is to increase jumping strength by making a number of jumps in sequence rather than a single explosive jump. The take-off can be one-footed or two-footed. The jumps can be made over a single obstacle or over a series of obstacles. This drill can be carried out in a forward or sideways direction.

Specific jumping strength

Drill 14: The heading gallows
A heading gallows is a ball suspended on a rope. The height of the ball can be varied easily. The players must run up, jump and head the ball powerfully. The take-off should be one-footed. The height of the ball can be progressively increased to force the players to jump higher. At the same time they must continue to head the ball properly (technique).

Drill 15: A ball through the middle
Player 1 has the ball in his hands and stands 5 meters away from players 2 and 3. He repeatedly throws the ball in the air for player 3 to jump and head it back. Player 2 tries to hinder player 3. Later player 1 can kick the ball 15 to 20 meters and player 2 can participate actively. He must try to head the ball on. Players 2 and 3 must take care not to clash heads. The jumps can be made from a standing or running start.

Drill 16: A ball from the flank
Defenders and attackers must be paired off. Wingers, or right or left midfield players, hit crosses from both flanks. The attacker must try to jump to meet the cross and head it into goal. The defender must try to prevent this by heading the ball out or at least jumping to challenge for the ball.

4.6.5 Conditioning for strength in the challenge
A soccer player must have a well developed upper body to be able to win challenges for the ball, but the lower body also plays an important role. A player must be steady on his feet. General strength in the challenge is therefore needed. The frequent physical contacts during a game are a constant threat to a player's balance. This may result in the player being passed by an opponent, or losing the ball. A player must therefore practice

his physical coordination and agility. This is referred to here as general strength in the challenge.

General strength in the challenge
Conditioning for strength in the challenge is concerned with the development of pure strength with which the ball can be shielded or won.

Drill 17: Pushing
Two cones are placed 10 meters apart. Two players stand between them. One player tries to push the other past one of the cones. This drill can be carried out with the players facing towards or away from each other.

Drill 18: Pulling
Two cones are placed 10 meters apart. Two players stand between them. One player tries to pull the other past one of the cones.

Drill 19: Squatting
Two players stand back to back and sink gradually into a squatting position. This position is maintained for a few seconds then the players stand again.

This is repeated several times.

Specific strength in the challenge
Conditioning for specific strength in the challenge involves teaching the players to use their body strength adroitly and to apply it as efficiently as possible in challenges for the ball.

a. The block tackle

Drill 20: Bracing

A tackling player frequently tries to block the ball just as the other player wants to pass it or shoot. This is a block tackle, and the tackler must know exactly when to make it. Otherwise he may commit a foul or, in the worst case, injure himself or his opponent. Timing is therefore crucial. Conditioning for this aspect of the game starts with bracing. The drills teach the players the difference between a relaxed and a braced body, and the advantages of the latter. The block tackle is made at far less than full strength. The emphasis is not on applying strength but on developing a "feel" for the moment when the various muscles have to be tensed. As this aspect improves, the emphasis can be gradually shifted towards strength.

b. The shoulder charge

Drill 21: The shoulder charge during a sprint
Two players stand close to each other. About 10 to 15 meters away are two cones, 10 inches apart. At a signal from the coach the players sprint to the cones. The first player to place his foot between the cones is the winner. During the sprint each player can shoulder charge the other to try to gain an advantage.

Drill 22: Shoulder charge during an airborne challenge
Two players calmly dribble towards each other, jump in the air and give each other a push with the shoulder. This drill also involves bracing the body. Players must learn how it feels to collide with an opponent in the air. They must learn how to use their body at the right moment to block an opponent in the air.

c. Shielding the ball

Drill 23: The "1 against 1" challenge
One player has the ball and the other is at his back. The objective of this drill is that the player with the ball learns to use his body to shield the ball. The other player tries to exert continuous pressure on the player in possession through physical contact, without committing a foul. Physical coordination and agility are at the heart of this drill.

4.6.6 Conditioning for starting strength

Starting strength is the push-off strength of the first 3 or 4 strides. This strength is supplied by the fast muscle fibers. The more muscle fibers, the greater the starting strength. Unfortunately the number of fast muscle fibers is determined by heredity, and cannot therefore be influenced by conditioning. Another way of improving starting strength is to get the combined muscle fibers to produce more starting strength or, expressed another way, to make the fast muscle fibers in the legs thicker by means of conditioning drills.

Shielding the ball

This is possible to a certain degree. The muscles are conditioned qualitatively and not quantitatively. Timing and technique play a large role in the above-mentioned components of soccer strength, and the most progress can be achieved by improving coordination. This is not the case, however, with starting strength. This involves pure push-off strength. A few general strength drills are therefore used, after which starting strength has to be placed in a soccer context (see Chapter 6). Soccer players must also learn the right moment to start a sprint.

Conditioning method

Duration:	1 to 2 seconds (3 to 4 strides)
Intensity:	100%, from a standing position
Repetitions:	8-10
Sets:	2-4
Rest:	30 seconds between repetitions
	4 to 6 minutes between sets

Drill 24: Uphill sprints
During a short uphill sprint the player also has to overcome gravity. This extra resistance puts more emphasis on the push-off strength.

Drill 25: Upstairs sprint
When a player runs up a set of stairs, gravity is again an extra resistance that has to be overcome.

Drill 26: Plyometrics
With one foot on a raised (maximum of 16 inches high) surface, jump down, jump forward, land on the ball of the same foot and make a short sprint.

Drill 27: Sprinting out of a backward dribble
Dribble backwards. On a signal from the coach, make a short forward sprint.

Drill 28: Stand up and sprint
The player lies on his back or stomach, or sits, then jumps up and makes a short sprint. The fact that he has to jump up makes the character of the drill more explosive.

4.6.7 Conditioning for eccentric soccer strength
It has already been explained that the speed developed by soccer players is braked by eccentric muscle work (see section 4.5.1). This frequently involves absorbing a considerable jolt. The muscles must be conditioned for this.

a. Braking after a sprint
Drill 29: Slalom sprint
The players sprint from cone to cone. Because the cones are not in a straight line, the players constantly have to brake and change direction.

b. Landing after a jump
Drill 30: Plyometrics
The eccentric muscle work of the quadriceps during the landing after a jump can be conditioned as in drill 12. The only difference is that in this case the player does not have to jump again directly after landing. This step can be replaced by, for example, a short sprint. A series of jumps in the forward direction are also a form of plyometrics.

c. Braking the lower leg
Drill 31: Reverse leg curl
It is difficult to put the emphasis on braking the lower leg during shooting. This facet must therefore be practiced with the help of a more general drill. Player A lies face down with one leg stretched out and the other bent at 90 degrees. He tries to bend the bent leg still further, but does not tense it completely. Player B tries to prevent this and stretches the leg very carefully. This drill must be carried out with both legs, because in principle a player should be able to shoot with both feet.

4.6.8 Integrated strength conditioning

The aspect that makes soccer so fatiguing is that all kinds of strength-sapping activities have to be carried out in rapid succession and sometimes merge into each other. A jump might be followed by a sprint, and the sprint might end in a sliding tackle. In short, everything that has been described above must be integrated into a whole and must be conditioned as such. In this way players develop "coupling ability."

Drill 32: Hopping + sprinting
Drill 33: Jumping + sprinting
Drill 34: Jumping forward or backward + sprinting
Drill 35: Jumping left or right + sprinting
Drill 36: Skipping sideways + sprinting
Drill 37: Dribbling backward + jumping + sprinting
Drill 38: Jumping + shoulder charge + sprinting
Drill 39: Jumping + shoulder charge + lying down + sprinting
Drill 40: Pushing competition + sprinting

4.6.9 Dosing soccer-related strength conditioning

The biggest problem associated with soccer-related strength conditioning is how to dose it correctly. The resistance is much more difficult to define than in strength conditioning with weights. Usually work is carried out against the body's own weight or that of another player. Only in the case of plyometrics and conditioning for starting strength is a specific method also defined. For the other (often more complex) drills the coach has to rely on his intuition. He must observe his players closely to ensure that the workload and the work-to-rest ratio are sufficient. Generally it is best to work with sets of 8 to 12 reps, with 2 or 3 sets per drill. Strength conditioning can be carried out ideally on the field in circuit form. The coach selects a drill for each component of soccer strength. The group of players is split up into as many smaller groups as there are drills. Each group performs a drill. After a while each group moves to the next drill. The coach must ensure that successive drills exercise widely different groups of muscles. This helps to avoid fatigue. No rest period is needed between the drills.

4.6.10 Position-specific strength conditioning

The central focus of attention in Chapter 1 was the workload of the players, and the differences in workload from position to position. One of the aspects of soccer-related work that was clearly emphasized was that defenders and attackers have to jump to head the ball more often than midfielders. There are also differences in the number of challenges for the ball, and midfielders are more dependent on strength in the challenge than defenders or attackers. There is also a difference in the type of strength in the challenge. In midfield, most challenges are aimed at winning the ball. Challenges between attackers and defenders are often concerned with getting into good positions for crosses, corners and free kicks. These are off-the-ball challenges. These aspects have to be taken into account during training sessions.

4.7 GENERAL STRENGTH CONDITIONING FOR SOCCER PLAYERS

Although general strength conditioning is of subordinate importance, it is nevertheless worthy of consideration. In the few situations where it is useful, conditioning for general strength must be carried out properly. If general strength drills are not carried out in a technically correct manner they can damage the body more than they strengthen it.

General strength conditioning only in special situations

Every athlete and sportsman needs basic strength. Nevertheless, a soccer player's proper place is on the pitch and not in a gym. Players' strength conditioning must be carried out on the pitch. Sometimes, however, a player's basic strength is too low, or suffers a sudden deterioration, or the balance of strength between the muscles is distorted. In such cases, general strength conditioning can be the remedy.

a. Shortage of strength

It may happen that a player has insufficient strength to maintain his performance during a match. This is the case with small players. They can be pushed off the ball too easily by physically stronger opponents. They are also at a big disadvantage when challenging for the ball in the air. It is therefore worthwhile to encourage these players to work on increasing their body strength under specialist supervision. By cultivating "body", a soccer player can compensate for his lack of height. Another example of an exceptional case is a player who lacks starting speed.

Such a player can practice short sprints in any number of soccer situations but this will not help to eliminate his shortcoming. A greater overload is necessary than can be imposed on the field. The player will have to follow a special program of strength conditioning to help him with his problem. Lack of starting speed can prevent a player from having a professional career.

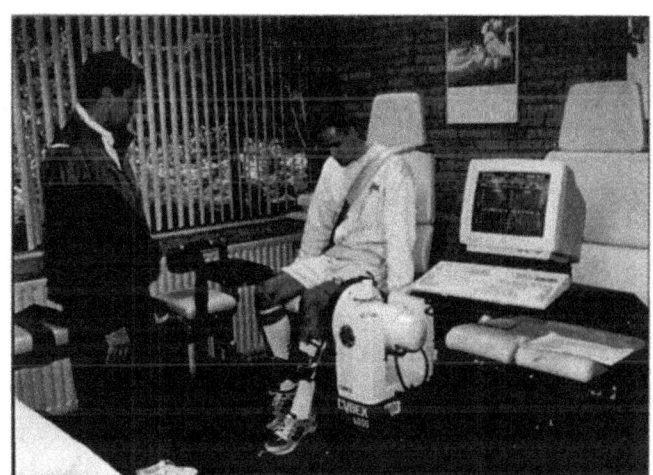
General strength exercises have a clear part to play in the rehabilitation process.

b. The rehabilitation process

Basic strength is lost when a player is inactive for a long period due to a serious injury. In the case of a leg injury the muscle strength in the injured leg can deteriorate considerably. Before the player can start to play again, this strength must be restored to its former level during a rehabilitation process (Chapter 14). This can be achieved more efficiently off the field. This is because all sorts of factors are difficult to control in such a situation. In the first place, of course, great care should be taken after a serious injury. General strength conditioning provides a way around this problem. Factors such as the workload intensity and extent can be more easily controlled. When the player has regained his basic strength, he can switch to soccer-related strength conditioning.

c. Imbalance in the body's strength

It is important that the strength in a soccer player's body is symmetrically distributed. The strength in the left leg should be the same as in the right. The muscle strength within the leg must also be well balanced. The relationship between the hamstrings (back of the upper leg) and the quadriceps (front of the upper leg) is of considerable importance. As a general rule, the strength of the hamstrings must be equal to at least 70% of the strength of the quadriceps. The strength of the stomach and back muscles must also be in relationship to each other. An imbalance in the body's strength can lead to injuries. A knowledge of how such imbalances can occur is needed to prevent this. Soccer players always tend to use their "stronger" side when they can. They always lead with the same shoulder when they turn away, or they always take off on the same foot. This is also true of shooting. Players always tend to shoot with the same foot. Usually this does not cause any problems, but it is as well to keep an eye on this aspect. Chronic muscle problems, for example, are often the consequence of imbalance in muscle strength. In this case the player must occasionally carry out specific strength conditioning in isolation. A coach can ensure that the player's strength increases step by step, so that injuries are avoided.

4.8 DRAWING UP A STRENGTH CONDITIONING PROGRAM

A soccer player who is faced with a problem situation can sometimes benefit from training with weights. In such cases the problem must be discussed and analyzed in depth with an expert in the field of strength conditioning before a start can be made on gen-eral strength conditioning. A step-by-step plan must then be drawn up on the basis of the analysis.

4.8.1 Step-by-step plan

It is not advisable to start with strength conditioning before a step-by-step plan with a number of objectives has been drawn up.

Step 1: The first step is to ascertain the extent to which strength conditioning is relevant for a sportsman or athlete. It is clearly relevant for a soccer player.

Step 2: If the player wants to develop muscle strength, a detailed analysis must be carried out to identify the muscles that are active during the sport-specific movements, and how they produce strength and how much. This information must be incorporated into the conditioning program.

Step 3: The sportsman's or athlete's current level of muscle strength must be measured. This can best be done with the help of a maximal test (see section 4.8.2).

Step 4: On the basis of the current level of strength, objectives must be set that the sportsman or athlete can aim to achieve during the strength conditioning. These objectives must be realistic, otherwise they can have a demotivating effect.

Step 5: The resistances should be light during the first phase of strength conditioning. Good muscle coordination must first be developed by practicing. When all the drills can be carried out correctly, the resistance can be slowly increased. This is when the development of basic strength starts.

Step 6: When a good basic strength is present, a cautious start can be made on sport-related strength conditioning. Conditioning for strength that is specifically related to soccer movements (soccer strength) is carried out on a foundation of general strength.

Step 7: The workload during the various drills is related to the maximal strength that can be produced during the particular drills. A player's maximal strength will increase as a consequence of strength conditioning. It is therefore worthwhile to carry out a maximal test on all muscles every 1 to 2 months. In this way the new maximal strength of each muscle can be determined and the conditioning program can be adjusted accordingly.

4.8.2 The maximal test

In a strength conditioning program, the load that has to be overcome in a drill is expressed as a percentage of the maximal strength that a muscle can produce during the drill. This maximal strength can best be determined with the help of a maximal test. The aim of this test is to determine the load when the muscle has just enough strength to carry out a drill once. This maximal strength must be estimated before the test is carried out (e.g., 60 kilograms). After a thorough period of warming up, the drill can be carried out with a somewhat lower load (e.g., 50 kilograms). If the drill can be carried out more than once, the load must be increased in 5 kilogram steps until the drill can only be carried out once. A minimum of 5 minutes rest must be allowed between the attempts. A careful estimate of the maximal strength ensures that the real maximal strength is reached with the fewest possible attempts. If the maximal test lasts for too long, fatigue may set in and the measured maximal load will be too low.

4.9   METHODS OF CONDITIONING FOR GENERAL STRENGTH

Dynamic concentric muscle strength is conditioned by working with weights. As already mentioned, this consists of four components. There is a conditioning method for each component.

Conditioning method for maximal strength
Load: 80-95% of maximal strength
Repetitions: 5
Sets: 6-8
Rest: 3-4 minutes between sets

Conditioning method for fast strength
Load: 60-80% of maximal strength
Repetitions: 8-10
Sets: 6-8
Rest: 1-2 minutes between sets

Conditioning method for explosive strength
Load: 80-100% of maximal strength
Repetitions: 1-8
Sets: 2-6
Rest: 4.5-6 minutes between sets

Conditioning method for strength endurance
Load: 40-60% of maximal strength
Repetitions: 15-25
Sets: 3
Rest: 45 seconds between sets

If a soccer player has to develop more "body" he must carry out conditioning for maxi-mal strength. Maximal strength conditioning is also used when there is an asymmetry in the body. If a player's starting speed is too slow, the emphasis must be on explosive strength in the muscles of the legs. Conditioning for strength endurance ensures that a player is stronger during the final phase of a game.

4.10 ORGANIZATION OF GENERAL STRENGTH CONDITIONING

Training sessions should always be well structured. This is essential if the conditioning effect is to be achieved. There are a number of organizational structures available for strength conditioning.

4.10.1 Station drills

The session consists of various types of drills. At each station a number of series of a drill are carried out. One or more groups of muscles have to carry out work. The next station is then selected. There are a number of organizational variations of this method (also referred to as the repeat method), each of which has its own conditioning objective.

Constant load and repeats

This method is eminently suitable for exercising and improving a specific strength component. The choice of load, number of repetitions and number of series is central. Strength endurance, for example, requires a low load, lots of repetitions and several series, whereas explosive strength conditioning requires a high load, less repetitions and only a few series. This method is very useful, especially during the first part of a conditioning period. More complex drills can subsequently be used.

e.g. $\dfrac{80\%}{8x} + \dfrac{80\%}{8x} + \dfrac{80\%}{8x}$ etc.

Variable load and constant number of repeats

This method is used mainly to condition players for fast strength. There are relatively few repetitions, a low load and high speed of movement.

e.g. $\dfrac{50\%}{10x} + \dfrac{40\%}{10x} + \dfrac{50\%}{10x}$ etc.

Constant load and variable repeats

This method can best be used to improve explosive and fast strength. Here too the speed of movement must be high and the load and the number of repetitions relatively low.

e.g. $\dfrac{70\%}{8x} + \dfrac{70\%}{12x} + \dfrac{70\%}{8x}$ etc.

Small pyramid drill

The objective of the small pyramid drill is to improve explosive strength and fast strength. This conditioning drill is eminently suitable for acyclic sports. The practice pattern is characterized by an increase in the load and a decrease in the number of repetitions. When the peak has been reached, the load is gradually reduced and the number of repetitions increased (see Fig. 4.7A).

e.g. $\dfrac{80\%}{8x} + \dfrac{85\%}{5x} + \dfrac{90\%}{3x} + \dfrac{95\%}{2x} + \dfrac{90\%}{3x} + \dfrac{85\%}{5x} + \dfrac{80\%}{8x}$

This method will have a positive effect on muscle coordination due to the constantly changing character of the drill. The demands on the nervous system change constantly. This drill can best be carried out at the end of a training session.

4.10.3 Broad pyramid drill

The objective of the broad pyramid drill is to improve strength endurance together with explosive strength and fast strength. The emphasis is therefore more on the number of repetitions and the high speed of movement, and less on the load (see Fig. 4.7B). This drill is of less importance than the small pyramid drill for soccer players.

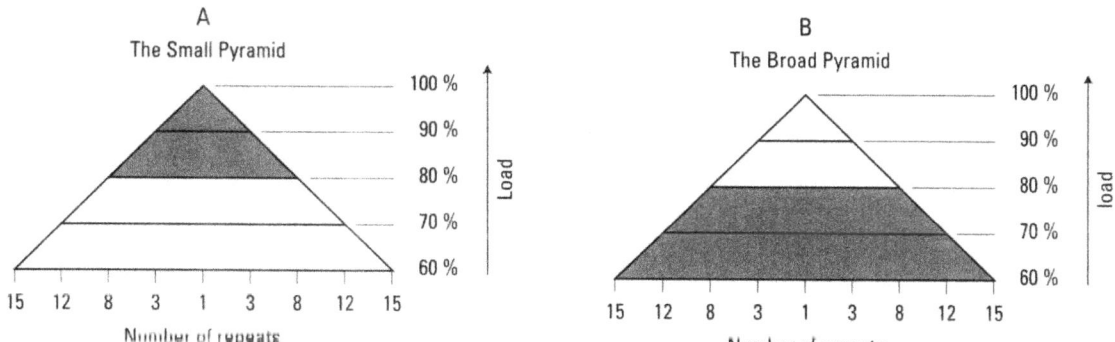

Figure 4.7: *The emphasis of the small pyramid is on a heavy load and a limited number of repetitions (A). The broad pyramid is concerned with lots of repetitions and a lower load (B).*

e.g. $\dfrac{60\%}{15x} + \dfrac{70\%}{12x} + \dfrac{80\%}{8x} + \dfrac{70\%}{12x} + \dfrac{60\%}{15x}$

4.10.5 Contrast method

The objective of this method is to confuse the nervous system. The load and the number of repetitions are varied considerably from series to series. Such large fluctuations prevent the nervous system and the rest of the body from "rusting up" and becoming set in familiar patterns. This method makes use of all sorts of elements from other conditioning methods. The speed of movement depends on the load during a given series.

e.g. $\dfrac{80\%}{5x} + \dfrac{40\%}{10x} + \dfrac{80\%}{5x} + \dfrac{40\%}{10x} + \dfrac{80\%}{5x}$ etc.

This drill is suitable for breaking through a strength barrier when a player cannot achieve any further progress in his strength development. The contrast method makes new demands on the nervous system, thus "shaking it awake."

4.10.5 Circuit training

Circuit training involves working with different drills. All muscle groups that are of importance for sport movements are exercised in a given sequence. During each drill only one group of muscles is exercised, so there is no need for a rest period between successive drills. This method is therefore very suitable for improving strength endurance, in view of the fact that the metabolic process and the blood circulation have to function continuously while the body is performing work. The workload can be varied by varying a number of factors:

> *You can develop a muscle by practicing. You make it carry out a lot of work, you maintain it in good condition and in time it gains strength of its own accord. That is absolutely simple. But such a muscle is a "stupid" muscle. Now you can also strengthen a muscle with your thoughts, by focusing your brain on the muscle.*
>
> **Joris van den Bergh**

- the load per drill
- the number of repetitions and series of a given drill
- the rest period between repetitions and series
- the speed at which the drill is carried out
- the recovery time between drills
- the number of drills per circuit
- the number of times the circuit has to be repeated

The above strength conditioning methods are especially suitable for more general strength conditioning. Considerable use is made of clearly quantifiable external loads (weights). The more soccer-related methods mainly make use of soccer-related resistances, for which the strength factor is very difficult to quantify. Moreover, soccer movements involve a mixture of maximal strength, explosive strength, fast strength and strength endurance. Because these four components are produced by varying patterns of concentric, eccentric and static muscle work, there is in fact a complex play of forces. The application of conditioning methods to soccer-related conditioning will therefore always be difficult. The coach's intuition and experience will therefore always be the most crucial factor determining the content of the conditioning program.

4.11 DRILLS FOR GENERAL STRENGTH CONDITIONING

General strength conditioning is done with weights. These can be individual weights or weights attached to a piece of equipment. There are a variety of drills for conditioning the various muscles and groups of muscles. The most suitable of these are shown on the following pages.

Drills for Arms

Dumbell Curl (biceps)

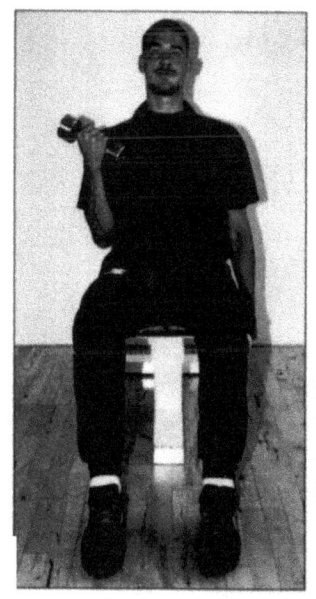
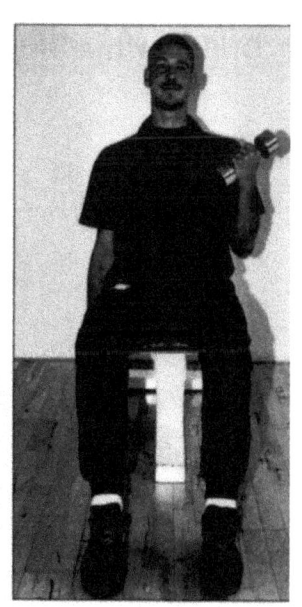

Kickback (triceps)

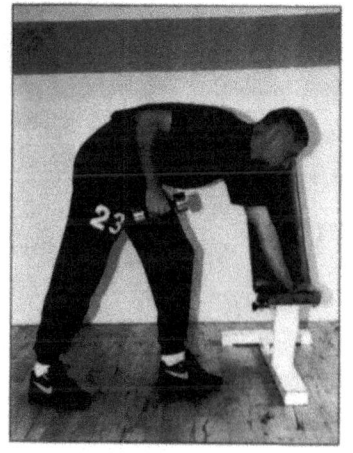

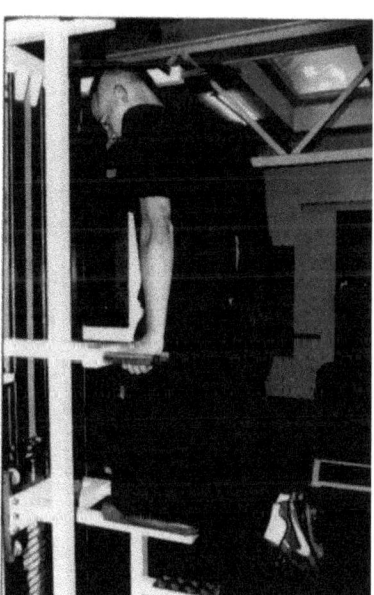

Dips (triceps)

Drills for the Shoulders

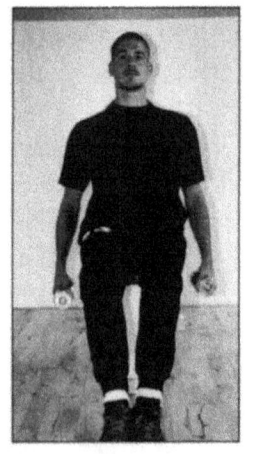

Side Raises

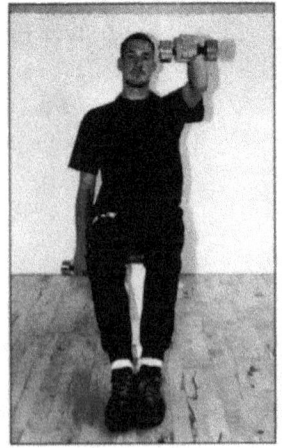

Front Raises   **Shoulder Press**

Drills for the Chest

Bench Press

Flyers

Drills for the Back

Easy Power Station **Lat Pull Down**

Lat Pulleys

Drills for the groin (adductors)

Standing Adduction

Adductor Machine

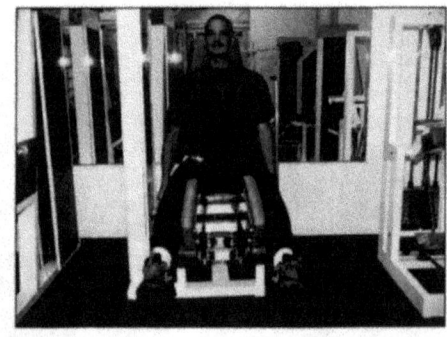

Drills for the Hips (abductors)

Standing Abductor

Abductor Machine

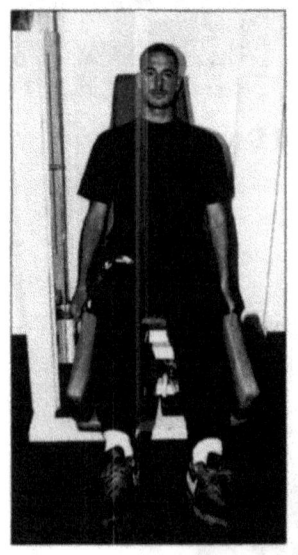
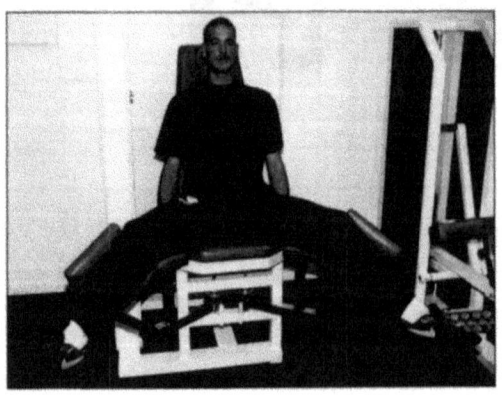

Drills for the Stomach

Crunch Machine

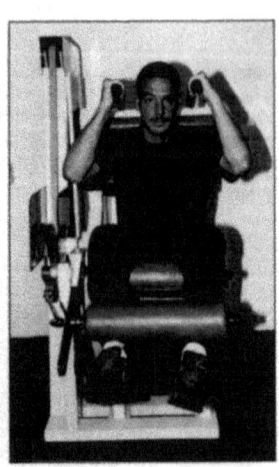

Drills for the Quadriceps

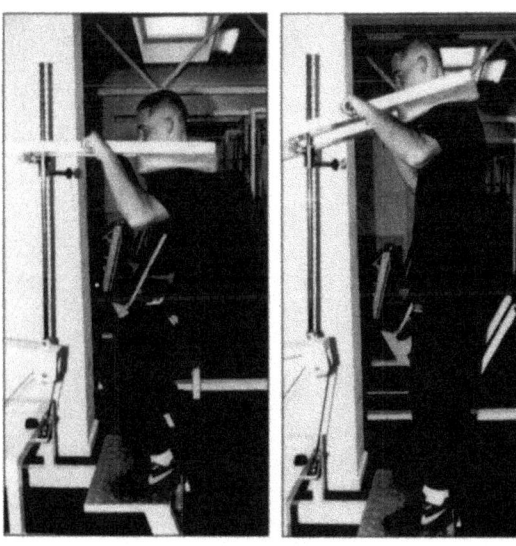

Squats

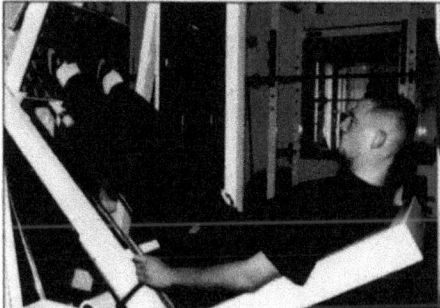

Leg Press

Drills for the Hamstrings

Leg Curl

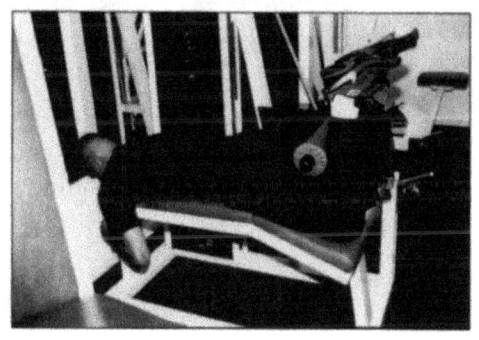

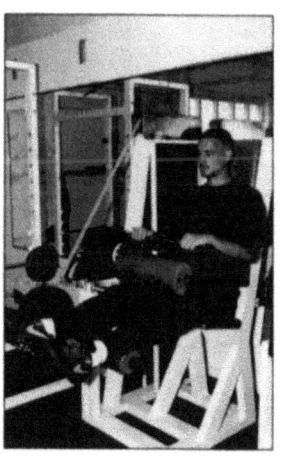

Hamstring Curl

Drills for the Calves

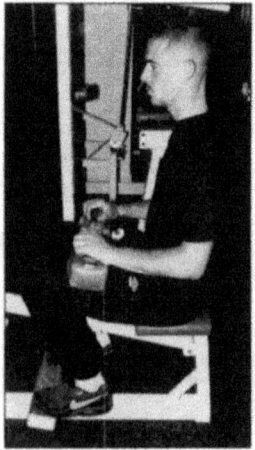 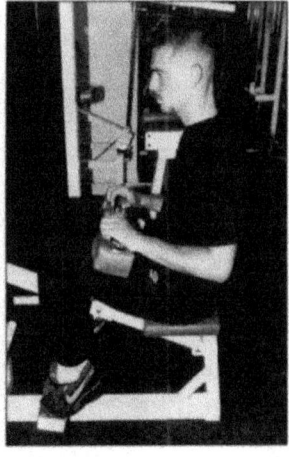

Calf Raises

Push Down

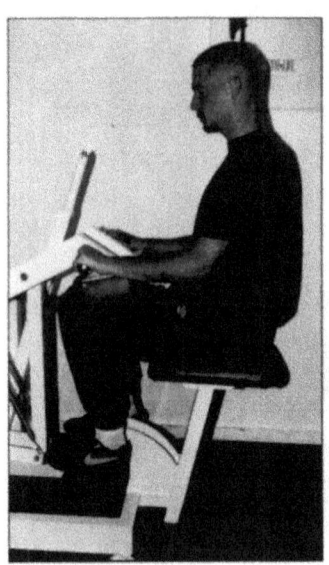 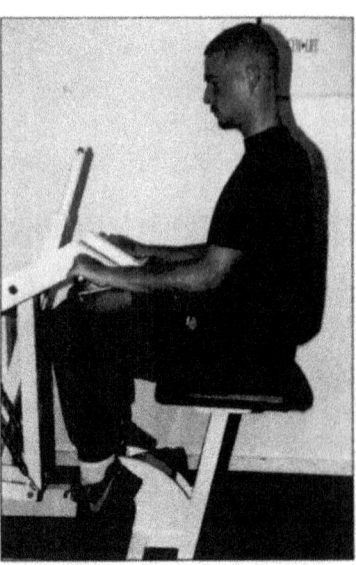

SUMMARY

- General strength is the basic strength that is needed to participate in a sport. Specific strength is the strength needed to carry out sport-related actions.

- There are two types of muscle work: dynamic and static. During dynamic muscle work the muscle develops strength while it contracts (concentric) or stretches (eccentric). During static work, strength is developed without any change occurring in the length of the muscle.

- Strength conditioning has two effects. First of all muscular coordination improves (increase in stimulus strength and frequency). Only then does the size of the muscle increase.

- Soccer strength consists of basic strength, kicking strength, jumping strength, strength in the challenge and starting strength.

- During soccer actions the muscles first perform concentric work to develop speed. At the end of such an action the speed of the body or part of the body has to be braked. This is done by performing eccentric muscle work. Static muscle work is performed when a player shields the ball, carries out a block tackle, makes a shoulder charge or shoots at goal.

- In soccer it is essential to translate existing basic strength into soccer actions. The better a player's coordination, the more of his basic strength he can effectively use during the soccer action. Strength conditioning is therefore initially coordination conditioning.

- General strength conditioning in a gym is only suitable in special situations, when a player lacks strength, or is undergoing rehabilitation, or has an unequal balance of strength.

- A step-by-step plan should be drawn up first when a conditioning program is being worked out.

- General strength conditioning can be carried out through station drills, a small or broad pyramid, or circuit training.

FIVE PRACTICAL QUESTIONS

1. What is a safe age to start with strength conditioning?

Before children have gone through their growth spurt they should only work against their own body weight. During the growth spurt the amount of testosterone in the body increases. This hormone makes strength conditioning possible. A start can be made on strength conditioning at age 16. It is not advisable, however, for youngsters in the soccer world to train in a gym. Youngsters with professional clubs should only carry out general strength conditioning under qualified supervision.

2. Must the muscles be stretched after strength conditioning drills?

There is a tendency to stretch the muscles after a strength conditioning session to prevent them from becoming shorter. Muscle shortening is avoided by carrying out drills across the full range of motion, and stretching is therefore unnecessary. It should be remembered that stretching may aggravate any muscle damage that is present.

3. Is it worthwhile taking the whole group of players to a gym?

General strength conditioning is only worthwhile if it is carried out regularly two or three times each week. This is almost impossible in amateur soccer. Moreover the purpose of general strength conditioning is to increase basic strength. Players must learn to translate the basic strength they already possess into explosive strength. Just for a change it is worth going to a gym now and again. Variety keeps the players fresh.

4. Is it true that muscle tension must be developed during the final training session before a match?

Increased muscle tension does have a positive effect on soccer performance. In amateur soccer, however, the final training session is usually two days before the match. The muscle tension built up during this session cannot be maintained for 48 hours. The answer, therefore, is no.

5. Which muscles are most important for a soccer player?

The most important muscles, which are also the muscles that are most often involved in injuries, are the hamstrings, the quadriceps, the stomach muscles and the muscles in the groin.

INTERVIEW WITH FRANK RIJKAARD (A.F.C. Ajax and A.C. Milan)

As a player you always gave an impression of strength. Did you deliberately work on this, and if so how and from what age?

Only later in my career did I start with strength training. Before that I was always one of the biggest and strongest players. When I was about 28 I noticed that I felt more balanced when I did a certain amount of conditioning for strength. I concentrated mainly on my upper body (chest and shoulders). My arms and legs were naturally well developed.

In contemporary soccer, winning challenges is viewed as the key to success. Do you agree, and what is the best way to train for this aspect of the game?

Winning duels, together with a good playing system, is certainly very important. I find the best way of training for this is to set two goals not too far apart and play 3 against 3. Each side has a goalkeeper and two other players. Because the playing area is small (for example, the size of the penalty area), the game is fast and there are lots of challenges for the ball. This sort of drill is very tiring. Each game should not last for longer than 4 minutes, and there must be sufficient rest between games.

It is said that strength, speed and endurance have become more important in the course of time. Have you yourself found that soccer has become more physical, and how does this manifest itself?

Yes I have. You can see that the team as a whole has steadily become more important. The top clubs are no longer dependent on two or three players who run things. The "ball distributor" type of player, who used to be able to fit into a top team without any problems, is now often found wanting in terms of strength, speed and endurance.

It is known that Italian clubs pay a lot of attention to the physical side of the game. How does AC Milan condition its players for strength. Do the players just work on the training field, or do they also work in the gym?

Conditioning for endurance, speed and explosive strength was carried out on the train-ing field. There was also a gym with all sorts of apparatus. This was ideal because everyone could work on his own special needs in the area of strength. Everything was done under qualified supervision. I don't think there is a lot of difference between the approaches to strength conditioning in the Netherlands and Italy.

There are large differences in the amount of running carried out by defenders, midfielders and attackers. What position requires the most physical strength?

I can believe that the amount of running varies. Personally I think that strength is useful in any position, irrespective of the amount of running you have to do. Nowadays teams play 1 against 1 over the whole field, so there are challenges for the ball wherever you play.

Were some games more physically demanding than others?
The top matches were fatiguing. It makes no difference whether you talk about top league games, European Cup games or international games. Top games are top games and they all cost a lot of strength.

You have played in teams that used different styles of play. What style is physically the most demanding?
Playing the "Ajax style" required more strength than playing the "Milan style." AC Milan played a 4-4-2 system with zonal marking. If an opponent left your zone he was simply marked by someone else. At Ajax you had to go with him. The Ajax system required the right and left halves in particular to do a lot of running. This is also true of the system played by the Dutch national team.

What combination of pure strength and physical coordination/agility is needed to win challenges for the ball?
I think that pure strength without physical coordination and agility is not much use on a soccer field. A player with only good physical coordination and agility can pass and shoot reasonably well, but for a player with only pure strength this is impossible. I would therefore say that the relationship between pure strength and physical coor-dination/agility needed to win challenges for the ball is about 30-70%.

Intensive strength conditioning makes heavy demands on soccer players' bodies. The body needs extra energy and nutrients. How much attention did you pay to the subject of nutrition?
In Italy in particular, thanks to the numerous training camps, players are made more conscious of good eating habits. At home I always ate everything I liked without thinking about it. I didn't pay much attention to what I ate during the summer months either. I didn't do much to maintain my physical condition either. I just liked to be able to switch off for a while.

Are there specific aspects of strength conditioning that you would use if you became a coach?
In strength conditioning the emphasis is always on the physical requirements of each separate player. Work must be carried out on an individual's shortcomings under qualified supervision. I am also a supporter of strength conditioning if it is properly dosed.

LITERATURE

1. Fitness training in Football - a scientific approach.
J. Bangsbo.
ISBN: 87-983350-7-3
Ho+Sotrm, Bagsvaerd.

2. Sports Fitness and Sports Injuries.
T. Reilly.
ISBN: 0-7234-1830-6.
Wolfe.

3. Buibspiertraining .... zinvol of zinloos?
F.B. van de Beld.
Richting/Sportgericht.

CHAPTER 5

SPRINT AND COORDINATION CONDITIONING FOR SOCCER PLAYERS

Dr. Raymond Verheijen

5.1 INTRODUCTION

In the context of soccer, running is a complex activity. Players continuously have to react to changing game situations by varying the direction and speed of their motion. In addition, soccer is becoming faster and the space in which the play takes place is becoming smaller. Players have to make more runs and feints to escape from close-marking opponents. No matter how many sprints a player makes, hardly any of them will be in a straight line. Now and then a player suddenly has to turn though 180 degrees when he is moving a top speed. Most soccer sprints are over distances between 1 and 40 meters. Some sprints are longer, but only rarely are they in excess of 60 to 70 meters. Speed is a complex concept and is made up of a number of different components. Practicing one component does not automatically improve the others. Special attention must therefore be focused on each component. Specific conditioning methods have been developed for this purpose. This chapter is devoted to conditioning for pure speed. General soccer-related drills are therefore used. Chapter 6 describes conditioning for speed in soccer situations. A soccer player must be fast and he must learn to recognize the right moment to start a sprint. This latter aspect can only be learned in specific soccer-related sprint drills. This chapter deals with coordination conditioning as well as sprint conditioning. To a large degree, speed is dependent on coordination.

Speed off the mark is all about the push-off strength of the first 3 or 4 sprint strides.

5.2 GENERAL SOCCER-RELATED SPRINT CONDITIONING

Figure 1.1 3 (on page 19) gives a good overview of the various possible phases of a sprint. Each of these phases has its own characteristics, which must be taken into account during conditioning.

5.2.1 Starting speed

Recent scientific research into improving starting speed has demonstrated that the greatest gains can be achieved in the first sprint stride. During conditioning for starting speed the emphasis must be on developing strength in the first push-off stride(s). This can best be done by practicing standing starts. The first stride costs most strength, the second a little less, and the third less again. Conditioning for starting speed has already been dealt with in detail in the previous chapter. It is really a form of strength conditioning.

5.2.2 Acceleration

Sometimes a sprint has to be made over a longer distance (20 to 50 meters), and the aim is to reach peak speed as quickly as possible. Usually this occurs after about 30 meters. The starting speed is the basis from which the body is accelerated. Accelerating the body requires a high stride rate. The higher this is, the more often each foot pushes off the ground per unit of time. The nervous system controls the frequency with which sprint strides are made. This can be conditioned with the help of coordination drills.

Conditioning method
Duration: 2-6 seconds
Intensity: 100%, with flying start
Repetitions: 6
Sets: 1-2
Rest: 1-2 minutes between reps.
4 minutes between sets

Acceleration depends on the stride rate that can be developed by the nervous system.

Always make a flying start
If a sprint is made from a standing start the first few steps cost a lot of strength. As the body gets moving, less push-off strength is required. By making use of a flying start during conditioning for acceleration, the body is gradually brought up to top speed instead of experiencing an initial "explosive" acceleration. The strength that is saved by not making an explosive start can be used to achieve faster sprint speeds. The stride rate will be higher than when a sprint is made from a standing start.

Make use of as many soccer elements as possible
It has already been mentioned that soccer players rarely sprint in a straight line. They constantly have to change direction, swerve and even turn in their own tracks at full speed. This is because they always have to anticipate the consequences of changing game situations. Sprint drills of 20 to 40 meters should incorporate these elements.

Drill 1: Slalom
The player gradually accelerates from A to B, so that when he reaches B he can make a flying start into a sprint to C, slaloming between the cones.

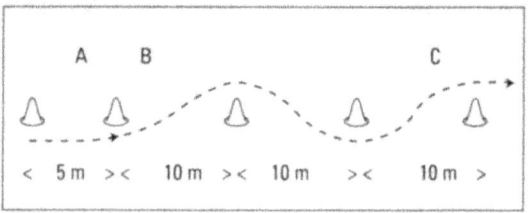

Drill 1:

Drill 2: Change of direction
The player gradually accelerates from A to B, then sprints from B to C. Just before he reaches C the coach at D plays a ball to the right or left. When the player reaches C he sprints after the ball and then tries to score.

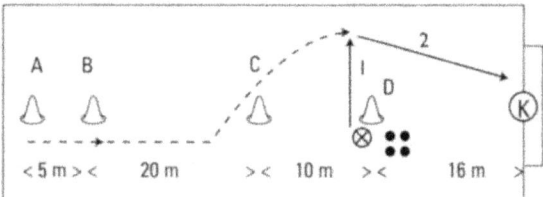

Drill 2:

Drill 3: Turning
The player gradually accelerates from A to B, then sprints from B to C, where he plays a one-two, then turns as fast as he can and goes back over his tracks. He sprints from B to A.

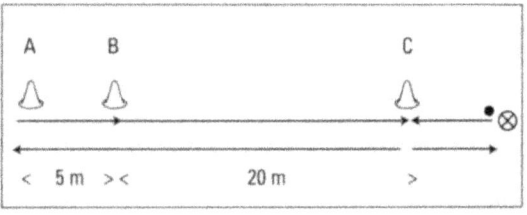

Drill 3:

The method of accelerating must always be related to the game situation. A player without the ball can accelerate by making long strides. When he has the ball at his feet this is more difficult. He must always be able to react instantaneously to an opponent's attempt to take the ball. In this case he has to shorten his stride, so that he has more contact with the ground and can, if necessary, react quickly. These two types of acceleration must be practiced, and this can be done with the help of obstacles. The purpose of the obstacles is to force the player to adjust his stride length while accelerating. The distance between the obstacles must be varied. The coach must take the age of his players into account when he decides on the distances between the obstacles.

Drill 4: Small strides
The player gradually accelerates from A to B, then sprints from B to C. A number of bars are placed close together on the ground between B and C. The player is therefore forced to accelerate using small strides. Only one bar can be crossed with each stride.

Drill 5: Long strides
The player gradually accelerates from A to B, then sprints from B to C. The bars between B and C are now further apart. Because the player has to cross one bar with each stride he is forced to lengthen his stride.

Breaking the speed barrier

A player's acceleration capacity is subject to the same sort of hereditary limitations as his starting strength. His starting strength is limited by the number of fast muscle fibers that he is born with. Acceleration capacity is limited by the speed with which the nerve stimuli from the brain pass through the nerve fibers before they reach the muscles.

The faster the stimuli are transmitted, the higher the stride rate. There is a speed barrier in the nervous system, however, which is very difficult to break through. Nevertheless, there are a number of drills with which some progress can be made.

Drill 6: Downhill sprinting

One of the drills for teaching the nervous system to coordinate fast leg movements is downhill sprinting. The stride rates achieved during this drill would be inconceivable on flat ground. This is therefore a way of breaking through a barrier in the nervous system. The nervous system is forced to transmit signals faster to the leg muscles otherwise the player will fall. The slope should not be too steep to allow a technically correct sprinting style to be adopted. An acceleration drill must be carried out on flat ground immediately after this drill, to allow the faster stride rate to be translated into the normal situation.

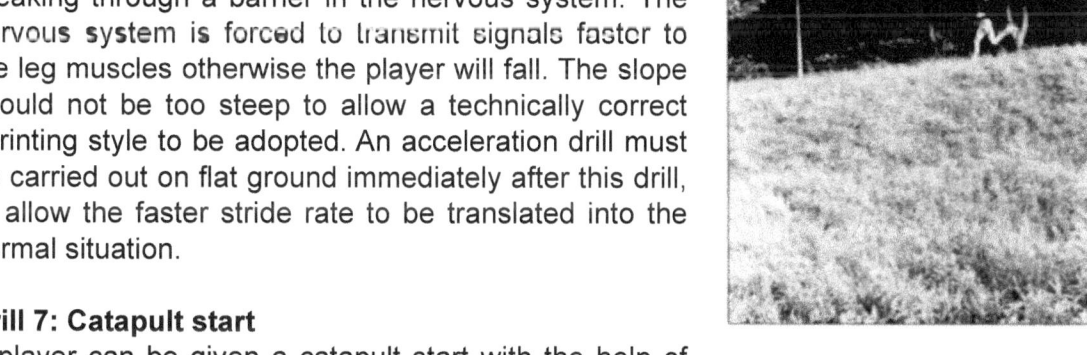

Drill 7: Catapult start

A player can be given a catapult start with the help of an elastic belt. The extra impetus applied to the body ensures that a higher peak speed is reached.

5.2.3 Speed endurance

Only rarely does a soccer player have to sprint 60 or 70 meters. When he does, he has to maintain his peak sprinting speed for as long as possible. The better his speed endurance, the less the deterioration in his sprinting speed during the last part of the sprint. This can make all the difference between just reaching the ball in time and being just too late, in both defensive and attacking situations. The longer the sprint, the smaller the chance that it will be made in a straight line. All sorts of soccer elements must therefore be included in the drills again.

General soccer-related sprint drills incorporate soccer ingredients such as turns and changes of direction.

Conditioning method
Duration: 6-10 seconds
Intensity: 100%,
Repetitions: 4-6
Sets: 1-2
Rest: 2-4 minutes between repetitions
6 minutes between sets

Drill 8: Sprint duel

Two players stand 60 meters apart. At a signal from the coach they sprint towards each other. Player 1 arrives at a cone after 25 meters. He runs round the cone and sprints back to his starting position. Player 2 continues running past the cone and tries to catch up with player 1. By swapping roles, both players condition their speed endurance, also when they have to turn.

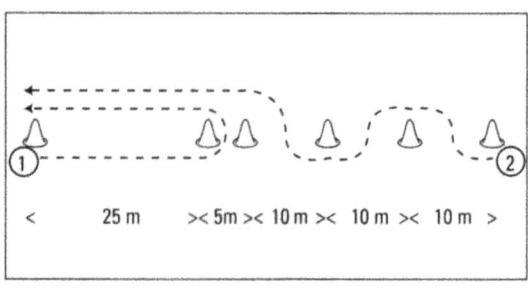

Drill 8:

The position of the cone may have to be varied to take account of the sprinting capabilities of the players in the group.

5.2.4 Repeated short sprint capacity

Soccer players make lots of short sprints. Sometimes they have only very little time between sprints. They must therefore be able to recover quickly. The better they recover, the more time it takes before fatigue has a negative effect on their sprint performance. This ability to recover is also referred to as repeated short sprint capacity. Conditioning for repeated short sprint capacity is similar to that for starting strength. The only difference is that there is a shorter rest period between repetitions. This is logical, because learning to sprint when tired is precisely the aim of this conditioning method.

Conditioning method
Duration: 1-2 seconds
Intensity: 100%,
Repetitions: 6-10
Sets: 2-4
Rest: 10 seconds between repetitions
4-6 minutes between sets

> *We miss the street. Now you see players running for the whole 90 minutes with only one objective: to go down in the penalty area. Before, when everyone used to play in the street, you couldn't let yourself fall down. That hurt. You had to have a good technique to stay on your feet.*
>
> **Johan Cruyff**

Drill:
The drills used for conditioning starting strength (see Chapter 4) can also be used for repeated short sprint capacity, except that the above method must be applied.

5.2.5 Planning sprint conditioning

The time to introduce sprint drills into a training session depends on the particular speed component.

> *You can only be explosive when you are totally calm.*
>
> **Christine Aaftink**

Starting speed

The objective of conditioning for starting speed is to increase a player's push-off strength during the first 3 or 4 sprint strides. One of the conditions for raising a player's threshold is that he must reach this threshold during each repetition. Because the body can only become stronger if it is challenged to go to the limit, fatigue must be avoided as far as possible. A fatigued player cannot apply his maximum push-off strength, much less increase it. Such drills must therefore be carried out at the start of a training session.

Acceleration

Starting speed depends on the maximum push-off strength, and acceleration depends on the maximum stride rate. This "speed barrier" can only be broken if it is constantly challenged. Acceleration drills must therefore also be carried out at the start of a training session, when the players are not tired and can sprint at their best.

Speed endurance

During a sprint over 50 to 60 meters it is important to maintain peak speed for as long as possible in the face of approaching fatigue. Players have to learn how to sprint when they are tired, and it is therefore not necessary to carry out these drills at the start of a training session. The middle of the session is suitable. The players must still be able to reach their peak sprinting speed.

Repeated short sprint capacity

This is the ability to make a lot of short sprints in sequence with only short intervals of rest in between. Sometimes players have little or no time to recover before they have to make the next sprint. Conditioning for repeated short sprint capacity is nothing more than learning to sprint despite fatigue. These drills must therefore always be carried out at the end of a training session.

5.2.6 Position-specific sprint conditioning

In Chapter 1 it was explained that there are considerable differences in the number and type of sprints made by players in different positions. Attackers have to make the most sprints, and because most Dutch teams play a "man marking" system, defenders have to sprint almost as much as attackers. Midfielders make far fewer sprints per match. The differences in the total distances sprinted are much smaller. This indicates that, on average, midfielders make longer sprints. This is logical in view of their linking role between defense and attack. Attackers and defenders tend to make shorter sprints, and to rely more on their starting speed and acceleration. Midfielders do this too, but they also have to make more calls on their sprint capacity. Players who make a lot of sprints have to rely on their repeated short sprint capacity. All of these aspects have to be incorporated in a sprint conditioning program.

5.3 COORDINATION CONDITIONING

Soccer differs from athletics in that running is not an end in itself but simply a means to an end. Running is one of the means of achieving soccer objectives. Because soccer players have to do a lot of running during a game, it is logical that special attention should be paid to practicing running technique. Good running technique saves strength that can then be used to run faster and more often. An improved running technique has the greatest effect in terms of sprinting capacity. Progress can be made with the help of a number of specific coordination drills to improve certain aspects of sprinting. Before this is dealt with it is necessary to explain what good sprinting technique involves.

5.3.1 The ideal sprinting technique
A technically good sprinting style can be described as follows:
- The head is always steady.
- The arms swing alternately forward to chin height in front of the body but the shoulders remain steady.
- The knees are raised powerfully during each stride.
- The ankles are well stretched each time the foot pushes off.
- Only the front part of the foot touches the ground.

A soccer player needs to be aware of what is happening around him on the field, even when he is running at full speed. If his head is in motion while he runs, he has a less clear picture of his surroundings and he will react less quickly to changing game situations. The swing of the arm supports the push-off leg. A powerful arm swing gives extra impetus to the body. The swing must be in the forward direction. A sideways swing is an unnecessary waste of strength. It is important that the shoulders remain steady during the swing, otherwise the upper body

Good awareness requires the head to be kept steady even during a sprint.

will be cramped and this will have a negative effect on the blood circulation. All sorts of (capillary) blood vessels are squeezed shut. The same considerations apply to raising the knees. Vigorously raising the knees in a forward direction also gives extra impetus to the body. Another advantage of a high knee-raise is that it increases the stride length. If the upper leg is raised higher, the lower leg can swing further forward. A longer sprint stride means a faster sprinting speed. A characteristic of many soccer players is that they do not use their ankles when they sprint. They push off with their feet flat. Stretching the ankles results in a more powerful push-off and therefore a faster sprinting speed. Perhaps the most important aspect is that soccer players should run on the front part of the foot. A player who is standing on the front of the foot can change direction faster than a player whose feet are flat on the ground. Because players have to continuously react to repeatedly changing game situations, it is important to run on the front of the foot. This also has the advantage that the ankle can be stretched more efficiently.

5.3.2 Coordination conditioning to improve speed
Coordination conditioning can be used to improve raising the knees and stretching the ankles in particular. During all coordination drills the head must be steady, the arms must

support the push-off, the shoulders (and therefore the rest of the upper body) must be steady, and the players must run on the front of the foot. These aspects do not need to be specially practiced, but the coach must pay attention to them.

Raising the knees

Raising the knees powerfully during running does not just mean raising the upper leg. The heel must also be jerked upward. After each push-off the push-off leg has to be swung forward as fast as possible. The faster the swing, the higher the stride rate. If the heel is jerked upward after the push-off to make the angle between upper and lower leg as small as possible, the push-off leg can be swung forward faster than when the lower leg is left to "dangle" from the upper leg (see Fig. 5.1). The "heel jerk" is the first aspect that needs to be practiced on the way to a higher and more powerful knee-raise.

Figure 5.1: *Making a heel-jerk (A) reduces the time and energy needed to swing the lower leg forward than if the lower leg is left "dangling" from the upper leg (B). Situation A illustrates one of the conditions for developing a high stride rate.*

Drill 9: Drawing-up the heel

The player runs from A to B (20 meters) and jerks up the heel sharply at each stride. The heel-jerks follow each other in rapid sequence. The upper body is inclined slightly forward. As a variation the player can be required to make a short, explosive, heel-jerk with the left or the right leg on each third stride. Remember: the head and upper body must be steady, the arms must be swung forward powerfully, and the player must run on the front part of his feet.

The knee-raise must then be practiced. This can best be done with the help of high and half-high skips.

Drill 10: Skipping

Skipping involves simultaneous knee-raises and heel-jerks. High skips require the upper leg to be drawn up horizontally. Half-high skips require it to be at an angle of about 45 degrees. The player skips at speed from A to B (20 meters), performing left and right half-high skips in sequence. This is a technically difficult exercise and requires a certain amount of practice. When the player has mastered the half-high skips he can move on to high skips.

Drill 11: Skip and swing

One purpose of the high knee-raise is to give the lower leg the opportunity to swing forward. This can be practiced by "skipping and swinging." The players skip forward, making high skips, swinging the lower leg forward each time the upper leg is raised. This is a good way of practicing long strides during a training session.

Finally the players can move on to real sprinting with a powerful knee-raise. This can best be done with the help of obstacles.

Drill 12: Sprinting over high obstacles
The drill is the same as drills 4 and 5, except that the obstacles are higher. A start must be made with low obstacles. The hurdles can only be raised if the player's sprint technique remains intact. The players can be required to sprint with short or long strides.

Stretching the ankles
Stretching the ankles gives an extra impetus to the sprint push-off. To be able to stretch his ankle efficiently, a player must run on the front part of the foot. A number of coordination drills are available for practicing stretching the ankles.

Drill 13: Heel and toeing
The player heel and toes lightly from A to B (20 meters), stretching his left and right ankles quickly in sequence, bending the knee slightly each time.

Drill 14: Spring strides
The player makes a fast series of short "spring" strides from A to B (20 meters), stretching the ankles as much as possible. The whole drill must be carried out on the front part of the foot.

5.3.3 Integrated coordination conditioning
The aim of the above coordination drills is to improve the player's sprinting technique. In the initial stages the focus has to be on one technical aspect at a time. As all of these aspects are gradually mastered, they can be integrated into one drill:

heel-jerk - half-high skips - high skips - skip and swing - sprint.

In addition, drills 10, 11, 13 and 14 can be coupled with a sprint as a form of integrated coordination conditioning.

5.4 GENERAL COORDINATION CONDITIONING
This chapter has focused on speed in relation to coordination. Coordination, however, is required for more than just speed. Technique is needed for carrying out all soccer actions, and good coordination results in good technique. In soccer, technique is always more important than strength.

5.4.1 A soccer action can never be viewed in isolation

In soccer, technique conditioning is primarily a matter of learning to carry out various soccer actions in a technically correct manner. However, soccer actions can never be viewed in isolation. The "how" and "when" of an action must always be seen in relation to the game. In youth soccer, however, technique is frequently taught in isolation. Technique must be learned in soccer-specific situations, because a large number of elements play a role in the execution of these actions.

In soccer, technique always triumphs over physique.

Speed of reaction

Soccer players never act without a reason. What they do is often a reaction to something that happens on the field during the game. In many cases it is not enough simply to carry out an action; it also has to be carried out as fast as possible. Players also have to learn when a certain action has to be carried out. Pure speed is of no avail if a player has no feeling for when he must use his speed. This feeling can only be acquired by playing a lot of soccer.

Linking ability: a sprint is followed by a shot at goal.

Linking ability

This is the ability to coordinate a series of soccer actions. It is especially concerned with the transition from one action to the next. Soccer players rarely carry out just one action. A cross, for example, might be preceded by a run, a feint and an acceleration. A soccer player has to learn to link one action to the next in rapid succession. After all, a soccer match is a sequence of soccer actions.

Orientation

This is the ability to change posture in space and time on the basis of awareness (orientation). The choice of a specific action and the execution of that action cannot be viewed in isolation. They are always influenced by other aspects of the game. As they gain in experience, soccer players come to recognize what to do in a given situation, and when to do it. A player must be aware that his direct opponent in a one against one situation has no one backing him up, and it is therefore worthwhile trying to beat him with the help of a feint. The feint must be well timed. If it is made too early the opponent has time to recover. If it is made too close to the opponent, he may be able to intercept the ball. Orientation is based on choosing the right action and the right moment to carry out the action.

Differentiation
This is the ability to carry out all the elements of a movement very precisely. Each movement can be broken down into a number of elements that are carried out in sequence. An opponent will always try to prevent a player from carrying out a soccer action. He can do this by means of, for example, a push or a tackle. At the moment when the opponent attempts this, a player must know which element he was carrying out and which element he has to carry out next to complete the action.

Balance
A player must be able to remain in balance, or to maintain or recover his balance after a movement. As mentioned above, players are frequently pushed or tackled during a game with the aim of knocking them off balance. Soccer actions should therefore not be practiced in isolation but under match conditions. A player can be made to lose his balance without any bodily contact occurring. A feint, for example, is carried out to throw an opponent off balance.

A feint can cause an opponent to lose his balance.

Agility
This is the ability to adjust a movement to take account of a perceived change in the game situation. Sometimes a player realizes that he has chosen the wrong action, or that the timing of an action is not good. At that moment he must adjust the action and ensure that he does not lose control of the ball.

Rhythm
Every dynamic movement has its own rhythm. If a movement is carried out with the correct rhythm, it looks supple and natural. A good example is the "scissors" movement. This is often less effective if it is carried out too slowly or too quickly. "Dragging" the ball also has its own rhythm as demonstrated by the Danish player Laudrup.

5.4.2 It is never too soon to learn
Although coordination conditioning is suitable for both youth players and adults, it is better to start as soon as possible. The nervous system of youngsters is still developing and is therefore open to outside stimuli. During this phase, speed and coordination drills must be included in training sessions. The nervous system then learns to carry out actions quickly. As a player grows older the nervous system gradually becomes less receptive to such stimuli and the effect of these drills is less noticeable. During the growth spurt the nervous system "opens up" again. The body undergoes a period of explosive growth when the bones, and subsequently the muscles and tendons, become longer. The nervous system therefore has to learn to coordinate all sorts of movements anew. It is advisable to take advantage of this (temporary) opening up of the nervous system by making young players take part in specific speed and coordination drills during the growth spurt. The nervous system is especially "keen to learn" during this phase.

5.4.3 The growth spurt

Children are usually confronted with the growth spurt between the ages of 11 and 14. Their limbs become longer and their coordination worsens. It is clear to see how young players start to make larger strides and their rate of stride decreases. Their footwork deteriorates, so that they cannot react as quickly to changing game situations. A lower rate of stride means that the player has less contact with the ground. He therefore has less chance to correct his soccer actions, can be made to lose his balance more easily and is taken in more quickly by a feint. Coordination conditioning offers a solution to these problems at this age.

> *When I was a player they never had to run after me when I scored a goal. I was not fast enough.*
>
> **Willem van Hanegem**

5.4.4 When should coordination conditioning be carried out?

The ideal situation would be to assign one training session each week to coordination conditioning. Unfortunately this is almost impossible. Especially in amateur soccer, coaches simply do not have the time to devote a whole training session to this aspect. They would have less time for the more important soccer coaching. The best alternative is to integrate coordination drills into the warming-up periods before 2 or 3 training sessions each week. The first 15 to 20 minutes of the session can be used to prepare the body for the coaching drills and to improve coordination. Make sure that the drills are varied. This promotes a broad range of development and prevents the players from becoming bored. This is especially advisable for youth players. Modern youngsters take part in only a limited amount of physical activity as a consequence of the restricted number of physical instruction lessons at school and the distractions of computer games. Additional coordination conditioning prevents youngsters' motor development from stagnating. Many adults also get too little physical exercise because they generally have a "sitting" job. Extra stimulation of the nervous system is therefore beneficial for them, too.

SUMMARY

- Speed consists of a number of components: reaction speed, starting speed, acceleration, speed endurance and repeated short sprint capacity.

- Conditioning for starting strength involves increasing the push-off strength of the first 3 or 4 sprint strides.

- Conditioning for acceleration involves teaching the nervous system how to develop faster stride rates. In this way the time taken to reach peak speed can be reduced.

- Conditioning for speed endurance improves a player's ability to maintain peak speed as long as possible.

- Conditioning for repeated short sprint capacity involves improving the ability to recover in the interval between two successive sprints. The faster a player recovers, the better the following sprint will be.

- Conditioning for sprinting must be precisely planned. Drills for starting speed and acceleration must take place at the start of the training session. Speed endurance drills should be included in the middle of the session. Drills for repeated short sprint capacity can be held at the end of the session.

- The ideal sprinting style is characterized by: head held steady, arm swing forward to chin height, powerful knee-raise at each stride, ankle-stretch at each stride, and running on the front of the foot.

- Soccer actions are never undertaken in isolation. The manner and the moment of execution are always related to the game situation. Drills must therefore incorporate elements of these game situations. In this way players develop fast reactions, linking ability, orientation, differentiation, balance, agility and a feeling for rhythm.

- Conditioning for coordination should be started at a young age, when the nervous system can still be influenced. This type of conditioning should be carried out for 20 minutes 2 or 3 times each week (for example, in the form of warming-up drills).

FIVE PRACTICAL QUESTIONS

1. What is the best surface for carrying out sprinting and coordination drills with young players?

Sprinting and coordination drills can be carried out on grass, artificial turf or even asphalt, provided the players have the right type of footwear. If the surface is hard they should wear shoes with efficient shock-absorbing soles. Naturally it is best, and comes closest to match conditions, to practice on grass, but it is better to practice on asphalt with sports shoes than on a hard field with soccer shoes.

2. Must this type of conditioning be carried out during the whole season, or only at certain periods?

Consistent application of sprinting and coordination conditioning brings results. Lots of repeats enable the nervous system to adapt to the demands made during these drills. Sprinting and coordination conditioning should therefore be carried out during the whole season.

3. Do sprinting drills involve an increased risk of injury?

Explosive soccer actions require considerable strength to be developed in a very short period of time. If the body is not used to this, the chance of injury is greater. A gradual build-up and a carefully dosed amount of work are therefore essential. A player must first learn good sprinting technique by means of coordination drills. The emphasis is then shifted to speed. Explosiveness becomes important at a later stage.

4. When will any progress become visible?

Conditioning effects in the field of speed are difficult to predict. They depend partly on a player's aptitude in this field and his fitness level when the conditioning is started. Nevertheless, some progress should always be visible after three months of consistent speed conditioning. Coordination is simpler. Children in particular quickly learn how to carry out soccer actions with a better technique. Because the nervous system is "eager to learn" at this time of life, results are visible within a month.

5. 5. Is this type of conditioning worthwhile for someone who has absolutely no aptitude?

If there is no aptitude, you will not be able to achieve miracles with sprinting and coordination conditioning. Nevertheless, coordination conditioning in particular is worthwhile. The player will never become very supple, but improvement is always possible. In any case this will have a positive effect on his daily functioning. Improved physical control influences a person's motor movements.

INTERVIEW WITH DANNY BLIND
(A.F.C. Ajax)

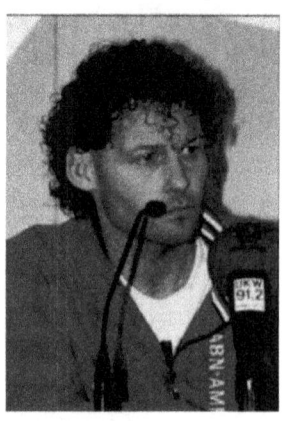

Do you, as a player, think that soccer has become faster?
I certainly think that soccer is becoming faster, although I am not sure whether the game itself is faster. The players are faster, fitter and more versatile. You see more and more soccer players who are naturally very strong. We at Ajax play against more and more teams who are technically inferior to us but make life difficult through their physical fitness, together with a tactical concept.

Do you think it is right that speed should be used as a scouting criterion?
Due to tactical developments in recent years, players now have less space in which to maneuver. Opponents mark you more closely, so you have to act more quickly. It is also more difficult to escape from your direct opponent. If you are fast off the mark, that is a big advantage. I would not like to claim that you can no longer become a professional soccer player without speed. That depends to some extent on the other qualities you possess. If you have a good tactical brain you can anticipate well in advance and you need not necessarily be fast. Not for nothing do you see that the less fast players have a better soccer brain. They often know exactly what is going to happen on the pitch. Fast players usually have to rely on their speed, and therefore make mistakes and are inconsistent. It is true that the "playmaker," who could direct the play without ever changing his pace, now finds life more difficult. It may even be impossible to play that way any more.

Can you briefly explain how sprinting and coordination conditioning has developed at Ajax?
This sort of conditioning was carried out at Ajax 15 years ago under Cees Koppelaar. It was a mixture of fitness, running and coordination drills. Since Lazio jambor arrived this type of conditioning has been geared more to the game situation. The emphasis is more on short, explosive work and less on continuous work. All of this seems to be new because the media have suddenly discovered it, but we have trained this way for years.

Have you become faster and a better runner in the course of time?
Twice each week we do 30 minutes of sprint and coordination drills, but I am not sure whether I have made a lot of progress. I was 25 when I came to Ajax. By then my style of running and my coordination were firmly established. The progress you make is minimal in comparison with the possibilities of improvement when you are 12 or 13 years old. In addition, speed never used to be tested, so I have no points of reference. Nowadays we do a variety of sprint tests with changes of direction, turning, flying starts and standing starts. There is therefore sufficient data available and you can see that the young players in particular become gradually faster. I think it is important for youngsters to be confronted with this type of drill as early as possible. This is the period when they are being formed and can learn the most. Even youths of 17 and 18, who come to Ajax without ever having had this sort of conditioning, make enormous progress during their first year. They are suddenly much faster and more nimble. You can therefore make a lot of progress, provided you do this in the right way and, especially, at the right time.

Do you know how many sprints a professional player makes during a game?
As a player you are never aware of this, but it appears that you make 180 to 200 sprints and that is a lot. This just confirms how intensive soccer is at the top level, in contrast to what many people think. It often annoys me how people compare soccer with other sports. Naturally long-distance runners, etc., have to go to the utmost, but you cannot make such a simple comparison. Soccer is more variable. First of all you have to use your feet and that is more difficult than using your hands. Then you have to use your brain, because tactics now play a large role. There is a lot of physical contact and you are regularly knocked to the ground or fall. On top of all this there are the 200 sprints. This demonstrates that soccer is very complex and very strenuous. After a game you need a lot more time to recover from damage to muscles, tendons and ligaments.

Do you think there are differences in the amount of sprinting work carried out by players in different positions?
In the Ajax system everyone has to be fast. I can imagine that attackers make more sprints because they have to escape from their markers. But if I look at myself, then I have to chase after my opponent if he makes a sudden sprint to escape from me. So I think there is not much difference between attackers and defenders. Midfielders have to switch between attack and defense and probably make fewer sprints. When they sprint, the distance is probably longer. On the other hand midfielders are always in motion and therefore have less chance to recover between moments of peak exertion. Our wingers have an easier time of it. They have to make more explosive runs, but they have enough time to recover. These are aspects that a coach has to take into account. Sprinting drills must also incorporate elements of the game itself.

Each player sprints less in the second half. Is this your experience?
I am a player who relies on thinking rather than running. If I am exhausted after 60 minutes then there is something wrong with me or it has been a very unusual game. For players who run more than I do, it is logical that they become more fatigued in the second half. A soccer player must be able to husband his strength over the whole game. If you could do this perfectly you would not experience any deterioration in the second half. In practice this is almost impossible. During the second half players are often less disciplined in their play, and start to run more with the ball, for example. This results in more loss of possession than in the first half and the team has to switch over to trying to recover it more often. These are moments of intense exertion when a lot of strength is unnecessarily wasted. The logical consequence is fatigue.

In soccer, pure speed is less important than the timing of the sprint. What is the best way of practicing this?
The best way is to play lots of small sided games of 3 against 3 or 4 against 4. In these games the players have to learn to take up position so that they can watch their opponents and intervene to help their colleagues when necessary. If you are frequently confronted by these situations you come to recognize them and you react automatically. At Ajax we also play 6 against 7. The side with one man less is forced to think of ways of compensating for this disadvantage. You have to learn to push out conceitedly to right or left as a unified "block".

LITERATURE

1. Coordination, Agility and Speed Training
(2 tape video series)
REEDSWAIN Videos.

CHAPTER 6

CONDITIONING FOR SOCCER FITNESS

by Foppe de Haan

6.1 INTRODUCTION

The first three chapters of this book sketch a picture of the work involved in playing soccer, the physiological systems that enable this work to be carried out, and the conditioning methods with which these physiological systems can be stimulated. The following chapters explain the role of strength, speed, coordination and flexibility, and how each of these physical parameters can be brought to an acceptable basic level by general soccer-related conditioning. We now come to the last of the basic motor properties, i.e., endurance. Although the drills chosen for conditioning acyclic aerobic endurance focus on this basic motor property, they also address soccer strength, speed, coordination and flexibility. In fact, all of the physical parameters that are of importance to a soccer player are integrated into one soccer-specific drill. All aspects of soccer fitness are simultaneously stimulated. Hence the chapter's title: "Conditioning for soccer fitness." This chapter also focuses on soccer-related sprint drills. Conditioning for speed is dealt with in detail in Chapter 5, but only in respect of pure speed. A good soccer player is, however, not only fast but also knows exactly when to use his speed. Good timing can only be learned in the context of soccer situations. These are the only settings in which a player can learn to recognize the instant to start a sprint.

6.2 SOCCER FITNESS

Soccer fitness is the ability of a soccer player to perform well in his chosen sport. This ability includes all sorts of elements such as technique, tactical insight and ability to communicate, as well as physical, psychological and social factors. This chapter is devoted to the physical factor, but always in relation to the other factors that go to make up soccer fitness.

6.2.1 The utility of good soccer fitness

The physical aspect is only one of the many aspects of soccer. It is therefore unwise to take the physical factor out of its soccer context and overexpose it. Physical fitness is only a means of achieving soccer objectives. It is a fact that, as a soccer player's physical fitness improves, this has a positive effect on all of the other elements that influence soccer performance. The less fatigued a player is during the final part of a game, the better his physical coordination and awareness of what is going on around him. This has a direct effect on factors such as his speed of action and his ability to read the game. It is important not to perform isolated drills. Soccer fitness must be built up with the help of soccer-related drills. These do not just have to be drills with the ball, as many people imagine. Soccer-related conditioning means conditioning in a soccer situation (both with and without a ball). During a game a player is in possession of the ball for no more than 30 to 60 seconds. The rest of the time he carries out all sorts of off-the-ball actions. Conditioning must therefore be linked to a soccer objective. The body's various physiological systems are stimulated during the process of solving all sorts of soccer problems.

6.2.2 How should soccer fitness be conditioned?

In youth and amateur soccer, coaches have only a limited number of training sessions each week in which to deal with a host of various elements. The advantage of soccer-related conditioning is that it increases the return on these training sessions. Fitness, technique and tactical insight can be conditioned simultaneously. It is important to apply the overload principle to achieve improved fitness. This means that the situation in which the players perform must be made more difficult than usual. Players must regard drills as a challenge. In practice the overload principle is totally or partly neglected. If the greater part of a training session fails to measure up to this principle, the players cannot make progress. The "danger" of carrying out conditioning drills with the ball is that the players can let the ball do the work. Usually this is one of the aims of the game, but not during specific conditioning. If the ball does the work, the body is insufficiently stimulated and there is no overload.

An "overload" situation is a little more difficult than the players are used to.

The correct dosage of soccer-related conditioning

The element of difficulty in soccer-related game drills and competitive drills must be steadily increased, without losing sight of the soccer objectives of the drills. There are a number of ways in which a coach can vary the intensity and extent of a soccer-related drill. He can put players in situations where they are forced to carry out certain work. For example, he can:
- give the players specific tasks;
- change or adjust the rules of the game;
- change the degree of soccer resistance (number of opponents);
- vary the work:rest ratio (intervals);
- vary the size of the playing area;
- vary the number of players in a team.

If a coach wants to condition certain physiological systems during soccer drills, he must not simply ask the players to run faster and/or more. The players must be assigned soccer-related tasks that will evoke the required physiological response. This means that the coach must have a good knowledge of his subject and a degree of creativity. A coach must be familiar with general principles of conditioning and be able to apply them in a soccer context. If the objective of a training session is to improve the players' physical fitness, the coach must ensure that they are subjected to an overload, without exceeding their physical limits. Without this overload, a player's fitness can only be maintained or may even deteriorate.

A coach can manipulate soccer resistance by changing the size of the pitch.

Intensity of conditioning

The most important difference between conditioning methods is their intensity. This can be quantified by measuring the heart rate. The higher a player's heart rate, the more intensely he is working. It is advisable to let the players check their heart rates occasionally during a training session to monitor whether they are reaching the required intensity. This can serve as a check on whether the objective of a drill is being achieved. The best time to measure the heart rate is during the rest periods between two blocks of intensive work. The heart rate can be measured by placing a finger over the artery in the neck or the wrist and counting the pulses. The heart rate is the number of heartbeats per minute. You can count the number of pulses over a period of 10, 15 or 30 seconds and then multiply by 6, 4 or 2. The longer the counting period, the more accurate the result. On the other hand the heart rate can decrease considerably over a period of 30 seconds, and this can give a distorted picture of the intensity with which a player is performing. A period of 15 seconds is therefore advisable.

6.3 ENDURANCE

Endurance plays an important role in soccer. Without endurance, even the best players would find a 90-minute game too long. A player with good endurance can also recover more quickly after intensive exertion. Endurance, however, is a general concept. It is therefore essential to identify the precise form of endurance needed by a soccer player. This is important for the choice of conditioning methods. It has already been mentioned that soccer players need:
- acyclic aerobic endurance,
- acyclic anaerobic endurance.

6.3.1 Conditioning for acyclic aerobic endurance

Acyclic aerobic endurance is dependent on the oxygen system. The conditioning methods described below are all intended to improve the efficiency of all or part of the oxygen system. Conditioning the heart, lungs and blood vessels must not be an aim in itself. Coaches must select drills with soccer-related objectives, whose execution will also inevitably lead to an improvement in the above-mentioned systems. Most drills for practicing technique (dribbling, running with the ball, shooting) are eminently suitable for aerobic conditioning. Positional games are also suitable for endurance conditioning, provided the playing area is relatively large. The workload can be increased by making the various lines in the team link up quickly with each other, or by introducing small sided games (3 against 3) in the form of line soccer. A number of methods are used for conditioning endurance, because soccer need to carry out both intensive and extensive conditioning.

Endurance can be conditioned through drills that involve passing and shooting.

Continuous extensive conditioning

This method involves working for 30 to 90 minutes continuously, without any peak loads. The session should be interrupted as little as possible, and preferably not at all. The heart rate should remain constant at 140 to 160 beats per minute.

Conditioning method
Duration: 30-90 minutes
Intensity: 50% of maximal workload (180 beats per minute, depending on age)
Repetitions: None
Rest: No breaks

Drill: Training Situation 1 (page 155)

Continuous intensive conditioning

Playing soccer requires continuous but The breaks allow continuous intensive conditioning to varied exertion. There are repeated incorporate both extensive and intensive work. moments of peak

The breaks allow continuous intensive conditioning to incorporate both extensive and intensive work.

effort. Continuous intensive conditioning should therefore be a fixed part of soccer conditioning. There is a mix of extensive and intensive elements. The drill is relatively extensive (30 to 40 minutes) but is divided up into blocks of 6 to 8 minutes. Intensive drills can be car-ried out in the blocks, because the breaks between blocks allow the players sufficient opportunity to recover. They will therefore not become extremely fatigued.

Conditioning method
Duration: 30-40 minutes (5x6 or 6 x 8 minutes)
Intensity: 160-180 beats per minute
Repetitions: 5
Rest: 5 minutes between each repetition

Drill: Training Situations 1-5 and 20 (pages 155-159, 174)

Extensive interval training
The emphasis during extensive interval training is on intensity. The breaks are an extremely important aspect of this method. They are also referred to as "reward" breaks.

Conditioning method
Duration: 30-60 seconds
Intensity: 170-180 beats per minute
Repetitions: maximum of 8 per sets
Sets: 2-5
Rest: 45-90 seconds between reps.
4-6 minutes between sets

> *What do you get if you squeeze an orange? Orange juice, of course. You can only find out what someone has in them when you put them under pressure.*
> **Pat Riley**

Drill: Training Situations 6-8 (pages 160, 162)

Fartlek training
This is a combination of continuous extensive conditioning and extensive interval training. Intensive exertion on the continuous extensive level alternates with short periods of intensive work (no lactic acid formation). This combination conditioning can best be given by means of circuit training.

Conditioning method
Duration: 2-3 blocks of 10-15 minutes
Intensity: 180 beats per minute, depending on age
Repeats: none
Rest: no breaks

Conditioning effects
1. Better supply of blood to the active muscles through an increase in the number of blood vessels in and around the muscles. The diameter of the blood vessels increases. This means that more nutrients and oxygen can be supplied, and more carbon dioxide, heat and lactic acid can be carried away.
2. Better respiration because the respiratory muscles become thicker and stronger.

> *A game of tennis-soccer used to be a matter of life and death. We played for a buck when the weekly win bonus was a thousand guilders. Spectators were brought in to act as referee. Today's generation of players has too little enthusiasm, they are content just to get by.*
> **Willem van Hanegem**

3. Increased glycogen reserves. Muscles can store more carbohydrates (see Chapter 11).
4. Better capacity for burning up fats, so that the glycogen reserves are called on less often (see Chapter 11).
5. Increased thickness of the walls of the heart, especially the wall of the left ventricle. A larger volume of blood (and therefore oxygen) is pumped per heartbeat.

Continuous extensive and intensive conditioning mainly achieve conditioning effects 1,2,3 and 4. Rest is a very important element of extensive interval training. The heart rate decreases rapidly during the breaks, but a large volume of blood continues to flow into the heart. The same volume of blood must be pumped around the body with fewer heartbeats. The heart therefore has to work harder. The volume of blood pumped per heartbeat increases, and the heartbeat becomes stronger. If this conditioning method is regularly applied, the cardiac muscle becomes bigger and thicker. The heart receives a powerful stimulus during these breaks, which are also termed "reward" breaks. Fartlek training can be used to achieve all five of the above-mentioned conditioning effects.

6.3.2 Conditioning for acyclic anaerobic endurance

If intensive exertion lasts for more than 10 seconds the body has to call on its acyclic anaerobic endurance. The lactic acid system then becomes active. This form of energy production is characterized by the generation of lactic acid. This waste product has a negative effect on a player's capacity to perform, because it disrupts all kinds of bodily processes. Anaerobic "periods" occur during a game when a full back moves forward 40 or 50 meters and then has to sprint back again because his team has lost possession, or when a team is pressuring its opponents, or when strikers have to retain possession while under pressure from opponents. Usually such periods do not last longer than 30 seconds. During training sessions, therefore, players should not be expected to exert themselves to the utmost over periods of 2 or 3 minutes, which would result in the formation of considerable amounts of lactic acid. There are two very suitable methods of conditioning players for acyclic anaerobic endurance. These are block training and intensive interval training.

Block training
Intensive work must be carried out for 15 seconds during block training. This completely exhausts the phosphate system.

Conditioning method
Duration: 15 seconds
Intensity: 100%
Repetitions: 4-8
Sets: 2-4
Rest: 15-30 seconds between repetitions
4-6 minutes between sets

Drill: Training Situation 9 (page 163)

Interval speed training

This is a genuine "acidifying" drill. Because the players have to go full out for 45 to 60 seconds, considerable demands are made on the lactic acid system and lactic acid is formed in the muscles. Although this only rarely happens during a game of soccer, this is a psychologically useful drill. The players learn what it is like to be put through the mill. Acidifying drills should never last longer than 60 seconds. Excessive concentrations of lactic acid harm the muscles and are too far removed from soccer reality.

Conditioning method
Duration: 45-60 seconds
Intensity: 90-100%
Repetitions: 6-8
Rest: 4-5 minutes

Training situation 9.

Drill: Training Situations 10-13 (pages 164, 167)

Conditioning effects

Conditioning for anaerobic endurance has two conditioning effects. During block training the phosphate system is completely exhausted. This acts as a stimulus, causing an increase in the capacity of the phosphate system, so that help from the lactic acid system is not needed so quickly. The moment

> *A sportsman who only focuses on physical fitness is like a painter who only colors things. Just as you paint with your brain, with your heart, with your thoughts and your emotions, so you can train for your sport with your brain and with your heart.*
>
> **Joris van Bergh**

when the lactic acid system takes over as the main energy supplier is delayed, and more intensive work can be carried out before lactic acid is generated. Interval speed training sharply activates the lactic acid system, which promptly generates large amounts of lactic acid. As a consequence of this method of conditioning, the body acquires greater resistance to lactic acid (lactic acid tolerance). The disruption to all sorts of energy processes becomes less. The lactic acid system also becomes "stronger." It can deliver more energy per unit of time. When lactic acid is formed, this must be "compensated for" in the form of as much energy as possible. Soccer players gain more "power" during long periods of intensive work, e.g. when they are pressuring their opponents. During intensive interval training it is important that each repetition can be carried out at full intensity. Recovery is therefore essential. The levels of lactic acid in the blood and muscles must decrease considerably before the next repeat can be started. Active rest between repeats is important, because it promotes recovery (see Fig. 3.7, page 71). It is, however, impossible to recover completely between repeats. More than 15 minutes rest would be necessary.

6.4 SOCCER-RELATED SPRINT CONDITIONING

Chapter 5 deals at length with speed and coordination conditioning, and the relationship between them. Most of the drills are general in nature. In this chapter more soccer-related drills are described, with which the various speed aspects can be conditioned.

6.4.1 Reaction speed and starting speed

In soccer a player often has to make a choice between a number of possible reactions in a given game situation. Reaction conditioning teaches the central nervous system to arrive quickly at a plan of action and carry it out. Lots of drills ensure that the plan of action gradually becomes almost automatic. The player can therefore react more quickly (speed of reaction). Players have to act quickly as a consequence of changes in the game situation and not in response to, for example, a signal from the coach. Turning to starting speed, a player needs to condition a lot more than just his push-off strength in the first few strides. Soccer players must learn when to start a sprint. In general a sprint does not occur in isolation. It is usually followed by another soccer action. He might, for example, have to take a pass and then shoot at goal. This requires linking ability, and that too can only be conditioned in a soccer context.

Training situation 15.

Conditioning method
Duration: 1-2 seconds
Intensity: 100%, from a standing start
Repetitions: 8-10
Sets: 2-4
Rest: 30 seconds between repetitions
               4-6 minutes between sets

Drill: Training Situations 14-15 (pages 168-169)

6.4.2 Acceleration

Good acceleration relies on a high stride rate. This is why the central nervous system has to be taught how to control higher stride rates. Players are not usually able to accelerate without resistance in a straight line. During a long sprint a player continuously has to anticipate what is going to happen as the game situation changes. The ball may change direction **(motor agility)** or an opponent may sprint with him and offer resistance **(differentiation ability and balance)**.

In these situations, too, it is important to keep building up as much speed as possible. A player should not sprint blindly. He must keep his eyes on what is happening around him **(orientation)**. These are all good reasons for conditioning acceleration not only in a general sense but also in soccer-related situations.

Conditioning method

Duration: 2-6 seconds
Intensity: 100%, from a flying start
Repetitions: 6
Sets: 1-2
Rest: 1-2 minutes between repetitions, 4 minutes between sets

Drill: Training Situation 16 (page 170)

6.4.3 Speed endurance

Speed endurance enables a player to maintain his sprinting speed for as long as possible. Occasionally a player needs to sprint 60 or 70 meters. Think of a midfielder, who has to get forward quickly to link up with his forwards during a counterattack, but then has to get back quickly to help his defense if the attack breaks down. The direction and duration of this sequence of sprints depends on a number of game factors. This is why conditioning must be carried out in situations that occur in real games.

Training situation 16.

Conditioning method

Duration: 6-10 seconds
Intensity: 100%, from a flying start
Repetitions: 4-6
Sets: 1-2
Rest: 2-4 minutes between repetitions
6 minutes between sets

Drill: Training Situations 17-18 (pages 171-172)

6.4.4 Repeated short sprint capacity

As mentioned above, a sprint is often followed by another soccer action. A player's repeated short sprint capacity must therefore also be stimulated in this way.

Conditioning method

Duration: 1-2 seconds
Intensity: 100%
Repetitions: 6-10
Sets: 2-4
Rest: 10 seconds between repetitions
4-6 minutes between sets

Drill: Training Situation 19 (page 173)

6.5 PERIODIZATION

A variety of conditioning methods and drills are described in this chapter. However, when should what methods be used? To put this another way, what aspects should a coach focus on during a specific period of the season? The correct distribution of

> *The stop-watch is a more efficient version of the whip.*
>
> **Julien Vangansbeeke**

the various conditioning elements in a good schedule is the most difficult part of the science of coaching. Depending on the sport concerned, basic motor properties must be conditioned in the correct sequence and relationship. In soccer, technique and tactics must be central. Before a conditioning plan is drawn up, a number of objectives must be defined for the short, medium and long term. This must be done on the basis of information over the starting situation of the individual and the team, the available time and the available facilities.

6.5.1 Conditioning plan

Each coach must have a clear conditioning plan in his mind. Such a plan consists of a number of cycles.

Macrocycle

This is concerned with long-term objectives. A specific objective is pursued over a number of years. This might be perfecting a certain style of play or improving all sorts of general technical and tactical skills.

Mesocycle

This is the soccer season, which consists of a number of periods:
- preparation for the first half of the season
- first half of the season
- winter break/vacation
- preparation for the second half of the season
- second half of the season
- summer break/vacation

Within this framework, the correct planning and periodization must ensure that the players are fit at just the right time, so that they can give their all in the coming game(s). All of the games that are to be played must be listed. League games, friendlies and cup games determine the working rhythm. The number and extent/intensity of the training sessions depends in part on the number of games.

Microcycle

Each period of a mesocycle consists of a number of weeks and is termed a microcycle. In such a cycle the training sessions are all closely geared to each other. The one starts where the last one left off. A mesocycle is characterized by closely intermeshing training sessions.

Daily planning

Professional soccer players train almost daily. Naturally the content of each training session depends on the period of the season, but it also depends on the condition of the individual players. Some players must be allowed to rest, while others need stimulation. A coach must monitor his players closely, so that he is always aware of their individual needs.

6.5.2 The extent and intensity of training sessions

It has already been pointed out that extent and intensity are in principle opposites. If the training intensity is high, its extent is often much less so. And if training is extensive, its intensity must be kept low to prevent fatigue. In the run-up to a game, the extent must be cut back and the emphasis must be on intensity. In periods when there are only a few games, the extent of the training sessions can again be increased. During the preparation period, coaches try to bring their players into top form for the start of the first half of the season. Even if training sessions are properly "dosed," this top form can only be maintained for about eight weeks. Because there are only limited opportunities to train extensively, the players' endurance will then start to deteriorate. During the second part of the first half of the season, therefore, more extensive training must be carried out and less intensive training. Just before or during the winter break this extensive training must be cut back again and the training intensity must be increased. The same applies during the second half of the season. Figure 6.1 gives an overview of the pattern.

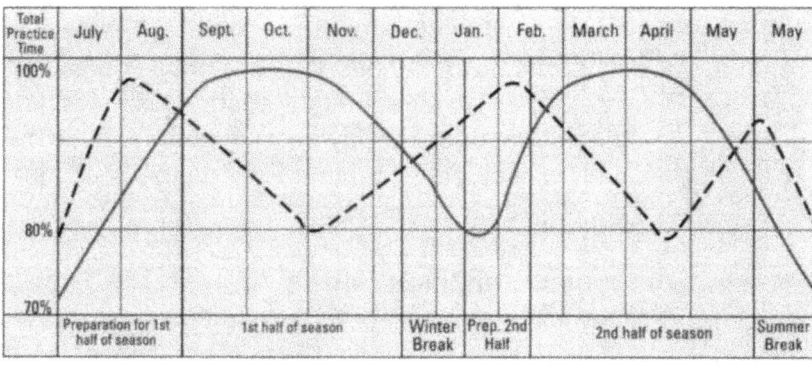

– – – = Extent of training sessions
―― = Intensity of training sessions

Figure 6.1: *Overview of when extensive and intensive conditioning are needed during the various periods of the soccer season.*

6.5.5 General and Specific Conditioning

The discussion around general soccer-related fitness conditioning and specific soccer-related fitness conditioning is at the heart of this book. The message that is emphasized in each chapter is that conditioning should be as specific as possible. The only purpose of general conditioning is to bring a player's basic fitness up to a certain level and maintain it there, for example, during the summer and winter breaks, when players cannot train with their clubs. Figure 6.2 shows that as soon as the preparation period for the first or second half of the season begins, the coach must switch as quickly as possible to specific conditioning. However, it is necessary to make a few comments about specific conditioning for soccer fitness.

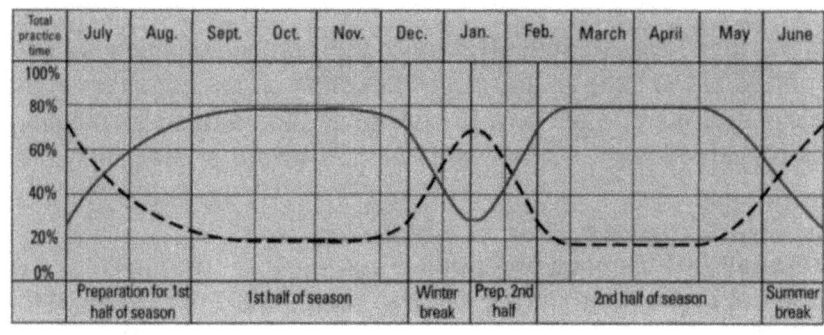

Figure 6.2: *Overview of when general conditioning and soccer-related conditioning are needed during the various periods of the soccer season.*

Position-related conditioning for endurance

just as for strength (soccer-related work) and sprint work, chapter 1 also gives the total amount of running that is carried out per position. Midfielders cover the most distance during a game. This difference is mainly attributable to jogging. Attackers and defenders can sometimes walk or even remain stationary, but midfielders are almost always in motion. They do this by jogging. Sometimes a midfielder jogs further than the total distance covered by a defender during a game. During a game the acyclic aerobic endurance of midfielders is put to the test much more than that of players in other lines of the team. The best way to take account of this difference during training sessions is to play small sided games with 6 or more players and to modify the rules to put the emphasis on the stamina of midfielders. A goal might only count, for example, if all the midfielders of the scoring team have linked up with their forwards. Or a goal might count double if one of the midfielders of the defending team has not got back quickly enough to defend his own goal. This sort of change to the rules forces midfielders to continuously run back and forth between attack and defense, just as they do during a real game.

Marginal remarks on soccer-related fitness conditioning

The objective of this chapter is to give coaches an idea of how the conditioning of soccer players can be carried out in a match-related context. There are, however, some disadvantages associated with this type of conditioning. When a player's physical fitness is improved with the help of soccer drills, there must always be an obvious soccer objective. Before this objective can be achieved, a certain level of soccer ability is required. If this is not present, the players will constantly be unable to stop the ball from running out of play, or will play it in wrongly, or will be unable to control it during the various game drills. As a consequence the game will be frequently interrupted and the physical objective will not be achieved. It will be almost impossible to subject the players to an overload. This problem manifests itself at lower levels of play in amateur soccer. Coaches of such teams must take this into account. They can adjust the drills described in this chapter by increasing the size of the playing area or reducing the level of difficulty of the obstacles. This will give the players more space and time, and they will therefore have more chance of achieving their soccer objectives. After a while the level of difficulty of the obstacles can be increased again and the players can also try to achieve the physical objective.

Match conditioning

Soccer fitness can be conditioned during games as well during training sessions. If the opposition is weaker, for example, the team can be required to apply pressing tactics for the whole game. The players are therefore required to work harder than the game itself requires. If the opposition is stronger and the team has to wait for chances to counterattack, the coach can require his players to push up quickly after the ball has been played to the center forward, so that the lines remain close to each other.
(page 155 Training Situation 1)

SUMMARY

- The physical aspect is only one of the many aspects of soccer. It is therefore unwise to take the physical factor out of its soccer context and overexpose it. Physical fitness is only a means of achieving soccer objectives.

- Soccer fitness must be built up with the help of soccer-related drills. These do not just have to be drills with the ball, as many people imagine. During a game a player is in possession of the ball for no more than 30 to 60 seconds. The rest of the time he carries out all sorts of off-the-ball actions. Conditioning must therefore be linked to a soccer objective.

- If the objective of a training session is to improve the players' physical fitness, the coach must ensure that they are subjected to an overload. The body must always be asked to do a little more than it is used to.

- The intensity and extent of a training session can be moderated by adjusting the rules of the game and the size of the playing area.

- The intensity of the drills can be checked by measuring the heart rate.

- There are four suitable methods of conditioning for acyclic aerobic endurance: continuous extensive and intensive conditioning, extensive interval training and fartlek training.

- There are two suitable methods of conditioning for acyclic anaerobic endurance: block training and intensive interval training.

- A coach must know which aspects to focus on during a specific period of the season. The correct distribution of the various conditioning elements in a good schedule is the most important and difficult part of the science of coaching. It is also referred to as periodization.

- Each coach must have a clear conditioning plan in his mind. Such a plan consists of a number of cycles: the macrocycle (years), the mesocycle (months), the microcycle (weeks) and the daily plan.

- The extent and intensity of conditioning are in principle opposites and must fluctuate during the course of the season.

- If the soccer ability of a group of players is limited, it is difficult to use soccer-related drills to condition the players' physical fitness. Much simpler drills must then be used.

FIVE PRACTICAL QUESTIONS

1. Can acyclic aerobic endurance be maintained through the whole year just by carrying out soccer conditioning?
This depends on the "dosage." If the conditioning methods described in this book are applied, there will be no problem. It is, however, very important to alternate overloading with quiet recovery periods. The coach must also take into account the work carried out during matches.

2. Training sessions at the end of the season are always less strenuous. Should they not be more strenuous, so that the players will have a better basic fitness at the start of the next season?
In the last phase of the league competition, conditioning should be carried out at normal intensity, otherwise the players' physical fitness will deteriorate. When the season is finished it is advisable to carry on with conditioning, although less frequently and intensely. Basic fitness can be broadened by introducing a lot of variety into training sessions, and a start can be made on building up strength. The players then have a higher level of fitness when they go on vacation, and therefore come back at a higher level. Less emphasis then needs to be laid on physical fitness during the preparation for the new season.

3. How large a workload can an amateur coach impose on his players?
This depends mainly on the situation in which the coach has to work. How do the older and younger players get on with each other? How many new players have to be integrated into the squad? What is the players' basic level of fitness? If there are only two training sessions per week, it is better simply to train hard, but avoiding lactic acid formation. Always take the ground conditions and the match schedule into account.

4. When is it better to train without the ball?
General conditioning drills without the ball can be used to allow the players to recover after a game. Just carry out relaxed running exercises in different surroundings. General conditioning drills without the ball can also be useful for bringing an individual's basic fitness up to scratch. For the rest, soccer conditioning is fitness conditioning and vice versa. The amount of work with the ball can differ from drill to drill.

5. Have any research results been published on lactic acid measurements during training sessions, and are such measurements useful?
German and Swedish researchers have measured lactic acid levels during training sessions. They found that some lactic acid is formed in soccer players' muscles during training sessions, but these levels are well below those measured in 400 meter and 800 meter runners or 1500 meter skaters. This is a consequence of the type of work they perform. It is therefore not really worthwhile carrying out such measurements on soccer players. You might want to measure lactic acid if a particular individual does seem to "acidify" unusually quickly.

INTERVIEW WITH RONALD KOEMAN
(F.C. Barcelona and PSV Einhoven)

Are you aware that there are wide differences in the distances covered by players in different positions?
In the early years of my career I played in midfield, and I realized that I had to do a lot more running than defenders or attackers. A midfielder has to help in both attack and defense. Later I played as a sweeper, where I had more work to do giving instructions than running. But there are differences even there. At PSV Eindhoven I played in the sweeper position but I was also expected to push up into midfield when I could, so I had to do more running. When I only had to stay behind the defensive line, I hardly felt tired at all by the end of the game.

Have you ever known a coach to take this into account during training sessions?
I have never known coaches to make certain players do more running work during training sessions because they had to run more than other players during games. I always had to do just as much work during training as non-stop runners like Dick Schoenaker, Berry van Aerie and Eric Gerets. Even during warming-up runs they were always far in front of the rest.

In recent years a lot of progress has been made in the field of conditioning for soccer players. How has this affected you, as a player?
The major difference between now and fifteen years ago is that the coach himself used to take all the training sessions then, whereas specialist coaches now tend to be in charge of conditioning. Fitness tests were unknown in those days. Coaches worked on the basis of their instinct. Nowadays there are all sorts of aids available for obtaining additional information. As far as the content of training sessions is concerned, it is clear that everything is now related to what happens when you play soccer, and you no longer just set off running without any fixed objective. We know a lot more now than we did 20 years ago. Coaches have a better foundation on which to build.

Do you think that soccer has become physically more strenuous?
It is very clear that today's players are stronger, faster and have better endurance. A lot more is demanded of them during a game than 15 years ago. Certainly I notice this. There are more tasks associated with each position in the team. It is just a pity that a team with a good defense, whose players are very strong and can keep on running, can beat a team that relies mainly on technique. Such teams are not pretty to watch but they win their games.

How far will this trend go?
The danger is that these methods will be copied because they can bring success. I don't see this happening in the Netherlands, because we tend to judge players on their technical ability. But the temptation is certainly there in countries where the level of skill is not so high. That is a shame, because this is the least attractive way of playing.

What is the most physically demanding style of play?
The more attacking the style of play is, the more strength it costs. Attacking soccer means gaining possession as quickly as possible. You have to be extremely fit to keep playing like this for 90 minutes. It is easier if you can just fall back into your own half, and wait for your opponents to come at you when you lose possession. You let the other team do the work then. The style played by Ajax, with the opposing team being penned into its own half, demands an awful lot from the players.

Is the Spanish league more strenuous than the Dutch league?
Spanish soccer is more strenuous. This is mainly because of the long journeys that have to be made between games. Moreover you spend a lot of time in hotels, where you cannot relax as well as you would at home. The training sessions take this into account. You probably do less work on the training field. However, I had a Dutch coach in Barcelona, so I cannot really say anything about the overall situation in Spain.

Are the games in Spain more strenuous?
Spanish league games are a lot more strenuous. In general, the teams are more evenly matched than in the Netherlands, so the games are more competitive. You rarely have a game against easy opposition. You have to go full out in every game, and if you are in the lead you cannot rely on the team's superior routine to just play the game out and conserve strength.

Are there differences in coaching methods between the Netherlands and Spain?
Not really, although the weather in Spain is much better and more time is therefore devoted to stretching exercises. More use is also made of weight training. Spanish players focus more on their physical development. They are also stronger by nature. You can see this when you watch youth international games. In countries such as Spain and Italy, 17 and 18 year-olds are physically more developed than in the Netherlands. I don't think that this is due to conditioning.

How did you keep fit in the summer months?
I always started with two weeks vacation, during which I did absolutely nothing except relax. I then began to play a few leisurely games of tennis, and in the last week before the pre-season preparations began, I used to do some running on my own, together with a few stretching exercises.

As a coach, will you take charge of the players' conditioning work yourself?
I will work in a team, in which everyone is specialized in his own field. Although the coaching course does deal with conditioning, I do not think that I will have enough knowledge to achieve as much as a conditioning specialist. But even if I let someone else take charge of this, conditioning will still have to be soccer-related and involve a lot of drills with the ball.

What things have you picked up in your career that you will be able to use in your coaching work?

The most important thing I have learned is that there is not just one way of getting players fit for the coming season. I have known coaches who relied on lots of continuous work, and others who put less emphasis on continuous work and more on working with the ball. I felt physically fit in both situations. For me that proves that there is more than one way of ensuring that a squad of players is fit when the new season starts. I would also use finishing drills and drills that have to be carried out at high speed.

LITERATURE

1. Waarde van conditietraining in het (top) voetbal.
F. de Haan.
De Voetbaltrainer nr. 23.

2. Is conditietraning verboden?
F. de Haan.
De Voetbaltrainer nr. 24.

3. Workshop conditietraining B. van Lingen.
De Voetbaltrainer nr. 23.

4. Conditioning for Soccer - Dutch Soccer School video REEDSWAIN Videos.

Training Situation 1

Objective:
- Conditioning for acyclic aerobic endurance with a variable workload.
- Practicing technique (passing, controlling the ball, one-touch passing, crossing the ball).
- Practicing tactics (ball speed).

Method:
- Continuous extensive conditioning.
- Continuous intensive conditioning.

Dosage:
- Duration: 30-90 minutes.
- Intensity: 50% of maximal load (180 heartbeats per minute, depending on age).
- Repetitions: none.
- Rest: no break.

Organization:
- A player passes the ball to the lay-off player(1), takes the return ball (2) and passes out to the wing (3). The lay-off player runs in the direction of the pass and the passer becomes the lay-off player.
- A player dribbles the ball down the wing (4) and crosses it.
- After he has crossed the ball the player runs into the middle so that the goalkeeper can throw the ball out to him (5).
- The player dribbles the ball to the starting point.

Buildup:
- Introduce strikers.
- Resistance from opponent(s) when trying to score.

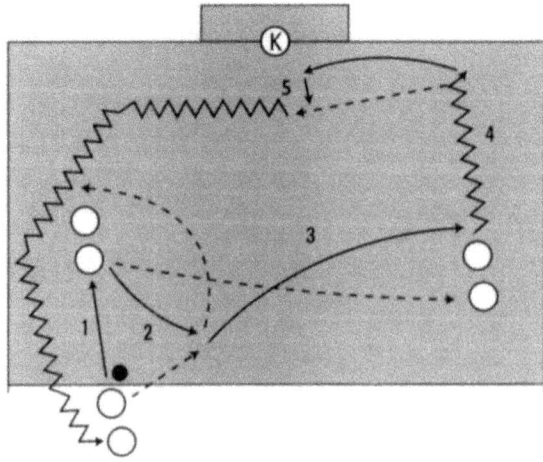

Training Situation 2

Objective:
- Conditioning for acyclic aerobic endurance.
- Practicing technique (one-touch passing, controlling the ball).
- Practicing tactics (getting the ball forward, switching when there is a change of possession).

Method:
- Continuous intensive conditioning.

Dosage:
- Duration: 30-40 minutes (5x 6-8 minutes).
- Intensity: 160-180 heartbeats per minute.
- Repetitions: 5.
- Rest: 5 minutes between repetitions (the work:rest ratio is incorporated in the drill).

Organization:
- Positional game of 2 against 2, with 4 lay-off players (A, B, C and D).
- Team △ plays from A to B and B to A.
- Team O plays from C to D and from D to C.

Scoring:
- When the lay-off player makes a pass to the third player.

Buildup:
- No rules, two-touch, one-touch (also on the flanks).

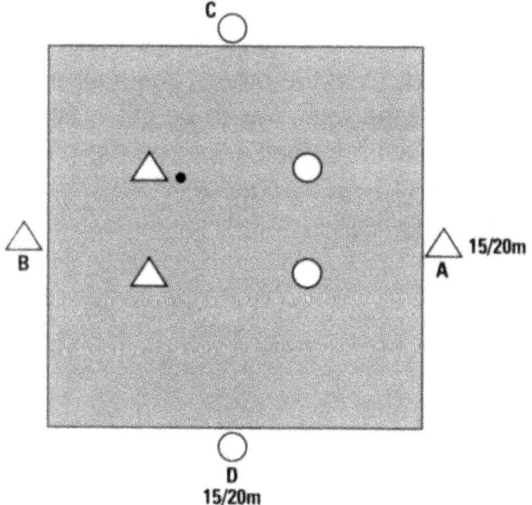

Training Situation 3

Objective:
- Conditioning for acyclic aerobic endurance.
- Conditioning for strength in the challenge.
- Practicing tactics (improving positional play when in possession, challenging/pressing at the right moment, getting the ball forward after an interception, switching when there is a change of possession).

Method:
- Continuous intensive conditioning.

Dosage:
- Duration: 30-40 minutes (5x 6-8 minutes).
- Intensity: 160-180 heartbeats per minute.
- Repetitions: 5.
- Rest: 5 minutes between repetitions.

Organization:
- When team △ has possession there is a 5 against 4 situation, with team O defending.
- Team O tries to win the ball by challenging/pressing. When in possession (4 against 5) it tries to play the ball to the player in the other zone and to link up with him. The situation in the other zone then becomes 5 against 4 for team O because a player from team △ must remain in the zone as a target man.

Scoring:
- By playing the ball to a player in the other zone or by scoring a goal.

Buildup:
- 3-2 touch, larger playing area, more players.
- 2 against 1 in the other zone instead of just one target man, so that the pass has to be more accurate.
- A goal with a goalkeeper on the goal line. **Score from 2 against 1** (goal: change of roles; no goal: start again in the other zone).

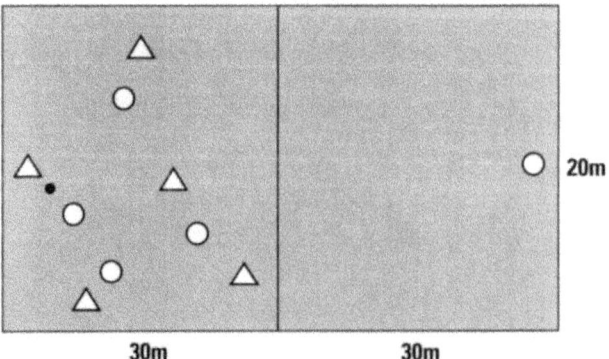

Training Situation 4

Objective:
- Conditioning for acyclic aerobic endurance.
- Practicing tactics (improving positional play when in possession and not in possession, switching when there is a change of possession).
- Practicing shooting quickly at every opportunity.

Method:
- Continuous intensive conditioning.

Dosage:
- Duration: 30-40 minutes (5x 6-8 minutes).
- Intensity: 160-180 heartbeats per minute.
- Repetitions: 5.
- Rest: 5 minutes between repetitions.

Organization:
- Small sided game of 5 against 5.
- Restrict the number of ball contacts (2-3) up to the center line so that the ball has to be played forward quickly. The game must be played with full effort. This is why extra balls are ready on the sideline and behind the two goals.

Scoring:
- In accordance with the normal rules.

Buildup:
- Two points for scoring after an interception in the opposition's half.
- A goal can only be scored if all the scoring team's players have crossed the center line. If there are still defenders in the other half when a goal against is scored, this goal counts double.
- The goalkeeper must play a backpass with one touch.

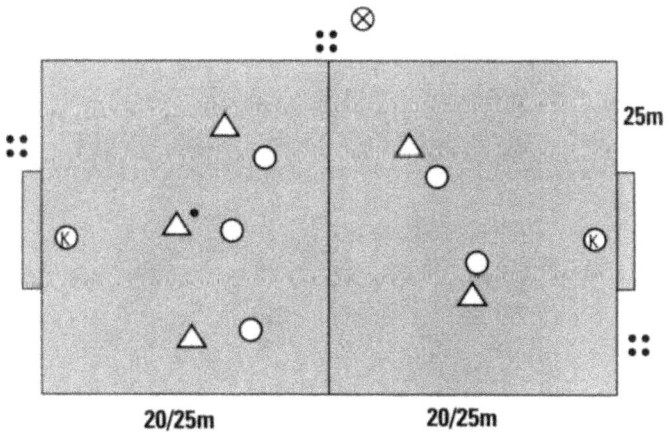

soccer conditioning

Training Situation 5

Objective:
- Conditioning for acyclic aerobic endurance.
- Specific coaching for the right and left flank, based on 4-3-3.
- Practicing technique (passing, controlling the ball, crossing).
- Practicing tactics (choice between one-touch play and controlling the ball, cooperation between players on the same flank).

Method:
- Continuous intensive conditioning.

Dosage:
- Duration: 30-40 minutes (5x 6-8 minutes).
- Intensity: 160-180 heartbeats per minute.
- Repetitions: 5.
- Rest: 5 minutes between repetitions.

Organization:
- Player 5 takes up position on the wing to receive the ball, takes a pass from player 1, passes to player 11, and goes around player 11 on the outside.
- Player 11 meanwhile passes to player 8, who makes a forward pass to player 5.
- Player 5 sends the ball directly in front of goal, or takes the ball on a short distance and crosses to the near or far post, where players 9 and 10 are running in.
- The players then change roles:
    - player 1 becomes player 5,
    - player 5 dribbles the ball back and becomes the new player 1.
- Players 8, 9, 10 and 11 must be capable of fulfilling these roles in the team, but they too must be replaced every 6 to 8 minutes.
- A work period of 15 to 20 seconds and a rest period of 40 to 60 seconds are built into this drill.

Buildup:
- Resistance in front of goal (1 or 2 defenders).
- Resistance to 11 so that better choices have to be made.

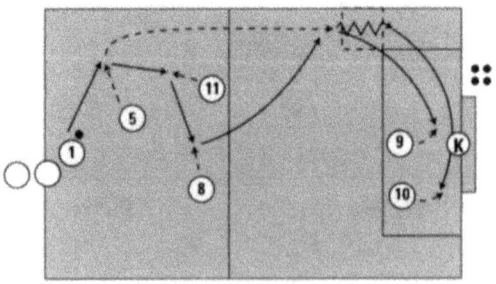

Training Situation 6

Objective:
- Conditioning for acyclic aerobic endurance.
- Practicing technique (passing, laying the ball off, controlling the ball).

Method:
- Extensive interval training.

Dosage:
- Duration: 30-60 seconds.
- Intensity: 170-180 heartbeats per minute.
- Repetitions: Maximum of 8 per series.
- Sets: 2-5.
- Rest: 45-90 seconds between repetitions.
  4-6 minutes between sets.

Organization:
- Player 1 plays the ball to player 2, who controls it.
- Player 1 runs round the cone by player 2 and takes the ball on (adjust speed).
- Player 1 plays a one-two with player 3 and dribbles around the cone.
- Player 1 plays the ball to player 3 again, takes the return and plays a long ball to player 2, etc.
- The players change roles every 30 to 60 seconds.

Buildup:
- Vary the distances and work periods.
- Variation in techniques.

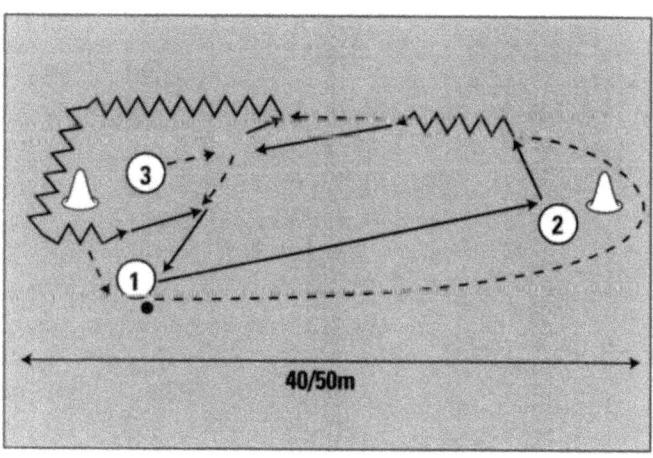

Training Situation 7

Objective:
- Conditioning for acyclic aerobic endurance.
- Practicing technique (passing, dribbling, changing direction and turning through a full circle).

Method:
- Extensive interval training.

Dosage:
- Duration: 30-60 seconds.
- Intensity: 170-180 heartbeats per minute.
- Repetitions: 2-5.
- Rest: 45-90 seconds between repetitions.
  4-6 minutes between sets.

Organization:
- Players in a circle, in pairs, each with a ball.
- The players with a ball (Δ) dribble to the middle of the circle, turn with the ball and play the ball to their teammate (O) on the outside of the circle.
- After the link up, the ball is played to them again. The ball must be controlled on the turn and taken to the middle again, etc.
- The two players forming a pair change roles every 30 to 60 seconds.

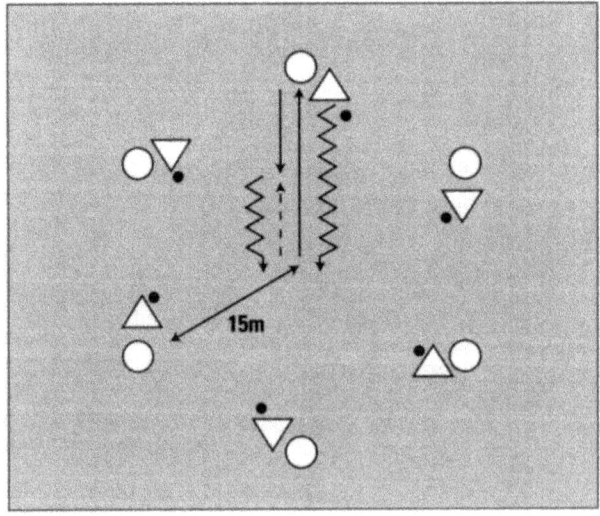

161
soccer conditioning

Training Situation 8

Objective:
- Conditioning for acyclic aerobic endurance.
- Practicing technique (dribbling, changing direction and turning through a full circle, speed of action).

Method:
- Extensive interval training.

Dosage:
- Duration: 30-60 seconds.
- Intensity: 170-180 heartbeats per minute.
- Repetitions: Maximum of 8 per set.
- Sets: 2-5.
- Rest: 45-90 seconds between repetitions. 4-6 minutes between sets.

Organization:
- △ dribbles at speed from A to B and back.
- O runs towards the player who is dribbling the ball and tries to take the ball from him..
- △ prevents this by repeatedly changing direction towards the outside and placing his body between the ball and O.
- △ and O repeatedly change roles.

Buildup:
- Vary the distances (long distances mean more dribbling at speed; short distances put the emphasis on more braking and turning and therefore on strength and technique).

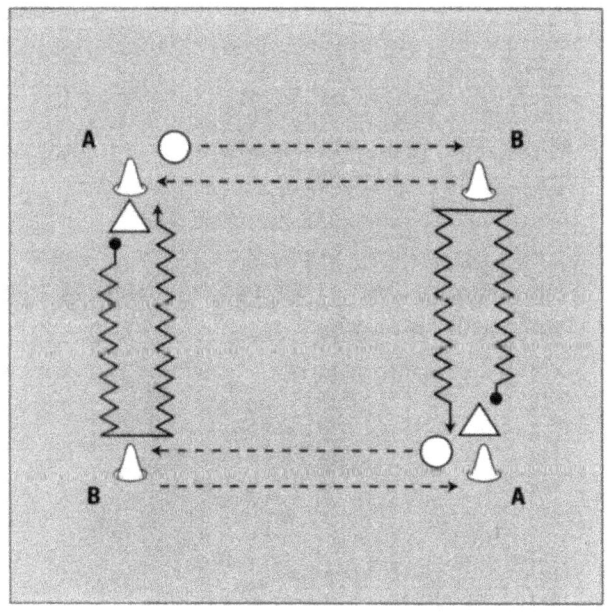

Training Situation 9

The remarks made above must be taken into account for anaerobic conditioning. Care is essential. The number of repeats per series and the number of series depend on the playing standard and the chosen buildup.

Objective:
- Conditioning for acyclic anaerobic endurance.
- Conditioning for strength in the challenge.
- Practicing technique (controlling the ball in the face of considerable resistance).
- Practicing tactics (timing the run towards the ball to receive a pass).

Method:
- Block training.

Dosage:
- Duration: 15 seconds.
- Intensity: 100%.
- Repetitions: 4-8.
- Sets: 2-4.
- Rest: 15-30 seconds between repetitions.
  4-6 minutes between sets.

Organization:
- Ⓐ serves △, who has his back to his marker O.
- △ tries to beat his marker, 1 on 1, and dribble the ball over the line (1). He can also try to do this by playing a one-two with Ⓐ (2 and 3).
- The drill is started and stopped at a sign by the coach (always 15 seconds).
- If the ball runs out of play a new ball must be played in.
- The attacker becomes the server, the server becomes the defender, and the defender becomes the attacker

Scoring:
- △ can score by dribbling the ball over the goal line. O can score by dribbling the ball over the center line.

Buildup:
- Make the zones smaller or bigger.
- Start with a throw-in.
- Goal with goalkeeper on goal line.
- Relatively relaxed break when roles are switched, whereas the breaks between the series should be filled with drills for practicing technique.

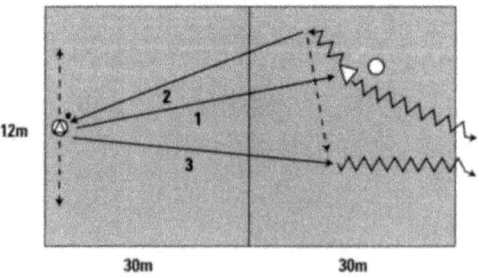

Training Situation 10

Objective:
- Conditioning for acyclic anaerobic endurance.
- Conditioning for strength in the challenge.
- Practicing technique (controlling the ball in the face of considerable resistance).
- Practicing tactics (positional play with and without the ball in combination with target players, switching when there is a change of possession).

Method:
- Interval speed training.

Dosage:
- Duration: 45-60 seconds.
- Intensity: 90-100%.
- Repetitions: 6-8.
- Rest: 4-5 minutes.

Organization:
- The ball is played to △ who has O at his back. He must try to take the ball over the goal line by dribbling directly or playing a one two.
- The ball can be played back to a layoff player Ⓐ but each lay-off player must play it directly to the player in the middle or the other lay-off player.

Scoring:
- Both △ and O can score by dribbling over the goal line.

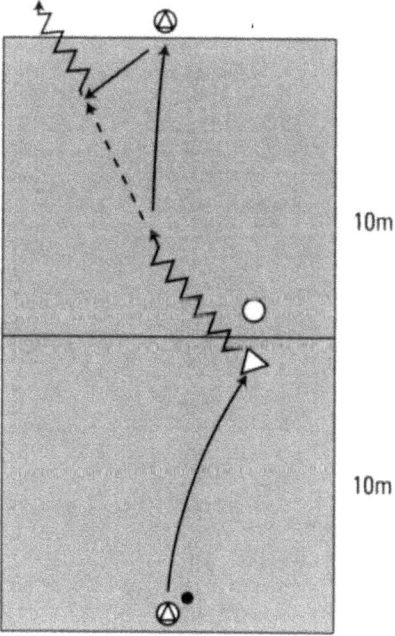

Training Situation 11

Objective:
- Conditioning for acyclic anaerobic endurance.
- Conditioning for strength in the challenge.
- Practicing technique (speed of action, controlling the ball).
- Practicing tactics (pressuring attackers; cooperation between defenders).

Method:
- Interval speed training.

Dosage:
- Duration: 45-60 seconds.
- Intensity: 90-100%.
- Repetitions: 6-8.
- Rest: 4-5 minutes.

Organization:
- The most central player of team O plays the ball to the most central player of team △.
- Team O then exerts pressure on the flank to which △ team plays the ball. The player from team O on the other flank ensures that there is defensive balance.

Scoring:
- Team O can score by winning the ball, while team △ can score by dribbling the ball over the center/goal line.

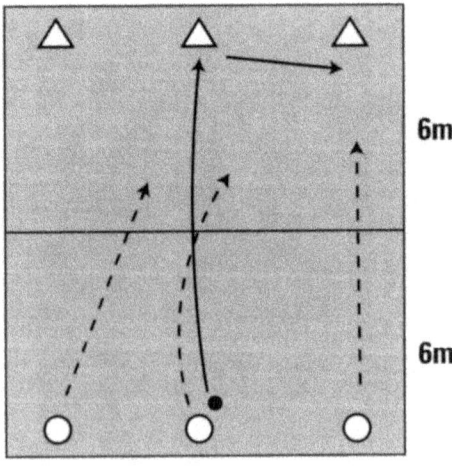

Training Situation 12

Objective:
- Conditioning for acyclic anaerobic endurance.
- Conditioning for strength in the challenge.
- Practicing technique (speed of action, controlling the ball).
- Practicing tactics (pressuring attackers; cooperation between defenders).

Method:
- Interval speed training.

Dosage:
- Duration: 45-60 seconds.
- Intensity: 90-100%.
- Repetitions: 6-8.
- Rest: 4-5 minutes.

Organization:
- The two neutral players ⊛ alternately play the ball to the attackers △.
- A 3 against 3 situation results after the pass, in which the defenders (O) exert pressure on the ball.
- The attackers must try to score.
- Change of roles after 45-60 seconds (attackers become defenders, defenders become neutral players, neutral players become attackers).

Scoring:
- The attackers must try to score in the full-size goal defended by a goalkeeper, while the defenders can score by dribbling the ball over the line between the cones.

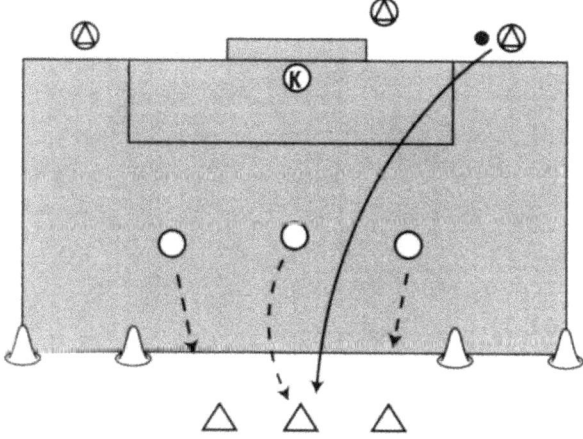

Training Situation 13

Objective:
- Conditioning for acyclic anaerobic endurance.
- Conditioning for strength in the challenge.
- Practicing tactics (strikers' tactics in the penalty area, defensive play by markers in and around the penalty area in cooperation with the goalkeeper).

Method:
- Interval speed training.

Dosage:
- Duration: 45-60 seconds.
- Intensity: 90-100%.
- Repetitions: 6-8.
- Rest: 4-5 minutes.

Organization:
- The ball is played from the center line into the zone in front of the penalty area. A 2 against 2 situation results.
- Team △ must try to shoot into the full-size goal defended by a goalkeeper, while team O must try to dribble the ball over the line between the cones.
- If the ball runs out of play, a new ball must immediately be played in.

Scoring:
- △ can score in the full-size goal. O can score by winning the ball and dribbling it over one of the two lines between the cones.

Buildup:
- Players waiting for a pass on the wings, who can cross the ball against resistance.
- Introduction of a free defender and an attacker who moves up to create a 3 against 3 situation in front of the goal.

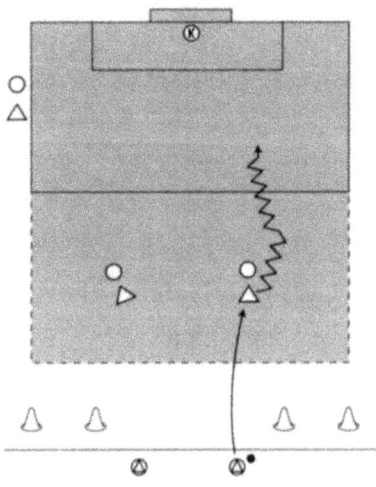

Training Situation 14

Objective:
- Conditioning for reaction speed and starting speed.
- Conditioning for strength in the challenge.
- Practicing technique (lay-off, passing, finishing).

Method:
- Reaction speed and starting speed.

Dosage:
- Duration: 1-2 seconds.
- Intensity: 100% from a standing start.
- Repetitions: 8-10.
- Sets: 2-4.
- Rest: 30 seconds between repetitions.
  4-6 minutes between sets.

Organization:
- △ sprints away from O into space to receive the ball.
- He receives the ball and lays it off in one touch to the coach.
- The coach plays the ball in one touch to △ and O, who sprint forward and compete for the ball.
- This drill must be carried out down the right and left flanks.
- Both players must defend four times and attack four times.

Scoring:
- The two players forming a pair can compete against each other. The attacker is awarded a point when he scores and the defender when he wins the ball.

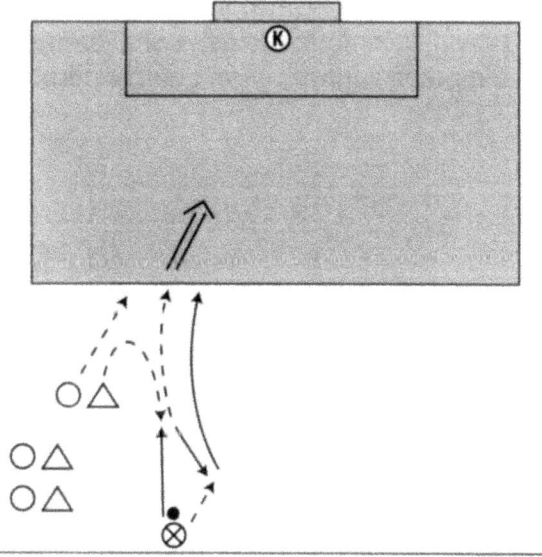

Training Situation 15

Objective:
- Conditioning for reaction speed and starting speed.
- Conditioning for strength in the challenge.
- Practicing technique (finishing).

Method:
- Reaction speed and starting speed.

Dosage:
- Duration: 1-2 seconds.
- Intensity: 100% from a standing start.
- Repetitions: 8-10.
- Sets: 2-4.
- Rest: 30 seconds between repetitions.
  4-6 minutes between sets.

Organization:
- The coach plays the ball in along the ground or through the air.
- This is the signal for △ and O (who starts 3 meters behind △) to sprint after the ball and compete for it.
- Shoot at goal from outside the penalty area or try to take the ball round the goalkeeper.
- Alternate series on the left and right.

Scoring:
- The two players forming a pair can compete against each other. The attacker is awarded a point when he scores and the defender when he wins the ball.

General:
- These drills have not only a conditioning aspect but also a soccer objective (controlling the ball, one-touch play, finishing, 1 against 1 challenges, sprinting away from a marker, running in on goal, accurate passing).

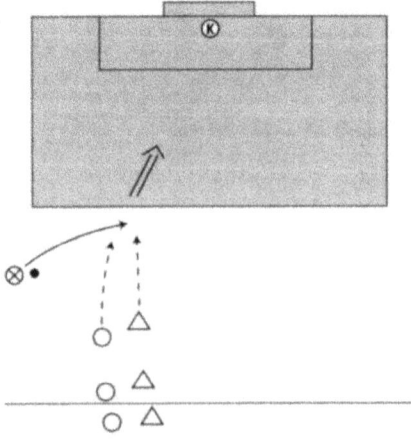

Training Situation 16

Objective:
- Conditioning for acceleration (with and without a ball).
- Conditioning for strength in the challenge.
- Practicing technique (passing, finishing).

Method:
- Acceleration.

Dosage:
- Duration: 2-6 seconds.
- Intensity: 100% from a flying start.
- Repetitions: 6.
- Sets: 1-2.
- Rest: 2-6 minutes between repetitions (depending on the work period).
  4-6 minutes between sets.

Organization:
- △ dribbles and plays a one-two with the coach.
- △ takes the ball on and accelerates towards the goal under constant pressure from O, who starts to sprint when △ plays the ball to the coach.
- This drill should be carried out over the left and right flanks.
- In each series, each player has the attacker's role three times and the defender's role three times.
- Work over a distance ranging from the center line to the penalty area (sometimes even the goal line).

Scoring:
- The attacker gets a point if he scores, and the defender gets a point if he wins the ball.

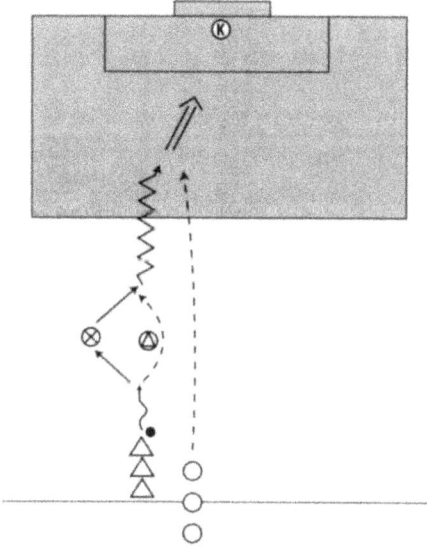

Training Situation 17

Objective:
- Conditioning for speed endurance.
- Conditioning for strength in the challenge.
- Practicing technique (passing, laying off, crossing, finishing).

Method:
- Speed endurance.

Dosage:
- Duration: 6-10 seconds.
- Intensity: 100%.
- Repetitions: 4-6.
- Sets: 1-2.
- Rest: 2-4 minutes between repetitions.
  6 minutes between sets.

Organization:
- From the left, △ plays the ball firmly to the striker (10), who lays it off into the path of △ who makes a forward run down the wing under pressure from O.
- △ takes the ball to the goal line and hits a hard high/low cross to the other striker (9).
- Repeat the above on the other flank.

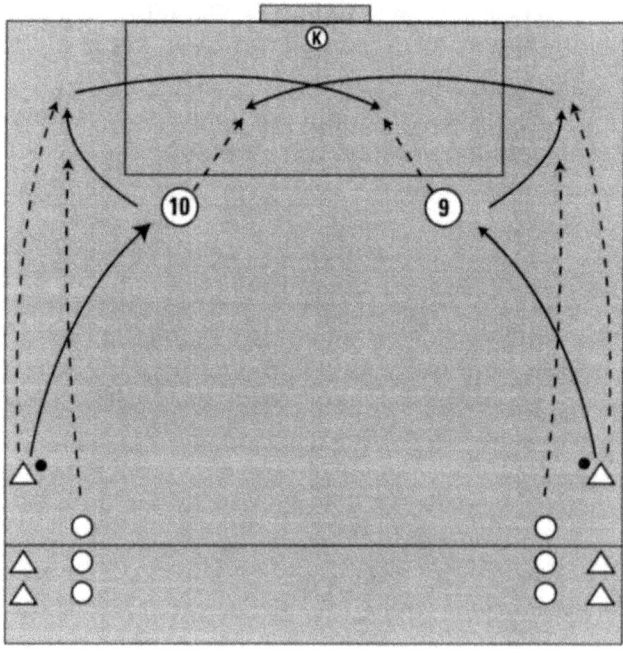

Training Situation 18

Objective:
- Conditioning for speed endurance.
- Conditioning for strength in the challenge.
- Practicing technique (passing, crossing).

Method:
- Speed endurance.

Dosage:
- Duration: 6-10 seconds.
- Intensity: 100%.
- Repetitions: 4-6.
- Sets: 1-2.
- Rest: 2-4 minutes between repetitions.
  6 minutes between sets.

Organization:
- △ plays the ball to the left winger (1) and runs towards the goal.
- △ plays the ball to the center forward (2), who flicks it on (3).
- The left winger (△) and a defender (O) contest the ball before the winger crosses (4).
- There is a 2 against 1 situation in front of goal.
- Repeat the above on the right wing.

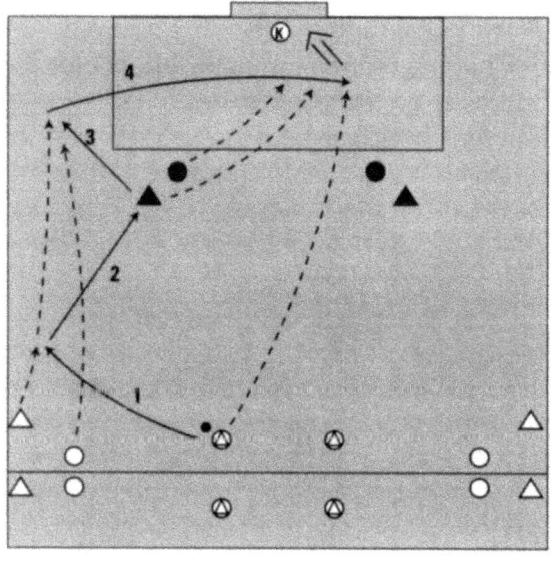

Training Situation 19

Objective:
- Conditioning for repeated short sprint capacity.
- Practicing technique (lay-off, passing).

Method:
- Repeated short sprint capacity.

Dosage:
- Duration: 1-2 seconds.
- Intensity: 100%, from a standing start.
- Repetitions: 6-10.
- Sets: 2-4.
- Rest: 10 seconds between repetitions.
  4-6 minutes between sets.

Organization:
- Circle formation. The players are paired off, each pair with a ball. One player from each pair (O) stands on the perimeter of the circle and the other (Δ) runs inside the circle.
- The player in the ring runs towards the ball (1) played towards him by his partner, lays the ball off (2) and sprints away (3).
- Each drill must be carried out over both right and left.
- After 6-10 repeats the two players swap roles.

Buildup:
- The ball is thrown in and has to be headed back (with or without a jump).
- The player in the middle can ask for the ball from any player on the perimeter.

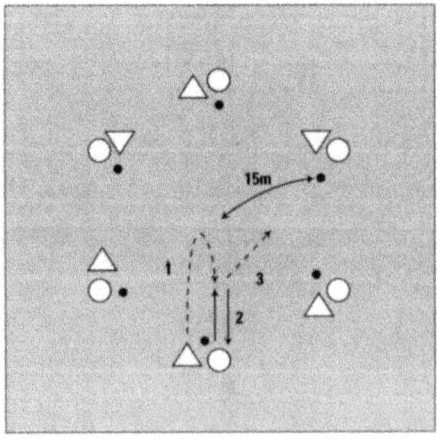

Training Situation 20

This is an example of a complex drill, in which work is performed at a continuously intensive level with links to speed endurance. This cannot be carried out in fixed doses. The coach must monitor the drill and call a break when neces-sary, sometimes after 4 minutes, sometimes after 6.

Objective:
- Conditioning acyclic aerobic endurance and, to a lesser degree, sprinting capacity and strength in the challenge.
- Practicing tactics (positional play).

Method:
- Small sided game of 4 against 4 with 2 goalkeepers. There are also 4 neutral players at the ends of the playing area.
- The neutral players are advanced target players. They have to play the ball with just one touch.
- The other players can touch the ball 2 or 3 times, depending on the standard of play.

Scoring:
- Normal goal = 1 point.
- Goal from a cross = 2 points.
- Goal from a one-two with a target man = 2 points.
- Goal scored by the third man = 3 points.

General:
- Within this drill, the aim is to adjust the rules and organization to put the emphasis on conditioning objectives. Players must therefore have good soccer ability.

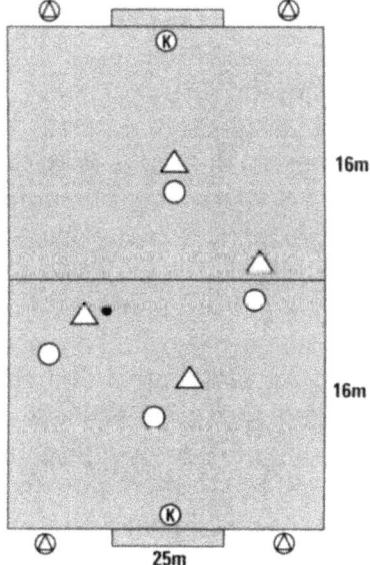

CHAPTER 7

PREPARATION FOR A NEW SEASON

Dr. Luc van Agt

7.1 INTRODUCTION

Soccer players are well acquainted with the phenomenon of preparation. After a (summer) break of one or two months they have a relatively short period of time to regain match fitness, i.e., to get back to the level of technical, tactical and physical fitness that is necessary to compete effectively. A coach only has an average of four to eight weeks to prepare his players for a new season. The type of buildup he selects is therefore of crucial importance. He has to take account of aspects such as the number of available training sessions per week, the loading capacity of the players and therefore, indirectly, their level of ability. Naturally his objectives for the coming season also play a role. This chapter deals with the structure of the preparation program, the extent and intensity of the work, and the work-to-rest ratio. A key aspect is the transition from general to specific soccer-related endurance, strength and sprint conditioning. Factors that can make the preparation successful or unsuccessful are also explained.

7.2 THE PURPOSE OF PREPARATION

7.2.1 The vacation break

Between two soccer seasons there is a break, when soccer players generally play no matches, train little or not at all, and enjoy a vacation. The duration of the summer break varies from four to ten weeks. This period gives soccer players the opportunity to allow their body to rest. In this way reserves can be built up for the following season and slight injuries at last have the time to heal completely. The interval between two seasons also has another function. Soccer players can think about other things than soccer, and can recharge their mental batteries. The physical loading capacity of the players decreases during this period. This is why it is necessary to plan a preparation period in which the players can build up their fitness again before a new season starts.

7.2.2 Building-up match fitness

After a period of relative inactivity, players are not physically prepared to start playing immediately. Inactivity causes their physical fitness to deteriorate. The longer the summer break, the more important it is to have a period of preparation. The players have to be gradually brought up to match fitness. Coaches must not make the mistake of pushing them too hard during the preparation period. Players should not have to work harder than they will need to during the season. They must be confronted with a workload that is equivalent to that of a game of soccer, and not more or less. After all, they are going to be required to play a game of soccer, not run a marathon. The players often find the preparation period strenuous, but that is a consequence of the deterioration in their physical fitness. This chapter explains how soccer players can be made match fit by means of a selective program of conditioning.

7.2.3 Changes in the squad and/or the style of play

Changes often take place with a squad. New players come and others leave. Sometimes the players are even confronted with a new coach at the start of the season. As a consequence of these changes, new agreements have to be reached within the team and automatic patterns of play have to be established. This requires a lot of time and work, for which the preparation period is also suitable.

Sometimes the players are confronted with a new coach at the start of the season.

7.3 A FIT START SAVES TIME

After a long season the players enjoy a hard-earned vacation. Nevertheless, it is important for a soccer player to monitor his fitness during this period. This means that he must resist temptation during the summer break and ensure that he does not put on too much weight. A slight increase in weight may be unavoidable, but haphazard eating and drinking habits, in combination with relatively little exercise, can soon cause a sportsman to balloon up. This is extremely inconvenient at the start of a new season. Moreover the excess pounds put an unnecessary additional strain on the joints. A soccer player should therefore try to keep his weight reasonably steady even during his vacation, and remain physically active in a more relaxed sort of way. Professional and top amateur players must have the discipline to do the necessary "homework" to maintain their basic fitness. The coach then does not need to spend much time on this at the start of the pre-season preparation period and can quickly move on to technical and tactical aspects. In youth and amateur soccer, in particular, preparation time is limited. If soccer players are not fit when the preparation period starts, more time has to be devoted to physical conditioning. Inactivity during the vacation period also increases the chance of injury. The body moves from a period of relative inactivity to sudden exertion. All kinds of minor muscle injuries can occur and this can disrupt the whole preparation period.

What can soccer players do during their vacation?
Soccer players must remain active during the summer break. Many players carry out programs with the emphasis on long-distance running. At first sight there seems to be no harm in this. The player's endurance and weight remain reasonably stable and he feels fit.

Soccer volleyball is an ideal way of maintaining fitness during the summer break.

However, a few words of warning are necessary. The long-distance runs are often delayed until the final days of the summer break. A lot of ground is then covered in just a few days. One disadvantage of this is that the player does not have time to recover completely from his hasty and intensive runs before he participates in the first training sessions for the new season. A second disadvantage is that players often do their running on the road while wearing unsuitable footwear. Soccer players are not used to this sort of surface, and may therefore suffer any of a variety of complaints or injuries. Many typical soccer actions such as starting, accelerating, stopping, turning, jumping and shooting involve the fast muscle fibers. During long-distance running the slow muscle fibers do most of the work, which involves continuous repetition of the same sort of movement. This is referred to as cyclic movement. Soccer, however, is characterized by an acyclic form of movement. Soccer players should therefore mainly use their muscles to carry out acyclic activity during the summer break. Sports such as tennis, soccer volleyball, beach volleyball and squash are much more suitable for preparing the body for acyclic movement.

7.4 STRUCTURE OF THE PREPARATION PROGRAM

Many coaches use the conventional form of preparation program, in which continuous work is followed by speed work and then sprint work. There is a long tradition of viewing endurance as the basis for participating in most sports. In addition, sprinting ability is viewed as the most important basic motor property for a soccer player. This explains the above program, because the theory of coaching stated that there should be a progression from the general to the specific and from extent to intensity. This requires a more detailed explanation.

7.4.1 From general to specific conditioning

In conditioning theory, from the general to the specific means that conditioning work is initially general and gradually becomes more like the sport in question. A physical basis must be established before sport-related aspects can be introduced. In soccer this means that a coach must start with general soccer-related conditioning and move towards specific soccer-related conditioning. It has been stated above that endurance

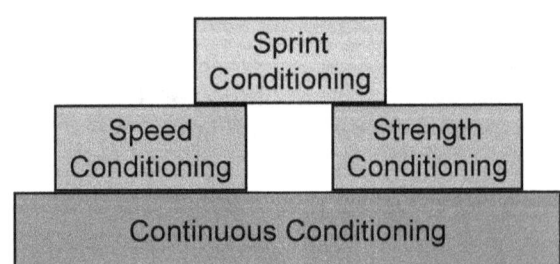

Figure 7.1: *Conventional conditioning buildup. Endurance used to be regarded as the foundation on which fitness had to be built.*

used to be viewed as the foundation on which fitness had to be built (see Fig. 7.1). Good endurance was taken as the starting point from which to work towards more sport-related conditioning. In the case of soccer there was a gradual shift from continuous and speed conditioning to sprint conditioning. The modern view is that all basic motor properties that are of importance for a soccer player must be conditioned from the very start, Here too, however, there is still a transition from general soccer-related conditioning to specific soccer- related conditioning. In the initial preparation phase the emphasis is on general aerobic and anaerobic endurance, general strength and general speed. Subsequently there is a gradual move towards using more specific soccer-related drills (see Fig. 7.2). During the general phase the characteristics of the sport of soccer must be taken into account. Aerobic and anaerobic endurance must be acyclically conditioned. Strength drills must primarily be explosive, and speed drills should consist mainly of sprints over distances of 5 to 30 meters, with lots of turns and changes of direction. General conditioning drills are only useful if these soccer "ingredients" are present.

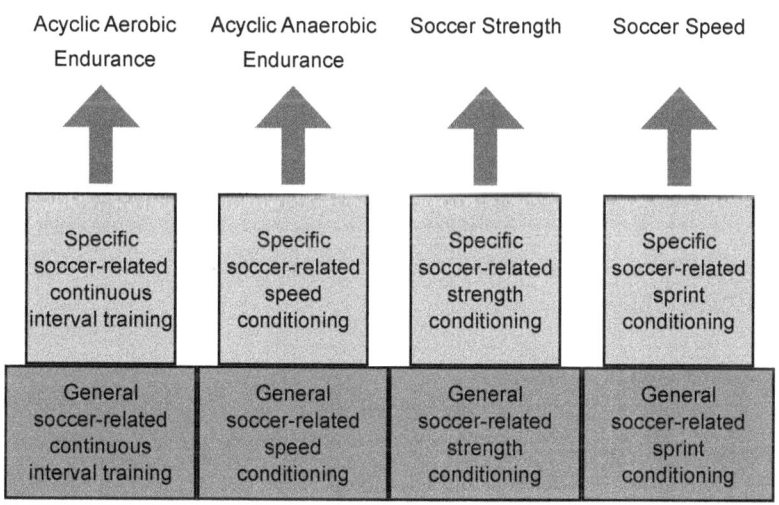

Figure 7.2: *Modern conditioning buildup. The general physical parameters together make up the foundation on which specific sport-related conditioning can be built.*

7.4.2 From extent to intensity

Extensive and intensive conditioning are difficult to reconcile together. Intensive drills result in fatigue, which makes carrying out extensive drills difficult. Nevertheless, both aspects are part of soccer conditioning. A game of soccer lasts for 90 minutes and involves many moments of peak exertion. According to the science of conditioning, it is more sensible to focus on extensive work and then to increase the intensity. The body of a soccer player must again become accustomed to playing soccer for 90 minutes. During the first week of preparation the training sessions will be long (90 to 120 minutes), with only a few intensive moments. During the second week the number of peaks can be gradually increased within training sessions that last no longer than 90 minutes. From weeks 3 and 4 the training sessions will be about 75 minutes long. The intensity of the sessions will then have reached match level.

7.4.3 The work-to-rest ratio

During the first weeks of the preparation period, the coach and players often feel that they have something to prove. Players want to secure their places in the team and the coach wants to set the tone for the coming season and take advantage of every conditioning opportunity. The work-to-rest ratio (or the relationship between exertion and recovery) has steadily attracted more attention in recent years. Initially there is a tendency to work hard and to lose sight of the relationship between extent and intensity. Carrying out a lot of intensive training sessions shortly after each other has a negative conditioning effect (see Fig. 3.3D). Sore

> *Run with a smile.*
> *You will feel good.*
>
> **Wim Verhoorn**

muscles, muscle damage and injuries result. The relationship between work and rest is important with respect to successive training sessions and to the workload within a single session. After a strenuous training session the players need time to recover. It must therefore be succeeded by a more relaxed session or by a session that focuses on a completely different energy system. Intensive interval training, for example, should be followed by a session of moderately demanding continuous drills with the emphasis on technique. There should also be a specific relationship between work and rest in a single training session. During interval work in the first phase of the preparation period, the ratio of work to rest should be 1:3 or 1:2. At a later stage this will have progressed to 1:1.5 or 1:1. Naturally this depends on the type of conditioning, but it also depends on the playing level of the group. A coach must observe his players closely during training sessions to ensure that the workload is not too demanding or even undemanding. In general it is more difficult for coaches to cancel a training session and give the players more rest than to have the players carry out more work. Above all, coaches do not want to do too little. Nevertheless, allowing the players to rest at the right moment can be more effective than the additional work. Unfortunately there are no hard and fast rules here, and the coach's intuition plays an important role.

7.4.4 Building-up acyclic aerobic endurance

The first phase of the preparation period (first two weeks) is used for continuous general conditioning. This running work must be geared to the acyclic character of the sport. Runs of 5 to 10 kilometers at the same pace should be taboo in soccer. Elsewhere in this book it is explained that they can have a harmful effect on both the muscles and the nervous system. During a game, soccer players have to do at a lot of running at varying intensities. Running work is useful during the first week of the season as a means of building up basic fitness, provided the runs are relatively short (2 to 3 kilometers) and the pace is constantly varied (speed up/slow down every 30 to 60 seconds) and they are not carried out during each and every training session. This variation in pace is the most important soccer aspect of such running work. Short, relaxed runs also have a role in the context of training sessions primarily aimed at allowing the players to recover. The circulation of the blood through the muscles is optimal, thus promoting recovery. During the second week the emphasis must shift towards soccer-related drills for conditioning acyclic aerobic endurance. The continuous extensive and intensive drills and interval training described in chapter 6 are suitable for this purpose (training situations 1 to 8 and 20). Games of 11 against 11 or 10 against 10 or 8 against 8 on a full pitch are also eminently suitable. A coach can make the players' workload heavier or lighter by varying the size of the playing area or changing the rules.

7.4.5 Building-up acyclic anaerobic endurance

The conventional buildup from continuous to speed and then sprint conditioning has already been mentioned above. Speed conditioning deserves special attention in this context. Although soccer players regularly call on the lactic acid system during a game, no considerable acidification occurs. The lactic acid system is never active for more than 20 to 30 seconds in succession, so only a limited amount of lactic acid is produced. It is therefore not particularly meaningful to make soccer players carry out the same type of speed conditioning as athletes (for example, 8 x 400 meters or 5 x 800 meters). This also applies during the preparation period. The purpose of such conditioning is to cause acidification and to go to the very limit. Apart from the mental aspect of learning to cope with this, such conditioning has no specific influence in respect to improving soccer fitness.

Intensive conditioning must be of short hydration, otherwise acidification occurs.

Soccer players do not typically produce large amounts of lactic acid. However, although the lactic acid system is active to only a limited degree during a game, the conditioning of this system must have a place in the preparation program. The drills last for no more than 30 to 45 seconds, so that extreme acidification cannot occur. Maximum intensity is not required at this stage. A suitable drill for the first week of the preparation is speed work over 100 meters (2 to 3 series, 6 to 10 repeats). Each run should be timed at 18 to 20 seconds. The runs need not be in a straight line. Soccer ingredients such as braking, turning and accelerating can be introduced by making the players run round a cone placed 50 meters from the start. During the second week the soccer-related drills described in chapter 6 (training situations 9 to 13) can be introduced. From week 3 only these drills should be used, as a means of stimulating acyclic anaerobic endurance.

> *Thorough preparation is a thousand times better than a pep talk. In a sense, I want to say to the players: I trust you completely, so I am going fishing.*
>
> **Hans Westerhof**

7.4.6 Building-up soccer strength

Building up strength is just as important as improving endurance. It might be thought that lots of hours of weight training are necessary, but that is not the case. Weight training is only worthwhile if it is done regularly over a long period of time, and not just during the few weeks of pre-season preparation. During the season only a limited amount of time is available for conditioning, and it is better to devote it to soccer-related conditioning. Weight training can have a place in soccer, but usually it is more worthwhile for soccer players to carry out strength conditioning on the field. All sorts of general and specific drills for strength conditioning are described in chapter 4. These are eminently suitable for the preparation period. There are drills that make use of the body's own weight, drills for pairs of players, drills that make use of simple materials, drills with the ball and circuit training. Strength conditioning should be included in the training sessions from the very start of the preparation period. Initially the emphasis is on basic strength. General strength drills (drills 1 to 10 and 17 to 19 in chapter 4) must be part of every training session. As soon as the players' general strength reaches the required basic level, a switch must be made to specific conditioning for the strength needed for soccer actions (drills 12 to 16 and 20 to 40 in chapter 4).

7.4.7 Building-up speed

Speed must be conditioned in parallel with strength. Speed and strength have so much in common that they can best be dealt with together (just think of conditioning for starting strength). After weeks of relative inactivity, sprinting flat out would put too great a strain on the muscles and tendons and result in injuries. The muscle system must be gradually accustomed to fast and above all explosive sprints. This can best be done with preparatory drills. These include running drills such as drill 1 (but also drills 9 to 14 in chapter 5)

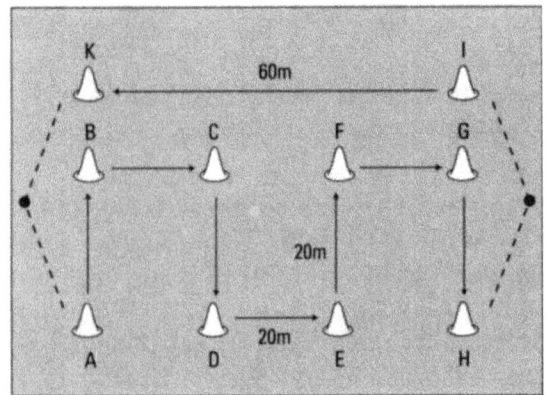

During each series:
BC + DE + FG + HI: jogging
IK: 60 meter run to top speed
KA: walk

Series 1:	AB + EF:	skip sideways to the left
	CD + GH:	skip sideways to the right
Series 2:	AB + EF:	skip
	CD + GH:	lift heels
Series 3:	AB + EF:	cross steps left
	CD + GH:	cross steps right
Series 4:	AB + EF:	hop left
	CD + GH:	hop right
Series 5:	AB + EF:	running jumps
	CD + GH:	acceleration

Drill 1: Interval training with the emphasis on running technique and coordination.

Before players sprint full out, they should carry out preparatory exercises. The body can then become accustomed to explosivity.

and "intensification." Intensification is especially suitable. The players are required to run a certain distance, within which they have to reach maximum speed. Initially there is no question of making an explosive start. During the first training session the distance should be 50 meters. In each successive training session the distance can be reduced by 10 meters, so that in each session the players have to reach their maximum speed in a shorter time. The drill therefore becomes gradually more explosive. From the fourth session the players can sprint full out over 5, 10 and 20 meters within the framework of general soccer-related sprint drills (see drills 24 to 29 in chapter 4 and drills 1 to 8 in chapter 5). By then the body is sufficiently prepared, and is accustomed to explosivity. In the third week the transition can be made to specific soccer-related sprint drills with genuine soccer resistances as described in chapter 6 (training situations 14 to 19).

7.4.8 Integrated conditioning

The conditioning of acyclic aerobic and anaerobic endurance, speed and strength have all been referred to above. At the start of the pre-season preparation period, complete training sessions or parts of them can be devoted to improving a single basic motor property. The further the preparation period progresses, the more the sessions include specific elements of real games of soccer. As far as physical capacity is concerned, training sessions will always be a mixture. Aspects such as strength, speed, flexibility and coordination can be dealt with especially effectively in "mixed" drills. In chapter 6, in particular, training situations are described during which almost all elements of soccer fitness are stimulated. The most important physical aspects of a game of soccer can be raised to a higher level by means of such integrated conditioning.

7.4.9 Linking soccer conditioning to soccer objectives: specific soccer-related conditioning

Conditioning must be linked to the objectives that a coach wants to achieve during a given phase of the preparation period. If a coach chooses a physiological objective such as improving acyclic aerobic endurance, drills must be selected that also focus on a specific "soccer problem." In this way acyclic aerobic endurance can be conditioned with the help of drills in which passing and "bringing the third man into the play" are practiced. Such drills are described in chapter 6. It is not just a matter of choosing the right conditioning methods. The content of the training sessions must be geared to the way the team plays. The training sessions must be specific in character in relation to both the physical objective and the style of play.

7.5 GENERAL GUIDELINES FOR PRE-SEASON PREPARATION IN RELATION TO THE STANDARD OF PLAY

In chapter 1 it was explained that soccer players at lower levels perform less work during a game. It was also pointed out that, in general, these players have a lower level of physical fitness. In other words, they have a lower loading capacity. Because workload and loading capacity always have to be in equilibrium, all of the above must be taken into account during the preparation period. This information must play a role in shaping the conditioning program, especially in terms of the duration and extent (i.e. the number and duration of the training sessions) and the intensity (work-to-rest ratio) of the preparation period. The content of the program differs from playing level to playing level. A rough distinction can be made between:

- professional soccer players;
- top amateurs (the top class, 1st class and 2nd class Dutch Soccer Association leagues);
- competitive amateurs (3rd to 5th class Dutch Soccer Association leagues);
- recreational amateurs (6th class Dutch Soccer Association leagues and lower).

7.5.1 Professionals

Duration of the preparation period:
At least 6 weeks;
no more than 8 weeks.

Number of training sessions each week:
Daily and sometimes twice daily. One rest day each week.

Number of games each week:
One or two.

> *When I think about running I always think about pain.*
>
> **Bart Veldkamp**

At each playing level, the training sessions should last for 75 to 90 minutes. If soccer players train twice daily, the two sessions should not last longer than 150 minutes (for example, 2 x 75 minutes, or 1 x 90 minutes and 1 x 60 minutes).

7.5.2 Top amateurs

Duration of the preparation period:
At least 4 weeks;
no more than 6 weeks.

Number of training sessions each week:
Three or four.

Number of games each week:
One or two.

If only one game is played in a given week, four training sessions can be held. If two games are played, the number of training sessions in that week must be restricted to three.

7.5.3 Competitive players

Duration of the preparation period:
At least 4 weeks;
no more than 6 weeks.

> *You cannot become a chamion without breaking a sweat.*
>
> **Epiktetos**

Number of training sessions each week:
Two or three.

Number of games each week:
One or two.

If only one game is played in a given week, three training sessions can be held. If two games are played, the number of training sessions in that week must be restricted to two.

7.5.4 Recreational players

Players at this level regard the game as part of their social life. There is therefore little point in giving guidelines for the preparation period. The most important thing for players at this level is to pay attention to injury prevention (see chapters 12 and 13). Ambitious teams that want to get into the higher regions of amateur soccer as fast as possible can best apply the guidelines for the competitive amateurs. For these teams a thorough period of preparation is essential. It is important for coaches at all levels of play to realize that the above guidelines are only general. Each coach must adapt them to the specific circumstances with which he is confronted and in which he must work. The coach's experience and intuition play an important role here.

7.6 STRENUOUS TRAINING SESSIONS AND MATCHES: A POSSIBLE CONFLICT

If a training session is held during the day and there is a game in the evening, a coach will have to define his priorities. If the objective of the training session is to improve physical fitness, he cannot expect as much as usual from his players during the match in the evening. If the preparation game takes priority, however, the intensity of the training session will have to be moderated. Such an approach helps to avoid physical problems (such as overstrain and muscle injuries) and unrealistic expectations. The frequency of the training sessions in the preparation period is higher at the top amateur level than during the season. Coaches at this level must take great care to avoid overstrain. Their players have to work all day. It is advisable not to plan strenuous training sessions on the last two days before a game. There must be sufficient recovery time to allow the players to perform well. The game itself can be used to give the players an extra stimulus.

7.7 THE WINTER BREAK

In many European countries there is a winter break. This is because snow, cold and ice often make it impossible to play properly. It is usual, and also sensible, to give the players a short period of additional rest during the winter break. This gives minor injuries the time to heal, and the players can also recharge their mental batteries for the coming months when the prizes will be won. However, this break does mean that the rhythm of training sessions and matches is interrupted, so another period of preparatory buildup is needed. This second period of preparation differs considerably from the first one at the start of the season. The break is shorter, as is the available preparation time. The deterioration in the players' fitness is also not as marked as during the summer. Coaches can therefore start with intensive rather than extensive conditioning immediately after the break. There is also more emphasis on technical and tactical work with the ball.

SUMMARY

- A period of preparation is necessary at the start of each season to build up the players' fitness. Often some players have left and others arrived, and a period of familiarization is therefore needed. Sometimes a new coach has arrived, with new ideas, and new agreements have to be reached.

- If players remain active during the summer months, an earlier start can be made on technical and tactical work during the preparation period.

- Endurance used to be regarded as the foundation on which fitness had to be built. In soccer there was a conditioning progression from continuous work to speed and then to sprinting. In accordance with the modern ideas of conditioning science, more emphasis is placed on strength, speed and endurance from the very start of the preparation period.

- However, there is still a transition from general to specific conditioning. During the initial preparation phase the focus is on conditioning for general acyclic aerobic and anaerobic endurance and general strength and speed. Subsequently more use is made of soccer-related drills. Even during the general phase, due account must be taken of the characteristics of the sport of soccer.

- In accordance with the modern ideas of conditioning science, it is advisable to focus first on extensive conditioning and then step up intensive conditioning.

- During preparation close attention must be paid to the work-to-rest ratio. There must be time for recovery during a single training session and between two successive training sessions.

- Conditioning for acyclic aerobic endurance should start with short runs of 2 to 3 kilometers with a change of pace every 30 to 60 seconds. There should then be a switch to continuous extensive and intensive conditioning, extensive interval training and fartlek training.

- Conditioning for acyclic anaerobic endurance should start with intensive runs over 100 meters. There should then be a switch to block training and intensive interval training.

- Conditioning for soccer strength should start with conditioning for basic strength as well as technique and coordination. A link must subsequently be established between general and specific conditioning for strength. Finally only specific conditioning for strength should be carried out.

- Conditioning for speed must start with preparatory drills. Then comes conditioning for pure speed and finally conditioning for speed in soccer situations.

- It is advisable not to schedule strenuous training sessions on the two days prior to a match. The players must have enough time to recover so that they can perform well. Such an approach prevents physical problems and false expectations with regard to the match.

- During the winter break the rhythm of the training sessions and games is interrupted. A buildup period is therefore necessary after the winter break. This is much shorter because the break is also shorter. The emphasis is soon placed on intensity and technical and tactical work.

FIVE PRACTICAL QUESTIONS

1. In general six weeks are assigned to the preparation period, with the emphasis gradually shifting from physical fitness to the technical and tactical level. Would it not be better to have two weeks of intensive conditioning, then a week of rest, then four weeks of specific soccer-related conditioning?

No. Specific soccer conditioning must be carried out from the very start. There should not be two weeks of just general conditioning. Moreover there is a good chance that the workload would be too much for the players in the first two weeks.

2. Must players be in top physical condition at the end of the preparation period?

This is probably impossible. They can only reach top form after a number of matches have been played. In top soccer the demand for players to reach top form quickly is increasing.

5. How should a youth coach deal with players who miss a couple of weeks of the preparation period because they are on vacation?

For the players, their "homework" is more important because they are inactive for a longer period. When they arrive back they must be gradually integrated into the team training sessions by letting them train partly on their own and partly with the others. During games they must slowly but surely be given more playing time.

4. When should the first practice game be scheduled?

Preferably after a full week of conditioning, and against a weaker opponent. During such games the coach should make maximum use of substitutions. As a result, players are not put under too much strain.

5. The physical aspect is less important in youth soccer, so the preparation period could be shorter. Is this correct?

The preparation period for youth players must certainly be shorter. Not just because the physical component is less important in youth soccer but because youth players suffer less of a deterioration in fitness during the vacation. The natural growth process also continues, which is not the case with adults.

INTERVIEW WITH DICK ADVOCAAT
(Coach of PSV Einhoven)

When does the preparation period for a new season start for you, as a coach?

For a coach, the preparation period for a new season begins during the previous season. That is when the first plans are made. Shall we go to a training camp, and where? How many games should we play, and against which opponents? If you leave these questions until after the end of previous season, you are already too late. When the players take their vacation the coach is often working on the composition of his squad for the following year. An ideal vacation situation is when you have won something, and you know that your squad for the following year is already complete. Then you can relax. Unfortunately that does not happen very often.

What happens during the first week of your preparation period?

During the first two days all kinds of tests are made in the hospital. We do this to get an insight into the players' physical condition. The intensity of the training sessions depends on the results of these tests. Then we have two training sessions on each of the three succeeding days. On the Saturday we carry out a shuttle test on the field. Sunday is a rest day.

To what extent do you expect your players to maintain their level of fitness during their vacation?

The players are given a list of activities to take with them. I regard this list as important, because it lets the players know what they can and cannot do. To what extent do they conform to the list? Obviously this is up to the players themselves and their own sense of responsibility. I think that most of the players are sufficiently active during the summer months. Those who do too little experience problems during the preparation period and only have themselves to blame..

Is the preparation period divided into phases?

The first one and a half weeks we train at our own complex. Then we go to a training camp somewhere in the Netherlands for a week. During this phase we work fairly intensively. Practice games are usually played against amateur teams from the 2nd class Dutch Soccer Association league or higher. These games are mainly used to practice routine patterns of play. They also serve as a change from the training camp. Playing games against relatively easy opponents relieves the everyday routine. This is important because the emphasis at a training camp is on the physical aspect. In addition there is a certain form of teambuilding, because you are all together. The most important part of the preparation is therefore the training camp. In the third week we start with more serious practice games, and the training rhythm is adjusted accordingly. From that moment there are less days with two training sessions, and the focus shifts gradually from physical fitness to technique and tactics.

How long does the preparation period usually last?
The total preparation period is six weeks, including the test days. I think that is long enough. Too much time should not go by before the first competitive match. If a coach has to make a lot of changes within the squad he might need more time to allow the players to get to know each other. More rest periods are then necessary.

The preparation period is gaining in importance because it is becoming more difficult to train during the season. Do you agree with this?
Not being able to train during the season is a complaint voiced by a lot of coaches, and I have this problem at PSV too. This makes the pressure on the preparation period greater. It becomes more important to lay a foundation that will endure until the winter break. Some intensive conditioning is possible during the season, but only when the fixture list permits. It is not often that we do not have to play in the middle of the week, but there are a few occasions. Unfortunately these rest periods usually occur because the Dutch national team is playing. Most of PSV's players can be given a conditional stimulus during such weeks, but not the internationals who have been picked to play for their country. There is therefore a danger of a conditional imbalance within the team.

Is there a big difference between the preparation periods you experienced earlier as a player and those you program now as a coach?
Nowadays not only the coaches but also the players are more knowledgeable with regard to conditioning. Over the years soccer has naturally become more of a profession. The players therefore take it more seriously, and this is reflected in the pre-season preparation. Previously we did a lot more continuous work and long-distance running. If we played on the Sunday we had a relaxed 30 or 45-minute run through the woods on the Monday. There was less emphasis on sprint conditioning. The tendency nowadays is to do everything in short bursts. We do this too. I can see the sense of this because soccer consists of a lot of short actions. On the other hand I think it is no bad thing if the players are occasionally made to go to their physical limits. Continuous work is very suitable for this. Not so much to improve their basic physical fitness, because that is maintained sufficiently just by playing matches, but to make them mentally tougher. Timed runs are also suitable. The players know that they have to finish within a certain time and therefore have to push themselves very hard.

Did you do any coaching in amateur soccer?
In the early 1980s I was the coach of DSVP in Pijnacker. The club plays on Saturdays. I had three fantastic years there. We were once unbeaten for 55 consecutive games. It was a village team and the players were all 22 and 23 years old and extremely keen. Due to their will to win, we twice won the championship. We held two training sessions each week, on Mondays and Thursdays.

What factors make it difficult for an amateur coach to prepare his team properly?
First of all you have less time. I suspect that my pre-season training sessions at that time were probably more strenuous than now. Because we had fewer training sessions we worked flat out for 90 minutes. At PSV the sessions are usually 75 minutes long and we can monitor the work-to-rest ratio much better. We simply have more time. We can spread the work out better. At PSV we look at the training program from week to week. At DSVP, however, the program was fixed from the very start. For five weeks we held three

training sessions per week and played one game. Naturally the players had day jobs. In addition, at amateur clubs you often have a large group of players, and that makes things more difficult. Finally the facilities are not always ideal, so you sometimes have to improvise because you can't use the field.

How did the Dutch international team prepare for major tournaments when you were the coach?

During the preparations for the World Cup in the United States in 1994, we were naturally confronted with the difficult circumstances under which we would have to play. It was important to acclimatize the players as well as possible. Together with our doctor, Frits Kessel, and physiotherapist Rob Ouderland, I tried to gain as much information as possible. Of course, there is always the question of the players' fitness when they come to you at the end of the season. After the end of the league competition, we first of all gave them a week's rest. When the players reported back afterwards you could see that they were eagerly anticipating the coming tournament. At that moment there is no question of fatigue as a consequence of the long and strenuous season. That feeling sets in when the European Championship or the World Cup is over. As a consequence the players' clubs often have to deal with this. We started the preparation period by testing the players to determine their physical condition. On the basis of the test results we decided to spend the first phase of the preparation period working very hard in the Netherlands. We knew that we would not be able to work like this under the prevailing weather conditions in the United States. I put myself in charge of the physical fitness sessions. There was no special fitness coach, although the conditioning program was drawn up with the help of the medical staff. Each evening we evaluated the day's activities again. It is clear that the players gradually became fitter as the tournament progressed.

What do you feel about the winter break?

Personally I am not in favor of a long winter break. A break of fourteen days would be sufficient. A long winter break has the disadvantage that two preparation periods are necessary during one season. During the first of them the players are very keen and will do whatever you ask of them. This is not always the case after the winter break. The players' basic fitness would remain intact during a short winter break and there would be less need to carry out a second preparation program. The only advantage of a long winter break is that there is time for all sorts of injuries to heal properly, so you can start the second half of the season with a relatively fit squad of players.

What would be the ideal duration and structure of a preparation period after a winter break, in your opinion?

During the pre-season preparation the working conditions are ideal. During the preparation for the second half of the season, however, it is virtually impossible to implement a planned buildup. Usually you have to improvise, so things do not run as smoothly as you would wish. The duration of the preparation period depends on the length of the winter break, and the number of free weeks that the players are given.

A lot of muscle injuries always occur during the preparation period. Have you encountered this problem?

It is unavoidable that players will have minor muscle ailments during the preparation period. The question is how you deal with this. I have never known players to suffer torn muscles. It also depends on how you coach. One of my main priorities is to keep the squad fit. If a number of key players drop out with injuries during the preparation period, you are forced to start again. This is why periodization is so important. If you start at maximum intensity and a few players pick up injuries you have a problem. We evaluate everything during the preparation period. How was the training session, was it too hard/too easy, how was the game? During the season we carry out hardly any tests, because you have no opportunity to react appropriately. We test at the start and end of the preparation period to enable us to evaluate it. Incidentally, you have to be very careful that you do not send the players the wrong signals when you carry out tests. If you test a player who is out of form, you can create the impression that perhaps there is a physical problem.

LITERATURE

1. The physiology of soccer,
J. Bangsbo.
ISBN: 87-983350-5-7.

2. Basis voor verantwoord trainen.
J. Vrijens.
ISBN: 90-70870-12-6.

3. Optimale training.
J. Vrijens.
ISBN: 90-70870-12-6.

4. Conditietraining zonder bal.
L. van Agt.
De Voetbaltrainer nr. 32.

5. Een voetbalprobleem met een conditionele doelstelling in de voorbereiding.
F. de Haan.
De Voetbaltrainer nr. 28.

6. Krachttraining in de voorbereiding.
F. de Haan.
De Voetbaltrainer nr. 32.

CHAPTER 8

TESTING SOCCER PLAYERS' FITNESS

Dr. Raymond Verheijen

8.1 INTRODUCTION

Fitness tests are important for all coaches. When a coach holds a training session he should always take a critical look at whether the desired effect has actually been achieved. Naturally a match is the best yardstick, but the fact that a match is won does not mean that every player also performed well. Soccer players can "hide" during a match, and in this way they can disguise a physical shortcoming. In the long term a lack of fitness is disastrous.

A coach must therefore ensure that he detects it quickly. Periodic fitness tests are an excellent aid in this respect. Soccer fitness is, however, extremely complex. This chapter is devoted to the testing of speed and endurance.

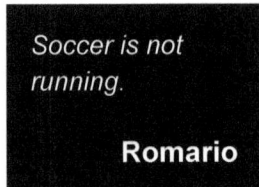

Soccer is not running.

Romario

8.2 THE UTILITY OF FITNESS TESTS

As stated above, tests can reveal a possible lack of fitness. However, such tests also have a number of other advantages.

Collecting information for drawing up a conditioning program

The content of a (fitness) conditioning program must always take account of the actual fitness of the players. This must be the starting point. The only way to obtain a picture of the physical condition of the players is to test them. This is important at the start of the preseason preparation period, when the players have just returned from vacation.

Assessing the effect of a conditioning program

The objective of soccer conditioning is to improve a player's ability to perform. This also applies with regard to the physical part of soccer conditioning. Specific conditioning stimuli are applied for the purpose of encouraging a supercompensation response in the body. It is advisable to check whether this really occurs by holding tests every 2 to 3 months. Naturally the tests used must measure the physical parameters that have been conditioned.

Measuring match fitness

Especially at the end of a long recovery process, it is often difficult to assess the exact moment when a player is ready to rejoin the group training sessions or even to play a match. A player's progress and his fitness deficit can be monitored by testing him on a number of aspects and comparing the results with those of tests carried out when he was fully fit.

Motivating soccer players

A competitive element can be introduced into fitness tests. No soccer player wants to be the worst in the group when a test session is held. As a result, all the players try to do their best. If one of them does score badly, this may be the motivation he needs to work extra hard on his weak points during training, so that he will score better when the next test is held.

8.3 WHAT PHYSICAL PARAMETERS SHOULD BE TESTED?

In the context of soccer players' speed and endurance, it has already been explained in Chapters 5 and 6 that the emphasis should mainly be on:
- speed off the mark;
- acceleration;
- speed endurance;
- repeated short sprint capacity;
- acyclic aerobic endurance;
- acyclic anaerobic endurance.

These are the physical parameters that have to be tested. The best way to do this is described below.

No one has yet devised a test to measure soccer ability.

8.4 SOCCER-SPECIFIC FITNESS TESTS

The most familiar fitness tests are the Cooper test and the maximal test (on a treadmill). In both tests the players run at an almost constant speed. The tests measure cyclic aerobic endurance, and are therefore not soccer-specific. The results of scientific research have recently been used as a basis for devising fitness tests that are more closely related to the realities of soccer. The starting point for the development of these tests was the physical work carried out by soccer players during a match (see Chapter 1).

8.4.1 Speed off the mark: the 10-meter sprint test

Speed off the mark is one of the most important physical attributes that a soccer player can possess. Soccer players have to make a lot of sprints over short distances during a game. The 10-meter sprint is eminently suitable for measuring the speed that soccer players can reach during the first 3 or 4 sprint strides.

Organization

The players sprint over a distance of 10 meters three times. The first time they do not run flat out. The best time of the second and third sprints counts. There must be a rest period of at least 3 to 4 minutes between two successive sprints. This prevents fatigue from influencing the test results. If large groups are involved, the players are bound to get sufficient rest because they have to wait until all of the others have had their turn. An electronic (infra-red) system should be used rather than a stopwatch to time the players, because the measured times will then be more accurate. Manual timing can result in errors ranging from 0.1 to 0.4 seconds. Changes in players' performances (for the better or worse) may fall into this margin and therefore remain unnoticed, or an improvement or deterioration may be detected when none has in fact occurred.

What does the 10-meter sprint test measure?

This test lasts about 2 seconds and gives an indication of the peak power that the phosphate system can supply. The greater the peak power, the more energy the phosphate system can produce per unit of time (in this case 2 seconds). A considerable energy flow is a prerequisite for explosivity during the first few sprint strides.

8.4.2 Acceleration: the 30-meter sprint test

A player requires about 25 to 30 meters to accelerate to his maximum sprinting speed. The 30-meter test is therefore suitable for measuring a player's rate of acceleration.

Organization

The players sprint over a distance of 30 meters three times. The first time they do not run flat out. The best time of the second and third sprints counts. There must be a rest period of at least 5 minutes between two successive sprints. This prevents fatigue from influencing the test results. In this case, too, an electronic (infra-red) system should be used in preference to a stopwatch.

> *The ball dictates the pace. There has never been a soccer player who is faster than the ball.*
>
> **Johan Cruyff**

What does the 30-meter sprint test measure?

This test lasts about 4 to 5 seconds and the score is a measure of the power and capacity of the phosphate system. This can perhaps be made clearer by comparing the phosphate system to a car. The power is then the maximum speed that can be reached and the capacity is the content of the fuel tank.

8.4.3 Speed endurance: the shuttle sprint test

The shuttle sprint test can be used to measure speed endurance. Sprinting over 10 meters five times reveals how well a player can retain his speed over a longer period. Initially the shuttle sprint test involved ten sprints over a distance of 5 meters, because players have to sprint over 5 meters more often than over 10 meters during a match, but in practice this proved problematical. The sprint distance is so short that players with long legs can often cover it in one stride. Sometimes the players started to turn while sprinting, and put their hands on the ground to help them to turn faster. In short, this test did not measure just speed endurance but also timing and agility. It was therefore decided to sprint five times over a distance of 10 meters, thus shifting the emphasis towards speed.

Organization
The players carry out the shuttle sprint test three times. The first time they do not run flat out. The best time of the second and third attempts counts. There must be a rest period of at least 5 minutes between two successive tests. This prevents fatigue from influencing the test results. An electronic (infra-red) system should be used in preference to a stopwatch.

What does the shuttle sprint test measure?
The test lasts about 10 to 12 seconds and the test score gives a clear indication of the capacity of the phosphate system. The greater the content of a player's "phosphate tank," the more capable he is of covering the final 10 meters at top speed.

8.4.4 Repeated short sprint capacity: the interval sprint test
The interval sprint test was developed to provide an indication of soccer players' powers of recovery between sprints. Five sprints of 10 meters are made, with an interval of 10 seconds between successive sprints. The best and the average sprint times can be determined, as well as the deterioration in the sprint times. This final aspect can be taken as a measure of a player's powers of recovery between sprints. The deterioration is of course a consequence of fatigue. The smaller the decrease, the better the player's powers of recovery. Figure 8.1 shows how the results of the interval sprint test can be processed.

Figure 8.1: An example of how the results of a 5x10 meter interval sprint test can be expressed.

	SPRINT 1	SPRINT 2	SPRINT 3	SPRINT 4	SPRINT 5
Time (sec.)	1.91	1.98	2.02	2.14	2.20
Best Time:	1.91 seconds				
Average Time:	2.05 seconds				
Decrease:	0.29 seconds				

Organization
The players carry out the interval sprint test twice. The best time counts. Two "timers" are needed for this test. One registers the sprint time, while the other signals when the 10-second pauses are finished and the following sprint has to start. The players must rest for at least 7 or eight minutes between tests to ensure that the results are not influenced by fatigue. In this case, too, an electronic (infra-red) system should be used in preference to a stopwatch. The 10-second pauses can be timed manually.

What does the interval sprint test measure?

The test lasts about 50 seconds (5x2 seconds + 4 x 10 seconds). The phosphate system supplies energy during the 10-meter sprints. After each sprint the phosphate system is partially depleted and has to be replenished. The faster this happens, the less chance there is that the phosphate system will become exhausted during the test. A small decrease in sprint time indicates that the phosphate system recovers quickly. The size of the "phosphate tank" also plays a role here. A player with a large "phosphate tank" will not be confronted with an exhausted phosphate system so quickly, and will experience a smaller decrease in performance during the test.

8.4.5 Acyclic aerobic endurance: the shuttle run test

It is clear that acyclic aerobic endurance is important for a soccer player. This is why the shuttle run test - a more soccer-specific version of the Cooper test - was specially developed. This test also measures endurance, but in this case the players have to continuously brake and accelerate.

The shuttle test involves running to and fro between two lines. The player is therefore continuously forced to brake and accelerate.

Organization

During the shuttle run test the players have to run up and down between two lines, which are 20 meters apart, at a steadily increasing speed. The players' running speed is specified by acoustic signals from a prerecorded cassette. Alternatively the coach can give signals by whistling. The coach has a specially developed list, which indicates exactly when he must give each signal. The players start to run with a speed of 8 km/hour. The speed is then increased by 0.5 km/hour after each elapsed minute. The players are informed of this by means of special acoustic signals. The increase in running speed is carried out in steps. The players must not run faster or slower than is indicated by the signals, and they must touch the lines with at least one foot. If a player has not reached the line when the signal comes, he must continue to the line and touch it with one foot before he turns and runs back. This is only allowed once. If a player arrives too late at the line a second time, the test is finished as far as he is concerned. He must then leave the test track as quickly as possible, without impeding the remaining players. The test result is expressed as the number of steps completed by the player, to the nearest half step. The last completed half or complete step counts as the result.

What does the shuttle run test measure?

During the shuttle run test the players' heart rate is gradually (and acyclically) brought to its maximum. The flow of blood through the muscles and rate of respiration also increase slowly but surely to a maximum. When the maximum heart rate is reached the body is producing the greatest possible amount of energy per unit of time. At that moment there

The match itself is the best and only test of a soccer player.

Bobby Robson

are no further sources of energy available. It is therefore not possible to accelerate to the next step of the shuttle test. The maximum heart rate, coupled to the step reached in the shuttle run test, is a measure of a player's aerobic endurance.

Heart rate measurements
It is worthwhile to measure the players' heart rates during the shuttle run test. The shuttle run test is a good, standardized test. A coach can use it to determine whether the heart rate at step 1, 2, 3, 4 etc. has changed since the previous test was held. If a player's heart rate at various shuttle steps is lower after a period of conditioning, then his endurance has improved. A player's heart rate can best be measured with a heart monitor.

Submaximal test
The players are expected to go to the limits of their capacity during a shuttle run test. However, this is not always necessary. A coach may decide to let his players run to step 10 or 12. The heart rate values measured during such a submaximal test provide sufficient information about any improvement or deterioration in endurance. The submaximal version of the shuttle run test can be used for players who cannot yet be pushed to the limits of their capacity after illness or injury. They can be tested without having to go to their limits.

8.4.6 Acyclic anaerobic endurance: the shuttle tempo test
The shuttle tempo test is used to measure soccer players' acyclic anaerobic endurance. However, a few words of caution are necessary with regard to this test. During the shuttle tempo test the players have to run 10 meters and back again, then 20 meters and back again, and so on until the distance reaches 50 meters. A total of 300 meters are covered. The test lasts for about 60 to 70 seconds. All the players who carry out this test experience considerable acidification. There is a buildup of lactic acid in the muscles and blood, and the players therefore experience extreme fatigue. Acyclic anaerobic endurance is tested in a manner that is of no relevance for a soccer player. During a match a player's anaerobic endurance is never subjected to the demands made on it in this test. At most, the shuttle tempo test should be used as a test of mental strength. The (too) extreme acidification exhausts the players, and it can be of interest for a coach to see how they cope with this. However, it is not advisable to subject soccer players to this test.

8.5 WHEN MUST ALL OF THESE VARIOUS TESTS BE CARRIED OUT?
If a coach decides to test the fitness of his players, he should do so regularly (3 or 4 times per year). It is, however, impossible to carry out all the above mentioned tests in one day. Not only would they take too long, but fatigue would influence the scores. It is therefore advisable to draw up a list of priorities, indicating which tests are most important and must certainly be carried out:

1. Acyclic aerobic endurance.
2. Speed off the mark.
3. Repeated short sprint capacity.
4. Acceleration.
5. Speed endurance.

A proper game is still the best test.

A test session should always consist of at least the first three tests. The following guidelines should be followed to prevent fatigue and avoid making the test session too long. Start with the 10-meter sprint, making each participant complete the test 3 times. Allow the players to rest for 5 minutes and then start the interval sprint. After all of the participants have completed this test twice, allow them 10 minutes to rest. Conclude the session with the shuttle run test. Such a test session should be held 3 or 4 times each year, e.g., at the start and end of the preseason preparation period and at the start and end of the winter break. Alternatively a test session can be held in the middle and at the end of the season. The other tests can be carried out now and then with individual players, if the coach finds this necessary. It is not necessary to do this in the form of a special test session.

8.6 STANDARDIZATION

It is important to carry out the tests under almost the same circumstances each time, so that the results will be genuinely comparable. Only then can changes in test results be regarded as a consequence of an improvement or deterioration in a player's fitness. A number of factors must be standardized to achieve this.

The surface underfoot
Differences in the surface underfoot can easily cause differences in test results. Synthetic turf is a surface that remains the same under almost all circumstances. A possible alternative is a gravel pitch. Of course, synthetic turf is not very soccer-specific, but holding tests on a grass pitch can be a very unpredictable business. In summer and winter the pitch is hard, while in autumn there is often a lot of rain and the pitch is therefore frequently soft. The contribution of the surface to the test results is then always an unknown factor.

Weather
Although the weather cannot be controlled, it is important that test sessions should, as far as possible, always be held under the same weather conditions. This means that a session must be postponed if the weather is very hot or very cold. Similarly it is advisable to postpone a session if there is a strong wind or heavy rain or snow.

Injuries and fatigue

Players who are carrying a minor injury should not participate in test sessions. First of all there is a risk of aggravating the injury. Secondly an injured player cannot perform at his best. A deterioration in such a player's results, in comparison with the previous session, may suggest that the player is less fit than he should be, whereas in fact his injury is to blame. Another factor that can cause poor test scores is fatigue. Players must be reasonably rested when they start a test session. The tests should not, therefore, be held during a week when, for example, the team has to play two matches.

Footwear

Careful attention must be paid not only to the surface on which the tests are held but also to the players' footwear. It is important that players have the correct footwear. It is advisable to wear specially developed sports shoes on synthetic turf, but such shoes are unsuitable for tests on grass; they provide too little grip.

8.7 TEST STANDARDS

The above mentioned fitness tests are a relatively recent development. There are therefore not enough data to indicate what is a good or bad result for players at a specific level. It is important that such data become available; the standards of physical fitness that suffice for a team in a lower league cannot be applied to a top level team. Moreover, the standards within a team differ (for example, between a goalkeeper and a midfielder). At the moment the test results can at least be used to check whether players are making progress or slipping back. The following rough guidelines apply to the shuttle sprint test and the shuttle run test.

	shuttle-sprint	shuttle-run
very good	<10.5 sec.	>13.30 min.
good	<11.0 sec.	>12.30 min.
moderate	<11.5 sec.	>11.30 min.
poor	>11.5 sec.	<11.30 min.

8.8 POST MORTEM

It is advisable to hold a "post mortem," in which the players' test results can be discussed. This is the moment to impress the players with the utility of the test sessions. The players will gradually come to appreciate the value of their own test results. They will know whether they have scored well or badly. This can encourage them to accept more responsibility for their own fitness. The players will feel more involved. The players can also be motivated during testing by introducing a competitive element. They will compare their scores.

SUMMARY

- Fitness tests are a useful means of obtaining information for drawing up a conditioning program, evaluating a conditioning program, checking match fitness and motivating players.

- The factors that should be tested are speed off the mark, acceleration, speed endurance, repeated short sprint capacity and acyclic aerobic and anaerobic endurance.

- The Cooper test and a maximal test (on a treadmill) are not soccer-specific.

- Speed off the mark can be tested with the 10-meter sprint test.

- Acceleration can be tested with the 30-meter sprint test.

- Speed endurance can be tested with the 5x10-meter sprint test.

- Repeated short-sprint capacity can be tested with the 5x10-meter interval sprint test.

- Acyclic aerobic endurance can be tested with the shuttle run test.

- The shuttle tempo test is not a good way of testing soccer players' acyclic anaerobic endurance.

- Speed off the mark, repeated short sprint capacity and acyclic aerobic endurance should always be tested during a test session (3 or 4 times each year). The other tests can be used occasionally.

- The following test elements must be standardized to enable the results of the tests to be compared: the surface underfoot, the weather conditions, and the players' footwear. Players should not participate in the test session if they are fatigued or injured.

FIVE PRACTICAL QUESTIONS

1. In soccer clubs there are often a large number of players in the group. What is the best way of testing them without taking too long?

It is best to work with a maximum of 16 players. The test session then lasts for 60 to 90 minutes. The group often consists of 25 to 30 players. One possibility is then to test the first and second teams separately. Another is to form two groups, with players from both teams in each group. This introduces a competitive element between first and second-team players.

2. Is it worthwhile submitting young players to fitness tests?

The growth process of children often varies widely. Young players of the same age are often in different phases of development. It is therefore difficult to use the results obtained from young players as a means of comparison between them. The most important function of fitness tests is therefore to document the development of each young player, and to check whether anything out of the ordinary occurs. It is meaningless to compare the players with each other.

3. Is it worth testing fitness during the preseason preparation period, and when is the best time to do so?

It is very worthwhile to use fitness tests in the preparation period. The first test should be held just after the preparation starts. This shows the basic fitness of the players when they return from vacation. Because the players have to give their utmost during the tests, it is better not to hold them on the first day of preparation. After one or two training sessions the players are more prepared for the tests and the chance of injuries occurring is smaller. The second test session should be held one week before the league competition resumes. This is the moment when the preparation work can be evaluated and when it can be seen whether the players have built up to proper match fitness.

4. An amateur coach does not always have the resources to carry out the fitness tests described in this chapter. Is there an alternative?

There are lists with times for the shuttle test. The coach can read them off and give a whistle to signal when the players should be at the other end. This is a good alternative to the prerecorded tape with whistle signals. For the other tests you only need cones and a stopwatch. That should be no problem for a coach.

5. Are there also tests of "soccer ability"?

Various attempts have been made through the years, but no suitably applicable battery of tests has been developed yet. One reason is that soccer is a very complex sport. A good test would have to address all the components of the game (technical, tactical, physical, etc.) and that is very difficult.

INTERVIEW WITH RONALD DE BOER (Ajax Amsterdam)

When you returned to Ajax from F.C. Twente you had to pass a number of fitness tests. What was that like?
I was surprised that I suddenly had to take the tests. I had never carried out that type of test and it was all new for me. First I had to do the shuttle sprint test, then the shuttle tempo test, and finally the shuttle run test. There was no specific reason for testing me. Van Caal was taking an interest in fitness tests, so it was logical that I should take them. At that time my fitness was better than it had ever been, so there were no problems with my transfer.

The tests were subsequently introduced for the whole squad. How did the players react?
The coach explained why we were being tested and what the results would show. The players therefore knew what was happening. Moreover the shuttle sprint test gives rise to a sort of contest, and soccer players like that. You always want to do better than the others. The shuttle tempo test was very hard though. Fortunately it is not used any more now. The acidification you were confronted with during the test had nothing to do with soccer. Most players did not like it because you had to run until you were exhausted.

Are the players aware of the principle behind the use of the heart monitor during the shuttle run test?
The heart rate is the most important aspect of the shuttle run test. By checking your heart rate during the various steps you can see how good your fitness is. If you have a lower heart rate after five minutes than the last time, you know that you have become fitter. A lower heart rate indicates that it costs you less effort at that step. The players know this and they therefore carry out the test very conscientiously. After all, they can immediately see for themselves how their fitness is progressing.

How often are you now tested?
Every three or four months we do a shuttle run test. We never have to go to our maximum though. We usually stop after seven minutes. The support staff look at our heart rate after the seven minutes. You can immediately see whether your fitness has improved or deteriorated. So there is no need to run to the 12 or 13-minute step. This is also a key reason why we do this test so often. If you have to run until you are exhausted every month, you gradually lose your motivation and at a certain moment the test also becomes meaningless. The shuttle tempo test is not carried out any more. Every three months we are tested for speed. The percentage of body fat is also measured. On such a test day we often work with two groups of 12 to 14 players. This is faster and means that you are finished within an hour.

What happens to the test results?
The result of each test is compared with the result obtained in the test session at the same time in the previous year. You can therefore see whether you are at the same level

as you were last season. The results of the shuttle run test, in particular, show that your endurance deteriorates in busy periods when there are a lot of games. Because there are always only three or four days between games, it is almost impossible to carry out intensive conditioning, or to put in enough hours of conditioning work in general. As a result your heart rate is higher during the shuttle run test. I was once ill when we had to do this test. My heart rate was consistently 10 beats too high for each minute. This is why you should only carry out these tests when you are fully fit. Injuries, fatigue, or in my case illness, can give a totally distorted picture of your fitness.

Are there marked differences in the test results of players in different positions?
I do not think that there are big differences. You do see that strikers and wingers score better in the sprint test. They need speed over the first few meters to carry out their task of escaping a marker and then taking the ball past their direct opponent. The players who wear the number 4 and 10 shirts do a lot of running during a game as a result of their linking role between defense and midfield, and midfield and attack. These players get good scores in the shuttle run test. That is logical, because if they did not have the physical capacity they would not be able to play in these positions. The task or function associated with a given position may require speed or endurance or even both of these together. I always finish in the top four when we carry out this test. That has a lot to do with the fact that I can run a good time. If I have to achieve 12 minutes, then I can do it. It is simply a question of mentality. Moreover I always want to win. Before we carry out the shuttle run test I am never very enthusiastic about it, but once we start I put everything into it. I think it is very difficult to compare players with each other. Some of them have a heart rate that only goes up to 165. That is a big difference in comparison with someone who has a heart rate of 200.

Do the test results show that you have become fitter during the last five years?
In the sprint test I now score better than five years ago. That is true of most players. In the shuttle run test my heart rate is much lower than it was a few years ago. I do not think that the shuttle test gives a complete picture of a player's soccer fitness. The way that you run during the test is not the same as during a match. I see that players who score just as well as, or better than, me are sometimes exhausted much earlier than I am during a match, although they have not run much more. In the shuttle test you run up and down after each other, while in a match there is a lot more variation.

Do you think that your improvement is due to the fact that you do a lot of sprint and coordination drills at Ajax?
Of all the innovations at Ajax in recent years, sprint and coordination drills have been the best. You can see that some players run much better and more easily over the pitch. It is a fact that Ajax players are often a stride faster. I think that this is due to the way we train. It is important that you concentrate fully on these drills. You have to focus consciously on placing your feet, pushing off for each stride, etc. If you do this you notice that you become faster. If you just regard training as a necessary evil, none of the drills will have any effect. You have to put everything into it when you carry out the short sprints.

LITERATURE

1. The MOPER-fitness test: manual performance scales.
J.H.F. Bovend'eert, H.C.C. Kemper and R. Verschuur.
De Vrieseborch, Haarlem.

2. The validity of testing soccer players.
K.J. Schilder and F.M. d'Herripon.
Faculteit der Bewegingswetenschappen, Vrije Universiteit Amsterdam, 1996.

3. Introduction to measurement on physical education and exercise science.
J. Safrit and T.M. Wood.
ISBN: 0-8016-7849-8.
Mosby.

4. Trainen met een hartslagmeter.
Sally Edwards.
ISBN: 90-73510-03-1.

CHAPTER 9

THE PHYSICAL ASPECTS OF GOALKEEPING

Frans Hoek

9.1 INTRODUCTION

Just as for field players, aptitude, technique, insight, communication and psychological and physical aspects are the factors that determine the performance of a goalkeeper and are the components of his overall fitness. This chapter deals in detail with the physical aspects of a goalkeeper's fitness. What a goalkeeper does during a game depends on how his team plays. The way in which a goalkeeper functions - also physically - is therefore dependent on the coach's philosophy. The philosophy of Frans Hoek is reflected throughout this chapter. A central tenet of this philosophy is that the goalkeeper must be accepted as a team player, equal in all ways to all the other players. The chapter starts by giving a brief description of the basic ideas of Frans Hoek's philosophy. This is followed by an explanation of the physical capabilities needed by a goalkeeper, and how to condition these capabilities.

9.2 WHAT DOES A GOALKEEPER DO DURING A GAME?

There is not much data available on the work carried out by goalkeepers during a game, although this information is of vital importance. The content of training sessions depends on what will be asked of the players during a game. The work carried out by a goalkeeper, just as the work carried out by a field player, is mainly dependent on his team's style of play and the strength and abilities of the opposition. This is the case when his team has possession, when the opposition has possession, and when possession changes.

Soccer philosophy as a basis for all goalkeeper conditioning

The manner in which a team plays and the strength of the opposition largely determine how a goalkeeper functions. Because goalkeeper conditioning must reflect what happens in real matches, the philosophy of play also determines how a team trains. The work of all goalkeeping coaches should be guided by a soccer philosophy. This philoso-phy is the starting point for each game (and training session) and leads, according to the coach, to the best results. Everything that a coach does must be geared to it. The task and function of each player, including the goalkeeper, should be described in detail as part of such a philosophy. Moreover, everyone should be aware of the philosophy and should apply it consistently during training sessions and matches. This is true of the coaches as well as the players. Good cooperation is essential, and communication plays a central role in this. At the start of the season, all those involved must have a clear idea of their ultimate objective and how this is to be achieved. If this is not the case, it will never be possible to achieve this objective in an organized manner.

9.3 THE FRANS HOEK PHILOSOPHY

The starting point of the Frans Hoek philosophy is that the goalkeeper is a team player, not just in word but also in deed. The goalkeeper is part of the team and is one of the links that lead to ultimate success. Just as every other player, the goalkeeper can be the decisive factor in a match, in either a positive or negative sense. Because the goalkeeper is just as important as every other player in the team, he has a right to receive optimal training and support. The creation of optimal working conditions for a goalkeeper demands a number of qualities from both the coach and the goalkeeping coach. They must have a good knowledge of, and insight into, everything connected with goalkeeping. They must also be able to impart this knowledge in the right way. One of the objectives of goalkeeper coaching is to improve the goalkeeper's fitness, so that he is able to carry out his function in the team as well as possible.

9.3.1 The task and function of the goalkeeper in the team

The Frans Hoek philosophy includes a very clear description of the task and function of the goalkeeper. Just like his teammates, the goalkeeper must make a positive contribution to the objective of the game - winning. As part of achieving this objective, the goalkeeper has two general tasks:

1. He must make the chance of conceding a goal as small as possible.
2. He must make the chance of scoring a goal as large as possible.

The specific description of the task of a goalkeeper is based on the three key situations of the game and the associated aims of the whole team. The general and specific tasks of the goalkeeper in each of these three situations are derived from these aims. The three situations are:

1. Possession
2. Opposition in possession
3. Change of possession

The general and specific tasks of the goalkeeper in each of these situations cannot be described before the general and specific task of the team as a whole is defined. The goalkeeper is a part of the team, and his functioning is therefore an aspect of the general and specific tasks of the team.

9.3.2 Possession

What is expected of the goalkeeper when his team has possession depends on the intentions of his team. The general and specific tasks of the team will therefore be described first.

The general tasks of the team as a whole
- Retain possession.
- Create chances.
- Score goals.

The specific tasks of the whole team
- Make the playing area as large as possible (width/length).
- Always aim to get the ball forward when possible.
- Play the ball wide in preparation for a through ball or a forward pass.
- The team must keep its shape.

The general tasks of the goalkeeper
Depending on what his teammates do, the goalkeeper must help to facilitate the buildup play so that goals can be scored or chances created. He must be able to send the ball to his strikers. He must not play the ball to teammates who are closely marked, and therefore have little chance of controlling the ball or holding it. He must certainly not do this in the vicinity of his own goal, where the buildup play should be kept as safe as possible.

- He must always aim to get the ball forward when possible.
- He must keep possession.
- He must take no risks in the buildup near his own goal.

The goalkeeper's specific tasks
When the goalkeeper is in possession, he must take the following considerations into account:

a. When to play the ball, bearing in mind the rules of the game (5 or 6 second rule, etc.).

b. The technique he will use:
- drop kick;
- volley;
- rolling the ball forward and then kicking it;
- rolling the ball out to a teammate;
- round-arm throw;
- over-arm throw;
- dribble (for instance, when he receives a backpass);
- goal kick;
- free kick.

c. Communication
- With the player he wants to send the ball to (in word and gesture).
- With the players who have to link up or close the gaps after the ball has been played.

When a player in the defensive line has the ball, the goalkeeper must take up position so that:
- his teammate can play the ball to him;
- he can react adequately if his team loses possession.

The goalkeeper must also communicate with the player in possession and the players around the ball.

When a player in the midfield line has the ball, the goalkeeper must take up position so that he can react adequately if his team loses possession. He must also communicate with the defensive line and, possibly, the midfield line.

A goalkeeper should also have good soccer technique

9.3.3 Opposition in possession

The task or function of the goalkeeper when the opposing team is in possession depends on the opposition's style of play. However, a number of general and specific tasks have to be carried out by the team as a whole and by the goalkeeper in particular.

The general tasks of the team as a whole
- Disrupt the opposition's buildup play.
- Win the ball back.
- Prevent goals and prevent the creation of goalscoring chances.

The specific tasks of the team as a whole
- Keep the playing area as small as possible.
- Defend towards the ball (pressing).
- Defend closer to goal (fall back).
- Defend towards the sidelines (squeezing).
- Pressure the player in possession.
- Mark closely in the vicinity of the ball and mark positionally further away from the ball (cover; zonal marking).

The goalkeeper's general tasks
Depending on where the opposition has possession, and the strength and abilities of the goalkeeper, he must intervene as best he can by:
- communicating, organizing and instructing;
- positioning;
- intercepting the ball as early as possible.

The goalkeeper's specific tasks

The goalkeeper's three above mentioned tasks can be elaborated on for two specific situations when the opposition is in possession. In one situation the ball is in play, while in the other the play has been stopped and must be resumed by the opposition. When the ball is in play (game situations), the goalkeeper must take the following considerations into account:

a. He must communicate with his teammates when:
- the ball is far away from his goal;
- the ball is in the danger zone (through ball, cross, shot);
- the ball is between him and a teammate.

b. He must take up position for:
- through balls;
- lobs;
- 1 against 1 challenges;
- crosses;
- shots and headers at goal.

c. He must deal with the ball with the help of the following techniques:
adopting the correct initial posture;
- footwork;
- jumping;
- catching;
- falling;
- tipping the ball over the bar;
- punching;
- challenging for a high ball;
- 1 against 1 challenge.

> *A goalkeeper must be vain. If he is not, he is unreliable. A good goalkeeper must pay attention to his appearance. He should want to look like a young god. That gives him confidence, and his teammates as well.*
>
> **Heinz Stuy**

When play is resumed, the goalkeeper must organize his teammates and communicate with them when the following situations arise:
- drop ball;
- kick off;
- throw in;
- free kick;
- corner;
- penalty.

9.3.4 The moment when possession is lost to the opposition

At the moment when a team loses possession, its players must rapidly switch from attacking to defensive mode. If no clear agreements have been made, organizational chaos may occur. The opposition can profit from this and score a goal by means of a well executed counterattack. The field players and the goalkeeper must therefore know exactly what they have to do in this situation.

The general tasks of the team as a whole
- The player nearest the ball must pressure the player in possession so that he cannot make a forward pass or take a shot at goal. This forces the player in possession to play the ball square, hold the ball, run with the ball, play the ball back or seek some other solution.
- All of the players must switch to defensive mode and make a contribution towards preventing the opposition from scoring, by:

a. Containing the opposition on the flanks. Players can block a shot or take up position to prevent any direct threat to goal.
b. Exerting pressure on the ball. If there are enough players in the immediate vicinity of the ball, the opposition players are closely marked.
c. Delaying the opposition players. If there are insufficient players in the immediate vicinity of the ball, they can adopt positional/zonal marking. Their main aim is to prevent the opposition from going forward rather than to win the ball back.

The goalkeeper's general tasks
The goalkeeper also has to switch over to defensive mode in terms of his positioning and thinking. He must avoid being surprised by a fast counterattack, a long ball forward or a through pass. He must communicate with his defenders and keep them alert.

9.3.5 The moment when possession is won from the opposition
When a team wins the ball it is important to switch as quickly as possible from defensive to attacking mode. The faster this is done, the harder it is for the opposition's defense to get organized in time. A rapidly executed counterattack can expose defensive disorganization and possibly create a scoring chance. This can only be achieved if everyone in the team is aware of his role.

The general tasks of the team as a whole
- The player who intercepts the ball or wins the ball back looks to play a long ball forward.
- Players who are further away from the ball take up position to receive the long ball forward. This may be the task of players from the midfield line, to reduce the risk of offside.
- The player who wins the ball can also push it forward and run on to it himself as a means of overcoming the offside trap.
- The players of the team in possession spread out to make the area of play as big as possible.
- The players of the team in possession try to remain out of the field of view of their immediate opponent.
- The teammates of the player in possession must try to anticipate his intentions and to distract the opposition's attention from him.

The goalkeeper's general tasks
The goalkeeper must always be prepared to intervene, whether by communicating with his teammates, receiving a backpass, intercepting the ball or, when he gains possession, restarting the play quickly.

9.3.6 Technique, insight, communication

In each of the three main situations in the game, the goalkeeper's tasks include elements such as dealing with the ball (technique), choosing the right position, being prepared to send a long ball forward (insight), and communication.

Goalkeepers must also have TIC (technique, insight and communication)

Technique
The goalkeeper makes use of his technique in dealing with every type of situation. Not only when he defuses a scoring attempt by the opposition but also when he or his team is in possession.

Insight
Goalkeepers and players must develop and exploit their soccer insight. The earlier a goalkeeper reads the intentions of the opposition in general and individual players in particular, the sooner he can react, for example, by taking up the correct position. The goalkeeper must also be able to recognize the strong and weak points of the opposition. Such knowledge can play an important role, for example, when the goalkeeper sends the ball into play.

Communication
This is not simply a matter of language but of gesture and eye contact. The basis for good cooperation between a goalkeeper and his defense is good communication. Being able to judge a bouncing ball is also a form of communication.

9.3.7 The match ingredients from a goalkeeper's point of view

During a match a goalkeeper is always confronted by a number of ingredients:
- the ball;
- his teammates;
- opponents;
- the rules of the game;
- the drive to score goals;
- tension/stress;
- time;
- space;
- goalkeeping materials.

9.3.8 Conclusion

Now that a sketch has been given of the goalkeeping philosophy behind this chapter, together with the goalkeeper's tasks and function, it is time to define the components of the goalkeeper's soccer fitness. The resistances that a goalkeeper has to overcome during a match have been clearly explained. A goalkeeper's fitness reflects his ability to overcome these resistances. It is not enough just to have a philosophy. A coach must be able to translate this philosophy into practice. In other words, he must work in a way that allows this philosophy to come to the fore.

9.4 THE FRANS HOEK METHOD

The Frans Hoek method recognizes a number of principles that apply at all times and in all places. The starting point of the method is the question, "What are the demands made by the game?" It is pointless to practice situations that never occur, or that have no clear relationship to the game itself. The task and function of a goalkeeper have been described in detail above. All of these elements must be incorporated in a coaching program. The translation of match-related information into practice and coaching drills is essential. The things that happen during

Goalkeepers also communicate with the ball.

a match must be recreated on the training field. Obviously they cannot be recreated identically, but the ingredients must be present. A central problem is the degree to which goalkeepers should be coached with, and in isolation from, the other players. In what sort of situations must they be coached with the other players, and how must this be done? Specific goalkeeping drills must be used. Goalkeepers should not be made to carry out drills that have nothing to do with what happens during a real game. Coaching and support must be provided in such a way that the goalkeepers and the other players do what both they and the coach think is best for them. If the players and the coach disagree about the soccer philosophy and methods being used, they have a problem. Youth players will be coached and supported differently than adult players. Field players and goalkeepers have to meet different challenges at every stage of their development.

> *I know from experience how it works. When you stand between the posts, you are in an environment where absurd laws apply. Outsiders cannot understand this at all. I can well imagine that they find goalkeepers disturbed, crazy and mad.*
>
> **Frans Hoek**

9.5 THE FRAMEWORK CONDITIONS

A coach may have an excellently thought out philosophy and method of working, but these will be of no avail if the necessary framework conditions are not in place. The framework conditions must therefore be examined before a start is made on coaching.

9.5.1 The coaching staff: composition and cooperation

It is always questionable whether goalkeepers are being given the coaching they need when they are put in the charge of an assistant coach. Such a coach is frequently given the task of "doing something with the goalkeepers." This is an unnecessary and extremely amateur approach. Nowadays enough information is available to allow coaches to work with a well structured program. There must be a good relationship and good cooperation between the chief coach and the assistant or goalkeeping coach. A joint philosophy is the basis for everyone's work. There must be mutual understanding. The chief coach must be approachable, even for criticism. Everyone must be aware of his tasks or function. Everyone must be aware of his responsibilities. What is expected of him, and how must he achieve this? A goalkeeping coach must always be accountable to the chief coach. After all, the chief coach always bears ultimate responsibility. The chief coach must indicate how he wants his team to play, and what he expects of his goalkeeper(s). The goalkeeping coach must indicate how this can be achieved with the current goalkeepers). The chief coach and the goalkeeping coach must be in agreement about how they will work together. The goalkeeping coach must know what he can and cannot do. Is he given separate coaching sessions to work with the goalkeeper(s), or does he have to wait until the chief coach gives him a signal? Can the chief coach suddenly interrupt a coaching session with the goalkeeper(s) if he needs a goalkeeper for his own coaching session? The latter situation is far from ideal.

9.5.2 Training resources

What resources and facilities are available? Are there enough balls to work with, and what is the condition of the training ground? Can training sessions be held during the day, or at night under artificial light? These are also factors that can influence how a coach's philosophy is translated into practice. The following minimum resources must be available:

- 10 to 20 balls (so that no one has to wait long for a ball to become available);
- 20 to 30 cones to mark off the training area;
- 10 to 20 small cones as markers and as goal posts;
- 2-4 lengths of cord (for goalkeeper tennis, etc.);
- 1 or 2 kickbacks (for warming up and practicing technique);
- goals (preferably portable and in different sizes);
- 1 or 2 soccer/goalkeeper tennis nets;
- 1 or 2 free-kick walls (for practicing how to deal with free kicks);
- 1 tactics board (for explaining game situations);
- 1 Top Coach file per coach.

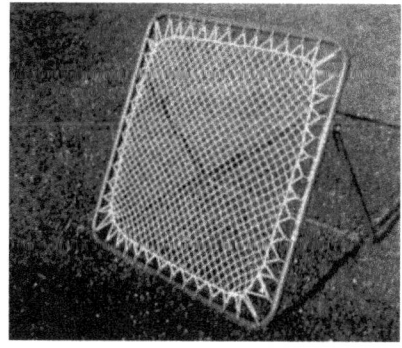

The kickback: ideal for practicing technique.

The Top Coach file is especially useful. It enables the coach to explain all kinds of game situations and restart plays. He can also use it to document all necessary information concerning training sessions and games.

9.6 THE GOALKEEPER'S SOCCER FITNESS

Just as field players need soccer fitness, goalkeepers need goalkeeping fitness. Although both types of fitness are based on the same five basic motor elements (strength, speed, endurance, coordination and flexibility), the importance of the individual elements is different. There are also differences between field players and goalkeepers in the way in which elements such as strength and speed are called upon. This is a consequence of the different tasks and functions of field players and goalkeepers. It is not the case that all the conditioning methods used for field players are equally suitable for goalkeepers. The content is different.

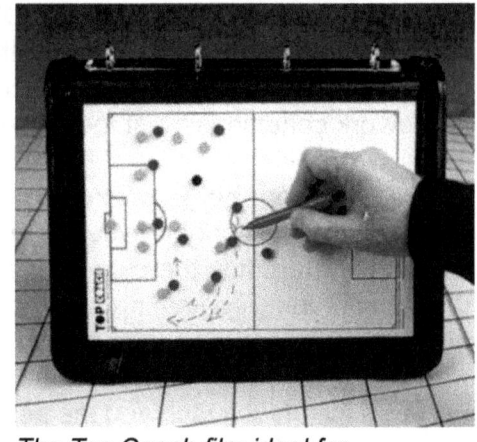

The Top Coach file: ideal for explaining game situations.

9.6.1 Speed

It has frequently been mentioned that soccer is becoming faster. This also affects goalkeepers. They too have to take decisions and act more quickly. In Chapter 1 it is explained that speed consists of five components. How important are these components for a goalkeeper?

Speed of reaction

This is the ability to react quickly to a local stimulus. In the goalkeeper's case such a stimulus can be the ball, an opponent, a teammate, the referee or the referee's assistant. Speed of reaction is crucial for a goalkeeper, because everything that he does during a game is in principle a reaction to a stimulus (e.g. a shot from close range, deflected shots or crosses, a long ball forward, a fast through ball). Speed of reaction must never be considered in isolation, however, but always in combination with other components of speed.

Speed off the mark

Speed off the mark is the speed with which the first few meters of a sprint are covered. For a goalkeeper this is important, because he often needs to take up a new position as quickly as possible, or to intercept the ball quickly before an opponent can become dangerous. In practice he makes very short sprints of no more than 5 meters. Speed off the mark is essential.

Acceleration

Acceleration capacity is the ability to extend a sprint to 20 or 30 meters. Sometimes a goalkeeper is forced to extend a sprint to 15 or 20 meters. This is the case if he comes out to deal with a long ball outside his penalty area. If the goalkeeper arrives a second or two too late, the player who has broken through may be able to run in on an open goal. There will also be a risk that the goalkeeper will pull down his opponent and be given a red card. Acceleration capacity is therefore a "must" for goalkeepers.

Speed off the mark means getting to the ball just before your opponent.

Speed endurance
This is the ability to maintain speed over a long sprint (6 to 10 seconds, 50 to 90 meters). A goalkeeper rarely has to make such sprints. He only needs speed endurance if he comes a long way out of his goal and then has to sprint back to deal with a lob. This is the least important component of speed for a goalkeeper. It is not, therefore, a significant part of goalkeeper conditioning and will not be mentioned again in this chapter.

Repeated short sprint capacity
This is the ability to make short, explosive sprints with only a short period of rest in between. More so than field players, goalkeepers tend to make short, explosive sprints followed by long(er), relatively restful intervals. Sometimes a goalkeeper has to sprint 2 or 3 times in a relatively short space of time. A well developed short sprint capacity ensures that he can carry out the final sprint in almost the same time as the first.

9.6.2 Endurance

Acyclic aerobic endurance
Aerobic endurance is the ability to maintain an effort for a long period. This is also important for goalkeepers. As part of the Frans Hoek philosophy, the goalkeeper is expected to change his position frequently and to move in response to the movement of the ball and the team. The goalkeeper must constantly take up new positions. Aerobic endurance is of less importance for a goalkeeper than for a field player, because the intensity of his movement is less, but a goalkeeper should be in motion for the whole 90 minutes of the game. Goalkeepers and field players are alike, in that the intensity of their movement fluctuates. Goalkeepers must therefore carry out conditioning for acyclic aerobic endurance. Monotonous long-distance runs are of no value for a goalkeeper.

Acyclic anaerobic endurance
Anaerobic endurance enables a player to maintain an intensive effort for a period of time (15 to 60 seconds) with hardly any rest. Such an effort results in the formation of lactic acid. A goalkeeper rarely or never has to work in this way. Anaerobic endurance is therefore of subordinate importance for goalkeepers, just as speed endurance, it will not be mentioned again in this chapter.

9.6.3 Strength

Strength should be used to overcome local resistance. A goalkeeper is confronted with a number of sources of resistance during a game:

- the ball;
- opponents;
- teammates;
- the condition of the pitch;
- the weather.

Despite these resistances, a goalkeeper must correctly carry out his task or function as described above. In addition to his basic strength he must therefore also possess good goalkeeper-specific:

1. Speed off the mark.
2. Jumping strength.
3. Catching strength.
4. Diving strength.
5. Punching strength.
6. Strength in the challenge.
7. Kicking strength.
8. Throwing strength.

From this list it is clear that a goalkeeper needs to develop both his upper body and lower body. Like speed, strength consists of a number of components. These are maximum strength, explosive strength, fast strength and strength endurance. For the conditioning of strength, it is important to know what role each of these strength components plays in the various actions carried out by a goalkeeper. In soccer it is not important who has the biggest and strongest muscles. A player's general strength must be brought to an acceptable level, but once this has been achieved it is better to focus on other strength components. In soccer it is not so important how much strength is available, but rather when strength is used, and with what speed or explosive power. This also applies with regard to goalkeepers.

9.6.4 Flexibility

It is important that a goalkeeper has good flexibility. This enables him to carry out specific goalkeeping actions technically correctly. A goalkeeper has to be able to twist in all sorts of directions to control the ball and prevent an opponent from scoring. This subject has been dealt with in detail in Chapter 3.

9.6.5 Coordination

Coordination is the technique that is needed to carry out all soccer movements and goalkeeping actions. Only the coordination that is needed for keeping goal should be conditioned. Coordination is not simply needed to deal with the ball. During a game, a goalkeeper sometimes has to move at great speed in all sorts of directions. His center of gravity switches alternately from left to right, and forward and backward. Physical coordination

Flexible hips are needed for goalkeeping actions.

is therefore very important if he is to retain his balance. The goalkeeper's footwork deserves special attention. A goalkeeper must always be able to adjust to the requirements of the changing game situation. Coordination is also important in strength conditioning (see Chapter 4). It is not enough for a goalkeeper to be strong; he must also be able to handle his strength adroitly. Considerable strength can be controlled with the correct coordination. Finally, good coordination is essential if injuries are to be avoided.

9.7 CONDITIONING GOALKEEPING FITNESS

Now that the components of goalkeeping fitness have been explained, it is time to turn to how goalkeeping fitness can be conditioned. A coach must always try to identify situations in which the learning effect will be at a maximum, so that the goalkeeper's capacities improve as much as possible. A number of aspects must be taken into consideration in this context. Soccer-specific or goalkeeper-specific elements, which bear a relationship to the requirements of the game, should be employed at all times and under all circumstances. Do not use general drills. There are plenty of books full of drills, each of which is more unnatural and further removed from reality than the other. Everyone should make his own choice of what is worthwhile, but, from the point of view of the Frans Hoek philosophy and method, the effect is far from maximal. Goalkeepers do not learn to play any better by performing all kinds of circus drills. Goalkeeping ingredients must be present in all drills. The objectives of a conditioning program must be clear. It must be well structured and understandable for all those involved. If there is a soccer problem, the coach must explain it, answer questions and communicate clearly, so that it becomes a problem of the individual goalkeepers or players, or of one of the lines that make up the team, or of the whole team. A coach can only be a presenter. It is not the coach who is important - it is the goalkeepers and the players. This is why making things understandable is so important. Coaching must be finely dosed, so that objectives can be achieved. Never present too much information at once. Try to set realistic objectives. What can be achieved, and what are the consequences? Sometimes a coach wants to achieve too much in too short a time. Consider how much the players can take in. If the above ideas are put into practice, it is possible to create an ideal learning situation, in which a goalkeeper's fitness can best be developed. This applies to all components of goalkeeping fitness.

9.7.1 Speed

Chapter 5 was largely devoted to speed conditioning. Speed conditioning is also one of the central aspects of goalkeeper conditioning. This factor occupies a crucial place in goalkeeping fitness. The conditioning methods and drills described below are all relevant to conditioning for (goalkeepers') speed components.

Speed of reaction

Speed of reaction is the ability to react quickly to something without consciously thinking about it. Speed of reaction is genetically determined and is difficult to condition. On the other hand a goalkeeper with good speed of reaction does not necessarily have good goalkeeping reflexes. Speed of reaction must be translated into the goalkeeping situation, and that can be conditioned. Drills must be used that translate speed of reaction into goalkeeping reflexes. A goalkeeper must be taught how to react instantly to match-specific situations, before he has the chance to make a conscious choice. Speed of reaction should never be conditioned in isolation but always in combination with goalkeeping actions. Speed of reaction is never an isolated phenomenon. A goalkeeper must react quickly, so that he can then carry out another action.

Conditioning method

Duration: less than 1 second
Intensity: 100%, starting with full concentration
Repetitions: 8 to 10
Sets: 2 to 4
Rest: 20 seconds between repetitions
2 to 3 minutes between sets

Drill 1: Reacting quickly to a shot from close range

Close-range shots are made at goal in rapid sequence, from all possible positions. Small goals can be used, so that most of the shots hit the goalkeeper's body. If full-size goals are used, the balls will automatically tend to be further away from the goalkeeper. The goalkeeper must adopt the initial posture at the correct moment and deal with the balls by means of reflex goalkeeping actions. The stationary or rolling ball can be kicked towards goal by the goalkeeping coach or by another player or another goalkeeper.

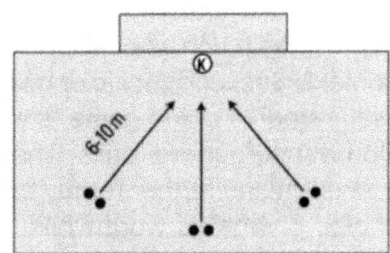

Drill 2: Reacting quickly to deflections

A row of cones is laid about 5 to 8 meters from the goal with the tips towards the player. The player then shoots at the cones. The goalkeeper has to anticipate the direction the shot will take after striking the cone. He therefore has to wait longer and react faster to prevent the ball from passing him.

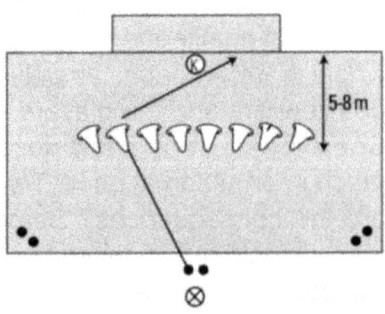

Variant: In place of cones, another player (or goalkeeper) can be told to stand in front of the goalkeeper to deflect the ball. This player need not stay in the same place.

Speed off the mark

The sprints made by a goalkeeper during a game are usually short (1 to 5 meters). Conditioning the push-off strength of the first stride is therefore important for a goalkeeper. The emphasis must be on explosive power. Chapter 5 deals with the conditioning of this aspect in detail. Speed off the mark is also genetically determined to a large extent. Speed can be conditioned better if the appropriate genetic endowment is present. Chapter 5 deals purely with speed off the mark. It must now be translated into goalkeeping terms, and this is why it is dealt with here in the section on speed off the mark. Speed off the mark in goalkeeping situations can best be conditioned by getting the goalkeeper to make a short sprint preceded and/or followed by a goalkeeping action. Incorporate recognizable game situations in such drills as much as possible.

Speed can make the difference between winning and losing.

Conditioning method

Duration:	2 seconds
Intensity:	100%, from a stationary start
Repetitions:	4-6
Sets:	2-4
Rest:	30 seconds between repetitions
	4-6 minutes between sets

Combining the short sprint with a goalkeeping action makes the drill harder. It is therefore necessary to give the conditioning method a different content to that for field players. The number of repeats per series must be decreased. Improving a player's speed off the mark is simply pushing back a threshold. If he is to reach this threshold during each repetition, he must be able to rest sufficiently between repetitions to allow him to recover completely.

Drill 3: Speed off the mark in the forward direction
An attacker pushes the ball a few meters ahead. At this moment the goalkeeper must sprint forward to narrow the angle. When the player shoots, the goalkeeper must have adopted the "ready" posture for dealing with the shot. The attacker can approach from left, right or through the middle. He should follow up after each shot to put additional pressure on the goalkeeper.

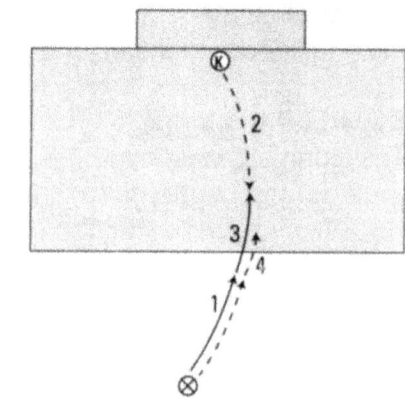

Variant: A player hits a volley into the penalty area. The goalkeeper must deal with the volley without letting it touch the ground.

Drill 4: Speed off the mark in the sideways direction
After a low or a high cross, the goalkeeper must sprint sideways in an attempt to narrow the angle for the attacker, who takes the cross and tries to score. The goalkeeper must sprint, narrow the angle, adopt the "ready" posture and then deal with the ball. The crosses can come from either right or left.

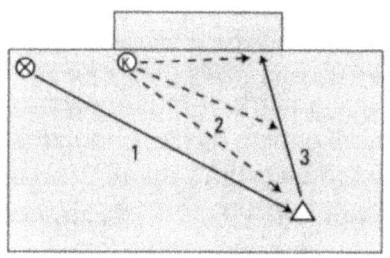

Drill 5: Speed off the mark in the backward direction
The goalkeeper stands 6 to 8 meters in front of the goal. The ball is lobbed over him and he has to spring backward to deal with it. The lobs can be made from left, right and through the middle.

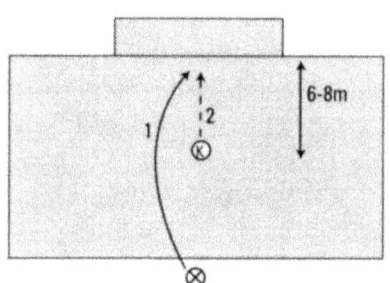

Drill 6: Getting back up and choosing position
The goalkeeper must dive to save a shot and then choose position again, adopt the "ready" posture and save the next shot. The shots can come from left, right and through the middle.

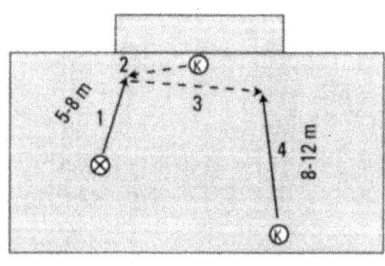

Acceleration
Once the body is in motion (speed off the mark), it is necessary to accelerate by increasing the stride rate. A number of acceleration drills for field players are described in Chapter 6. Naturally, more specific drills must be used for goalkeepers. The idea remains the same. Because goalkeepers have to make sprints of more than 20 meters less often than field players, the number of repeats is adjusted accordingly.

Conditioning method
Duration: 2-6 seconds
Intensity: 100%

Repetitions: 3-4
Sets: 1-2
Rest: 1-2 minutes between repetitions
4 minutes between sets

At higher sprint speeds, the period of contact between foot and ground steadily decreases. The time for generating push-off strength therefore becomes shorter. The emphasis is on fast strength.

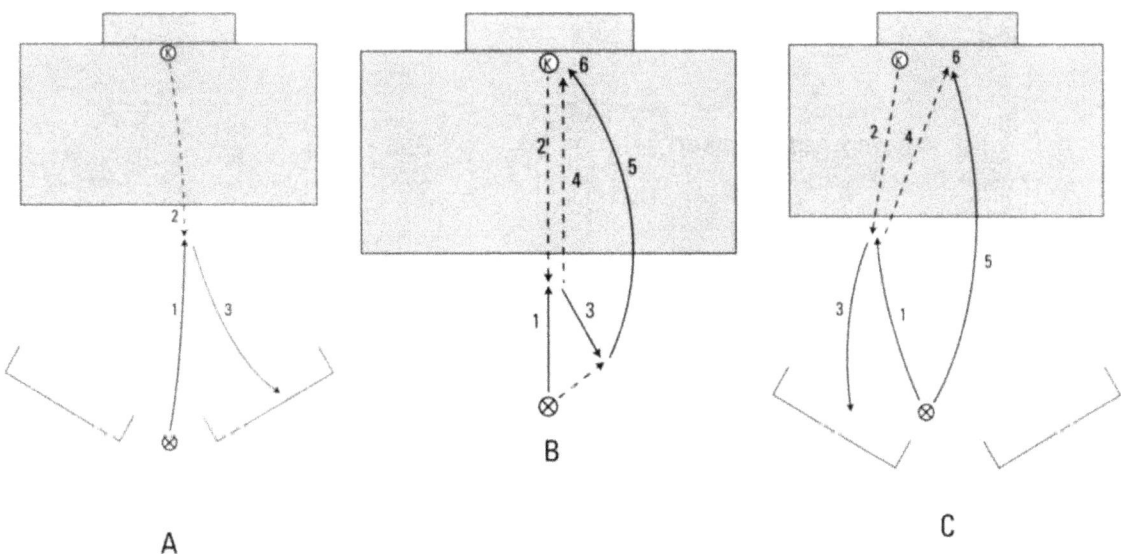

Drill 7A: Intercepting/dealing with a long ball forward
The goalkeeper must sprint from the goal area to outside the penalty area (15 to 20 meters) to deal with a ball played towards him. This can be a long ball forward or an underhit backpass. To practice putting the ball back into play after a long ball forward, the goalkeeper must place the ball in one of the goals after dealing with the long ball forward.

Drill 7B: Dealing with a lob from outside the penalty area
The goalkeeper sprints outside the penalty area, plays a 1-2 with the coach and sprints back towards his goal to deal with a lob. This situation occurs during games when a goalkeeper gives the ball away when he is out of his goal.

Drill 7C: Dealing with a lob from outside the penalty area
Instead of playing a 1-2, the goalkeeper must try to place the ball accurately by scoring in the goal.

Repeated short sprint capacity
Repeated short sprint capacity can be conditioned very well by combining short sprints and goalkeeper actions, in a similar way to conditioning for speed off the mark. Goalkeepers rarely have to sprint in isolation, but they often sprint before or after carrying out an action. In principle the same drills are used as for speed off the mark. The conditioning method

also remains the same. The difference is that, in this case, a rest period of 5 seconds is allowed between the repeats. Because the rest period is shorter, the emphasis of the drill is shifted towards its repeated character and away from pure speed. A complete recovery is not necessary. Conditioning for repeated short sprint capacity is about learning to sprint despite feeling fatigued.

Conditioning method
Duration: 2 seconds
Intensity: 100%
Repetitions: 4-6
Sets: 2-4
Rest: 10 seconds between repetitions
              4-6 minutes between sets

Drill 8: Goalkeeper tennis
This is played in two zones, with one goalkeeper in each zone. One goalkeeper has to kick (drop kick, volley) or throw the ball into the zone of the other. If it touches the ground in the other goalkeeper's zone he scores a point. The goalkeepers are therefore forced to make lots of short sprints in all directions, combined with goalkeeping actions.

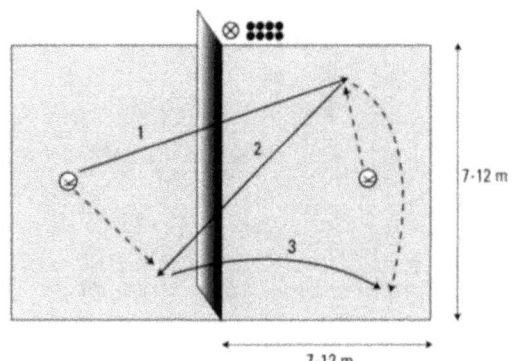

9.7.2 Acyclic aerobic endurance
Conditioning for endurance is always a matter of finding the right balance between the extent and intensity of the drills. The higher the intensity, the shorter the extent of the training session, because fatigue sets in. Aerobic conditioning for goalkeepers is described below in more detail. Use is made of conditioning methods with a variety of ratios of extent to intensity.

Continuous extensive conditioning
In continuous extensive conditioning the emphasis is on the extent of the drills. The goalkeeper's body is taught to be active for long periods.

Conditioning method
Duration: 30-90 minutes
Intensity: 50% of maximal work load (180 heartbeats per minute - age),
Repetitions: none
Rest: none

Drill:
In practice, any small sided game played on a large pitch for 30 to 90 minutes is continuous extensive conditioning for a goalkeeper, provided the play switches frequently from end to end and the goalkeeper is actively involved.

Continuous intensive conditioning

Continuous intensive conditioning is a type of conditioning in which both the extent and the intensity of the drills play a role. The players usually work in five blocks of 6 to 8 minutes. The goalkeepers therefore have to work for a long period (5 x 6-8 minutes = 30-40 minutes), but high intensity work is also possible because they are allowed to rest during the blocks.

Conditioning method

Duration: 30-40 minutes
(5x6 - 5x8 minutes)
Intensity: 160-180 heartbeats per minute
Repetitions: 5
Rest: 5 minutes between each repetition

Drill:

This type of conditioning is carried out during small sided games. The distance between the goals is shorter (30-50 meters). The intensity is higher for the goalkeeper because more is demanded of him. One of the ways in which this is reflected is in a higher heart rate. To maintain a high intensity during such drills, the game always starts with the goalkeeper and there are no corner kicks. Instead the goalkeeper of the team that would normally have been awarded a corner kick restarts the play at the other end of the pitch. There must be sufficient balls in and around each goal, so that the game never or hardly ever comes to a stop.

Whatever the situation, goalkeepers should only dive if it is absolutely necessary.

Extensive interval training

During extensive interval training the emphasis is on the intensity of the drills. As the name suggests, the emphasis is on working with intervals. Extensive interval training for goalkeepers can best be carried out with the help of finishing drills. Goalkeepers have to deal with all sorts of goalscoring attempts in rapid sequence. If such drills are carried out properly, the intensity of the goalkeepers' work is very high. It is therefore best to work with two goalkeepers per goal. One of them stands in goal for 30 to 45 seconds and is then replaced by the other. The work to rest ratio is then 1:1. Each goalkeeper takes 6 to 8 turns at standing in goal, and then has 2 to 4 minutes rest. The sequence is repeated 2 to 4 times.

Conditioning method
Duration: 30-60 seconds
Intensity: 170-180 heartbeats per minute
Repetitions: no more than 8 per sets
Sets: 2-5
Rest: 45-90 seconds between repetitions
4-6 minutes between each sets

Drill 9: Goalkeeper '1 against 1' with shots at goal ('war')
Two goals stand 20 to 30 meters apart. In each goal is a goalkeeper. Each goalkeeper must try to score past the other by shooting and throwing the ball. The goalkeepers thus fight a duel.

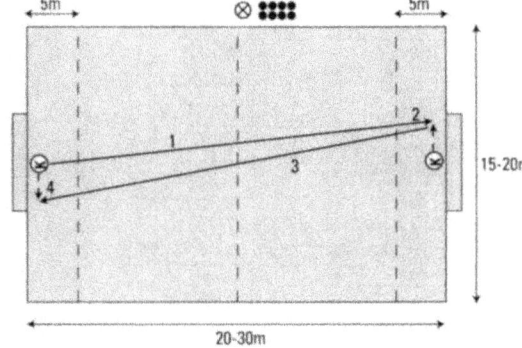

9.7.3 Strength
In Chapter 4 it is explained that muscle strength is made up of the following four components:

1. Maximum strength.
2. Explosive strength.
3. Fast strength.
4. Strength endurance.

In many sports, the purpose of strength training is to increase maximum strength. Although goalkeepers also need basic strength, strength training for goalkeepers is not primarily aimed at improving their maximum strength. It is more important that the strength that is already available can be translated into explosive power and speed during the whole 90 minutes of the game. The emphasis is therefore on explosive strength and fast strength. Many people find it difficult to explain the difference between these two components, which have already been dealt with in Chapter 4, on page 82. A goalkeeper needs explosive strength, for example, when he dives for the ball from a standing position. From a state of rest (speed 0), his body has to be moved to another position by means of a considerable explosion of strength. As the name suggests, fast strength is more concerned with speed than with strength. Sometimes a goalkeeper needs to exert strength when he is already in motion, for example, when he intercepts a cross after a short sprint. The strength he exerts to push off from the ground is much less than when he jumps from a stationary position, but because he is already in motion, and therefore has a higher starting speed, he can jump higher. Explosive strength is therefore called on when a goalkeeper requires explosive peak strength to carry out an action from a relatively stationary position. If a goalkeeper performs an action when he is already in motion, he needs to translate his speed into (push-off) strength. We will return to this point a number of times as this chapter unfolds. The intention is to point out that there is a difference in coordination. An 'explosive' goalkeeping action requires completely different coordination to a 'fast strength' action, and this must be taken into account during training sessions. During training sessions, players must practice what they have to do. Finally a goalkeeper must be able to do his job properly even in the final minute of a game. If he is to be able to call on reserves of strength for long periods of time without becoming (too) fatigued, he needs strength endurance.

Basic strength

Especially during the preparation period, the strength of the muscles of the arms, shoulders, chest, back, stomach and legs must be brought up to an acceptable basic level by means of general drills. Once this has been achieved, specific strength drills can be introduced. These are used to condition the strength component that is specifically needed for a given goalkeeping action. Some of the general strength drills described in Chapter 4 are also eminently suitable for conditioning goalkeepers. Each drill should be carried out in 2 or 3 series of 8 to 12 repeats.

Starting strength

Starting strength is listed here for the sake of completeness, but conditioning for general starting strength has already been described in detail in Chapter 4. These drills are very suitable for goalkeepers. For them, too, it is the case that choosing the right moment is important as well as pure speed. This can only be learned in real game situations such as those described in section 9.7.1.

Jumping strength

A goalkeeper needs jumping strength to enable him to intercept a cross or deal with a high shot at goal. With the help of good timing, this strength is translated into a jump. This can be made from a standing start or while already in motion. There is a crucial difference between the two. A jump from a standing start requires explosive strength and a jump while already in motion requires speed strength. The control of the muscles (coordination) is essentially different in the two cases. These are therefore different goalkeeping actions and must be practiced separately. As already mentioned, jumping drills are not just aimed at developing more strength. Technique is still the basis. Before jumping strength (or catching strength, diving strength, punching strength, throwing strength or kicking strength) is conditioned, the correct technique must have been mastered. This is where the most gains can be made.

Drill
- **From a standing start**

The ball is thrown above the head of the goalkeeper. From a standing start he must make an explosive jump to reach the ball.

Jumping strength from a stationary start: explosive strength.

- **From a moving start**

The ball is thrown to the side, in front of/behind the goalkeeper. The goalkeeper must therefore make a short sprint and then jump to reach the ball. His horizontal starting speed must be translated into vertical jumping strength. The goalkeeper must learn to take off on both the right and left foot.

Catching strength

The safest way to deal with the ball is to catch it. When the goalkeeper has the ball in his possession the opposition cannot do anything about it. It is important for the goalkeeper to get his body behind the ball. If this is not possible when catching a hard shot, the hands and arms must take the speed off the ball. It is not sufficient just to place the hands behind the ball to do this. At the moment when the ball enters the goalkeeper's hands, the arm muscles must be capable of maintaining the catching posture. This requires static muscle work.

Jumping strength from a mobile start: explosive strength.

Drill

The goalkeeper has to catch shots (e.g., drop kicks) from close range (8 to 10 meters) above and close to his body. In this situation he cannot get his body behind the ball. He therefore has to rely on good catching technique and the strength of his arms. Shots can be hit hard and low to give him practice in catching the ball with his fingers pointing downward. In this situation, it is also not always possible to get the body behind the ball.

Diving strength

Although diving and jumping have many similarities, diving is treated separately here. These are two completely different goalkeeping actions. Diving involves taking off in a more horizontal than vertical direction, and exactly the opposite applies to jumping. This makes a big difference in terms of coordination. Diving can also be carried out from a standing or a mobile start, although rather less so than is the case for jumping. The emphasis is again on, respectively, explosive and fast strength. It is important that a goalkeeper acquires a good diving technique before other coaching objectives are pursued. Poor diving technique can result in (chronic) injuries. Work on a good technique must start at a young age. A kickback is an ideal piece of equipment for this purpose.

Drill

From a standing or mobile start, the goalkeeper must dive onto the ball, which is played gradually further away from him (preferably by kicking it). He must only dive if it is necessary.

Diving strength from a stationary start: explosive strength.

Diving strength from a mobile start: fast strength.

Punching strength
Sometimes a goalkeeper cannot catch the ball. He may then decide to punch it away. The objective of punching the ball is to send it in another direction, preferably well away from goal, to a teammate. A special technique is required to carry out this action properly. The ball has to be punched correctly rather than strongly. Only when a goalkeeper can punch correctly should he try to punch it more strongly.

Drill
Punching the ball from a standing position is practiced first. An element of resistance must be introduced later, combined with a functional jumping action.

Strength in the challenge
A goalkeeper also has to challenge for the ball. When he intercepts a cross or a corner, and whether he has his feet on the ground or in the air, a goalkeeper runs the risk of being pushed by an opponent who is also trying to win the ball. Strength in the challenge is also necessary when a goalkeeper blocks the ball with his hands or body. It is

A goalkeeper must be strong in the challenge, whether in the air or on the ground.

important that the goalkeeper wins these challenges. He must therefore develop his upper body strength (see Chapter 4). At the same time he must remain supple and retain his technique. It is not simply a matter of developing more strength. A goalkeeper must learn to use his body when he challenges for the ball. Whenever possible, therefore, drills must include resistances that are similar to those encountered by goalkeepers during a real match.

Kicking strength

A goalkeeper can kick the ball in two ways: from his hands or from the ground. A keeper can use these kicks to send the ball to a teammate. Sometimes such a teammate will be a long distance away. In this case the goalkeeper must be able to call on his well developed kicking strength. As in all goalkeeping actions, the emphasis is on technique. The ball must not only be kicked over long distances but it must also be kicked accurately. Kicking strength alone is of little use. Clearly, the coordination required to kick the ball from the hands differs from that needed to kick the ball when it is on the ground. Both methods must therefore be practiced separately.

Drill 10: Kicking from the ground

When he receives a backpass, or a long ball forward, or taps the ball forward himself, a goalkeeper kicks the ball from the ground from a mobile start. This can initially be practiced in a fairly simple form. The goalkeeper plays the ball to the goalkeeping coach, who plays the ball back to him so that he can kick it to the goalkeeper in the other goal. The other goalkeeper then repeats the exercise.

Drill 11: Kicking out of the hands

The goalkeeper must kick the ball into one of the three goals (or goals formed by cones). He must indicate which goal he is going to aim at before he kicks the ball. By gradually moving the goals further away, the goalkeeper is forced to kick the ball harder and further. He therefore develops his kicking strength. The goals may only be moved when the goalkeeper can kick the ball (fairly) accurately over the current distance.

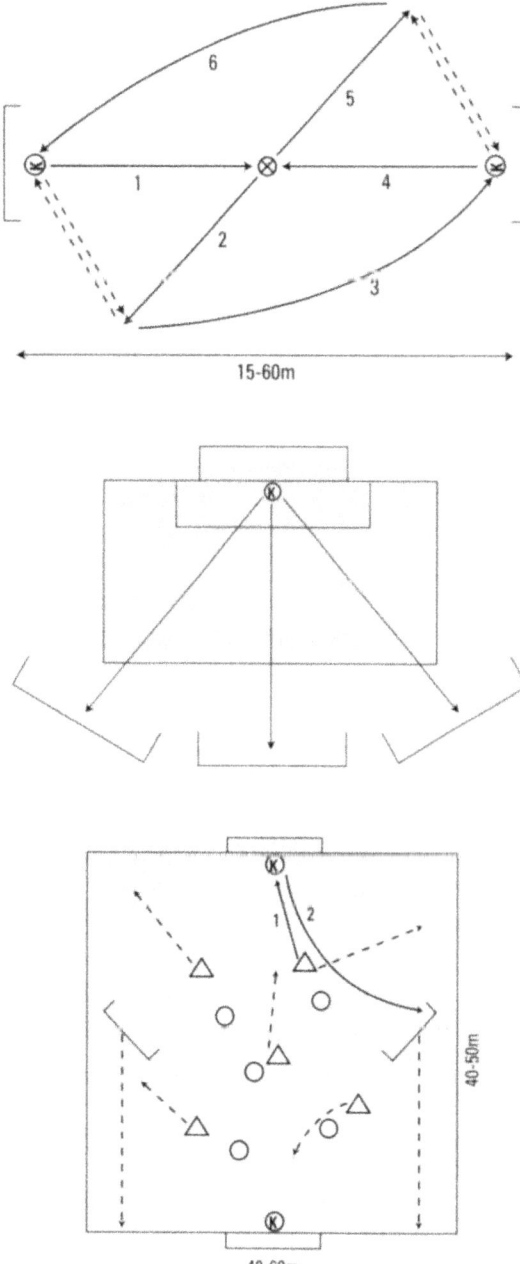

Drill 12: Kicking while under pressure

In a real game, a goalkeeper often has to pass the ball to a teammate when under pressure from an opponent. This must therefore be practiced in competitive drills. During a game of 4 against 4, the goalkeeper can score by kicking a backpass into one of the three goals. He must only do this if no better option is available. If there is a better option, he must play the ball to a teammate.

Throwing strength

The goalkeeper can also throw the ball to a teammate. Just as a kick, a throw may also have to be made accurately over a long distance. Again a combination of strength and technique is needed. There are a number of methods of throwing the ball (overarm, round arm, rolling). Each of these methods must be practiced.

Drill

Throwing strength can be practiced in the same situation as in drill 11. The goalkeeper must throw the ball into one of the three goals. The goals can be gradually moved fur-ther away to force the goalkeeper to develop more throwing strength. A cone can be placed in each goal to help improve accuracy. The goalkeeper must try to hit the cone. At a later stage the cone must be hit full on. The ball must not bounce just in front of the cone. A bouncing ball is more difficult for a teammate to control.

Goalkeeping drills = strength conditioning

Conditioning for physical strength in specific goalkeeping situations can be carried out ideally as an element of the goalkeeping drills on the training pitch. Strength can be integrated into drills for practicing and improving technique. All goalkeeper-specific running, jumping, diving, falling, throwing, punching and kicking actions are elements of strength conditioning. The body's own weight or some other resistance has to be overcome each time. Many goalkeepers still think that weight training is the best way to build up strength, but weight training plays absolutely no part in the Frans Hoek concept and method. The danger of weight training is that strength will be developed at the cost of technique, coordination and suppleness. The situations in which weight training is of benefit are described in Chapter 4, and in these cases such training should always be carried out under the supervision of an expert. This expert must be able to analyze the individual problem and identify the relationship to what is needed during a game. He must also possess the ability to establish the link with match requirements. Many sided development must also be at the heart of strength conditioning for goalkeepers. This means that the goalkeeper must learn to kick with both feet, to take off from both feet, to throw with either arm and to punch the ball with the right and left fist.

9.7.4 Flexibility and coordination

Goalkeepers must also concentrate on improving their flexibility and coordination. However, this will not be dealt with in detail in this chapter. Flexibility is treated extensively in Chapter 3 and coordination in Chapter 5.

Diving strength in the backward direction; footwork and coordination rather than larger muscles.

9.8 THE STRUCTURE OF THE SEASON FOR GOALKEEPERS

9.8.1 The structure of the season in terms of time
The structure of the season depends on the climate in the country concerned and the way the league competition is organized in that country. In the Netherlands the season lasts from August to May. The Dutch season is structured as follows:
- 1st preparation period;
- 1st half of the league season;
- winter break/vacation;
- 2nd preparation period;
- 2nd half of the league season;
- summer break/vacation.

This overall structure is the same for each club. The details depend on the level and the available time.

9.8.2 Content of the soccer season
The soccer season is broken into a number of phases. A goalkeeping coach must know exactly which aspects to focus on during his training sessions in each of these phases. There are three main aspects.

a. Goalkeeping aspects
1. Opposition in possession: Shots at goal, 1 against 1 situations, crosses, long balls forward
2. Own team in possession
   - 2.1 Goalkeeper in possession: Build-up play
   - 2.2 Team in possession: Backpass
3. Change of possession: Possession <--> Opponents in possession

Drills for these aspects can be general and/or specific. The purpose of general drills is to help the goalkeeper to improve generally. The purpose of specific drills is to improve the goalkeeper's abilities in relation to the team. The aims of this type of training are to learn, improve, maintain and perfect goalkeeping actions.

b. Physical aspects
The goalkeeper's fitness is made up of a number of elements: strength, speed, endurance, coordination and flexibility. The aims of conditioning for fitness are to build up, maintain and/or improve these elements.

c. Various influences
There are also a number of factors that can differ from situation to situation:
- the form of the goalkeeper/the team;
- the team's/opposition's style of play;
- the weather conditions;
- the conditions underfoot;
- the available resources

The coach must know which of these aspects is most important during a given phase of the season.

The 1st preparation period (July to August)
- Goalkeeping aspects: general and specific
- Physical aspects: buildup

During this period there is a lot of time, little pressure, and the weather and the conditions underfoot are ideal.

The 1st half of the season (September to December)
- Goalkeeping aspects: specific
- Physical aspects: maintain and improve

In this period, results are crucial. It is important that the goalkeeper and the team train together as a whole. The weather and the conditions underfoot remain good until November, but usually deteriorate quickly from November onward.

The winter break (December to February)
- Vacation and/or homework

The content of the homework program varies from individual to individual, and depends on the goalkeeper's self-discipline, his physical condition, whether or not he is injured, and how mentally fatigued he is.

The 2nd preparation period (January to February)
- Goalkeeping aspects: general and specific
- Physical aspects: buildup

During this period there is again a relatively large amount of time available, but the weather and the conditions underfoot are much poorer. Usually the pressure is off and the working atmosphere is relaxed.

The 2nd half of the season (January to May)
- Goalkeeping aspects: specific and general
- Physical aspects: maintain

In this period, results are again crucial. The pressure is on, because the number and importance of the games played increases. The weather and the conditions underfoot gradually improve from March onward.

The summer break (June to August)
- Vacation and/or homework

Just as in the winter break, the content of the homework program depends on aspects such as self-discipline, physical condition, injuries, and the level of mental fatigue.

9.8.3 Take the goalkeeper's phase of development into account
It is clear that the content of an annual plan depends on a large number of factors. The objectives must always depend on the level that a goalkeeper has already reached. Has he reached his expected level or has he still got some way to go? Goalkeeper coaching must always be seen in relationship to the needs of the team, and the goalkeeper's development as an individual in general and in relation to the team. Goalkeepers may find themselves in different phases of development. A goalkeeper who is 28 years old will usually have more conditioning and match experience than a goalkeeper of 20. This must always be borne in mind when individual objectives are set. These two goalkeepers cannot be given the same conditioning program, with the same expectations and demands. The ultimate objectives are the same, but care must be exercised on the way to achieving these objectives. The coach must draw up a plan that will ultimately result in the goalkeeper being able to satisfy the requirements of the team's game concept. The goalkeeper's abilities must also be taken into account. A goalkeeping coach must realize that nothing is absolute during a training session. Observe, analyze and listen at all times. Act on the basis of the information gained in this way.

9.9 PHYSICAL CONDITIONING OF YOUNG GOALKEEPERS
Young goalkeepers must first learn technique and insight. Only then should the focus be switched towards improving physical factors. Repeated execution of a technically incorrect movement can cause damage to joints, ligaments and tendons. The point of departure for every coach must be:
- What is the starting situation?
- What resources are available?
- Where are we (the coach and the goalkeeper) going?

It is important to take a number of factors into account in connection with the physical conditioning of young goalkeepers:
- their (biological) age;
- their physical (im)possibilities;
- their mental (im)possibilities;
- their social (im)possibilities.

Remember that children do not all grow at the same rate. Nor do they all experience the growth spurt at the same age. This is why a coach must look at a young player's biological age rather than his calendar age. The coach must vary the intensity of training sessions. Before a player goes through the growth spurt (age 11 to 15), the emphasis must be on technical development. Only afterwards can young goalkeepers be subjected to drills in which the emphasis is on physical fitness. If a start is made earlier they will lose their enjoyment of the sport. Girls mature earlier than boys and can therefore be subjected to the pressure to perform well at an earlier age.

Coaching plan for young goalkeepers

A coaching plan is needed to ensure that young goalkeepers get a good soccer educa-tion. Many clubs pay little attention to the selective coaching of this specialized task at the youth level. It is questionable whether a child should be encouraged to make the choice to be a goalkeeper at the age of 6 or 7. At this age it is better to allow everyone to take a turn in goal, and ensure that aspiring goalkeepers gain experience as field players. After all, a modern goalkeeper has to possess many of the skills of a field player. As children grow older, their soccer education can become more selective. This can best be done on the basis of a coaching plan for young goalkeepers. This must be properly integrated into the whole system of coaching and support within the club. There must be a clear line from the 8 year-old in the "D" team to the adult first team goalkeeper. At school, every student knows what he must do to gain his diploma, and this should also be the situation with regard to a goalkeeper's soccer education. An 8 year-old must know what will be required of him as the first

Youngsters should take turns in goal, and participate in the field of play.

team's goalkeeper. That is the ultimate objective he is working towards. Goalkeepers must be given an all-round soccer education, to prepare them to play in any system. This education starts at the age of 8 (for more information, see under "Literature", page 244) It is important to realize that young players must be allowed to make a lot of mistakes. As the youngsters get older their aim must be to make less mistakes, and ultimately to make as few as possible. It is inevitable that goalkeepers will always make some mistakes. Many amateur clubs cannot afford the luxury of a specialist goalkeeping coach. If they do have one, the plan of education must contain clear agreements on the cooperation between the goalkeeping coach and the youth coach(es). In principle there must always be a clear job description, defining the duties and responsibilities of the goalkeeping coach and the other coach(es). It must be clear who does what during the coaching, conditioning and supervision of young goalkeepers. The plan of education should include a description of the concept to be applied to the soccer education of young goalkeepers. The best point of departure is for the coach to make use of genuine soccer situations. The repeat principle is also important. There should be a lot of action, as little inactivity as possible, good planning and organization, and sufficient materials (balls, cones, goals).

9.10 HOW YOUNG GOALKEEPERS SHOULD LOOK AFTER THEMSELVES

A goalkeeper needs to be physically fit, but he also needs to look after himself if he is to perform to the best of his ability. Existing injuries must be treated, and good equipment is necessary to avoid further injuries.

9.10.1 How to handle injuries

Minor injuries should never be ignored. If scrapes, bruises or blisters are left untended, they can develop into serious, long-term injuries. Moreover, such minor injuries can disturb a player's concentration, causing a deterioration in performance, and increasing the risk of further injury. Goalkeepers must learn to look after themselves at a young age. They must know when it is possible to play and when not. Youngsters often cannot distinguish between injuries that prevent them from playing and those that do not. Injury prevention is very important even at a young age. In the long term, neglecting minor injuries results in problems.

9.10.2 Personal hygiene

A sportsman should always be clean and well groomed. If he does not look after his body he cannot expect it to perform at peak level. In practice this means that:

- players must always shower after a game or a training session;
- players should always wear sandals or footwear in the shower;
- players should dry themselves thoroughly after a shower, because eczema can also cause problems;
- players should keep their finger and toe nails short to prevent problems with ingrowing nails.

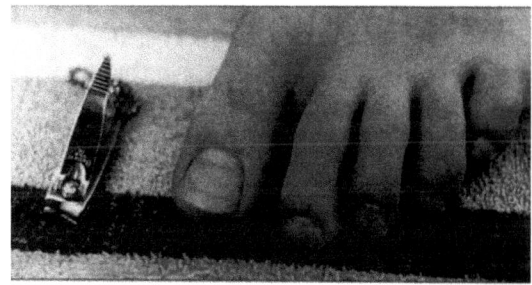

9.10.3 Good equipment prevents injuries

It is not generally appreciated how important good equipment is for a goalkeeper. Care should be taken with everything he wears:

- jersey;
- shorts;
- overall;
- sliding shorts;
- boots;
- gloves;
- shinguards.

As mentioned above, a goalkeeper has to overcome a large number of resistances dur-ing a match. It is therefore essential that he has good equipment, otherwise each resistance could endanger his health. Good equipment also gives a goalkeeper confidence.

Jersey

A goalkeeper encounters most resistance from the ground underfoot. He has to do a lot of diving and falling, and if he has a poor technique he may pick up hip and elbow injuries. A goalkeeper must develop good technique to be able to deal with the ball and also to avoid injuries. Modern goalkeeping jerseys are designed to offer good protection to the elbows. This is achieved with elbow padding, consisting of various layers of foam rubber. In extreme conditions - for example, if the pitch is hard (in winter or summer), or when playing on artificial turf or gravel - it is advisable to wear elbow guards. Most jerseys are now made of synthetic material, which cannot absorb moisture, so it is advisable to wear a cotton T-shirt under the jersey to absorb perspiration. This prevents cooling off and colds.

Shorts

Hip injuries can occur when a goalkeeper falls or dives. A goalkeeper's shorts must therefore offer protection to the hips. Foam rubber pads protect the hips when the pitch is hard. A goalkeeper's knees may also suffer during a match, and special long trousers are now available, which protect not only the hips but also the knees. The legs of such trousers contain padding for the knees, but in extreme conditions it is advisable to wear knee guards. In cold weather, long trousers keep the leg muscles warm, and therefore   help to avoid unnecessary muscle injuries. Long trousers should only be worn if the weather and/or the pitch make this advisable, because they restrict the goalkeeper's mobility.

Overall

A goalkeeper's overall is now available. This consists of a tracksuit top and long trousers in one garment. There is a cord at hip height, so that the trousers can be pulled up as high as required. The advantage of the goalkeeper's overall is that the trousers do not slip down, leaving the back exposed.

Sliding shorts

Sliding shorts first appeared in the soccer world a few years ago, and are now being worn more frequently by goalkeepers. Their function is to protect the skin at hip height when a goalkeeper performs an action such as, for example, flinging himself in

front of the ball. Such actions can result in hip scrapes, especially if the ground is hard. With sliding shorts, this can be avoided. Another advantage of such shorts is that they prevent heat from escaping, so that muscles of the upper leg and back are kept warm. The shorts also support the back, and provide an element of stability for goal-keepers with back problems.

Boots

It has been mentioned above that a goalkeeper's body weight is supported on the left or the right, and on the front or the back of the foot during a game. It is essential that a goalkeeper has a stable footing. This is an important function of soccer boots. Boots must not be too big for the feet. They must also stabilize the ankles when a goalkeeper lands on his feet after a jump. And they must give him a good grip underfoot, so that he will not lose his balance or slip. It is very important that a goalkeeper inspects the pitch before the game and then chooses an appropriate pair of boots with the correct stud length. He must chose the boots that give him the best grip and stability on the pitch where he is to play.

Gloves

Gloves are perhaps the most important items of a goalkeeper's equipment. A goalkeeper must be able to grip the ball firmly. He needs good technique to do this, but during recent years goalkeeping gloves have come to play an increasingly important role. At one time the ball was made of leather, but nowadays it has a layer of plastic around it. It is more difficult to get a good grip on this type of ball with the bare hands. This is why almost all goalkeepers now wear gloves. The palms of the gloves are their most important feature, and are usually made of foam rubber. There are a lot of gloves with various types of foam rubber on the market, and a special glove has been developed for every type of weather. It is often the case that, the better the gloves grip the ball, the faster the foam rubber wears through. A large number of varieties have been developed in this area too. Gloves are now available that provide protection for the fingers, wrist and palm. Their use is advisable to prevent injuries or protect weak points in the hand or wrist.

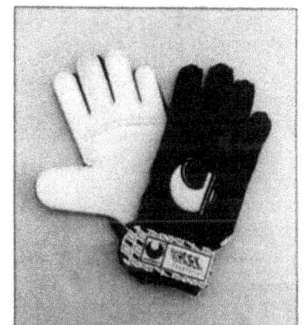

Shinguards

Many players, including goalkeepers, often regard it as a nuisance to have to wear shinguards. However, not only are they mandatory under FIFA rules but they are also necessary for goalkeepers, who often have to throw themselves in front of the ball. Goalkeepers should therefore wear shinguards to prevent bruises, wounds or even broken bones.

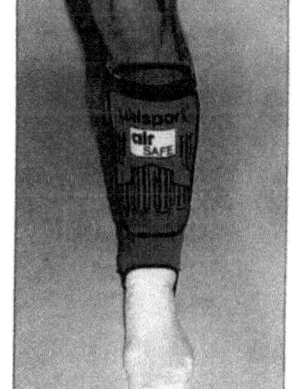

SUMMARY

- What a goalkeeper does during a game is largely dependent on the team's style of play and therefore on the coach's philosophy.

- As part of such a philosophy, the task and function of each playc (including the goalkeeper) should be described in detail. Everyone should be aware of his own tasks and function, and those of his teammates.

- The point of departure of the Frans Hoek philosophy is that a goalkeeper is part of the team, not only in theory but also in practice. A goalkeeper is part of the team and, just like every other player, is one of the links that contributes to its ultimate success.

- The Frans Hoek philosophy is associated with a defined method of working (the Frans Hoek method). Drills must include elements that are encountered during a real game, or are clearly related to a real game. What happens during a game must be reflected on the training pitch.

- A coach may have an excellently thought out philosophy and method of working, but they will be of no avail if the necessary framework conditions are not in place. The coaching staff must complement each other well, with the emphasis on communication. There must also be sufficient resources available.

- A goalkeeper's fitness is made up of a number of physical factors that he calls on during a game: strength (basic strength, starting strength, catching strength, jumping strength, diving strength, punching strength, strength in the challenge, kicking strength and throwing strength), speed (speed of reaction, speed off the mark, acceleration, and repeated short sprint capacity), and endurance (acyclic aerobic).

- Always use goalkeeper conditioning drills that incorporate elements related to playing soccer and to goalkeeping.

- Young goalkeepers must first learn technique and insight. Only then should the focus be switched towards improving physical factors. A coaching plan is needed to ensure that young goalkeepers get a good soccer education. Such a plan must describe the demands that a goalkeeper must satisfy in each age category. The plan must also specify how to work towards satisfying these demands.

- Goalkeepers must look after themselves properly. The emphasis must be on coping with injuries, personal hygiene and good equipment. The items of equipment that are important for a goalkeeper are: jersey, shorts, sliding shorts, boots, gloves and shinguards.

FIVE PRACTICAL QUESTIONS

1. At what level and age is it worthwhile engaging a specialist goalkeeping coach, and how often should training sessions for goalkeepers be held each week?

Everyone should be given a turn in goal until children reach the age of ten. I personally think that this is a good age to choose a permanent goalkeeper. Ideally there should be one training session per week with just the goalkeepers. During the other sessions they should be coached with the rest of the group. It is essential for goalkeepers to be coached in relation to the other players.

2. Is flexibility more important for goalkeepers than for the other players?

Flexibility is indeed more important for a goalkeeper than for a field player. Goalkeepers sometimes have to contort their bodies into all sorts of shapes to prevent a goal. Dynamic flexibility drills must therefore form part of a goalkeeper's conditioning. Just as for field players, however, flexibility is not a factor that determines a goalkeeper's performance.

3. Is it worthwhile making goalkeepers carry out "lactic acid" conditioning?

Lactic acid conditioning is pointless for goalkeepers. It has nothing to do with the game and just results in (temporary) physical damage. Coaches who drive their goalkeeper to exhaustion during a training session should ask themselves whether they are able to analyze a game properly. Acyclic anaerobic endurance is of no relevance to goalkeepers.

4. Should goalkeepers train with the rest of the group during the preparation period?

The physical work performed by goalkeepers during a game is so different to that performed by field players that it is pointless to make the goalkeeper carry out the running drills that the other players go through. During the first two training sessions the goalkeepers can participate in the continuous interval work, but they should then work on their fitness independently. A goalkeeping coach who knows what is demanded of a goalkeeper during a game is of course necessary.

5. How should a goalkeeper's strength be built up during the preparation period?

During the first week the goalkeeper must carry out general strength drills to bring his basic strength up to the mark. He should then practice the coordination and technique needed for the various goal-keeping actions. A goalkeeper must acquire the "feeling" for his task again. In the second week, the two types of drill must be combined. General strength drills for the legs can be followed by drills that focus on kicking (kicking strength). Similarly a "press-up" drill can be followed by a "throwing" drill.

INTERVIEW WITH EDWIN VAN DER SAR (Goalkeeper of Ajax Amsterdam)

What phases did you go through during your development period at Ajax?
During the first phase I had to work mainly on my general shortcomings. In addition a lot of attention was paid to aspects that are of specific importance for an Ajax goalkeeper, especially being able to join in as an eleventh field player, and restart plays in general. When I had been knocked into shape and had adapted myself to the Ajax system, everything had to be raised to a higher level. I had to work towards satisfying all the demands made on the goalkeeper of Ajax's first team. Now that this has been achieved, I have to ensure that I maintain this level and perfect my play. A goalkeeper can always improve.

What are the typical aspects of the Frans Hoek method?
First of all there is always a relationship to game situations. He never just takes a series of shots at goal. Other players were often involved in the goalkeeping drills. Frans was in charge of a group of players, so in fact the goalkeepers' training sessions took place within the group sessions. The advantage was that I could practice specific goalkeeping actions in a game context. In this way you learn to cope with resistances that you are also confronted with during a game. During the goalkeepers' training sessions he continuously emphasizes that you have to stay on your feet as long as possible. He feels that you should only dive if you need to. He also repeatedly points out that a goalkeeper must retain possession. This is why we frequently practiced restart situations. In his philosophy, you cannot just kick the ball blindly upfield. You must always have a purpose. Kicking the ball upfield is only useful if you are trying to reach a teammate.

How much attention is paid to the physical aspect during training sessions?
The basis of physical fitness is established during the preparation period. The training sessions are very intensive. The goalkeepers sometimes work with the group during the first few days of the preparation period, but most of the work involved in building up fitness is carried out during the separate goalkeepers' training sessions. In fact we carry out the same specific goalkeeping drills as usual, but more intensely and with fewer rest breaks. During the season it is almost impossible to do any conditioning work. Usually there is a goalkeepers' training session on Tuesday and Thursday. But because we often play a game on Wednesday, and there is therefore only a recuperation session on Thursday, I only have a goalkeepers' training session on Tuesday. This cannot be too intensive, however, because we are preparing for the game on Wednesday. You just train for the feel of it. If we do not play on Wednesday, the Thursday session is very tough. The rest of the time you simply try to maintain your fitness. You focus more on the technical and tactical aspects of keeping goal.

Because you have to function as an eleventh field player, do you have to have more endurance than a goalkeeper who is less involved in the play?
In the fitness tests that we do at Ajax, I always score fairly well for a goalkeeper. Usually the goalkeepers are the first ones to drop out of the shuttle-run test, but I manage to keep going for a long time. When we do long-distance runs I always end somewhere in the middle. I do not know whether good endurance is a "must" for a goalkeeper, but I do benefit from it during a game. Although I often join in the field play, I never have any conditional problems. Goalkeepers are conditioned for endurance primarily in small sided games with the goals close to each other. As a goalkeeper you are then continuously in action, because shots at goal come from all directions. Perhaps I have good endurance because we often carry out this type of drill at Ajax.

Do you do weight training?
I do exercises for the stomach muscles and press-ups. Sometimes I do weight training for two months, but that just involves four or five exercises. In my opinion a goalkeeper develops all the strength he needs during the goalkeepers' training sessions. A good example of this is the training I did to become two-footed. The kicking strength in my left leg has increased considerably, but my muscles have not grown in size. It is purely a question of technique. The same applies to throwing, punching, diving and jumping. As long as you have not perfected your technique, you know that you can still make progress in the area of strength.

Speed is an increasingly important factor for field players. Is this also the case for goalkeepers?
Because soccer has become faster, the goalkeeper also has to be faster over the first few meters. But even more important is that he takes up better positions. Because opponents are faster, the goalkeeper has to be faster to anticipate that, for example, an opponent is going to hit a long ball forward over the defense. It is essential to be in the right position when the long ball is played. At the same time you have to watch out for a lob over your head. A goalkeeper must also try to exploit the speed of his teammates. If you see that a teammate is in a 1 against 1 situation in the opposition's half, you must try to play the ball to him directly.

How much attention do you pay to your equipment?
The most important aspect is that you have to feel comfortable in what you wear. That applies to everyone, I think. I have no additional protective padding in my jersey or shorts. In my opinion that is not necessary if you have a good diving and falling technique. I only wear long trousers with padding and sometimes elbow guards if the ground is frozen hard. As regards the equipment developed by the club sponsors, I only have a say in the colors. I am satisfied with the equipment we use. I have more input to the sponsor of the Dutch national team. I am involved in developing models and choosing the material.

LITERATURE

1. Basisboek keeperstraining
Frans Hoek.
ISBN: 90-5121-002-7.
Tirion, Baarn.

2. Het keepersdagboek.
Frans Hoek.

3. The Soccer Goalkeeper
The Frans Hoek Method
(3 Part Video Series) REEDSWAIN Videos.

4. Developing A Goalkeeper Coaching Plan
Frans Hoek.
Developing Soccer Players: The Dutch Way (Chapter 4).

5. De warming-up voor de keeper.
Frans Hoek.
De Voetbaltrainer nr. 51.

6. Het analyseren van de keeper.
Frans Hoek.
De Voetbaltrainer nr. 62.

7. Training voor keepers/spelers.
Frans Hoek.
De Voetbaltrainer nr. 64.

CHAPTER 10

CONDITIONING FOR YOUNG SOCCER PLAYERS

Bert van Lingen
Vera Pauw

10.1 INTRODUCTION

It is generally recognized that physical conditioning does not have a dominant role to play in the soccer learning process of children. Factors such as strength and endurance certainly increase considerably between the ages of 11 and 14, but this is a consequence of the natural process of growth, and not of conditioning. In games of soccer at this level, moves do not break down due to lack of strength or endurance, but rather due to a lack of technical ability and insight into the game. The key problem is that the players are not on the same wavelength. There is a lack of understanding and insight into the intentions of others. The development of functional technical ability, focused on the soccer situation, must be central to the coaching of young soccer players. It is pointless, especially in view of the limited amount of time available and the low enjoyment value, to force children to carry out all kinds of drills with the purpose of improving their strength and endurance. This chapter examines the aspects that are important in youth soccer, and how to coach these elements.

10.2 WHAT ARE THE IMPORTANT ASPECTS OF YOUTH SOCCER?

Soccer is a game. Games have rules, which act as a framework within which the players can make choices. There are a huge number of ways of achieving the ultimate aim of the game (winning). The availability of so many options encourages creativity. It is a very complex game. In the first place it is complex because a large number of players are involved.

Soccer players must recognize game situations before they can take the correct decision.

Every situation in a game of 11 against 11 is characterized by an infinite number of possibilities. All 22 players make their own choices, and the player in possession also has to react to these choices. Secondly, in contrast to a sport such as basketball, in soccer the ball is "free". This means that the players of the team without the ball can try to take it off the player who is in possession. At one time the goalkeeper could function as a "safe haven," but since the backpass rule was changed, playing the ball back to the goalkeeper has proved to be a dangerous maneuver, especially in the youth game. Because the ball is free, soccer is a game of constantly fluctuating situations. Everything is continuously in motion, everything is continuously changing, except when the goalkeeper has the ball in his hands and when the ball is "dead." These "restart situations" (also known as "standard situations") are the only moments in the game when play is static, and are therefore the only situations that can be rehearsed precisely. In basketball, the player in possession is protected, and it is therefore easier to rehearse every pass and movement. A basketball player can always hold the ball safely in his hands. Soccer players need to be able to recognize certain situations if they are to make correct choices. The ability to recognize situations gives players a point of reference. They must know what is expected of them in different positions when their team is in possession, when their opponents have the ball, and when a change of possession occurs. And all of this must be put into the context of the match, the league competition, and the pressure exerted by the opposing team. Soccer is all about winning. To win, one team must score more goals than the other. A team can only score a goal if it is in possession, and it can only gain possession by taking the ball off the opposing team. When a team gains possession, it tries to build up an attack. If it loses the ball it tries to prevent the other team from scoring. It does this by disrupting its buildup play and defending against an attack. These basic aspects are fundamental to any analysis of the structure of the game. The elements on which the game is based, or rather the means by which the objective of the game (winning) can be achieved, are summarized in the so-called **TIC** principle. In the Netherlands we say that you must have **TIC** to play soccer. The more **TIC** you have, the better your soccer ability. Players who want to improve must increase their "soccer **TIC**." **TIC** stands for the basic elements of the game, namely technique, insight and communication. These elements can be **differentiated** from each other, but not **separated**. The importance of any given element varies according to a player's age.

TIC covers all of the resources that are needed to play the game, and all of the factors that influence the game. An additional complicating and influencing factor is the continual flux and movement of all these game ingredients. Situations change continuously as the game progresses, and the players must repeatedly reorient themselves and take new decisions. Awareness is the key. The quality (of the development) of a player's **TIC** determines the quality of his awareness. A soccer player must develop from seeing very little of the information in the large picture (the beginner) to seeing the large picture with very little information (the top player).

Technique
This is the skill needed to control the ball and to be able to play the game. No matter how small children are, or however elementary the standard of play, they possess a certain amount of technical skill.

Insight
Insight into the game is needed in order to understand what actions are appropriate or inappropriate in a given situation. Insight is largely a question of experience and soccer intelligence. A player's ability to anticipate what will happen in a given situation (the ability to "read" the game) depends on his insight into the situation.

Communication
A player communicates with all the resistances he encounters during a game: this includes not only verbal and non-verbal communication with teammates and opponents, but also communication: with the ball (speed/weight/whether it is hard or soft), the field of play (flat/bumpy/wet/dry), the spectators (cheering/jeering), the coach/referee, referee's assistant.

10.3 WHO ARE YOUNG SOCCER PLAYERS?

Each and every one of us is different. This maxim applies in equal measure to adults and children, and therefore also to young soccer players. Some people are reserved, whereas others are outgoing. Some children are mistrustful, while others are open and receptive to everything around them. Getting along together is often a question of experience. There are no text books or manuals that give easy solutions on how to get on well with everyone. This is an indication of the problems facing a coach. Of course, these problems are not restricted to youth coaches. Anyone who is involved with youngsters soon notices that certain behavior patterns may be characteristic of certain age groups. The words "may be" are chosen deliberately, because some children exhibit certain traits very strongly, while others show them hardly at all. Behavioral characteristics surface at an earlier or later age in some children than in others. The Dutch Soccer Association divides young soccer players into 6 different age categories: F, E and D beginners and C, B and A juniors. An overview of the possible characteristics of each age group is given below. Youth leaders and youth coaches should have a good knowledge of the typical characteristics of the different phases of growth, so that they can assess what can and cannot be expected of young players.

6 to 8 year-olds: (F)

At this age children are easily distracted and cannot concentrate for long periods. They are often too playful to approach soccer as seriously as some parents might expect from them. These children are egocentric, with no feeling for teamwork. Very young players all cluster around the ball. The only exceptions are the goalkeeper and one or two field players who have been repeatedly reminded to stay back in defense. It can hardly be called a proper game of soccer. The ball is rarely kicked cleanly, and it is chased around the pitch by a scurrying, flailing pack of enthusiastic youngsters. When boys and girls have

Players who want to improve must increase their 'TIC'.

spent some time with a club, the first signs of teamwork become noticeable. The ball is kicked around more purposefully. Nevertheless, the players abilities are largely limited to receiving passes, dribbling, pushing the ball forward, and shooting at goal.

8 to 10 year olds: (E)

The children are now much more willing to be part of a team. They can distinguish between good and less good players. They are capable of practicing a specific drill for longer periods. There is a noticeable improvement in ball control. This is the ideal age for mastering basic soccer skills. Skills are practiced with much more awareness and purpose than in the lowest age group. Teamwork takes the form of simple combinations. The concepts of marking and running into space are better understood.

10 to 12 year olds: (D)

At this age, players are more inclined to compare themselves with others. They are capable of pursuing objectives as part of a team. These youngsters have control of their own movements and work consciously at improving their game. D beginners play in teams of 11. The basis for learning technical skills is already in place, and the emphasis is now on developing insight into the game. In matches, the youngsters must become familiar with the size of the pitch, the rules of the game (e.g. offside), playing to a specific system (for example, 4-3-3) and, most of all, the principles of how to play when in possession and when the opposition has possession.

12 to 14 year olds: (C)

The youngsters' ability to read the game increases rapidly, and they now have minds of their own. Assertiveness increases, and there is a greater tendency to compare their own performance with that of others. Growth spurts can occur at this age, heralding the onset of puberty. Girls usually reach puberty before boys. In a relatively short space of time, girls may suddenly put on extra weight. Reasonable demands can be made on this age group with regard to the division of tasks within a team. C players are primarily occupied with skills they started to develop in the previous age groups, such as running into space and marking. Heading duels are taken more seriously, and there is less of a tendency for the players to close their eyes when heading the ball. Improvements in defensive play are apparent. The number of instances when several defenders all try to deal with one opponent are less frequent. The tasks assigned to a particular position become clearer and are gradually absorbed.

14 to 16 year olds: (B)

Boys broaden out, which may result in a discernible decrease in their control of their limbs. In general, girls have already reached full growth. Features of puberty, such as apathy, stubbornness and moodiness, are manifest in both boys and girls. Winning is more important than ever for boys, while girls seem more able to relativize its importance. Some youngsters may take enthusiasm to extremes in their quest to discover how far they can push themselves. B juniors are increasingly capable of playing genuine competitive soccer. Sometimes they try things that contribute little towards the team as a whole. They are sometimes too late with sliding tackles, or they may play the ball self- indulgently with the outside of the foot, just to prove they can do it. The pace is faster and the marking is sharper. Players have to learn to cope under pressure. This may cause problems. Individual skills must be used in the service of the team, so that the team as a whole can profit from them. This is difficult to learn.

16 to 18 year olds: (A)

At this age, youngsters are more mentally and physically stable. Players in this age group broaden out physically, and take a more businesslike approach to what is happening around them. This is usually the age at which players decide whether to take up the game seriously or simply to continue playing it for fun. The players are better able to deal with the problems they encounter when playing in a limited amount of space. Although an A junior is not yet a complete soccer player, this is now simply a question of growing maturity. The restlessness that typifies B juniors is replaced by greater restraint. Players keep a close eye on how their team-mates play. A certain amount of control becomes noticeable.

10.4 YOU LEARN TO PLAY SOCCER BY PLAYING SOCCER

It is difficult to formulate a step-by-step approach to learning how to play soccer, because the learning process depends largely on practice. You learn soccer by playing soccer. The time children spend playing the game is important for their soccer development. Lack of time is probably enemy number one, as far as learning to play soccer is concerned. Increased competition from other pastimes (other sports, computer games, television, etc.) has had an adverse effect. Children used to spend endless hours playing soccer in the streets. They devised all sorts of soccer games, from small sided games to games that depended on the presence of walls, sidewalks and trees. This was how children mastered the skills of the game. The constantly changing circumstances stimulated their creativity. They had to adjust their play to the features in their immediate neighborhood, such as the ditch that formed the sideline, the trees on the pitch, or the neighbor's yard (from which the ball might not always be returned). Progress always went hand in hand with growing insight, sometimes referred to as "soccer intelligence." Nowadays, however, soccer activities usually have to be squeezed into 1 or 2 hours of coaching each week at the local club, with games and drills which are devised, started and stopped by a coach. To enable youngsters to learn how to play soccer in a shorter time, the 11 against 11 game must be simplified, while still retaining as many characteristic aspects of soccer as possible. Under the direction of Rinus Michels, the technical staff of the Dutch Soccer Association carried out a theoretical

> *I am really a sort of junior soccer player, because I always want to be where the ball is.*
>
> **Flemming Povlsen**

and practical study, on the basis of which they formulated recommendations on how children can best learn soccer in the few hours of practice time that are available each week. This resulted in the Dutch Soccer Association's concept of youth soccer.

The Dutch Soccer Association's concept

This concept is a method of encouraging the soccer learning process in youngsters. We are convinced that it helps youngsters to become better soccer players and to enjoy their soccer more. Soccer players show their true colors in actual play. Their play demonstrates what they are really capable of, and reveals aspects of the game that they have not yet mastered. It also reflects their insight into soccer objectives. The Dutch Soccer Association's concept has a number of starting points.

a. Getting the most out of the game

The more enthusiasm that players show for the game, the more they will get out of it and the more they will learn. Youngsters will experience the game to the full if they get the feeling that they are really playing soccer. In days gone by, getting children interested in a knockabout on the streets was no problem at all. Kids would play for hours on end, day in, day out.

Optimal soccer enjoyment?

b. Lots of repetition

'Practice makes perfect' - children used to learn their soccer skills in the streets on the basis of this principle. The same game over and over again. The principle also applies to many other walks of life - if at first you don't succeed, try and try again. This is why soccer coaching needs little more than a few types of practice drills, in which all the elements of soccer are present: a ball, a field of play with a certain size, goals, teammates, opponents and, last but not least, the rules of the game. By constantly repeating these practice drills, the players will be able to master the game much quicker than when they practice all kinds of different exercises that do not contain the ingredients of the game.

c. The right coaching

In contrast to the street soccer situation, an adult is always on hand at a soccer club. Coaching sessions and matches take place under the supervision of youth leaders and coaches. Things aren't always as they should be. Players often fail to understand the remarks and instructions directed at them. The language used may be adult, properly suited to adult soccer but bearing little relationship to youth soccer. It is therefore important for coaches to understand exactly how youngsters experience the game, so that they can convey their message in a way that the players understand and act upon. A youth coach must also be capable of organizing coaching sessions and matches that satisfy the first two principles of the Dutch Soccer Association's concept. This means that coaches must be able to use soccer drills that get the most out of the players and can be used again and again. Coaching is all about influencing soccer performance, and a coach must be able to do this in such a way that his players learn better ways of solving soccer problems, and consequently play better.

10.5 BETTER SOCCER, MORE PLEASURE: '4 against 4'

Four against four embodies the key motto in the process of teaching youngsters to play soccer, namely 'You learn to play soccer by playing soccer.' Obviously, children have only a small chance of mastering the game and developing skills in games of 11 against 11. They have too little opportunity to actually play. The soccer situations are too complex for beginners, and they do not understand the objectives of the game. They are not involved enough, and the average number of ball contacts is too low. In short, these are all aspects that do not favor a child's learning process. This is why the technical staff of the Dutch Soccer Association decided to implement a form of drill that closely resembles a genuine game of soccer but is much easier for children to carry out. This is '4 against 4'.

Correct coaching - one of the basic principles of the Dutch Soccer Association's philosophy.

10.5.1 '4 against 4'

'4 against 4' is played by two teams of four players on a pitch 20 meters wide and 40 meters long. Each team defends a goal at least 3 meters wide, The choice of '4 against 4' is arbitrary, but it does conceal a worthwhile aim. The starting point for the present- day learning process for youth soccer players is that there are a number of basic drills that guarantee that these young players will play soccer at all times. The small sided game is the most suitable vehicle for this concept. It includes all the elements that soccer can offer (Technical and physical skills, Insight into the game, and Communication with teammates and opponents: in short, TIC). It was felt that '4 against 4' comes closest to the basic characteristics of a real match. '4 against 4' contains the most important characteristics of the game of soccer. The small number of players (four) encourages the proper use of the length and width of the playing area. A square pass can be assigned a function, by making a forward pass conditional on a prior square pass. Or a forward pass can be played, and the subsequent threat of a square or return pass can pull an opponent out of position. Here, too, the square pass has a clear function that is the same as in a real match. It is true that such situations also arise in games involving other numbers of players, such as 5 against 5 or 3 against 3, but in 3 against 3 they occur less often. The number of players defines the structure of the game. With 3 players there are less opportunities to exploit the function of the square pass as a condition for a forward pass, and there are thus less opportunities for learning. There is one less direction for distributing the ball. In '4 against 4', by contrast, there are options in all directions of play. In 5 against 5 a completely different problem arises. Because there are 2 more players on the field, there is less room to play a forward pass or a square pass. Situations arise in which several players play the same role and get in each other's way. The play then becomes chaotic and uncontrolled (without structure). '4 against 4' is the smallest manifestation of a real match. So many comparable situations occur in such a short period of time that children learn to solve these problems very flexibly. No two situations are identical, but the structure and the aim are always the same.

10.5.2 The rules of '4 against 4'
Whether they are beginners or juniors, young players need clear rules. '4 against 4' therefore has a number of rules that are intended to ensure that the objectives of the game can be achieved. The game must be played in such a way that it flows. For example, if each goal is so small that one player can completely guard it, then it becomes impossible to achieve one of the objectives that apply when a team is in possession, namely scoring goals. In such a situation the rules must be amended. The goals must be enlarged until they offer a reasonable chance of scoring. Irrespective of the applicable structure and rules, it is important to implement the rules strictly.

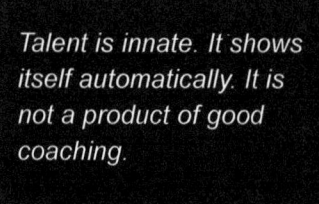

Talent is innate. It shows itself automatically. It is not a product of good coaching.

Rinus Michels

Starting the game
The kick-off is in the middle of the field. After a goal is scored, the game is restarted from the goal.

Ball goes over the sideline
The ball must be kicked into play rather than thrown in, because this is quicker and there is no need to wait until teammates have found space. The youngest players are usually not capable of dealing with a thrown-in ball, and this would lead to interruptions in the flow of the game, thus defeating the aim of the exercise, which is to play as much as possible. For older youngsters, a coach might deliberately decide to use throw-ins so that the players can learn about throwing in and its associated aspects such as timing, taking up position, feinting, etc. When a kick-in is taken the opponents must be at least 3 yards from the ball.

Ball goes over the goal line
The ball is played in from the goal line by dribbling it or kicking it

Offside
In principle no offside rule applies in games of '4 against 4.' However, it can be useful with older juniors or adults.

Corners
Children must be taught to take short corners with opponents at least 3 yards from the ball. In this way positional play can be resumed very quickly. No high crosses should be hit into the goalmouth of such a small goal from these short distances.

Free-kicks
Offenses such as dirty play, foul tackles and hands are punished with an indirect free-kick. The opposing players must stand at least 3 yards from the ball. Tapped free-kicks are best, so that positional play can be quickly resumed. Preventing a goal by handling the ball is punished by a penalty. The ball is placed 15 meters from the goal, and the goal is not defended by a goalkeeper.

What '4 against 4' is not
In recent years, '4 against 4' has sometimes become an objective in itself rather than a means to an end. This is usually the result of a lack of qualified supervision. In such cases, '4 against 4' becomes an instrument with which clubs, coaches or parents try, cost what it may, to gain prestige. This is nothing more nor less than the exploitation of children to satisfy their elders' thirst for success. '4 against 4' is not intended to be another competitive element alongside existing club competitions. The weekly match against another club must remain the highlight of the week. All the work, practice and coaching is focused on the weekly game. In this context, a game of '4 against 4' is simply a means to an end. If the '4 against 4' game is only used to fight soccer battles at full tilt, then it is not fulfilling its purpose. Its purpose is to provide a simple framework, within which a coach can focus on typical soccer situations, with the aim of teaching youngsters how to play soccer. The pace of a youngster's soccer development should not be forced. Children should be able to concentrate on their own play. Within the restraints of the small number of players and the small playing area, there are sufficient opportunities for them to shine, and to learn to recognize certain situations themselves and come up with solutions to the problems involved. '4 against 4' is a game played by and for children. The role of the adult in the street soccer of former years was restricted to confiscating the ball when the flowers in his yard were flattened for the umpteenth time. This, of course, also encouraged the development of technical skills.

10.6 SOCCER TRAINING IS CONDITIONING; CONDITIONING IS SOCCER TRAINING
Physical conditioning has no role to play in connection with children. It only becomes relevant when they reach puberty and go through the growth spurt. Hormones are then released that make it possible to develop strength, speed and endurance. A coach must have a knowledge and understanding of all of the problem areas before he can set up a coaching situation properly. However, this knowledge should never be seen in isolation, but always in relation to the actual game. Some forms of soccer conditioning, for example, are too often directly derived from theories of exercise physiology. Soccer training is conditioning and conditioning must be soccer training. Insights gained from exercise physiology need to be translated into drills that are suitable for soccer players. Conditioning is too often associated with fatigue, muscle pain, long-distance runs, being hot, sweating, sprinting, and exercises to build up strength. In short, all sorts of activities aimed at pushing back the limits of performance. A soccer player's performance is, however, more than the sum of his strength, speed, endurance, flexibility and coordination. These factors say nothing about the capacity of an individual to play soccer. What is more important is how players solve soccer problems and achieve soccer objectives. The most important source of information is perception. Conditioning used to be primarily focused on the muscles. Muscles, however, are the slaves of the brain. Muscles alone cannot learn

anything. Only the brain can learn. To learn how to play soccer, and therefore to increase soccer ability, soccer must not be reduced to movements but to the purpose of movement, and that is the realization of soccer objectives. If a player knows the purpose of solving soccer problems, the brains will control the muscles. If a player has a lot of experience in a certain situation, he will be able to decide what to do much faster. A coach must know the principles that have to be applied to develop strength, speed and endurance. These are the general principles of the science of conditioning.

A coach must know how to develop soccer ability.

Soccer ability is developed with the help of these principles, which are translated into soccer-related drills. It should not be thought that soccer players would be able to play better if they had a bigger lung capacity. Nor can players head the ball better if they have stronger leg muscles. And being able to run faster does not, by definition, improve a player's soccer ability.

In practice, conditioning is totally concerned with playing soccer. The coach must always try to create situations in which players are stimulated to carry out certain soccer actions better, longer or faster. The principle of becoming better is based on doing things that are always at a slightly higher level. In effect the circumstances under which a soccer activity is carried out must be just too tiring or too complicated. The players must want to start the drill, but they must also regard it with some apprehension. It must be a difficult, tiring task, which requires concentration and a specific attitude. In conditioning science, the term "overload principle" is used. Having to do more than you are used to. This makes a training session more like a real match. In practice (in matches and training sessions), this principle is often given too little (or no) content. If the main part of a training session does not conform to these principles, then the session is not a training (= improving the ability to perform) session but a form of maintenance (which can be useful) or occupational therapy (which is less useful), or is boring (which is totally undesirable). Naturally it is a good thing if a child is confronted with all kinds of movements and physical exercises. Especially now, when less and less physical education is given at school. Between the ages of 8 and 14 in particular, when children are receptive to this sort of stimuli (influences), the most varied possible program should be provided. However, the main aspect must remain that children in this age group must occupy themselves as much as possible with actually playing soccer. This is already challenging and difficult enough.

10.7 YOUTH SOCCER, SOCCER FOR BOYS AND GIRLS

10.7.1 Mixed soccer

In the Netherlands, mixed soccer is played on a steadily increasing scale. The term mixed soccer is intended to cover all situations in which boys and girls play soccer with or against each other. It also covers occasions when two girls' teams play against each other in the context of a league that also includes boys or boys' teams. Initially girls only played in segregated leagues. There was a lot of emphasis on the differences between boys and

This sort of situation is avoided in mixed soccer.

girls, along the lines of "Girls are different to boys, so they should play soccer separately." The problem in the Netherlands is that girls who play soccer are spread over the many clubs that were set up for the approximately one million male soccer players who are members of the Dutch Soccer Association. The number of girls per club is therefore small. As a consequence, girls' teams consist of players who vary in age from 6 to 15 years old. And if there are teams that are only made up of 6 and 7 year-olds, they have to play against teams with girls of 14 and 15. For this reason, many girls stop playing the game after only a few years. More and more people now realize that there are more similarities than differences between boys and girls, and the few differences that do exist often have no influence on the game of soccer. This is why mixed soccer came into being. After all, boys and girls are confronted with the same problems when they play soccer. Game situations must be mastered with the help of soccer actions. The performance of soccer players is judged on how well they carry out these actions in relation to the task or function that is associated with a position in the team. There is no difference between boys and girls in this respect. The learning process of girls and boys is also the same. If they both start to play soccer at 6 years of age, they go through the same stages of development.

Most people think, perhaps unconsciously, that this is not the case. They automatically assume that boys learn soccer faster and better than girls. Such attitudes imply that the ability to play soccer is genetically determined - that there are "soccer genes" and that boys have more of them than girls. This is nonsense, of course. The fact that most 6 year-old boys have a better knowledge of handling a football than many girls of the same age is due to the fact that boys are brought up to play with a ball, whereas girls are given dolls to play with and rarely have the chance of acquiring any sort of familiarity with a ball. When girls start to play soccer, they first of all have to develop a "feeling for the ball." Most boys already have this to some degree. Another advantage of mixed soccer is that boys and girls often influence each other. Boys are often focused on their own performance, whereas girls often try to achieve things by cooperating. By playing soccer in mixed teams, boys acquire a better social attitude both on and off the field, and girls learn to play soccer more purposefully.

Many children have to develop a feeling for the ball.

Girls are more oriented towards joint achievement.

10.7.2 Differences between boys and girls

By now it should be clear that there are more similarities than differences between boys and girls. One important difference is concerned with puberty. Girls usually experience puberty earlier than boys. Moreover, they are then often bigger and stronger. This can be seen in school. Anyone who has taught children knows that girls are physically and mentally more developed than boys between the ages of 12 and 14. This is often forgotten in discussions about sport. By the age of 15 the boys have caught up physically, but the girls are still mentally more advanced. This mental advantage is retained until the age of at least 18. This is reflected in the fact that 17 year-old girls often have boyfriends of 20 or 21. Only rarely does a 17 year-old boy have a 20 year-old girlfriend. Because they are mentally more mature, girls usually have more soccer insight than boys of the same age with the same amount of soccer experience. This is why 90 percent of the girls in mixed teams of 13 and 14 year-olds play in the backbone of the team (center forward or central midfield). It might be concluded that girls have more soccer aptitude than boys, but of course this is not true either. Girls can play soccer with boys up to the age of 18. Afterwards the physical difference is too great. It is the physical aspects that make mixed soccer impractical at the senior level. It is not a consequence of too large a difference in technique and/or insight.

10.7.3 The future of women's soccer

The history of women's soccer is much shorter than that of the men's game. In general women's soccer is therefore at a lower level of development. The gap between men's and women's soccer differs from country to country. In the USA, soccer was introduced to the women in the early 1970s. The Dutch situation is very different. In the Netherlands, men's soccer has been played for more than a century. Women's soccer was tagged onto it only a few decades ago. There is therefore no question of equality yet. One advantage of the Dutch situation is that the women can profit from the already existing infrastructure (pitches and organization). In the USA everything had to be built up from nothing In the coming years a lot of work will have to be carried out to attain a position of equality alongside men's soccer.

Role models

Role models have to be created for girl soccer players. This is something that is being encouraged by the Dutch Soccer Association. Girls must realize that coaches, referees and club officials can be either men or women. In other countries the top women model themselves on the top men. In the Netherlands, the top women model themselves first of all on the first team of their club. These are men in the 4th or 5th category leagues, who themselves only train once or twice each week. They do not model themselves on Ajax Amsterdam or PSV Eindhoven. The women players of Milan model themselves on the "great" AC Milan. They therefore have a different attitude to their sport. They would even train 5 or 6 times each week. The women's teams play in the same strips and on the same pitches. Women's soccer is viewed as part of a whole there. A club consists of a men's team and a women's team. The women's section of the club receives less money, but enjoys the same prestige and respect. In Norway, women's soccer is an accepted sport in itself, and games are shown live on television. The Norwegian women are the 1995 Women's World Champions. After ice hockey, women's soccer is the second most popular sport in Norway. Then comes men's soccer. The women's league is a professional league. In Germany the position of women's soccer within the German Soccer Association is even weaker than in the Netherlands, and yet the German women are the European champions. There is a lot of money in Germany, and even if it is "only" women's soccer, they want to be among the best. In England all of the professional clubs also have a women's team. Because women's soccer is linked to the professional clubs, it is taken much more seriously. In the Netherlands this would be unthinkable.

Role models must be created for girl soccer players.

Continuity in women's soccer
The quality of the development of a sport is largely dependent on the ex-players who work to support and promote their sport when they themselves retire from playing. Women must accept this responsibility in the world of soccer. Unfortunately, very few of them feel called upon to do so. Moreover, only a few of them are capable of performing such a function. Efforts are being made to raise the standard of women's soccer by giving a chance to those who not only want to but also can do such work. Here, too, quality is all important. The standard of most women coaches referees and officials is not high enough. This has nothing to do with being a woman. Because women have played soccer for only a relatively short period of time, it is the case that women referees, for example, have little experience and have not therefore acquired the ability to see what will probably happen on the pitch. By watching a lot of soccer (on television), it is possible to recognize patterns of play, and this knowledge can be exploited as a referee. From 1998, the Dutch Soccer Association will appoint a number of female national coaches to learn the job. These women will be chosen on the basis of quality. They must be qualified, committed to the Dutch Soccer Association's philosophy, and ambitious. If they satisfy these criteria they will be given a chance. The ultimate objective is to promote continuity in women's soccer. Women have often played women's soccer themselves. Male national coaches usually start by trying to reinvent the wheel, and in most cases are

then active for only a short time in women's soccer. This form of positive discrimination should not be necessary, but it is the only way to achieve anything. Nothing will happen of its own accord. A report "Women in sport, a step backwards" indicates that more women were active behind the scenes in sport ten years ago than now. It might be expected that the numbers would gradually increase. Fifteen years ago positive discrimination was "in." An organization did not count if it did not take any women into its ranks. But because the position of women is still not equal to that of men, when a women steps down from a position it is often argued that it is time for a man to be appointed again. But this does not apply in reverse. Men are not succeeded by women on the basis of this reasoning.

SUMMARY

- Physical conditioning does not have a dominant place in the soccer education of children. The development of functional technical skills, oriented towards soccer situations, must be at the heart of soccer coaching for youngsters.

- The elements a player needs to play the game, or rather the resources with which the objective of the game can be achieved (winning), are embodied in the TIC principle (Technique, Insight and Communication).

- In the Netherlands we say that you must have TIC to play soccer. The more TIC you have, the better your soccer ability.

- Certain patterns of behavior may be characteristic of the phase of growth that a youngster is going through. Anyone who works with young people should have a good knowledge of the typical characteristics of the different phases of growth, so that they can assess what can and cannot be expected of a youngster.

- It is difficult to describe how to learn to play soccer in a step-by-step manner, because soccer is primarily based on practice and on doing. Soccer is learned by playing a lot of soccer.

- The Dutch Soccer Association's philosophy is a method of accelerating the learning process of young soccer players. The starting principles are optimal soccer enjoyment, lots of repeats and correct coaching.

- '4 against 4' was developed as the vehicle for putting the principles of the Dutch Soccer Association's philosophy into practice. It is the smallest manifestation of a genuine match.

- Soccer training is conditioning; conditioning is soccer training. However, the principles of exercise physiology must be properly translated into soccer practice.

- Mixed soccer is now played widely in the Netherlands. More and more people now realize that there are more similarities than differences between boys and girls, and the few differences that do exist often have no influence on the game of soccer.

- Game situations must be mastered with the help of soccer actions. The performance of soccer players is judged on how well they carry out these actions in relation to the task or function that is associated with a position in the team. There is no difference between boys and girls in this respect. The learning process of boys and girls is precisely the same.

- By playing soccer together, boys and girls influence each other. Boys acquire a better social attitude both on and off the field, while girls play soccer much more purposefully.

- Role models have to be created for girl soccer players. Girls must realize that coaches, referees and club officials can be either men or women.

- The quality of the development of a sport is largely dependent on the ex-players who work to support and promote their sport when they themselves retire from playing. Women must accept this responsibility in the world of soccer. Here too quality is all important. The ultimate objective is to achieve continuity in women's soccer.

FIVE PRACTICAL QUESTIONS

1. How often should young soccer players exercise?

The soccer learning process of youngsters depends to a large extent on their stage of development. You therefore have to look at them in terms of their age and experience. The associated learning objectives and practice material must also be known. Exercise in the sense of maximal strength, speed and such like is not an option. A varied range of movements each day is desirable (coordination, activities connected with soccer technique, games).

2. Young players are sometimes pushed into a higher age category, where they encounter much more resistance. Is this sensible?

The criterion is whether they can hold their own, and whether their soccer ability is positively influenced. If it means that they learn to recognize soccer situation more quickly and to act and react appropriately, then there is no problem. But if the resistance they encounter in a higher age category is such that they cannot participate in the game on equal terms, this will stop the development of their soccer ability. They will mark time, be confronted with their physical inadequacies and experience mental blocks, and a brake will be put on their technical development.

3. Many people have the Impression that modern children do not get enough exercise. Is this true?

It is impossible to answer this question unless it is looked at within a defined framework. I am often amazed at the skill and agility of young children, both inside and outside the context of soccer (skateboarding, computer game skills, mountain bikes, inline skating and dancing).

4. When should young players be confronted with maximal physical work?

Each time of life has its own rules and limitations. Insight is needed into the charac-teristics of the development stages. Maximal physical work should play no part in the learning process of young soccer players. The development of individual TIC (Technique, Insight and Communication) should be the common theme at all ages.

5. Which physical factors should play a role in the scouting and selection of young players?

The scouting and selection of young players should be based, above all, on how they recognize and react to soccer situations. Soccer situations require them to react adequately. The physiological rules relating to factors such as flexibility, coordination, speed, strength and endurance play a role here. However, these factors alone cannot be the basis for judging a player's soccer qualities. The aim must be to look at a young player's actions in relation to the demands made for achieving soccer objectives. A lack of strength, speed or endurance can play a role in soccer, but is never a determining factor.

INTERVIEW WITH RINUS MICHELS

The Dutch soccer school is respected throughout the world. What are the visible signs of this?
The most important criterion for judging the quality of Dutch soccer is the results achieved by Dutch club and national teams at international level. For a number of years, the Netherlands has been in or around tenth position in the FIFA world listing. In view of the size of the Netherlands in comparison with soccer nations such as Germany, Brazil, England, France, Italy and Spain, this is a considerable achievement. Another criterion is the ideas and content of the total approach to youth soccer in the Netherlands. A very special feature of the Dutch school is its ability to make soccer a game that can be learned and taught. This approach has been elaborated in an extensive learning plan, which deals in detail with each individual age group. The way in which the learning process of young soccer players is put into practice is also unique. A finely meshed network of clubs, districts, administrators, commissions and technical officers guarantees the mutual interaction between the Dutch Soccer Association and its members. Other countries are envious of the youth soccer sit-uation in the Netherlands, with regard to not only ideas and content but also organization and infrastructure.

What is the situation abroad with regard to the organization and standard of youth soccer?
A recent survey compared the youth soccer situation in the Netherlands with that in other countries on the basis of a number of assessment criteria. If the number of players is left out of consideration, it appears that the Netherlands and France lead the field. The other countries lag behind in terms of coherent ideas about the learning process of young soccer players, the role of leagues, and the infrastructure of youth soccer.

It is often said that young Dutch players are physically and mentally less developed than their contemporaries in Spain and Italy. What is your opinion?
You need a number of objective criteria before you can answer this question. One objective criterion is, for example, that both of these countries have far more young soccer players than the Netherlands. This means that there are more potential top players, and therefore more competition between them, which has a positive effect on quality. Moreover it is a fact that, in these countries, young players are expected to play for a team result even at a very young age. Youth soccer therefore reflects the requirements and standards that apply in adult soccer, where the result is all important. It is known that young players in Italy and Spain generally reach competitive maturity earlier than Dutch youngsters. This is the case not only in soccer but also in many other sectors. Although Dutch youngsters initially seem to lag behind, they catch up at a later stage. And although they are slower to mature physically, they are often further developed in aspects such as technical skill and insight into the game. What ultimately matters is how mature adult players perform.

In international top soccer, the physical factor plays an increasingly important role. To what extent must this be taken into account during a young player's soccer education?

just as in other top sports that go to the limits of what is possible, soccer players are put to the test in all respects, and not simply with regard to team tactical elements. If it appears that there is an advantage to be gained by fully exploiting a player's physical potential, then this will not be ignored. However, it should be pointed out that the player's soccer ability must first be extensively analyzed. Bigger muscles do not make a player head the ball better.

The '4 against 4' project has now been in progress for 12 years. What are your impressions?

As a learning aid, '4 against 4' is the smallest simplification of the real game. It is an important step in the soccer learning process of young players. Considerable attention was initially focused on the 5 to 12 year-old age category in particular. Studies have been carried over many years to determine whether the ideas behind '4 against 4' can yield results. On the basis of these ideas about learning soccer and about youngsters in general, a development took place that resulted in important innovations in the education of coaches, even at the senior level. In the meantime, these ideas have become widely familiar through books and films. Throughout the world, there has been a lot of interest in this subject. As with everything else, there is always room for improvement. We must continue to evaluate the project and develop it further.

Is it sensible to expect very young players to function within a fixed system of play?

From an early age, right through to adulthood, an organizational form within which soccer (or derived forms of soccer) is played is an important means for achieving certain objectives or results. At the youngest age, when the main objective is learning to control the ball, an organizational form is needed that facilitates the achievement of this objective to the greatest possible extent. When youngsters are old enough to start playing '11 against 11' for the first time, it is important to have a system that enables them to play soccer as well as possible at this age. We decided on '1-4-3-3' or variations of it, such as '1-3-4-3.' At the absolute top, a system must be chosen that will yield the best match results. This is not the same as the result that is aimed for with youngsters. Naturally children want to win for their own satisfaction, but the main aim must be to create optimal conditions for youngsters in the given age category to learn the game. As long as the general basic elements of soccer still have to be learned, it is not sensible to tie youngsters to specific positions in the team at an early stage of their development (below the age of 12).

What is your opinion of mixed soccer?

In practice, it has been found that the decision to allow boys and girls to learn soccer together has been successful. Surveys have shown that both boys and girls have reacted favorably to this possibility. One recurring criterion is that the important thing in sport is, who can play his or her role at what level? Practice shows which boy or girl can reach what level. Soccer ability is the only criterion. This is why mixed soccer can be played until the age of eighteen, as long as the game remains a game. The limit is different for each individual, and the only limit is the natural limit. On average, a grown man runs faster, jumps higher and shoots harder than an adult woman. When it becomes important to raise the level of performance - in competitive leagues - the physical differences between men and women make mixed soccer impossible. I see no problems in the lower regions of adult soccer, where the principle of playing for pleasure still applies. Why should these men and women not be able to play soccer together?

LITERATURE

1. Coaching Soccer. The Official Coaching Book of the Dutch Soccer Association.
Bert van Lingen
ISBN: 1-890946-04-4
REEDSWAIN

2. De bal is rond... en dat is best moeilijk.
Bert van Lingen en Vera Pauw.
ISBN: 8-710966-040195.
KNVB.

3. Coachboek 'de bal is rond'.
Bert van Lingen en Vera Pauw.
KNVB.

4. The Dutch 4x4 Training Method KNVB (video tape)
REEDSWAIN Videos.

CHAPTER 11

NUTRITION FOR SOCCER PLAYERS

Dr. Raymond Verheijen

11.1 INTRODUCTION
Nutrition is of essential importance for a soccer player if he is to maintain a good nutritional status, function efficiently during (and recover after) physical exercise, and avoid health risks. Nutritional shortages can impair a player's ability to perform, lengthen the time he needs to recover, and possibly have a negative effect on the immune system. A (top) sportsman demands more of his body than an average person. He therefore needs more energy and body-building substances. However, it is often the case that (top) sportsmen have almost the same eating patterns as other people. This can result in shortages or excesses of certain substances, with the above mentioned consequences. It is therefore advisable to maintain good eating habits. This chapter contains information, guidelines and recommendations in the field of nutrition in relationship to soccer.

11.2 GENERAL NUTRITIONAL PRINCIPLES
In everyday life we encounter a number of fuels for specific machines. Examples include diesel oil for tractors, gas for automobiles, and kerosene for aircraft. Every machine needs its own specific fuel to provide it with the energy to carry out work. The human body is unique in that it can use a variety of fuels. The body can choose between carbohydrates, fats and sometimes even proteins to cover its energy needs at any given moment. A few general nutritional principles will now be explained, with a view to providing an insight into the specific requirements of soccer players. The role of carbohydrates, fats and proteins during exercise will be described, as well as the function of the body's fluid balance.

Simple sugars
(monosaccharides)
Glucose (grape sugar)
Fructose (fruit sugar)
Galactose (constituent of lactose)

Double sugars (disaccharides)
Saccharose (common sugar)
Maltose (malt sugar)
Lactose (milk sugar)

Polysaccharides
Starch (potatoes, rice, and pasta)
Glycogen (in muscles and liver)

Figure 11.1: *The various types of carbohydrates.*

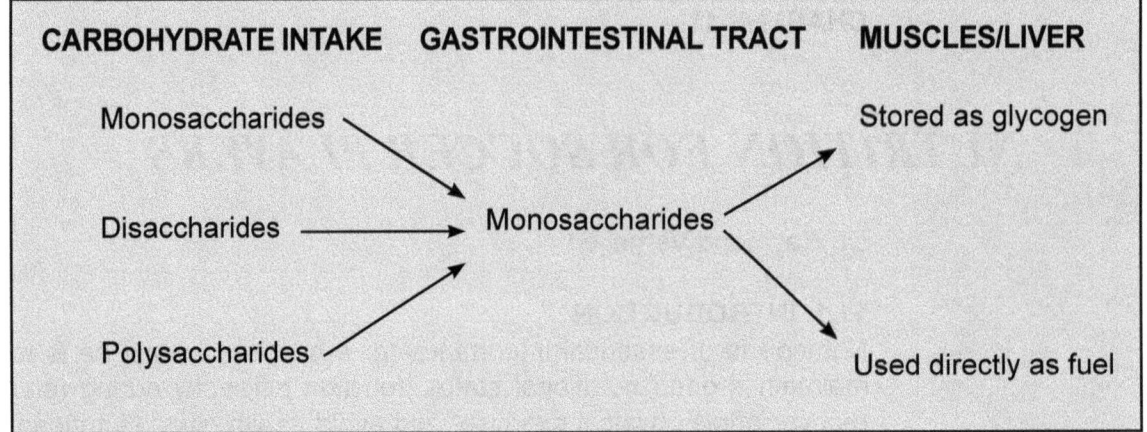

Figure 11.2: *Breakdown and utilization of carbohydrates.*

11.2.1 Carbohydrates

Carbohydrates consist of carbon and hydrogen. There are various types of carbohydrates, which contain different numbers of sugars (see Fig. 11.1). After they enter the body, all carbohydrates end up in the gastrointestinal system, where they are broken down into simple sugars. The glucose molecules are then absorbed directly into the blood. Fructose and galactose pass through the portal vein into the liver, where they are converted into glucose. All glucose molecules are either used directly as fuel by active muscles, or are stored in the liver and/or muscles in the form of glycogen. Figure 11.2 gives a clear picture of the path taken by carbohydrates after they enter the body.

Glycogen in the liver

The amount of glycogen in the liver is about 100-150 grams. The most important function of this glycogen reserve is to maintain the blood sugar level. Active muscles draw on sugar from the blood during physical exercise. When the concentration of sugar in the blood falls below a certain level, the body sends a signal to the liver. The liver then breaks down glycogen and transforms it into glucose molecules, which ultimately pass into the blood. There are, however, only limited reserves of glycogen in the liver. When they are exhausted, the active muscles have to fall back on their own glycogen reserves.

Glycogen in the muscles

On average, there are around 500 grams of glycogen stored in the muscles of the human body. In very fit individuals there may even be more than 500 grams. Muscle glycogen serves as fuel for active muscles. The speed with which the glycogen reserve is used up depends on the duration and intensity of the exercise and the sportsman's level of fitness. When the reserve is exhausted, the muscles have to switch over to burning up fat (and possibly proteins). It is known that work can only be carried out to 50 percent of maximal capacity because fat is a 'slow' fuel (see page 268).

Replenishing the glycogen reserves

When the glycogen reserves are exhausted through exercise, they have to be built up again by eating carbohydrates. There is a direct relationship between carbohydrate intake and the degree to which the reserves are restored. The larger the carbohydrate intake, the more the glycogen reserves recover, until they are finally completely replenished (see Fig. 11.3). When this point has been reached, any additional carbohydrate intake has no further effect. The excess carbohydrates are even converted into fat. Glycogen exhaustion takes place mainly in the muscles that are active. Right-handed handball players therefore experience glycogen exhaustion primarily in the muscles of the right (throwing) arm and left (takeoff) leg. Soccer players are mainly confronted with glycogen exhaustion in the muscles of the leg they use most. Glycogen replenishment only occurs in the muscles whose glycogen reserves have been drawn on.

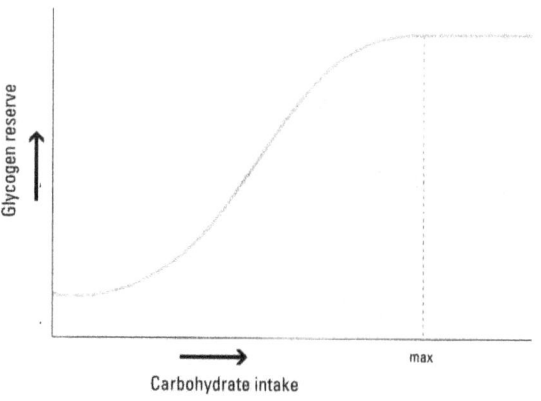

Figure 11.3: *The relationship between carbohydrate intake and replenishment of the glycogen reserve.*

What foods contain carbohydrates?

Simple sugars (monosaccharides) and double sugars (disaccharides) are present in fruit and vegetables, and above all in chocolate bars, candy, cookies and soft drinks. The last four, in particular, should be avoided as far as possible, on grounds of health. In general they contain no other useful nutrients and a lot of fat. It is better to eat food that contains polysaccharides (e.g., pasta, cereals, potatoes and bread). Together with fruit and vegetables, they supply all the necessary carbohydrates. Moreover, they also contain lots of vitamins, minerals and dietary fibers. Dietary fibers are indigestible components of vegetable foodstuffs. They contain very little energy, but are of crucial importance to the functioning of the intestines and, therefore, the digestion. Dietary fibers are present in whole-wheat bread, brown bread, rye bread, unpolished rice, potatoes, fruit and vegetables.

11.2.2 Fat

Triglycerides are the most important type of fat in the body. Fat is the second most important source of energy during exercise. It is sometimes referred to as the 'slow' source of energy in comparison with carbohydrates, because the body produces less energy per second from fat than from carbohydrates. Ten percent more oxygen is needed to produce the same amount of energy from fat as from carbohydrates. During intensive work, when the body's oxygen intake reaches its limit (see page 34), it is therefore much more economical to use carbohydrates. Fats function not only as a fuel, but also as a building material for cell walls, as protection for organs, as insulation for the body, and as a catalyst for the absorption of (fat-soluble) vitamins A, D, E and K by the body.

Fat reserves

In contrast to the carbohydrate reserve, the body has considerable reserves of fat. Triglycerides are stored in fat cells, which together form the fatty tissue. Fatty tissue is mainly located just under the skin. It also surrounds the organs in the zone of the stomach and abdomen. In addition, there are small amounts of triglycerides in the muscles and blood. On average, men have a body fat percentage of 10 to 20%. In women this figure is often higher (20 to 35%). People who are very fit may have a much lower percentage.

> *A clean and sober way of life is of overriding importance for every athlete.*
> **Roger Milla**

What foods contain fats?

Just as with carbohydrates, there are 'good' and 'bad' fats in our food. The 'bad' variety are the saturated fats. These are present in animal products and the above mentioned products such as candy and cookies. Excessive intake of saturated fats can cause constriction of the blood vessels, leading to cardiovascular disease. If too much fat is eaten, the percentage of fat in the body increases. The 'good' fats, known as unsaturated fats, are present in fish and vegetable products. These fats act to prevent constriction of the blood vessels. It is therefore advisable to eat fish oils, nuts and seeds. An exception to this rule is coconut. Intake of this vegetable product should be limited. The difference between saturated and unsaturated fats is in their structure. There is also a difference between essential and nonessential fats. Essential fats are fats that the body has to obtain through a proper diet, because it cannot make them itself. It can, however, produce nonessential fats, and these are usually present in the body in ample amounts.

11.2.3 Proteins

Proteins are the body's building blocks. They play an extremely important role in the growth of muscles and the repair of damaged tissues. Proteins also function as a fuel when a sportsman's reserves of glycogen are exhausted, and in this way they ensure that the brain is always provided with fuel, even in extreme situations. Proteins are made up of 21 different amino acids. The body can only make eleven of these itself (nonessential amino acids). The other ten (essential) amino acids have to be obtained from the body's food intake. In the case of children there are 12 essential amino acids. If too few (essential) proteins are eaten, there is a danger that recovery and adjustment processes (conditioning effects) will take place incompletely or not at all. After all, there will be too few building blocks. By contrast, excessive intake of proteins does not cause recovery and adjustment to take place faster. It even puts an unnecessary extra burden on the kidneys.

Protein reserves

Unlike carbohydrates and fats, a reserve of proteins is not built up in the body. All of the proteins in the body are functional. They all perform a function, and this cannot be said of all of the body's fats and carbohydrates. If more proteins are eaten than are needed, the excess is split into two parts. One part leaves the body in the urine, while the other is used directly as a fuel or is stored as glycogen or fat. Proteins serve as fuel if the glycogen reserves are exhausted and fat is not being burned up at a sufficient rate. Because all of the proteins in the body have a function, in extreme cases even muscles or organs are broken down to produce energy.

What foods contain proteins?

It is best to eat food in which the ratio between essential and nonessential amino acids is approximately the same as in the human body. Less protein-rich food then has to be eaten to obtain all the essential amino acids. Not only milk and dairy products, eggs, meat and fish, but also potatoes, rice, soybeans and green vegetables meet this requirement. Cereals, bread, nuts and most vegetables are less suitable. The problem with vitamin-rich food is that it often contains a lot of fat. For this reason, low-fat protein prod-ucts should be chosen when possible.

11.2.4 What fuel is used when?
In the introduction, it is stated that the human body can make use of different fuels (carbohydrates, fats and proteins). The choice of a particular fuel during exercise depends on a number of factors.

- the exercise intensity
- the exercise duration
- the fitness of the sportsman
- carbohydrate consumption during the exercise

Exercise intensity
The energy that is needed during exercise is mainly obtained by burning carbohydrates and fats. Depending on the exercise intensity, one of these two sources is dominant. During rest periods, for example, almost all the necessary energy is provided by burning fats. Only the brain (and other parts of the nervous system) make use of carbohydrates as fuel. As the exercise intensity is stepped up, the role of carbohydrates (glycogen) gradually gains in importance. Very fit sportsmen still use more fats than carbohydrates during jogging. During running, the relationship is already around 50-50%. During intensive exercise, carbohydrates are virtually the only fuel. Only by burning carbohydrates can the body obtain the energy it needs to rapidly carry out such activities as sprinting, shooting and jumping. Carbohydrates are therefore essential for a sportsman who has to make /successive short, explosive actions over a long period of time.

Carbohydrates are almost the only fuel for explosive actions.

Exercise duration
Not only the intensity but also the duration of the exercise influences the body's fuel consumption. During long-term exercise, the body's glycogen reserve is a limiting factor, because it is not very large. Intensive intervals of exercise (such as during a game of soccer) can exhaust this reserve after only 90 minutes. During less intensive exercise, relatively more fat is used and the sportsman's glycogen reserve is first exhausted after a number of hours. When the glycogen reserve is completely spent, proteins are also used as fuel. It is almost impossible to play soccer without glycogen. All kinds of actions can no longer be performed explosively. A soccer player cannot function on energy from fat,

because the rate of energy production is too slow. As a result he can only sprint at half strength.

A sportsman's fitness

The disadvantage of fat is that it takes a relatively long time to convert it into energy (ATP). Conditioning can ensure that the conversion proceeds faster. This makes fat a more attractive source of energy during intensive exercise. A fit person is able to use more fat and less carbohydrate at a given exercise intensity. His glycogen reserves are therefore expended more slowly. In addition, conditioning for endurance increases the body's capacity for storing glycogen. The glycogen reserve becomes bigger.

Carbohydrate consumption during exercise

Players who have a bigger glycogen reserve when they start a game are slower to experience a glycogen deficit, and can maintain intensive exercise for a longer period. The size of a sportsman's glycogen reserve depends on his daily intake of carbohydrates. Carbohydrate intake during exercise plays an important role. If the glycogen reserves are almost or completely spent, the body will start to use the carbohydrates that it has just ingested. The switch to 'slower' fat is therefore delayed or even avoided. The sportsman can therefore continue to perform at maximum capacity. Another consequence of eating carbohydrates during a match is that these carbohydrates are used to replenish the glycogen reserves during quieter moments in the play. If players stand still, walk or jog easily, no demands are being made on the glycogen reserve. This period can therefore be used to allow glycogen synthesis (glycogen formation) to take place.

11.2.5 Water

Water is often forgotten in the discussion on nutrition. It is possible, however, to survive for a very long time without carbohydrates and fats, but not without water. Water is the main component of the human body. Around 50 to 60 percent of the body consists of water. It is essential for all processes that take place in the body. Its most important role is to transport substances that are necessary for growth and energy production (metabolism). During intensive exercise, or exercise in hot surroundings, the body may lose a lot of water through perspiration. A water deficit can lead to a reduction in the volume of blood. The transport of oxygen and nutrients to the muscles therefore decreases, and less heat is carried away from the muscles. The result of a water deficit during exercise is more rapid fatigue.

What is the body's daily water requirement?

Everyone must ensure that his water balance remains in equilibrium. This means that the body's fluid output must be at least matched by its fluid intake. Participating in sport results in additional fluid loss, and it is therefore necessary to compensate for this. The amount of fluid lost depends on a number of factors:
- ambient temperature;
- atmospheric humidity;
- exercise intensity;
- exercise duration;

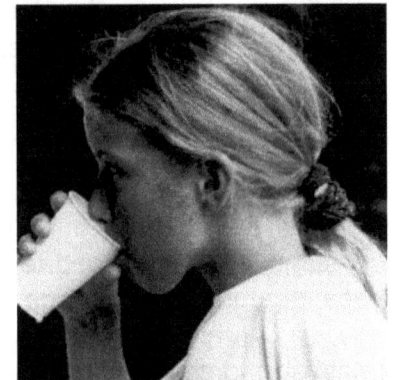

Thirst is a sign that the right time to drink is already past.

- clothing

(insulating material causes more perspiration and therefore more fluid is lost).

A fluid loss of 1% of the body's weight has a negative effect on performance. Larger losses result in a larger deterioration in performance. Sportsmen often regard thirst as a sign that they need to take in fluid. However, thirst is not felt until a fluid loss of 2% has already occurred. The obvious conclusion is that thirst is a warning signal, indicating that the right moment for taking a drink has already passed. Sportsmen must be taught to drink regularly during matches and training sessions, so that they will never feel thirsty. The amount of fluid that a sportsman loses while engaging in his sport can be measured easily by checking his weight before and after the match or training session. Naturally, clothing should not be worn when he weighs himself.

11.3 NUTRITION IN RELATION TO SOCCER PERFORMANCE

The diet that a sportsman needs depends on the type of exercise that he has to perform. Naturally this also applies to soccer players. At several points in this book, it has been stated that a game of soccer is a succession of short, explosive actions. Soccer players must continuously run, sprint, turn and change direction. The biggest source of energy for such actions is the carbohydrate reserve (glycogen). Between actions, the players often walk or jog. They usually use such moments to recover from the more strenuous actions. For players who are fit, fat is the most important source of energy when they are walking or jogging.

11.3.1 Glycogen: the 'soccer fuel'

Players with a larger glycogen reserve can carry out more sprint work.

The short explosive actions that characterize a game of soccer rely mainly on the players' fast muscle fibers. These fibers are capable of producing a large 'energy flow' and a rapid increase in muscle tension. The fast muscle fibers take sugars from the blood to generate the necessary energy. When the glycogen reserves in the liver and the muscles are exhausted and the blood sugar level falls, fast muscle fibers are no longer capable of performing work. The player can continue to work for some time by making use of the slow muscle fibers. However, these fibers work less quickly and strongly, because they mainly derive their energy from fat. The intensity and strength of the player's exertions therefore decrease. The player simply becomes fatigued. In Chapter 1 it was explained that soccer players perform less work in the second half of the game than in the first half. Although other factors also play a role (decreased motivation if a team is losing, or a change of tactics for the purpose of defending a lead), exhausted glycogen reserves are viewed as the most important cause of fatigue in soccer players. The 'soccer fuel tank' is empty.

11.3.2 The influence of glycogen on soccer performance

The influence of glycogen on the work capacity of soccer players was studied in Sweden as long ago as 1973. Five soccer players (one defender, two midfielders and two attackers) started a game with maximum glycogen reserves. Four other players (one defender, two midfielders and one attacker) only had half of their maximum reserve (they had car-ried out tiring exercises the day before the game). A film analysis of the game was made, with the aim of determining how much work each player carried out during the game. All of the players did less work in the second half. The decrease was lower for the players who started with maximum glycogen reserves. They covered a total of 19% more ground. A bigger difference was found in the intensity. The players with less glycogen covered 50% of the distance at walking pace and 15% at a sprint. The figures for the other group were 24% and 25% respectively. The conclusion was that more glycogen enabled the players to carry out more (sprint) work. Sprinting is a key performance factor in contemporary soccer. Such experiments were carried out another ten times, and each time the result was the same. Soccer players become fatigued because they have exhausted their glycogen reserves. At lower levels of play, less discomfort is experienced when the glycogen reserves are spent. The logical explanation is that less sprint work is carried out at lower levels. On the other hand, the players have smaller glycogen reserves and therefore exhaust them more quickly. Selective nutrition only becomes important at the level of the second class Dutch Soccer Association leagues. In the lower classes it is important that the players should not eat too much fat. The intake of specific carbohydrate preparations is then less critical.

11.4 NUTRITIONAL GUIDELINES FOR SOCCER PLAYERS

Starting a game with a full 'glycogen tank1 will delay the moment when fatigue sets in. For a soccer player, it is important to eat correctly, so that as much carbohydrate as possible is stored in the leg muscles. This can be achieved by including carbohydrates in the daily diet, and by eating carbohydrates just before, during and directly after matches and strenuous training sessions.

> *Fortunately it is still possible to deliver a top performance on the basis of a chocolate confetti sandwich.*
>
> **Ellen van Langen**

11.4.1 The daily diet

First of all, soccer players must ensure that they take in the right amount of energy. There are no fixed rules for this, because energy consumption can vary widely from person to person. The percentage of fat in the body is the best indicator of whether energy intake and energy consumption are in equilibrium (see section 11.5.3). As long as this factor is at the right level and also remains stable, the energy balance is in equilibrium. Soccer players have to train and play almost every day. The glycogen reserves are drawn on regularly and can therefore become exhausted. It is of great importance to top up the reserves completely again within 24 hours. The next day a player is expected to play a good match or to give 100 percent during training sessions. This is only possible with maximum glycogen reserves. Glycogen is formed from glucose molecules that originate in the carbohydrates in a player's diet. Glycogen cannot be formed from fat, and it can only be formed to a small extent from protein. It follows that the rate at which the glycogen reserve is replenished is in inverse proportion to the amount of fat and protein in the player's diet. Expressed in terms of fuel, it is obvious that you should not put diesel in the tank of an automobile that runs on petrol. If the body uses energy derived from carbohydrates, then it needs regular refills of carbohydrate-rich food.

The daily diet (breakfast, lunch, dinner and snacks) of most people in the Netherlands consists of 45% carbohydrates, 40% fat and 15% proteins. This is not sufficient to completely replenish a soccer player's exhausted glycogen reserves within 24 hours. The proportion of carbohydrates must be increased and the percentage of fat reduced. This was illustrated by a study of the players of Malmö FF during their preparations for a UEFA Cup match. After the team played a league game on a Sunday, the players' glycogen reserves were down to about 25% on average. In the days between this match and the coming UEFA Cup game (on the following Wednesday evening), the players' dietary patterns were recorded and their glycogen reserves were measured. The players had an 'average' dietary pattern, and as a result their glycogen reserves had only recovered to 39% of maximum by the Tuesday. No further measurements were carried out on the Wednesday, as this would have disrupted the team's preparations. Nevertheless, it can be assumed that the levels of glycogen reserves of the Swedish players were only half of what they should have been. The players of Malmö FF were thus far from ideally prepared for a UEFA Cup game. The indications are that many (professional) soccer players have a similar dietary pattern.

In short, a soccer player must eat more carbohydrates than he uses. The precise percentages differ from playing level to playing level. The higher the level, the higher the proportion of carbohydrates must be. The protein content of a player's diet should always be around 10 to 15%. The measure that is often applied is 1.2 to 1.4 grams of protein per kilogram of body weight. There is no point in eating more. This does not result in increased muscle growth. The excess is simply discharged from the body or stored as energy. During periods when the emphasis is on weight training, the protein content should be increased to 2 grams per kilogram of body weight. After all, muscles need building blocks to become stronger. The fat intake of players at higher levels must be restricted. An increase in the fat percentage has a negative effect on performance capacity (sprint capacity). Figure 11.4 gives a picture of the recommended amounts of carbohydrates, fats and proteins in the diet of soccer players at each playing level.

Playing Level	Carbohydrates (%)	Fat (%)	Proteins (%)
Professional soccer	65-70	15-20	15
Top class amateur	60-65	20-25	15
2nd class amateur	55-60	25-30	10-15
5th class amateur	50-55	30-35	10-15
18 year-olds juniors	60-65	20-25	15

Figure 11.4: *Contribution of carbohydrates, fats and proteins to daily energy consumption.*

Percentages on their own do not reveal very much. They are always percentages of 'something.' In this case the 'something' is the total amount of energy intake. From page 279 of this chapter, an explanation is given of how to determine the total amount of energy a person needs to take in each day. During busy periods of the season, players generally use more energy because they have to play more games. They need to step up the amount of carbohydrates they eat in the intervals between training sessions and games, because it is then more important to replenish the glycogen reserves. It is also essential that players who are ill or injured, and who therefore carry out less conditioning work for a long period of time, should adjust their dietary patterns to their reduced energy requirement. The same applies to all players during the winter and summer breaks. If they neglect to do so, their weight and fat percentage will increase unnecessarily (positive energy balance, see Fig. 11.9 page 280).

11.4.2 Carbohydrate intake before a match

Players should eat meals containing carbohydrates (pasta, rice or potatoes) on the 2 or 3 evenings preceding a match. This gives the glycogen reserves an extra stimulus. On the day of the match, the players must be very careful with their carbohydrate intake. A player must not have undigested food in his stomach when he starts a match. Care must also be taken with the blood sugar level, which drops immediately after carbohydrates have been eaten and requires some time to recover (60-90 minutes). If recovery is still incomplete when the match starts, the players will become fatigued sooner. The planning of the meals before a match is therefore crucial. The 'sport meal' is a crucial element of a match day. This is the players' final main meal before the match. This is an accepted routine nowadays. The meal is taken between 2 and 4 hours before the match, and is intended to provide the players with extra energy. The ideal sport meal for soccer players consists largely of carbohydrates, with as little fat, fibers and proteins as possible. If a sport meal is taken too shortly before the match, there is a danger that not all of the food will have been digested before the game starts. This may result in gastrointestinal discomfort. The digestive process is dependent on a flow of blood to the gastrointestinal tract. This is unfortunate, because during exercise as much blood as possible must be available for the active muscles and organs. Products with polysaccharides (such as cereals) can cause problems. They often contain a lot of fibers, which slow down the digestion process. Fatty foods must also be avoided as much as possible in the run-up to a match. Fats take a long time to digest. Only very lean meat (such as chicken) is suitable. Fatty sauces are also totally unsuitable for a sport meal.

Until two hours before the warming-up, only easily digestible 'carbohydrate snacks' (granola bars, bananas) should be eaten. Subsequently, no more carbohydrates should be eaten before the warming-up. This ensures that the blood sugar level is maintained. After the warming-up starts, it is advisable to eat carbohydrates again. This is because hormones that prevent a drop in the blood sugar level are released during exercise (in this case during warming-up). The most suitable form

Ambient temperature	Fluid intake
< 15 degrees Celsius	0.2 liters
15 - 25 degrees Celsius	0.4 liters
> 25 degrees Celsius	0.6 liters

Figure 11.5: *Amount of liquid that should be drunk between warming-up and the start of a match and during the break at various ambient temperatures.*

of carbohydrate intake just before (and during) a match is a (hypotonic or isotonic) energy drink. Intake of solid food has considerable disadvantages. The amount to drink depends on the ambient temperature (see Fig. 11.5). Players perspire more during warmer weather, so they need to drink more. However, the carbohydrate requirement

Ambient temperature	Carbohydrate concentration
< 15 degrees Celsius	90 grams of carbohydrate per liter (9%)
15 - 25 degrees Celsius	45 grams of carbohydrate per liter (4.5%)
> 25 degrees Celsius	0.6 liters

Figure 11.6: *Amount of carbohydrates per liter of fluid at various ambient temperatures. This takes account of the fact that more fluid has to be drunk at higher temperatures.*

remains the same. If the weather is hot, the carbohydrates should be dissolved in a larger amount of fluid. The carbohydrate concentration in the fluid will then be lower (see Fig. 11.6).

11.4.3 Carbohydrate intake during a match

The rules of soccer make it difficult for players to take in carbohydrates regularly during a match. A game of soccer only includes natural breaks. During a match, the players must not carry drinks on the pitch. Nor are players allowed to leave the pitch to take more energy on board. Despite these restrictions, the players must grasp every opportunity of taking in more energy. For one thing, an energy drink can yield a number of surprising advantages if it is consumed during a match. Towards the end of a match, a soccer player's glycogen reserves are low. He then has to make more and more use of energy derived from fat. Research has shown that, if players start to consume energy drinks when they start to perform work, this delays the moment when the muscles have to switch over to fat as the main source of energy. The carbohydrates in the drink pass into the blood stream. When the active muscles run out of (or have insufficient) glycogen, they absorb these carbohydrates from the blood. The carbohydrates from the energy drink are also used to replenish the glycogen reserves. This occurs during the brief moments when no demands are made on the glycogen reserves. When a player stands still, walks or jogs, fat is the most important source fuel. To prevent the carbohydrates from the energy drink from accumulating in the blood, some of them are removed from the blood, converted into glycogen, and stored in the muscles. The glycogen reserves therefore increase. After the game it seems as though the players have used up less glycogen than usual. Their 'net' glycogen consumption is lower. As a result of these two processes, soccer players' glycogen reserves are spent less quickly. The players are therefore capable of performing explosive actions even during

During a game of soccer, there are only a few natural breaks when players can take a drink.

the last part of a match. Fatigue caused by glycogen exhaustion expresses itself in, among other things, a loss of speed (off the mark) and an increase in recovery time between sprints.

During a match, the players must also drink regularly to ensure that their fluid balance remains in equilibrium. If they wait until they feel thirsty before drinking, they are too late. Feelings of thirst indicate that the body is in an early stage of dehydration, with all the negative consequences for performance capacity. Players should therefore aim, as far as possible, to take in 0.1 to 0.3 liters of energy drink every 15 minutes during a match. The exact amount depends on the weather (see Fig. 11.7). Although the consumption of energy drinks during a match is important, it should not be allowed to influence the match itself. Players should only drink when the match situation allows this. Small bottles of energy drink can be placed around the pitch, so that players can regularly exploit breaks in the play to take a drink. The advantage of this is that they do not need to run to the substitutes bench, and there is therefore less danger of being out of position when the play resumes. Even if the weather is not hot, it is advisable to make use of this strategy. The bottles must be positioned in such a way that they do not rep-resent any danger to the players.

Ambient temperature	Fluid intake
< 15 degrees Celsius	0.1 liters
15 - 25 degrees Celsius	0.2 liters
> 25 degrees Celsius	0.3 liters

Figure 11.5: *Amount of liquid that should be drunk every fifteen minutes during a match.*

11.4.4 Carbohydrate intake after the match

After a match, the players' glycogen reserves are very low (especially at the higher levels of play). They need to be replenished as soon as possible. To achieve this, the players have to do more than eat lots of carbohydrates. The carbohydrates must also be eaten at the right moment. Research has shown that more can be done to accelerate the recovery of the glycogen reserves in the first two hours after a match. A specific enzyme in the body is responsible for the recovery process. The lower the reserves become, the more active the enzyme is. After a match, the players have used up (almost) all of their glycogen. The activity of this enzyme is therefore at a peak during the next two hours. Its activity then decreases rapidly. The best results can be achieved by taking in carbohydrates immediately after a match. As a general guideline, players should take in 100 grams of carbohydrates during this time, followed by 25 grams per hour in the subsequent period. A total of 10 grams of carbohydrates per kilogram of body weight should be taken in within 24 hours. Soccer players are not usually hungry after a match, so they need to be encouraged to take carbohydrate drinks to ensure that the above levels of carbohydrate intake are achieved. In this way, they also compensate for the fluid they have lost during the match.

11.4.5 Carbohydrate intake before, during and after training sessions

Soccer players also use up glycogen during training sessions. Their dietary patterns must therefore be geared to the training schedule. Here, too, the actual match must serve as a model. In general, therefore, the match guidelines should also be applied to training sessions, even though the intensity and extent of training sessions vary considerably during the course of a week. Soccer players should not eat too much before a training

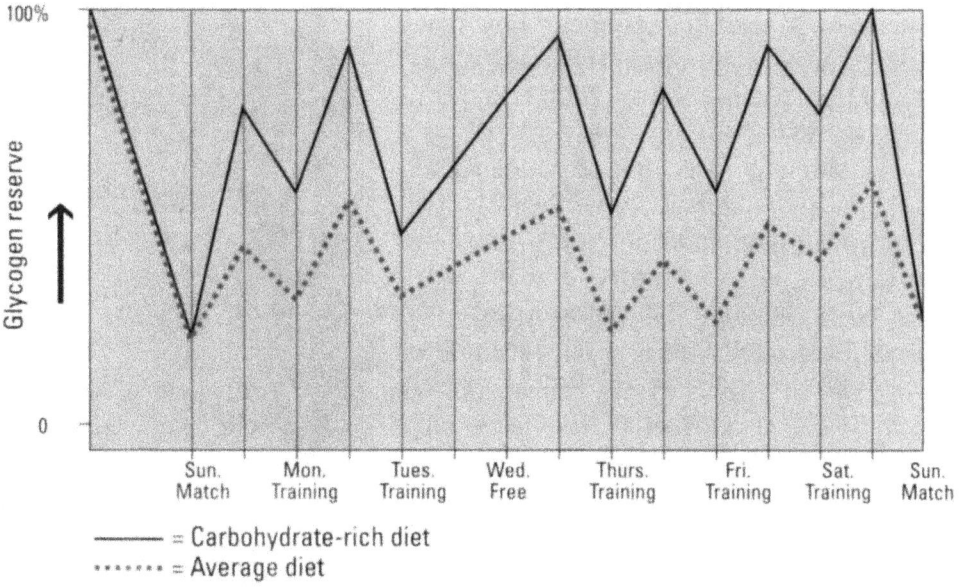

Figure 11.8: *An example of the flucuations in the glycogen reserve during a week of training sessions and matches. A player who follows the guidelines on carbohydrate consumption will start every training session and game with a virtually maximum glycogen reserve. If carbohydrate intake is insufficient the glycogen reserve will not be replenished before the next training session or match.*

session. Undigested food in the stomach causes the same problems during drills as during a match. The big advantage of training sessions is that drink breaks can be more easily incorporated. A coach should certainly make use of this opportunity. After the end of the session the players should take in carbohydrates, to ensure that their glycogen reserves are fully replenished when they start the next session. Figure 11.8 shows the fluctuations in the glycogen reserves of a player who takes in sufficient carbohydrates and a player who does not follow the specified guidelines.

11.4.6 The importance of fluid for soccer players

During long periods of intensive exercise, fluid loss will occur. This is a consequence of the production of heat in the body, and the process of cooling through perspiration. The amount of fluid loss depends on the ambient temperature, the atmospheric humidity, and the type of clothing being worn. The player's level of fitness and the intensity of the match or training session also play a role. It is very important to keep the body's fluid balance in equilibrium by drinking an adequate amount of fluid. The amount of fluid that a soccer player should drink at various temperatures has already been indicated in this chapter. It has been shown that a fluid loss amounting to 1 % of body weight (800 ml for a player who weighs 80 kilograms) is sufficient to have a negative effect on performance. Most of the fluid that is lost in the form of perspiration comes from the blood. The amount of blood circulating around the body, therefore, becomes gradually smaller when considerable fluid loss occurs. The blood flow in the muscles decreases, so the supply of nutrients and oxygen to the muscles (and the transport of waste products from the muscles) is restricted. The only way of preventing this is to harmonize the body's fluid intake with its fluid loss.

Energy drink: the ideal solution

Soccer players must take in a lot of carbohydrates before, during and after a match. However, eating a large amount of food before a match can cause gastrointestinal discomfort if the food is not completely digested by the kick-off time. Eating solid food during a match is inconvenient and can also result in gastrointestinal problems. After the match the players are not hungry, and therefore cannot eat large amounts of carbohydrate-rich food. All in all, it is clear that it is not practical to eat carbohydrate-rich solid foods before, during and after a match. A number of special energy drinks have been developed to solve this problem. An energy drink simply consists of water in which a certain amount of carbohydrate is dissolved. This carbohydrate solution is absorbed into the body much faster, and there is far less chance of gastrointestinal problems occurring. Another advantage is that the consumption of these energy drinks keeps the body's fluid balance in equilibrium. Soccer players lose between 2 and 5 liters of fluid during a match or training session, depending on

At lower levels of play, it is sufficient to drink water.

the ambient temperature and the work intensity. It has already been stated that fluid loss has a negative effect on performance. This can be avoided by taking regular drinks during a match. However, the ability of players to perform well when they have fluid in the stomach varies widely. Some players can drink a lot, but others cannot tolerate even small amounts of fluid in the stomach. For this reason, it is necessary to experiment with drinking during training sessions. In this way, it is possible to determine which drinking pattern best suits a player, and the players become used to playing when they have fluid in the stomach. This usually happens quickly. The fluid tolerance of the stomach during exercise can be conditioned.

11.5 THE ENERGY BALANCE

In the guidelines above, reference is made to percentages of the total energy intake. The question is, how can we determine the total energy that a person can or must take in each day? It is clear that energy intake has to match energy output. This is referred to as the energy balance. If energy intake is too high or too low, then the energy balance is positive or negative (see Fig. 11.9). An example of a good dietary pattern is shown in Figure 11.10. The player concerned plays in the top class Dutch Soccer Association league. Because it is almost impossible to measure energy intake and output each day, another (indirect) method must be found to ascertain whether the energy balance is in equilibrium. Body weight is frequently used as a criterion. It is known that a positive energy balance results in an increase in weight, and a negative balance causes loss of weight. If the body's weight remains constant, it is assumed that energy intake and output are in equilibrium. This is not always true. A player who is injured, and is therefore inactive for a long period of time, will experience some loss of muscle bulk. If his body weight remains constant, this means that the lost muscle bulk has been compensated for by an increase in the amount of fatty tissue in his body. Moreover, there is the question of what is a person's ideal body weight.

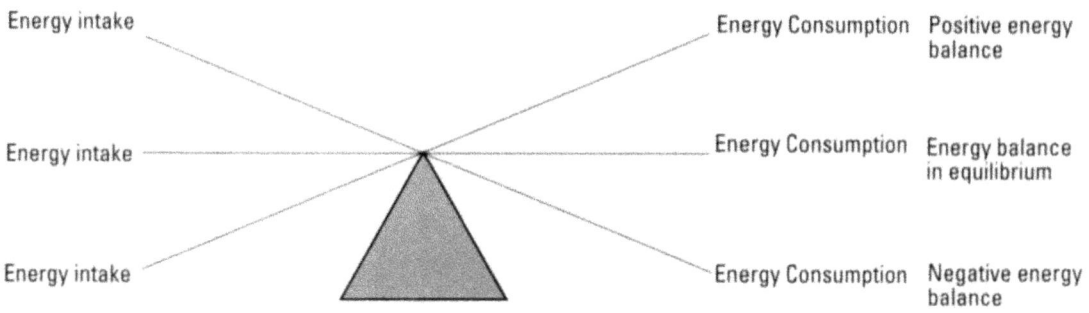

Figure 11.9: *An overview of the relationship between energy intake and consumption, and the associated energy balance.*

11.5.1 The ideal body weight on the basis of height

A number of methods have been developed for determining the ideal body weight on the basis of height. The very variety of these methods indicates that there is no single good way. The most familiar methods are those of Broca and Lorenz.

Broca's method
Men: ideal weight = height (cm) - 100
Women: ideal weight = (height (cm) - 100) - 10%

Lorenz's method

$$\text{Ideal weight} = (\text{height (cm)} - 100) \frac{\text{height (cm)} - 150}{4}$$

In practice very few people have an ideal body weight that corresponds to the weight determined by these two methods.

11.5.2 The Quetelet index

The Quetelet index (Q.I.) makes use of both height and weight. The Q.I. is a figure that is calculated by dividing an individual's weight (in pounds) by the square of his or her height:

$$Q.I. = \frac{\text{weight (pounds)}}{\text{height (ft/inches)} \times \text{height (ft/inches)}}$$

The Q.I. should be between 18.5 and 24.9, irrespective of height, age and gender. Figure 11.11 shows the range of ideal body weights for each height. However, this is still an

	Carbohydrates (grads)	Fat (grams)	Protein (grams)
Breakfast			
3 slices of whole-wheat bread	39.5	2.7	8.6
3 thinly spread with low-fat margarine	0.1	4.3	0.1
1 thinly spread with apple syrup	8.2	0.0	0.3
1 thinly spread of honey	12.0	0.0	0.0
1 thinly spread with jam	9.0	0.0	0.0
1 glass/mug of orange juice (unsweetened)	17.6	0.0	1.0
Snack (morning)			
2 biscuits	23.8	1.8	3.1
2 cups of coffee	0.6	0.0	0.0
Midday meal			
5 slices of whole-wheat bread	65.8	4.5	14.3
5 thinly spread with low-fat margarine	0.2	7.1	0.2
1 slice of cheese	0.0	6.2	5.9
2 slices of sandwich meat (average)	0.5	6.3	5.1
1 thinly spread with jam	9.0	0.0	0.0
1 thinly spread with apple syrup	8.2	0.0	0.3
2 glasses/mugs of low-fat milk	18.4	6.0	14.4
1 portion of fruit (average)	12.8	0.1	0.9
Evening meal			
5 potatoes (average, boiled)	42.0	0.0	5.8
300 grams of winter vegetables (cooked without salt)	10.2	0.6	5.1
10 grams of meat (average, less than 5 grams of fat, raw)	0.4	2.9	22.2
15 grams of cooking margarine	0.1	14.7	0.1
100 grams of low-fat quark	3.9	0.6	10.1
100 grams of vanilla tart	14.0	2.8	3.1
1 portion of fruit (average)	12.8	0.1	0.9
Snack (evening)			
2 glasses/mugs of tea	0.0	0.0	0.0
2 biscuits	23.8	1.8	3.1
After training session/match			
2 slices of whole-wheat bread	26.3	1.8	5.7
1 thinly spread with apple syrup	8.2	0.0	0.3
1 thinly spread with honey	12.0	0.0	0.0
During training session/match			
1 bottle of water	0.0	0.0	0.0
100 ml soft drink	54.0	0.0	0.0
2 bananas	57.1	0.6	3.4
General			
2 vitamin tablets	0.0	0.0	0.0
TOTAL	490.3 (65.3%)	64.9 (19.5%)	113.9 (15.2%)

Figure 11.10: *Diet of a player in the top class amateur league of the Dutch Soccer Association.*

indirect method. The amount of fat is not actually measured. This is why another method is usually employed, which is known as skinfold measurement. This gives an indication of the amount of fat that is stored in the body.

11.5.3 The percentage of body fat

Fat has a negative image. Many people immediately think of excess weight, and health problems. Fat, as such, has nothing to do with these problems. The body cannot survive without fat. But as with most things, fat can be harmful when it is present in excess. Excess fat is the cause of the problems referred to above. Most of the body's surplus energy intake is stored in the form of fat. The body has special fat depots (fat cells), especially under the skin, to enable it to do this. Thus, if the fat layer under the skin increases in size, this is a sign that more energy is being taken in than is actually needed (positive energy balance). In general terms, the body can be considered to consist of a fatty mass and a non-fatty mass (muscles, skeleton and organs). By measuring the percentage of fat, it is possible to calculate the fat mass. This method has considerable advantages in comparison with simply measuring the body's weight. It has already been stated that the body's weight can give a distorted picture of what is happening inside the body. A person who takes part in a lot of sporting activity as a means of losing weight will lose fat on the one hand and gain muscle bulk on the other. In this way the body weight may increase rather than decrease. Part of the reason is that muscle is heavier than fat. Such misinterpretation is avoided by measuring the fat percentage.

Height (m)	Q.I. = 18	Q.I. = 24.9
4' 10"	41	57
5' 0"	43	60
5' 2"	46	64
5' 4"	49	68
5' 6"	52	72
5' 8"	55	77
5' 10"	58	81
6' 0"	62	85
6' 2"	65	90
6' 4"	68	95
6' 6"	72	100

Figure 11.11: *For an ideal weight, the Q.I. must be between 18 and 24.9. This table shows the minimum and maximum weights for a range of heights.*

Skinfold measurements

Skinfold measurements must be carried out on the left side of the body for right-handers, and on the right side for left-handers. The measurements must be carried out with the subject in a standing position. The thumb and index finger of the hand that grasps the fold must be placed 4 centimeters apart on the measurement point. The skinfold must be grasped in alignment with the elastic fibers of the skin. No

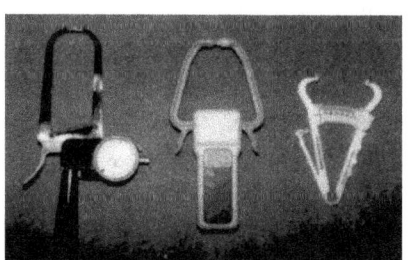

There are various types of skinfold meters.

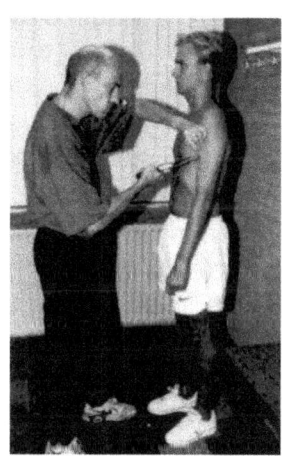

Skinfold measurements can be used to determine the percentage of body fat.

muscle should be grasped. If there is any doubt, the muscles should be tensed to check this. The skinfold calipers are then placed on the skinfold, about 2 centimeters from the thumb and index finger. After a few seconds the thickness of the skinfold can be read off. Each skinfold must be measured three times. The average thickness is recorded. The Durnin method is used in the Netherlands. This involves measuring four skinfolds. The percentage of body fat can be determined from the sum of the four skinfold thicknesses, and the age and sex of the subject.

1. The front of the upper arm (bicipital fold)
The arm hangs down in a relaxed fashion with the palm of the hand facing forward. The center of the upper arm is then determined. This can be done by marking the acromion and the olecranon. The acromion is a bony projection from the shoulder-blade and can be felt on the top of the shoulder. The olecranon is the point of the elbow. With the help of a tape measure, the middle of the line joining the two points can be determined. The skinfold is aligned longitudinally to the upper arm.

2. The back of the upper arm (tricipital fold)
This skinfold is directly above the olecranon, precisely in the center of the upper arm. This skinfold is also aligned longitudinally to the upper arm.

A skinfold on the back of the upper arm is measured.

3. Under the shoulder-blade (subscapular fold)
The lowest point of the shoulder-blade can be located by touch. A skinfold about 2 cm in length can be grasped at this point, and the measurement is carried out 2 cm away from the fingers. The elastic fibers of the skin run from 'top center' to 'bottom side' at an angle of 45 degrees at this point. The skinfold must run parallel to these fibers.

4. Above the edge of the pelvis (supra-iliacal fold)
A vertical line runs down from the center of the armpit. The intersection of this line and the edge of the pelvis is the measuring point. The elastic fibers of the skin run from 'top back' to 'front bottom' here. The skinfold must also run in this direction.

When the thickness of each of the four skinfolds has been measured, the four measurements are added together. The table in Figure 11.12 can then be used to read off the percentage of body fat. The table gives the figures for both men and women from the age of 1 7. Only very general guidelines can be given for boys and girls between the ages of 12 and 16 (see Figure 11.13). This is because children in this age group can differ widely from each other due to the growing process.

11.6   Nutrition in relation to health
The basis for good sporting performances is a healthy body. Nutrition is not only important during exercise. All kinds of processes also take place in the body when it is at rest. A shortage of nutrients such as vitamins, minerals and trace elements can disrupt these processes. As a consequence the body functions less efficiently, and health becomes

MEN

Sum of 4 skinfolds (mm)	Age 17-29	30-39	40-49	50+	Sum of 4 skinfolds (mm)	Age 17-29	30-39	40-49	50+
	Body fat (% of body weight)					Body fat (% of body weight)			
15	4.8				63	21.8	24.1	27.8	30.0
16	5.5				64	22.0	24.2	28.0	30.2
17	6.2				65	22.2	24.3	28.2	30.4
18	6.9				66	22.4	24.5	28.5	30.7
19	7.5				67	22.6	24.7	28.7	31.1
20	8.4	12.2	12.2	12.6	68	22.8	24.9	28.9	31.2
21	8.6	12.6	12.8	13.2	69	23.0	25.0	29.1	31.4
22	9.1	13.0	13.4	13.8	70	23.1	25.1	29.3	31.6
23	9.6	13.4	14.0	14.4	71	23.3	25.3	29.5	31.9
24	10.1	13.8	14.5	15.5	72	23.5	25.5	29.7	32.1
25	10.5	14.2	15.0	15.6	73	23.7	25.7	29.9	32.3
26	11.0	14.6	15.6	16.2	74	23.9	25.8	30.1	32.5
27	11.5	15.0	16.2	16.8	75	24.0	25.9	30.3	32.7
28	12.0	15.4	16.7	17.4	76	24.2	26.1	30.5	33.0
29	12.5	15.8	17.2	18.0	77	24.4	26.3	30.7	33.2
30	12.9	16.2	17.7	18.6	78	24.6	26.4	30.9	33.4
31	13.3	16.5	18.1	19.1	79	24.7	26.5	31.1	33.6
32	13.7	16.8	18.5	19.6	80	24.8	26.6	31.2	33.8
33	14.1	17.1	18.9	20.0	81	25.0	26.8	31.4	34.0
34	14.4	17.4	19.3	20.4	82	25.2	26.9	31.6	34.2
35	14.7	17.7	19.6	20.8	83	25.3	27.0	31.8	34.3
36	15.1	18.0	20.0	21.3	84	25.4	27.1	32.0	34.6
37	15.5	18.3	20.4	21.7	85	25.5	27.2	32.1	34.8
38	15.8	18.6	20.8	22.1	90	26.2	27.8	33.0	35.8
39	16.1	18.9	21.1	22.5	95	26.9	28.4	33.7	36.6
40	16.4	19.2	21.4	22.9	100	27.6	29.0	34.4	37.4
41	16.7	19.5	21.8	23.3	105	28.2	29.6	35.1	38.2
42	17.0	19.8	22.1	23.7	110	28.8	30.1	35.8	39.0
43	17.3	20.0	22.4	24.1	115	29.4	30.6	36.4	39.7
44	17.5	20.2	22.7	24.4	120	30.0	31.1	37.0	40.4
45	17.7	20.4	23.0	24.7	125	30.5	31.5	37.6	41.1
46	18.0	20.7	23.4	25.1	130	31.0	31.9	38.2	41.8
47	18.3	20.9	23.7	25.5	135	31.5	32.3	38.7	42.4
48	18.6	21.1	24.0	25.9	140	32.0	32.7	39.2	43.0
49	18.8	21.3	24.3	26.2	145	32.5	33.1	39.7	43.6
50	19.0	21.5	24.5	26.5	150	32.9	33.5	40.2	44.1
51	19.3	21.7	24.9	26.8	155	33.3	33.9	40.7	44.6
52	19.5	21.9	25.2	27.1	160	33.7	34.3	41.2	45.1
53	19.7	22.1	25.5	27.4	165	34.1	34.6	41.6	45.6
54	19.9	22.3	25.7	27.7	170	34.5	34.8	42.0	46.1
55	20.1	22.5	25.9	27.9	175	34.9			
56	20.4	22.7	26.2	28.2	180	35.3			
57	20.6	22.9	26.5	28.5	185	35.6			
58	20.8	23.1	26.7	28.8	190	35.9			
59	21.0	23.3	26.9	29.0	195				
60	21.2	23.5	27.1	29.2	200				
61	21.4	23.7	27.4	29.5	205				
62	21.6	23.9	27.6	29.8	210				

WOMEN	Age					Age			
	17-29	30-39	40-49	50+		17-29	30-39	40-49	50+
Sum of 4 skinfolds (mm)	Body fat (% of body weight)				Sum of 4 skinfolds (mm)	Body fat (% of body weight)			
15	10.5				63	29.8	31.2	33.8	36.3
16	11.3				64	30.2	31.4	34.0	36.5
17	12.0				65	30.3	31.6	34.1	36.7
18	12.7				66	30.4	31.8	34.3	36.9
19	13.4				67	30.6	32.0	34.5	37.1
20	14.1	17.0	19.8	21.4	68	30.8	32.2	34.7	37.3
21	14.7	17.5	20.3	22.0	69	31.0	32.5	35.0	37.5
22	15.3	18.0	20.8	22.5	70	31.2	32.5	35.0	37.7
23	15.8	18.5	21.3	23.0	71	31.4	32.7	35.2	37.9
24	16.3	19.0	21.8	23.5	72	31.6	32.9	35.4	38.1
25	16.8	19.4	22.2	24.0	73	31.8	33.1	35.6	38.3
26	17.4	19.9	22.7	24.6	74	32.0	33.3	35.8	38.5
27	18.0	20.4	23.2	25.1	75	32.2	33.4	35.9	38.7
28	18.5	20.9	23.7	25.6	76	32.4	33.6	36.1	38.9
29	19.0	21.4	24.1	26.1	77	32.6	33.8	36.3	39.1
30	19.5	21.8	24.5	26.6	78	32.8	34.0	36.5	39.3
31	19.9	22.2	24.9	27.0	79	33.0	34.2	36.6	39.5
32	20.3	22.6	25.3	27.4	80	33.1	34.3	36.7	39.6
33	20.7	23.0	25.7	27.8	81	33.3	34.5	36.9	39.8
34	21.1	23.4	26.1	28.2	82	33.5	34.7	37.1	40.0
35	21.5	23.7	26.4	28.5	83	33.7	34.9	37.3	40.2
36	21.9	24.1	26.8	28.9	84	33.9	35.0	37.4	40.3
37	22.3	24.5	27.2	29.3	85	31.0	35.1	37.5	40.4
38	22.7	24.9	27.6	29.7	90	34.8	35.8	38.3	41.2
39	23.1	25.2	27.9	30.0	95	35.6	36.5	39.0	41.9
40	23.4	25.5	28.2	30.3	100	36.4	37.2	39.7	42.6
41	23.8	25.8	28.5	30.7	105	37.1	37.9	40.4	43.3
42	24.1	26.1	28.8	31.0	110	37.8	38.6	41.0	43.9
43	24.4	26.4	29.1	31.3	115	38.4	39.1	41.5	44.5
44	24.7	26.7	29.4	31.6	120	39.0	39.6	42.0	45.1
45	25.0	26.9	29.6	31.9	125	39.6	40.1	42.5	45.7
46	25.3	27.2	29.9	32.2	130	40.2	40.6	43.0	46.2
47	25.6	27.5	30.2	32.5	135	40.8	41.1	43.5	46.7
48	25.9	27.8	30.5	32.8	140	41.3	41.6	44.0	47.2
49	26.2	28.0	30.8	33.1	145	41.8	42.1	44.5	47.7
50	26.5	28.2	31.0	33.4	150	42.3	42.6	45.0	48.2
51	26.8	28.5	31.3	33.7	155	42.8	43.1	45.4	48.7
52	27.1	28.8	31.5	34.0	160	43.3	43.6	45.8	49.2
53	27.4	29.0	31.7	34.2	165	43.7	44.0	46.2	49.6
54	27.6	29.2	31.9	34.4	170	44.1	44.4	46.6	50.0
55	27.8	29.4	32.1	34.6	175		44.8	47.0	50.4
56	28.1	29.7	32.4	34.9	180		45.2	47.4	50.8
57	28.4	30.0	32.6	35.1	185		45.6	47.8	51.2
58	28.7	30.2	32.8	35.3	190		45.9	48.2	51.6
59	28.9	30.4	33.0	35.5	195		46.2	48.5	52.0
60	29.1	30.6	33.2	35.7	200		46.5	48.8	52.4
61	29.4	30.8	33.4	35.9	205			49.1	52.7
62	29.6	31.0	33.6	36.1	210			49.4	53.0

Figure 11.12: *Overview of the percentage of body fat associated with various accumulated skinfold totals, by sex and age (Durnin and Womersley).*

Age	Low Score	Below Average	Average	Above Average	High Score
12					
Boys	< 21	22-26	27-30	31.38	> 38
Girls	< 26	27-34	35-42	43-51	> 52
13					
Boys	< 21	22-25	26-31	32-42	> 43
Girls	< 29	30-36	37-43	44-56	> 57
14					
Boys	< 21	22-25	26-29	30-40	> 41
Girls	< 33	34-39	40-44	45-54	> 55
15					
Boys	< 21	22-24	25-27	28-35	> 36
Girls	<51	52-55	56-59	60-64	> 65
16					
Boys	< 19	20-22	23-26	27-32	> 33
Girls	< 34	35-41	42-49	50-60	> 61

Figure 11.13: *Indication of the body fat of boys and girls aged 12 to 16 years.*

endangered. In the field of nutrition, it is carbohydrates, fats and proteins that always attract most attention. However, the consumption, transport and storage of these nutrients depend on vitamins, minerals and trace elements.

11.6.1 Vitamins

Vitamins are involved in almost every biological process in the human body. They usually function as catalysts. This means that, processes would occur more slowly, or even not at all, if certain vitamins were not present. Vitamins are divided into two groups on the basis of their solubility properties. The one group is soluble in water, and the other in fats. Water-soluble vitamins (C and B complex) must be obtained in the daily diet, because the body is not able to store them in large quantities. Fat-soluble vitamins (A, D, E and K) can be stored in the body (in the liver and fatty tissue). A vitamin deficit can have a negative effect on physical fitness and can cause sickness. A good, varied diet prevents this problem. Extra vitamin intake does not improve performance capacity. Surplus vitamins are eliminated from the body as far as possible. Some vitamins are even toxic when present in excess, and this can lead to problems (for example, an excess of vitamin C can cause kidney stones). However, intensive participation in sport increases the body's requirement for a number of vitamins. These are discussed below.

Vitamin A (retinol)

Retinol is important for seeing in the dark. It is also of importance for the mucous membranes. Sportsmen who eat almost no fat run a risk of suffering from a retinol deficiency. Retinol itself is present in animal products such as milk and dairy products, fish, meat and eggs. However, vegetable products contain a substance called beta-carotene, which the body can convert into retinol. Green vegetables as well as yellow and green fruits can also supply the body with vitamin A.

Vitamin B (thiamin)
Thiamin plays an important role in converting carbohydrates into energy. The higher the body's carbohydrate intake, the more thiamin it needs. Thiamin also plays a small role in the breakdown and utilization of proteins. If a person's diet consists of 30% fat, he needs a daily intake of at least 0.6 mg of thiamin per 4200 kj of energy. There are, however, only a few food products that contain thiamin. Thiamin occurs mainly in cereals, pulses, egg yolk, meat and meat products, and pork. The problem with pork, in particular, is that it also contains a lot of fat.

Vitamin B2 (riboflavin)
Riboflavin is very important in the breakdown and utilization of proteins. The body's riboflavin requirement depends on the amount of proteins it has to convert into energy. A daily intake of 0.025 grams of riboflavin per gram of consumed protein is recom-mended, with a minimum of 1.3 mg per day for women and 1.6 mg per day for men. Riboflavin is present in whole-wheat cereal products, milk and dairy products, and meat and meat products.

Vitamin B6 (pyridoxine)
Pyridoxine is essential for the breakdown and utilization of proteins and amino acids. It is thought that the body's pyridoxine requirement increases with protein consumption. An intake of 0.020 mg pyridoxine per gram of protein is required. The absolute daily minimum is 2 mg for men and 1.6 mg for women. Too much pyridoxine can damage the nervous system, causing lethargy. Pyridoxine is present in cereal products, potatoes, pulses, eggs, fish and meat. Here, too, it is necessary to monitor the fat content.

A nutritional expert can determine a person's eating habits with the help of special food analysis programs and recommend changes if necessary.

Engaging in sport does not increase the body's requirement for the other vitamins, although sportsmen regularly pay attention to vitamins C and E.

Vitamin C (ascorbic acid)
Plays an essential role in the formation of connective tissue in the body. It also stimulates the uptake of iron. Too much vitamin C, however, inhibits the uptake of copper. A daily intake of 70 mg is recommended. This vitamin is present in vegetables, fruit and potatoes.

Vitamin E

Plays an essential role in protecting the body against dangerous and toxic substances (such as free oxygen radicals). It improves performance at high altitudes. An excess of vitamin E has a damaging effect on all bodily tissues. Vegetable oils, vegetables, fruit, potatoes, and milk and dairy products are especially rich in vitamin E.

Sportsmen with a healthy and varied diet have a sufficient vitamin intake. Sportsmen lose no more vitamins than other people through perspiration, urination and defecation. Moreover, sportsmen need more energy and therefore have to eat more. This automatically increases their vitamin intake. Soccer players who regularly train for one hour each day form an exception. They should consult a (sport) dietician for personal advice. Any deficiencies can then be identified and remedied.

11.6.2 Minerals

Minerals are crucial for the formation of bodily tissues and for conducting impulses from the nerves to the muscles. The body loses minerals through perspiration. These have to be replaced. A fit person loses less minerals per liter of perspiration than someone who is less fit.

Sodium

One of sodium's important functions is to regulate the body's fluid balance. The body tends to maintain the amount of salt per liter of fluid at a constant level (homeostasis). If the body's salt intake increases, more fluid is retained. Conversely, if a lot of salt is lost through perspiration, the body also loses more fluid. The blood volume decreases, with all the negative consequences for performance capacity. Sodium is present in common table salt. A daily intake of 3 to 8 grams of salt is sufficient. In practice, the average salt intake is 10 grams per day. Too much salt results in an increase in bodily fluid and higher blood pressure.

Potassium

Together with sodium, potassium plays an important role in sending impulses between the brain and muscles. These two minerals ensure that all impulses can be transmitted quickly through the nerve paths. A shortage of these substances causes disturbances of the nervous system.

Calcium

Calcium is an essential component of bones. It also plays a role in muscle contraction. During perspiration the body loses not only fluid but also calcium. Bone and muscle problems can be prevented by consuming dairy products. A good bone structure depends on not only calcium but also vitamin D (sunlight) and physical exercise.

Phosphate

Phosphate, like calcium, is essential for bones. Perspiration has a negligible effect on the amount of phosphate in the body. Protein-rich foods in particular, such as cereal products, milk and dairy products, and meat and meat products, are rich in phosphate.

Magnesium

Magnesium is essential for almost all energy processes. It accelerates the conversion of nutrients into fuel for the muscles. Magnesium also has a considerable influence on the functioning of muscles. It keeps the muscles supple. A shortage of magnesium can cause muscle cramp. Nuts, cereal products, (green) vegetables, milk and dairy products contain sufficient magnesium.

11.6.3 Trace elements

The name 'trace elements' indicates that only very small amounts of these substances are present in the body. Nevertheless, they have a considerable influence on performance capacity.

Iron

Iron is an important constituent of hemoglobin. Hemoglobin is the protein in the blood that transports oxygen from the lungs to the muscles. An iron deficit causes the hemoglobin content of the blood to fall, resulting in the condition referred to as anemia. The symptoms of anemia are an increased heart rate, lethargy, loss of appetite, and muscle cramps. An iron deficit can be caused by a shortage of iron in the diet or by perspiration. Loss of blood during menstruation or defecation also plays a role. Iron is present, above all, in foods such as cereal products, (whole-wheat) bread, unpolished rice, apple syrup, syrup, meat and meat products. Drinking a lot of tea and coffee can inhibit the uptake of iron by the body. Vitamin C stimulates the uptake of iron.

Zinc

Not as much is known yet about zinc as about other minerals. It is thought that it plays an essential role in the breakdown and utilization of carbohydrates. The zinc balance is also disrupted during perspiration. Any deficits can be made good by eating vegetables, nuts, cheese and meat. Too much zinc inhibits the uptake of copper by the body.

Copper

Copper plays a part in the formation of new body tissues. It also protects the body against harmful substances such as free oxygen radicals. Finally, the presence of copper has a favorable effect of the body's uptake of iron. Perspiration during intensive exercise can result in a considerable loss of copper. Cereal products, nuts, potatoes and liver are all food products with a high copper content.

Chromium

This trace element stimulates the activity of the hormone insulin. This causes the muscles to absorb more sugar from the blood. A chromium deficit can lead to a shortage of oxygen in the muscles, causing premature fatigue. An increased chromium intake results in an increase in the body's glycogen reserves. The muscles are better able to absorb sugar from the blood and store it. Broccoli, mushrooms and oysters are good sources of chromium.

11.6.4 Conclusion

The body can be regarded as a chemical factory. As soon as something is sent into it, all sorts of processes start to take place. Hormones are liberated and substances are con-verted into other substances. The more a person knows about these processes, the more he can control them. As a result, a sportsman's (and therefore a soccer player's) perfor-mance capacity can be improved through specific nutritional advice. This is still an underrated subject, especially in professional soccer. Recovery processes could be accelerated and conditioning effects could be enhanced, simply because the body's loading capacity increases.

SUMMARY

- Good nutrition is of essential importance for a soccer player if he is to maintain a good nutritional status, perform well, recover quickly after a match or training session, and avoid health risks.

- A (top) sportsman demands more of his body than an average person. He therefore needs a higher intake of energy and body-building substances. An average dietary pattern is inadequate.

- The human body is unique in that it has a variety of options for burning fuels. It can choose between carbohydrates, fats and sometimes even proteins to cover its energy needs at any given moment.

- Carbohydrates are broken down inside the body and are then used directly as fuel or are stored in the liver and muscles in the form of glycogen. The extent of the glycogen reserve is, however, limited.

- Triglycerides are the most important type of fat in the body. Fat is sometimes referred to as the 'slow' source of energy in comparison with carbohydrates, because the body produces less energy per second from fat than from carbohydrates.

- In nutrition, a distinction can be made between 'good' and 'bad' fats and between 'essential' and 'nonessential' fats.

- Proteins are the body's building blocks. If not enough proteins are eaten, areas of weakness will form in the body.

- Proteins can also be divided into 'essential' and 'nonessential' varieties.

- The fuel used during exercise depends on: the intensity and duration of the exercise; the fitness of the sportsman; and the level of carbohydrate intake during the exercise.

- Water is often forgotten in the discussion on nutrition. It is essential for all processes that take place in the body.

- Glycogen is the 'soccer fuel.' If a glycogen deficit occurs, there will be a decrease in total running and sprint work.

- A soccer player needs to step up the amount of carbohydrates in his daily diet and decrease the amount of fats.

- Carbohydrate-rich meals must be eaten on the evenings before a match. A light carbohydrate-rich 'sport meal' must be taken around 3 or 4 hours before the match. Large amounts of carbohydrates must not be ingested during the last 2 hours before a match.

- Carbohydrate drinks must be taken during a match. This saves glycogen and thus delays or prevents fatigue.

- Players must start to take in carbohydrates immediately after a match. The first two hours after a match are critical for replenishing the glycogen reserves.

- Measuring the percentage of body fat is the best way to determine whether a player's energy intake is sufficient.

- The percentage of body fat can be determined by measuring the thickness of four skinfolds. The percentage of body fat can be read off from a table against the sum of the thicknesses of the four folds.

- The basis for good sporting performances is a healthy body. A soccer player must therefore have an adequate intake of vitamins, minerals and trace elements. None of the processes in the body can take place without these nutrients. A shortage of, for example, vitamins will disrupt all kinds of processes.

FIVE PRACTICAL QUESTIONS

1. Amateur soccer players often have to train at 7.30 or 8 o'clock in the evening. What is the best time for them to eat a hot meal?

Ideally they should eat a hot meal at lunch time. Unfortunately this is impossible for many people. It is therefore advisable to try to eat at 5.30 or 6 o'clock in the evening. Another possibility is to split the hot meal into two phases. One part before the training session, and one part after. It is not advisable to eat a compete hot meal after the training session. By then it might be 10.30 or 11 o'clock, and much of the food eaten at this time is converted into fat.

2. Energy drinks have a positive effect on soccer performance, but clubs do not have enough money to buy them in large quantities. Is there an alternative?

Energy drinks are the ideal solution to the problem of maintaining soccer players' energy and fluid reserves at an acceptable level. However, they do cost money. Top amateurs are advised to use energy drinks, but below this level it suffices - and is cheaper - to drink enough water during the match.

3. Should players eat different food during the preseason preparation period than during the season?

During the preparation period the players must, in principle, work just as hard during training sessions as during the season. They should therefore eat the same food as during the season.

4. What can be done with regard to nutrition at the youth soccer level?

The most important thing is, of course, to wean the youngsters away from the 'fast food' culture. Young children can still be influenced to some extent. At this age a sound basis can be established for later eating habits. The professional clubs should play an important role here. It is advisable to involve the parents.

5. If a coach wants to look at this subject in more detail, where can he obtain information about scientific research?

There should be a lot of information available at your local libraries.

INTERVIEW WITH YVONNE VAN DER POL (Dietician with Ajax Amsterdam)

Why did you study dietetics?
I used to practice rhythmic gymnastics for 25 hours each week, and I paid a lot of attention to nutrition at that time. I had no one to turn to for advice, so my approach was not very systematic and this was frustrating. I knew all the data by heart, so I was a walking mine of information. It was therefore a logical step to study dietetics, which I did in Amsterdam between 1989 and 1993.

How did you get in touch with Ajax?
During the third year of the course I had to gain practical work experience. Because I hoped to get a job in the sports world, I looked for a place in this sector. I was given the chance to gain work experience with the Dutch rhythmic gymnastics team in Papendal, but turned it down. It did not seem much of a challenge to make thin little girls even thinner. Because the nutritional aspects had already been thoroughly covered in sports that involve physical strength and stamina, I decided to focus on the benefits of nutrition in team sports. Not a lot was known about this. Because I was studying in Amsterdam, and soccer is the major team sport, I contacted Ajax. I thought it would be interesting to spend three months there and look at all of the possibilities. I had no thought of getting a job there. Together with a fellow student I drew up a plan of what I wanted to do at Ajax. When we first rang the club we were brushed off, but we persisted, and eventually the club doctor, Piet Bon, gave us the chance to unveil our plan. This was accepted, and Ajax agreed to let us obtain our work experience there.

What was the nutritional situation at Ajax at that time?
We found that the players were given nutritional advice at that time. In addition, they were asked to keep a record of everything they ate and drank over a period of seven days. Most players did this only partially, or not at all. We proposed that, instead of asking the players to keep a record, they should be interviewed about what they had eaten in the last 24 hours. The information obtained in these interviews could then be used as a basis for providing nutritional advice. We also suggested organizing information talks for players and parents, to explain the relationship between nutrition and soccer. Another proposal was to draw up special guidelines for tournaments abroad. We suggested that, on the basis of these ideas, we should draw up a list of what needed to be done. In addition to this, I wanted to learn more about nutrition and soccer. Does nutrition affect performance? At that time very little was known about this. I had not expected that there would be so much information, or that nutrition could have such a considerable influence on soccer performance and yet so little was done in this area in soccer. A questionnaire indicated that the players had very little knowledge of nutrition, but that the interest in learning more was greater than expected. This was a reason for going further.

What was the following step?

After the period of work experience, we went back to college. Soon afterwards Ajax rang to ask whether I could come and advise certain players. In fact, from that moment I spent one afternoon every week working at Ajax. I then indicated that I wanted to write my thesis at Ajax. You have 6-months to do this, so you can go into everything in more detail. Because they already knew me, and could see that Ajax would also benefit, this was no problem. The objective of the thesis was to determine what information a dietician must provide during individual consultations and in a brochure, with a view to optimizing the soccer performances of the Ajax Under 18 team. During our work experience period, we had found that it is not advisable to talk to youth players as a group. At that age they can be a pain in the neck. We had asked them what approach they preferred. Many of them wanted the information in the form of a brochure, and asked for individual interviews so that they could discuss personal matters that they could not broach in front of the group. With this in mind, we made the extension of individual guidance for soccer players one of the aims of our thesis. In addition, we carried out fluid measurements to demonstrate to the players how much fluid they lose during a match. When the scale showed that they had lost two liters of fluid, we confronted them with this, so that it would really get through to them. Usually they do not pay much attention, but now they could not avoid it.

How did you finally come to work for Ajax?

When my thesis was finished, this meant that my time at Ajax was, in principle, also finished. But because the players clearly wanted advice, and I was by then a familiar figure at Ajax, I was automatically offered a job there. As a result of my studies, I had in fact been working for eighteen months at Ajax before this was made known. We were then buried in publicity, because this was something unique, and unfortunately it still is. I really thought that other clubs would follow in Ajax's footsteps as a result of all the publicity. Because it is clear that you can influence performance through selective nutrition, also in soccer.

What attitudes did you encounter within Ajax initially?

Initially everyone had the attitude of, "What are these two women doing here?" This was true of the coaches and the medical staff. It took a long time before we were accepted. It was a real men's world. In the meantime there are more women working at Ajax. Moreover, at Ajax you first have to prove yourself in the youth soccer section before the professional section will take you seriously. Initially we were confronted with all the familiar preconceptions. When people think of dietician, they automatically think of terms of the stereotypical picture of 'bread and water' and 'raw vegetables.' They do not realize that you can eat everything, even potatoes. A dietician simply ensures that your diet is properly balanced. There is nothing that a player cannot eat. I simply try to dose the amounts and to compensate. The overall picture is important - "How much do you eat and how often?" If you only eat oranges for two weeks, that is unhealthy.

What do you do at Ajax?

I work part-time at Ajax. In practice, this means that I spend two days there each week. My most important task is the provision of nutritional information and advice. The youth players between the ages of 8 and 14 have to attend informational talks, and that works very well at that age. The 15 to 18 year-olds have to attend individual information sessions. They have been given general nutritional information during the earlier phase of their time at Ajax. I therefore go into the subject of nutrition in more detail with them. I tell them about the relationship between carbohydrates and soccer performance, explain what the glycogen reserve is, and how you have to replenish it. There is an information evening for the parents of each group of young players. They are expected to attend. This information evening is also held for the parents of new players. When a player has been with Ajax for a few years, his parents are taken on a tour of a supermarket. We did this last year, and the reactions were very favorable. This takes 90 minutes, of which 60 are devoted to walking through the supermarket. We provide information about all kinds of product groups, and repeat it during the information evenings. People can compare products by taking a good look at the labels. Anyone who has a question can ask directly. I am also available to provide advice for the first and second teams and the Saturday amateurs. It is up to the players. They can consult me if they wish to. There is no obligation, although I hope to change this in the future. Players who come through the club's youth teams know what they should and should not do. But new players should be spoken to individually to ensure that they know about the basic principles of fluid and nutrition in soccer. If a player is not interested, then that is the end of it. I cannot force them, because they will not follow my nutritional advice anyway. Finally the physiotherapy students who are gaining work experience at Ajax are informed about the support for players in the context of a match. Coaches and other Ajax employees can also approach me for advice.

What ideal situation do you aim for as a dietician?
Each player should have a basic knowledge of nutrition and fluid before, during and after a match and a training session. That should be obligatory. An intake talk makes it easier for the players to approach you later. Now they tend to think, "I do not need to speak to a dietician, because I am not fat." The idea that a dietician is concerned with losing weight is still prevalent. A soccer player would rather spend his time with a ball on the pitch than in a dietician's office. They often do not realize that proper carbohydrate nutrition can improve their performance on that same pitch. In professional soccer there is a lot to be gained on the basis of nutritional advice. It is simply very difficult to demonstrate this. If a player eats carbohydrates all week, he will not notice that he plays better. That is a shame. The effect of nutrition must be seen in the long term. Every club that plays European soccer should have a dietician on its staff, and the other professional soccer clubs should at least consult an external dietician. A dietician is also objective, whereas a food manufacturer primarily wants to sell his products.

LITERATURE

1. Voeding en sport.
A. van Geel.
ISBN: 90-6076-418-8.
De Vrieseborch, Haarlem.

2. Koolhydraten, spierglycogeen en voetbal: het belang van koolhydraten voor voetballers.
R. Verheijen.
Faculteit der Bewegingswetenschappen, Vrije Universiteit Amsterdam. 1995.

3. Voeding bij topvoetbal - een onderzoek naar voedingsbehoeften en -gewoonten bij topvoetballers.
V.L.M. Beunis.
haagse Hogeschool, Opleiding Voeding en Dietetiek.

4. Nutritional needs of athletes.
F. Brouns.
ISBN: 0-471-940079-8.
J. Wiley Publishers.

5. Sport en voeding.
P. Konopka.
ISBN: 90-6120-396-1.
Utigeverij Elmar, Rijswijk.

6. Een lange termijn-effect van creatine-suppletie.
J. de Ruiter and W. Pasman.
Richting/Sportgericht 51 (1996) 1 en 2.

7. Journal of Sports Sciences.
Volume 12 (special issue)
Summer 1994.

8. Foods, nutrition and sports performance.
C. Williams and J. T. Devlin.
ISBN: 0-419-17890-2.
E & FN Spon, London.

9. Soccer: Nourishments and Diet
Enrico Arcelli
REEDSWAIN Books

CHAPTER 12

INJURY PROBLEMS AT VARIOUS PLAYING LEVELS

Dr. Han Inklaar

12.1 INTRODUCTION

Physical exercise is essential to good health. We need exercise, but the technological developments in our 'western' culture are such that the amount of exercise obtained during the course of normal everyday life is steadily decreasing. As a consequence, 'diseases of civilization' are rife. Obesity and cardiovascular diseases are the most familiar of these. In recent decades, governments and sports bodies have launched all kinds of campaigns to encourage people to participate more in sport. However, it is increasingly clear that sport is not always good for the participants' health. It can also be a threat to health, especially when injuries occur. This is certainly the case in soccer. A lot of attention has therefore been focused on the prevention of sports injuries, and here, too, there have been a number of campaigns. Their aim was to reduce the number of sports injuries. The importance of injury prevention is steadily increasing. This chapter deals with the problems of soccer injuries. The soccer world is characterized by its diversity. Under the auspices of the Dutch Soccer Association, youngsters take part in games of soccer in a variety of age categories from the age of 6 upward. The Dutch Soccer Association has not only junior but also senior members, including a veteran category. Boys and girls play mixed soccer (see page 240). There are different levels of play at the junior and senior levels for both men and women. The difference in playing ability between the highest and lowest levels gradually increases with age. The most extreme form of selection takes place in professional soccer. It is worth taking a closer look at the phenomenon of selection in the light of the risk of sustaining an injury. However, first of all it is necessary to explain exactly what a soccer injury is, and how its seriousness and extent are determined, and what factors are the basic causes of soccer injuries.

12.2 THE SERIOUSNESS AND EXTENT OF SOCCER INJURIES

12.2.1 What is a soccer injury?

Many people regard a soccer injury as a physical impairment caused by an accident during a game of soccer. This is an unfortunate choice of words, however. To talk of an accident is to rule out the possibility of soccer injuries occurring over a long period of time through stress. It is therefore better to view a soccer injury as damage sustained as a result of playing soccer. This definition covers both acute and stress injuries. The damage must have one of four consequences:

1. Forced reduction in the amount of work carried out during a training session, or the necessity of withdrawing from the match or training session.
2. Inability to participate in the next match or training session.
3. Inability to work on the next workday.
4. Necessity for medical assistance (doctor, first aid).

A stress injury must conform to the following criterion:

5. Persistent pain or stiffness in a muscle, tendon or bony tissue for longer than ten consecutive days.

12.2.2 The extent of soccer injuries
Incidence

Before measures can be taken to prevent injuries, it is necessary to establish the extent of the injury problem. The measure used for this is the incidence of injuries. This can be determined in various ways. For example, the number of soccer players who are injured in a year can be divided by the number of active players. If the result is multiplied by 100, this gives the incidence as a percentage.

$$\text{Incidence of injuries} = \frac{\text{Number of injured players}}{\text{Number of active players}} \times 100\%$$

Incidence per 1000 hours of play

If, for example, out of a group of 100 soccer players, 45 are injured during one season, the incidence is 45%. In other words, a soccer player has a 45% chance of getting injured. If the incidence is calculated in this way, it is difficult to compare different sports with each other. Not every sport is practiced for the same amount of time each year. It is therefore better to relate the chance of injury to the number of hours that the sport is played. The incidence is then expressed as the number of sports injuries that occur per 1000 hours of sport activity. The figures obtained enable the sport in which the injury problem is greatest, and in which the need for prevention is thus also greatest, to be identified. Soccer scores high in all incidence studies. It is therefore clear that more attention needs to be paid to injury prevention in soccer.

12.2.3 The seriousness of soccer injuries

It is not sufficient to know how often players are injured. It is also important to study the seriousness of the injuries. A number of criteria are available for determining the seriousness of an injury.

The type and location of the injury

A diagnosis reveals the type of injury. A broken leg is, for example, more serious than a bruise. The part of the body that is injured must also be identified. This is important for establishing the seriousness of the injury. If a field player bruises his hand, this is far less serious than if a goalkeeper does so.

The duration and type of treatment of an injury

If, for example, a broken bone is compared with a blister, it is clear that the two injuries differ widely in terms of the duration of their treatment. A broken leg needs months to recover, while a blister can have disappeared within a matter of days. The type of treatment also differs widely. A blister must be looked after, but otherwise it heals naturally within a few days. A broken leg requires not only specialized treatment but also, in some cases, many months of intensive physiotherapy.

Inability to play due to an injury

The only thing that really concerns a soccer player is, how long he will be sidelined due to an injury. He wants to start training again as soon as possible. There are three levels of inability to play. If the period of inactivity lasts for less than one work-week, the player is said to have a slight sports injury. If he cannot play for between one and three weeks, the injury is viewed as moderately serious. A soccer injury is serious if it keeps a player on the sideline for more than three weeks.

> *As a substitute player, at some stage you become a hyena. You hope that someone will get injured or lose form, although really you do not want this to happen to anyone. It is the law of the jungle; the weakest don't survive.*
>
> **Ron Willems**

Inability to work due to an injury

Insurance companies express the seriousness of a sport injury in the number of days that the person concerned cannot work due to the injury. In the Netherlands there is currently some debate on who is responsible for the costs of this form of inability to work. Some people feel that the player himself should take out insurance to cover this risk. This would discourage people from playing soccer (and from participating in sport in general). This would be a danger to the general health of the nation, because research has shown that sport has a generally favorable effect on health.

12.3 THE CAUSES OF SOCCER INJURIES

Not only the extent and seriousness of an injury need to be established. It is also important to know how injuries occur, and the associated risk factors. This insight must be obtained by identifying the risk factors in soccer, and the relationship between them. This can be done by making use of the 'stress - stress tolerance' model.

A teammate can also cause an injury.

12.3.1 External risk factors

Stress depends on the external circumstances in which the soccer player finds himself. There are all sorts of external risk factors that can cause an injury. The total stress on a soccer player consists of a complex of external factors, which are dealt with below.

Teammates and opponents
Most injuries occur in team sports such as soccer, where physical contact is permitted. Opponents are injured by intent or accident during physical contact. However, injuries can also occur in the absence of physical contact. A player may be hit in the face by the ball, or his head may collide with a goalpost. A teammate may also be the cause of injury due to an accidental collision.

The tackle from behind - a serious injury risk.

Rules of the game; referees
A sport such as soccer needs clear rules to define the limits of physical contact. Sometimes certain rules must be made stricter to reduce the risk of injury. The tackle from behind, for example, is no longer permitted. It is also important that the referee applies the rules of the game correctly. If he does not, the risk of injury is known to be greater. The problem for referees is that they must comply with so many instructions during a match nowadays that the chance of making a mistake is greater than ever.

Type of sport
Each type of sport demands different physical abilities. This is why injuries are often sport-specific. Terms like 'tennis elbow1 and 'runner's knee' have even entered everyday language. In endurance sports the same movement has to be repeated over a very long period of time. As a result, stress injuries are a frequent occurrence in these sports. In sports where short, explosive movement is required, such as sprinting or shot putting, the stress is short but extreme. This can cause acute injuries. Soccer players need endurance as well as explosivity. They can therefore suffer both acute and stress injuries.

Coach

The coach is in a position to influence certain external and personal factors. He must have sufficient knowledge of risk factors and their role in causing injuries. He must seek to maintain a balance between stress and stress tolerance. A coach must work flexibly, always adjusting to the information he picks up from his surroundings. He must monitor the training pitch and the weather. Personal factors can be kept under control by maintaining good communication. A coach must be aware of his players' social and psychological circumstances. If necessary, he must inform and advise them in individual discussions.

> *Some soccer pitches are so indescribably bad that even photographers can injure themselves in the potholes.*
>
> **Loen Beenhakker**

Type of match

In soccer, there are friendly matches and competitive matches. Injuries occur more often during important games than during games whose result is irrelevant. Promotion and relegation matches are a good example. Due to the high degree of interest in such games, the players seem to consciously take more risks than usual and to be more willing to infringe the rules. The chance of injuries is therefore greater.

Number of hours played

The time spent playing soccer differs from playing level to playing level. Professionals train almost every day, and regularly have to play two games in a week. Amateurs often train only twice and play one match each week. This large difference in the number of hours means that there is a difference in the chance of sustaining an injury. Professional players are exposed to all kinds of risk factors for a longer period of time.

Intensity and level at which the sport is practiced

There are also differences in intensity between playing levels. A distinction can be made between leisure players, competitive amateurs, top amateurs and professionals (see page 146). The professionals, in particular, play very intensively.

Pitches

Uneven pitches are one of the main causes of soccer injuries. Training sessions are increasingly held on synthetic turf. This, however, may be too hard if it does not have the necessary shock-absorbing properties. It has been found that injuries tend to increase when a switch is made from grass to synthetic turf. A soft pitch is not ideal either.

Equipment

Good equipment is necessary to prevent sports injuries. There are three groups of sports equipment. First of all, there is the equipment needed to carry out the sport. Then there is the equipment that the players wear to protect themselves against injuries (for example, shinguards). The final category includes equipment such as clothing and shoes.

Weather

The weather conditions also play a major role with regard to injuries. The weather can have a negative effect on a sportsman, but it can also have an unfavorable influence on a number of external factors. The pitch, for example, may be in poor condition due to below-zero temperatures, snow or rain. A hard or slippery surface is dangerous.

12.3.2 Personal risk factors

A soccer player must be able to withstand stress. Whether or not he succeeds depends on his stress tolerance. The stress tolerance of a soccer player depends on the physical, psychological and social aspects of his makeup. There are therefore personal risk factors associated with each player.

The fitter the players the less the chance of sustaining an injury.

State of health

A healthy person is in a stable mental, physical and social condition. The higher the level at which sport is carried out, the better the health of its practitioners needs to be. A player must not represent a health risk for his teammates or opponents. In some circumstances, a player may be a danger to himself. If a player puts his health at risk, he needs to be protected against himself.

Fitness level

A good level of fitness reduces the chance of sustaining an injury. Proper conditioning can improve a soccer player's physical fitness (stress tolerance). A specific level of fitness is needed for each sport. This is also true of soccer. The better a player's soccer fitness, the smaller the chance that he will sustain an injury.

Gender

It is clear that the body of a man differs from that of a woman. Conditioning programs for men and women therefore need to be drawn up on the basis of a differentiated 'stress - stress tolerance' model.

Age

Age must be taken into account in the choice of a sport and the level at which to play it. Age largely determines the balance between stress and stress tolerance. Youngsters often have insufficient experience of soccer, and therefore cannot really assess the risks associated with playing this sport. Older soccer players frequently make the mistake of forgetting that their physical capacity is not what it used to be.

Physical build

Physical build is crucial to performance in some sports. This is not the case in soccer. However, it would not be advisable for someone with weak ligaments around his knees and ankles to play soccer. The chance of knee and ankle injuries would be too great. Soccer makes considerable demands on the support function of the ligament system of the leg joints.

Lifestyle

A healthy and active lifestyle is a prerequisite for good sports performance. Although this applies to everyone, it is especially important for those who make considerable demands on their body by playing soccer. It is important to closely monitor nutritional and drinking habits. Smoking, alcohol and medicines should be avoided as far as possible. Rest is also essential. Fatigue results in loss of concentration and coordination. This can be a cause of uncontrolled movements during play, with an injury as the consequence. Conditioning effects manifest themselves especially during rest periods. This is when the body builds up extra reserves, in case it will have to face such an extreme load again.

Good soccer fitness requires a healthly lifestyle.

12.4 THE PROBLEM OF INJURIES IN PRACTICE

The general information given above is now followed by more specific information on the extent of the injury problem in soccer. This is taken from the results of recent research into soccer injuries.

12.4.1 Selection: the creation of various playing levels

At the start of each season, soccer clubs put together their teams again. This process starts with the club's main teams - the first three or four senior elevens, and the first teams at each youth level. The teams are selected primarily on the basis of age (especially at the youth level), soccer ability and tactical insight. Other personal factors that play a role are attitude (motivation, aggression, fear of failure), physical performance capacity, communication skills, and physical build. Other criteria are sometimes applied to the selection of the other teams. Do the players suit each other, or have they indicated that they would like to play in the same team together? Are enjoyment and social contact the main reasons for playing? In the progression from the youngest to the oldest youth levels, differences in playing ability will gradually become clearer. At the senior level another phenomenon is observed. As players become older, more of them give up the game.

> *As a center forward in Italy, you cannot afford to wait for a pass. By then you will have lost your Achilles' tendon.*
>
> **Wim Kieft**

The reasons are usually social (study, work, family), but sometimes soccer injuries are the cause. The keenest and healthiest players are left over at the highest level. At the lower levels, the players are only interested in kicking a ball around for the enjoyment and social contact involved. They have already started to put on weight around the waistline. From the above, it can be concluded that the soccer world consists of all kinds of different groups of players, who practice their sport at their own levels. The personal and external risk factors will not be the same for each group. It is, therefore, not to be expected that the different groups will be exposed to the same risk of injury, or that the distribution of injuries will be the same, in terms of type, location and seriousness.

12.4.2 At which standard of play is the risk greatest?

More injuries occur at higher levels of play.

Teams at the higher levels of play usually have more qualified coaches, train and play on better pitches, and have the best equipment. Dutch Soccer Association referees officiate at their matches. Moreover, qualified coaches pay more attention to injury prevention by preparing their players properly for the next match, by insisting that they go through a good warming-up routine before a match and sometimes (but unfortunately not always) warming down afterwards, by making the wearing of shinguards obligatory, and by advising that unstable ankles should be taped. In addition, teams at the higher levels always have sports masseurs, physiotherapists and other backroom helpers (and even doctors, at the very highest level), who reinforce the emphasis on injury prevention. If, despite all of this, players do suffer injuries, they receive better and faster treatment at the higher levels. This improves the chances of a good recovery and reduces the risk of chronic residual complaints. There is, however, more chance of a player returning to action too soon at the higher level, simply because teams at this level are under more pressure to succeed. At lower levels the situation is very different. Players often do not train at all. They arrive just before the match and have neither the time nor the desire to warm up properly. After the game they shower as quickly as possible and head for the bar and the first beer. If injuries occur, there are often no support procedures in place, and the player has to make do as best he can. On the other hand, players at this level do often have the patience to wait until they have fully recovered from an injury before they start to play again.

It might be thought that a player from a 'pub' team is more likely to sustain an injury than a player from a professional team. However, this takes no account of the culture that prevails in top teams. Success is all that matters. The result comes first, sometimes at the cost of everything else. This means that there is a much more intense approach to the game and a far higher level of aggressiveness on the part of all concerned (players, coach, backroom staff, spectators). The manner of playing is much tougher. There is less readiness to accept the referee's decisions. Players are more inclined to show aggression towards each other and the officials. The incidence of violent behavior (kicking, holding, pushing, pulling, elbowing, tripping, etc.) is greater at the higher levels of soccer. Matches where there is a lot at stake are more likely to give rise to aggressive and emotional behavior, and therefore to injuries. All in all, it is not simple to decide which soccer players are most at risk of sustaining an injury. Only scientific research can provide an answer. This is why the results of a study carried out in the Netherlands are discussed below. The first part of the study compared the injury risk of soccer players at the higher and lower levels of the game. The second part looked at the type and location of the most common soccer injuries.

12.5 RESEARCH RESULTS

12.5.1 Differences between playing levels

A total of 477 soccer players participated in the study. All of them were members of two amateur soccer clubs. The study group consisted of 1 7 senior teams, 6 Under 18 teams, 6 Under 16 teams, and 6 Under 14 teams. The 7 senior teams that played at national level (in the Dutch Soccer Association leagues) were categorized as 'high playing level.' The other 10 senior teams, who played in local leagues, were categorized as 'low playing level.' The two top youth teams in each age group were categorized as 'high playing level,' and the third as 'low playing level.1 In general, it appeared that the injury risk associated with 'high level' teams was double that at the lower level. This was true of both seniors and juniors. Although more attention is devoted to injury prevention at the higher level, it was found that:

- more stress injuries are sustained by players at the higher senior level that at the lower level;
- more upper leg injuries are sustained by players at the higher level than the lower level in both senior and junior soccer;
- Under 18 players are more prone to injury than seniors, Under 16 or Under 14 players.

The main reason for the greater risk of injury at the higher level is the behavior of the players during matches. This is reflected in the fact that many more violations of the rules are recorded at the higher level.

Conclusion
The higher the playing level, the greater the pressures on the teams participating. Players are more success and result-oriented, and are more aggressive. Matches are experienced more emotionally by everyone concerned (players, coaches, referees and spectators). At the Under 16 and Under 14 junior level it was found that 'emotional' matches were frequently associated with incidents of injury. Behavior on the field is the main cause of soccer injuries. The injury prevention measures practiced at higher levels (warming-up, warming down, stretching, wearing shinguards, taping ankles, etc.) cannot fully compensate for this increased risk. Only by restraining the behavior of all concerned, on and around the pitch, can significant gains be made in the field of primary injury prevention.

12.5.2 The type and location of soccer injuries

An analysis was also made of the 1099 soccer players, with 1157 soccer injuries, who consulted the medical section of the Dutch Soccer Association from 1990 to 1992 (see

Fig. 12.1). It was expected that these would mainly be problem injuries. (These are injuries that require a long period of recuperation, and tend to recur, and prevent players from participating in matches at the level they aspire to.) In view of the time that passed between the manifestation of the injury and the visit to the medical section of the Dutch Soccer Association (0.7 years on average), the high percentage of recurrent injuries (48%), and the high percentages of players who had sought treatment from a family doctor (84%), physiotherapist (74%) or specialist (53%), this expectation appeared to be well founded. The most common types of injury were sprains, inflamed tendons, and chronic joint complaints. The most frequent loca-tions were the knee (45.5%), groin/upper leg (22.9%) and ankle (1 3.8%). Most players came for advice and referral to the correct specialist. A telephone survey of 1 34 of the original 1099 soccer players indicated that the Dutch Soccer Association's intervention was very effective. In 1994 (2 to 4 years after the consultation), 78% of the soccer players were playing soccer again. 60% were even playing at their former level (the level they played at before they were injured). These results underline the need for better, more efficient, sport-related care and support. This applies to the organization and quality of the professional health care service as well as to the organization and quality of health care within the soccer clubs.

Bad behavior on and around the field must be curbed if injuries are to be prevented.

> *Top sport is unhealthy and inhuman; otherwise it is not top sport.*
>
> **Wim Verhoorn**

Figure 12.1: *The 1157 problem injuries of the 1099 soccer players who consulted the medical section of the Dutch Soccer Association, listed by type and location.*

Sprained joints	523	45.2%
• knee	(363)	
• ankle		(116)
Pulled muscle	99	8.5%
• groin/upper leg	(77)	
Bruising	52	4.5%
Dislocations	5	0.4%
Broken bones	30	2.6%
Inflamed tendon	265	22.9%
• groin/upper leg	(147)	
• knee	(61)	
• lower leg	(44)	
Chronic joint injury	136	11.8%
Other injuries	47	4.1%
	1157	100%

SUMMARY

- A soccer injury is damage sustained as a result of playing soccer.

- The extent (incidence) of soccer injuries can be determined by dividing the number of injured soccer players by the number of active players and multiplying the result by 100. This percentage must then be related to the total number of hours played.

- The seriousness of an injury can be determined on the basis of the following four criteria: the type and location of the injury; the duration and type of treatment of the injury; inability to play due to the injury; and inability to work due to the injury.

- Soccer injuries are attributable to a number of external and personal risk factors.

- The external factors include: teammates and opponents; rules of the game; referees; type of sport; coach; type of match; number of hours played; the intensity and level at which the sport is practiced; pitches; equipment; and weather.

- The personal factors include: state of health; fitness level; gender; age; physical build; and lifestyle.

- Because players are scouted and selected at a young age, various levels of play come into being. The soccer world therefore consists of all sorts of groups of people, who play at their own level.

- The external and personal risk factors are, therefore, not the same for all groups. The question is, which group is most at risk?

- The teams at the highest level have the best medical support, and are also physically fitter. At the lower levels there is a lower standard of support and fitness. It might therefore be expected that a player from a 'pub team' stands more chance of sustaining an injury than a top amateur.

- Scientific research has shown that the injury risk of top players is twice that of 'leisure' players.

- The better conditioning, injury prevention and medical support at the higher playing levels do not adequately compensate for the increased injury risk due to aggressive play. The greatest improvements in injury prevention can therefore be achieved by curbing negative behavior on and around the pitch.

FIVE PRACTICAL QUESTIONS

1. Young players sometimes have to stop playing for 6 to 9 months due to growing pains.' Are there ways of maintaining their soccer development during this period?

Doctors who advise youngsters to stop playing for 6 to 9 months due to 'growing pains' are often over-reacting. In principle, it is often sufficient to temporarily avoid those soccer activities that cause pain. These are usually intense actions such as sprinting, jumping and kicking the ball hard, as when passing over a long distance or shooting at goal. Less intensive drills such as dribbling and pushing the ball, singly or in combination with other players, and drills aimed at practicing technique, can often be performed without any pain. Youngsters should not play matches during this time. In case of doubt, a sports doctor should be consulted.

2. What are the symptoms of Osgood-Schlatter disease, and how is this problem treated?

Osgood-Schlatter disease is a temporary condition affecting the growth centers of the tibia, at the attachment of the tendon from the upper leg muscles that cause the knee to stretch when they contract. The growth center is where the longitudinal growth of a bone occurs. In fact, Osgood-Schlatter disease is a sort of inflammation reaction due to the difference in the tractive force exerted by the tendon on the bone, and the force that the bone can withstand at this time of life. It usually affects boys between 9 and 13 years old. A symptom of this condition is pain in the knee joint when the knee is forcefully stretched, as when the soccer actions referred to in the answer to question 1 are carried out. Sometimes there is also tenderness and a rather hot swelling on the tibia just below the knee. This problem is handled as described in the answer to question 1.

3. Many coaches feel that waves of injuries occur more frequently than they used to, and are also more serious. Is this true?

In 1986/1987 and 1992/1993, two studies were carried out into participation in sport and the number of sports injuries in the Netherlands. The second study revealed a slight downward trend in the number of soccer injuries per 1000 hours played (and therefore a slightly reduced risk of sustaining injury while playing soccer). However, the risk is still very high in comparison with other sports, as reflected in the fact that soccer occupies third position in the list of 'risk sports.' As well as the general characteristics of soccer (contact sport, team sport with considerable emphasis on technique, strength, speed and endurance), the major cause of injuries is the behavior of the players during matches. Although increasing attention is paid to various aspects of injury prevention, the uncontrolled, aggressive, dangerous behavior of players during games, with little consideration for the health of opponents, stands in the way of any significant reduction in the risk of sustaining an injury (see also the answer to question 5).

4. Shinguards are obligatory in soccer. Does it make any difference which shinguards a player wears?

The Dutch Soccer Association has followed the rules of UEFA and FIFA in this matter. These rules do not include any criteria to which good shinguards have to conform. This is a weak point. In practice, a piece of foam rubber or cardboard cannot effectively protect the shin. For a shinguard to be effective, it must satisfy all kinds of requirements, such as good shock absorption, adequate size (surface area of lower leg, protection for the ankles), and it must be comfortable to wear. Studies have shown that most common types of shinguard do not meet these requirements. In particular, they offer insufficient protection against the impact forces that cause fractures of the tibia or the fibula. International standards for shinguards are now being developed. At the moment, only shinguards derived from ice hockey satisfy the requirements. However, it is still worthwhile wearing the current types of shinguard, if only to prevent annoying scrapes and bruises.

5. The rules of soccer have been made stricter, and referees are therefore officiating more strictly. Has this resulted in a reduction in the number of soccer injuries?

In view of the answer to question 3, it has to be concluded that question 5 cannot be answered one way or the other. The changes in the rules are recent. Another study may shed some light on this. However, it is questionable whether measures that have been taken for the purpose of confirming the referee's authority can be effective in moderating the behavior of the players and reducing the risk of injury. Our modern society is increasingly unwilling to accept authority, especially when there is no place for explanation and discussion and the referee is below standard. An authoritarian approach that is not backed up by the necessary competence is more likely to cause irritation, with all its consequences (including injuries). Better standards of refereeing through improved selection and training procedures, would probably be more effective. The players' behavior on the pitch cannot usually be influenced for the better by stricter rules. Other methods of influencing behavior are more effective, with the coach playing a key intermediary role. Exerting a positive influence on behavior should be part of a policy aimed at improving the quality of soccer in the widest sense of the term.

INTERVIEW WITH LEO BEEN-HAKKER (Technical Director of Vitesse Arnhem)

Have you ever been confronted with a wave of injuries during your career as a coach?
I have never had to deal with a situation in which half of my team was unavailable through injury. Of course, you might have more injured players during periods when the fixture list is crowded. That is normal. I have an antipathy to injuries sustained during training sessions, and perhaps this is the reason why I have never experienced this phenomenon. I am talking about injuries sustained without any form of physical contact. I have always tried to avoid pushing my players too hard. I take account of not only the fixture list but also the state of the training ground.

How can a coach avoid injuries during training sessions?
In the technical and tactical area we always distinguish between attackers and defenders, and between workers and creative players. But in the physical area this distinction is neglected. I can imagine that certain drills are suitable for one player but not for another, depending on their roles in the team and their individual characteristics. I think that you have to take this into account with regard to the work you ask your players to perform. Depending on the type of player, a coach must be able to let some players skip all or part of a training session. You can also take account of the physical requirements and characteristics of players by working with small groups. You try to put players with similar physical characteristics in the same group. I have often done this and it works very well. However, you cannot avoid working with your squad as a whole. You will then inevitably encounter problems. You have to find a happy medium. I have always been able to do that because I have studied this in detail. You can also draw on your own experience, because in the course of time you learn to know your players. In my opinion, every coach should study what his players can and cannot do. It is therefore important that a coach has good powers of observation. Body language can tell you a lot.

As well as 'acute' injuries there are 'stress' injuries. What can a coach do to avoid these?
Everyone, and therefore every player, has a certain reserve. In my opinion this 'extra something' should be held back for the match. If you draw on this reserve during training sessions, you will see that a player can give no more at a certain moment during the match, and you want to avoid that. If it does happen, you have to give the player the time to regain his strength during the following week. He has to remain active, but at a relatively light level of intensity. Rest is also very important. Players sometimes find this difficult to grasp. If you, as a coach, neglect this aspect, and allow the player to train at the usual level of intensity, he will suffer irreversible stress.

Are injuries more of a problem than they used to be?

Soccer players certainly have to cope with much more stress. Soccer today is faster and more physical. Players have less space and time. They also face more resistance. I cannot say whether this results in more injuries. Every player should be able to play on Sunday and Wednesday and then on Sunday again, provided you combine this with a good conditioning program. The problem is that coaches, and especially players, have no appreciation of this. You have a do a lot to play at the top, but you have to leave even more undone. Soccer players need to listen better to what their bodies tell them. No matter how much effort you put in, you should have no problems if you relax and recuperate. In Mexico, I used to follow a lot of American sports. When you see how many matches are played in such a short time, it is obvious that the body can take it. But the players get a lot of sleep between games. In soccer there is a tendency for players to let themselves go to a greater or lesser extent after a match, but this is exactly the time when they should be recuperating.

Does the problem of injuries differ according to the prevailing soccer culture?

In countries such as Spain, Mexico and Turkey, it is often very hot. This is a big advantage for the muscular system. The fact that players in these countries often lie on the pitch for a half-hour after a training session, just carrying out stretching exercises, is largely attributable to the weather. In addition, the climate is such that you almost never have to play on a heavy pitch. In the Dutch winter, you often play on very hard, uneven surfaces in the cold, while in autumn the pitches are very soft because it rains a lot. The chance of sustaining an injury during training sessions is therefore greater in the Netherlands. On the other hand, the style of play in Spain, Mexico and Turkey is more physical, and there are therefore more 'soccer injuries.' In these countries, on the day after a match, far more players need treatment for injuries they have sustained by being kicked than in the Netherlands. Despite the more physical style of play, the injury problem is not dramatic. Spanish players have naturally learned to defend themselves against the numerous kicks that they receive. They jump to their feet again immediately after almost every tackle, because they can take a lot of knocks. The problem in Spain was the amount of travelling. Players who had minor injuries after a game scarcely had time to recover. Three days later there was another game, and in the meantime there was a lot of travelling to be done. Of course, you cannot expect to play through a whole season without pain, but in these circumstances, minor injuries have a cumulative effect and eventually it becomes too much.

Have the recent changes in the rules had an effect on the injury problem?

I certainly think that it has had an effect. You still see tackles from behind, but not as often as before. That has been a good measure. As a soccer player, you can take a lot of knocks, provided you see them coming. You have no chance against something that comes from behind you. As long as it happens within your field of vision, there is room for tackles and challenges in soccer. On the other hand you have to be careful not to make too many changes, because one of soccer's main characteristics is its physical competitiveness.

Do you know anything about the injury problem in youth soccer?
The Under 18 level, in particular, is a decisive phase for most young players. This is when the decision is taken on whether they can stay with the club on the professional side. A lot of young players will therefore be highly motivated. I cannot tell whether this leads to more injuries. The growth process is a more important cause of injury problems in my opinion. When I see the situation at Vitesse, I find the number of growth-related complaints enormous. The whole skeleton makes a spurt, and the rest of the body often cannot keep up with it. It is always uncertain how youngsters will come out of this process of physical development. The increased muscular tension and the loss of coordination sometimes cause youngsters to play less well. In addition, they are under pressure from parents and friends. This is a difficult time for such a player.

What measures does the club take in this situation?
You often cannot do much about the complaints themselves. It is no solution to tell the youngsters to stop completely. During training sessions you should only ask them to carry out drills that do not cause them any pain. We devote a lot of time to putting them at ease. The players must realize it is a phase they have to go through. They should not get worried, or start doubting their own ability and trying to do too much. They should do what they can within the limits of their own possibilities, and above all try to enjoy their soccer. To get some control over all of this, we recently introduced coordination training and soccer aerobics in the youth section, with the purpose of ensuring that the players retain their coordination.

LITERATURE

1. The epidemiology of soccer injuries in a new perspective.
H. Inklaar.
ISBN: 90-900-8551-3.
Proefschrift, Universiteit Utrecht, 1995.

2. Voetbalbessures, hoe ga je er mee om?
H. Inklaar.
ISBN: 90-5513-212-8.
Uitgave K.N.V.B. - Zeist, 1995.

3. Nieuwe gezichtspunten met betrekking tot voetbalblessures.
H. Inklaar.
Richting/SPortGericht 52 (1996) 4-6.

4. Bewegen Gewogen, Measures in Motion.
W.L. Mosterd, E. Bol, W.R. de Vries, M.L. Zonderland, H.P.F. Peters, Th. C. de Winter, S.L. Schmikli.
Rapport vakgroep medische fysiologie en sportgeneeskunde, Universiteit Utrecht, 1996.

5. Sportblessures, nader uitgediept.
S. L. Schmikli, F.j.G. Backx, E. Bol.
ISBN: 90-313-2035-8.
Uitgever: Bohn, Stafleu, van Loghum. Houten/Diegem, 1995.

6. Blessures in jeugdvoetbal.
S.L. Schmikli.
Onderzoeksverslag, vakgroep medische fysiologie en sportgeneeskunde, Universiteit Utrecht, 1994.

7. Een vergelijkende studie bij veldvoetballers en niet-sporters: verschillen in gezondheid, opleiding, werk- en arbeidsverzuim.
S.L. Schmikli.
Onderzoeksverslag, vakgroep medische fysiologie en sportgeneeskunde, Universiteit Utrecht, 1996.

CHAPTER 13

THE EMERGENCY TREATMENT OF SOCCER INJURIES

Dr. Frits Kessel

13.1 INTRODUCTION
Injury prevention is an important component of medical support in soccer. Regardless of this, injuries are unavoidable. The severity of an injury must, however, be restricted as far as possible. An important step in this direction is the treatment of an injury immediately after it has been sustained. Correct diagnosis and first-aid treatment can prevent more serious consequences. This chapter therefore explains how to react in this sort of situation. It indicates what to do and, especially, what not to do, in all sorts of critical situations on the soccer pitch.

13.2 FIRST-AID ON THE SOCCER PITCH
Slight injuries can be treated by those nearest to the scene. However, if a player's injury appears to be serious, a doctor, the local medical service or hospital must be contacted immediately. If the injury may necessitate an operation, the injured player must not eat or drink anything. Bystanders who offer help must take eight rules into consideration.

1. Do everything possible to avoid any local panic.
2. Ensure that the injured player has sufficient space.
3. Calm the injured player by talking to him as a form of distraction (it may be possible to identify hat is wrong in this way).
4. Once it is known what is wrong, the necessary measures can be taken. Do not try to do anything immediately. Remember that a player may either understate the severity of an injury or exaggerate it.
5. Do not move the injured player. A stretcher is needed if the injury is serious.
6. Cover the injured player with a blanket or tracksuit to prevent him from cooling down.
7. Write down brief details of how the injury occurred, the first-aid measures carried out, and the symptoms observed. Other factor such as the weather conditions (temperature, rain, humidity) can also be noted.

8. It is best to contact the local medical service to ensure that expert help and transport are quickly available for serious injuries. Make sure that the telephone number is always within reach.

13.3 TREATMENT AND PREVENTION OF SOCCER INJURIES

The symptoms and emergency treatment of a number of common injuries are described below. Suggestions are also given for avoiding such injuries. A number of serious, but less common, injuries are also described.

13.3.1 Nosebleed

A nosebleed involves bleeding in one or both nostrils. There are many possible causes. The most usual cause is a nose injury. A nosebleed should be treated by pinching the player's nostrils and keeping them closed for one minute. The head should be inclined slightly forward. The nostrils can then be slowly and carefully allowed to open again. If bleeding resumes, there is a good chance that clotted blood is holding the edges of the wound apart. These clots of blood must be removed from the nose before another attempt is made to stop the flow of blood. This can be done by firmly blowing the nose into a handkerchief. The nostrils should then be pinched together again as described above. If there is still no

The shape and condition of the nose must also be examined when a nosebleed is treated.

success, one more attempt can be made. If this fails to help, it is advisable to consult a doctor or go to a hospital first-aid department. The shape and condition of the nose must also be looked at. The nose might be broken. If there is any suspicion of this, the player must be taken to hospital as soon as possible for examination.

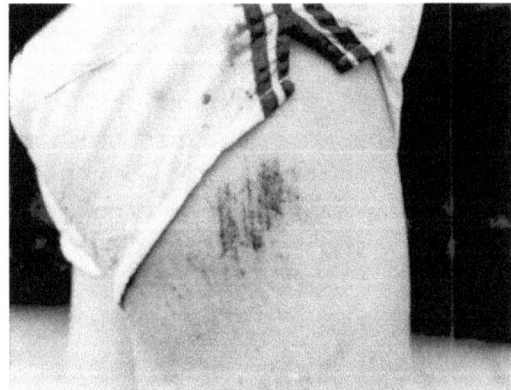

The main danger associated with scrapes is infection.

13.3.2 Scrapes

Soccer players frequently carry out sliding tackles, in the course of which they may scrape their hips or, to a lesser extent, their knees. The main danger associated with scrapes is that infections may occur through the open wound. This must therefore be immediately and carefully cleaned, removing as much dirt as possible. This can best be done with running water and disinfectant soap. Do not run water directly onto the wound. If necessary, use a clean, soft brush. When this has been done, apply iodine to the wound and the adjacent skin. The blood and pale yellow fluid subsequently dry and form a crust. The wound should never be dried with powders, because this would hinder the healing process. A scrape heals fastest by being exposed to the air. If clothing is worn over a wound, the wound must be covered with a bandaid or sterile gauze to prevent infections. If a wound is very badly soiled, a doctor should be consulted. Players are less likely to sustain scrapes if they wear protective clothing or other material. Coating the most vulnerable areas with a layer of Vaseline also has a preventive effect.

13.3.3 Blisters

Blisters are caused by excessive friction and pressure, especially on the heels, toes and ball of the foot. The surface skin is displaced with regard to the underlying layer, and moisture is therefore formed between the two layers. Friction between the skin and clothing can also cause blisters. This can happen when new boots are worn. An area of inflamed skin appears before a blister forms. It is advisable not to burst a blister. If this is unavoidable, the following procedure must be followed.

1. Apply iodine to the blister and the surrounding skin.
2. Sterilize a needle by, for example, holding it in a flame.
3. Prick the edge of the blister, then prick the opposite edge.
4. Use sterile gauze or absorbent cotton to press the moisture out of the blister, from the center outward.
5. If you have a pipette, drip a little iodine into the blister.
6. Squeeze the blister again until no more fluid emerges.
7. Apply iodine to the blister and the surrounding skin again.
8. Cover the blister with sterile gauze or a bandaid.
9. If necessary, spray a 'second skin' over the blister.

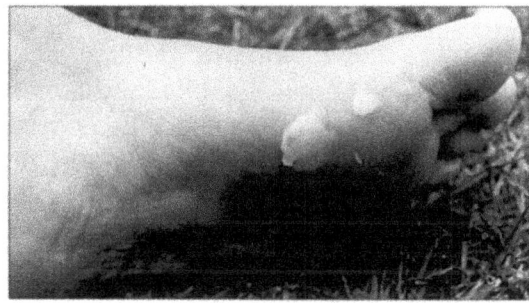
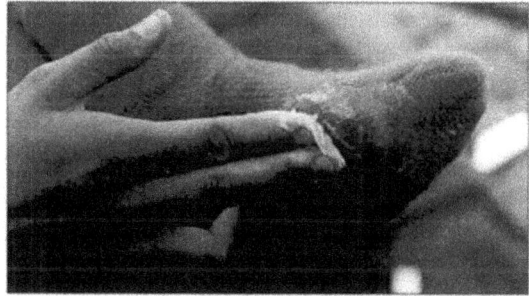

Blisters can be prevented by applying Vaseline.

If a blister is not a hindrance during a training session or match, it is better to cover it with layers of bandaid, arranged like tiles on a roof. The blister will dry out within a few hours or days, and will then present no more problems. If a blister is formed under a thick layer of horny skin on the foot, it is advisable to consult a doctor or chiropodist. Wearing comfortably fitting boots can prevent the formation of blisters. When new boots are worn, they should be 'run in' properly before they are worn during a complete training session or match. Soap or Vaseline can be applied to the inside of the heel to reduce friction. Wetting the socks and smearing them with soap is another good method.

13.3.4 Cuts

A superficial cut only affects the skin. Deeper cuts may damage the underlying structures. The cuts sustained by soccer players are often caused by studs with a ragged edge. Hygiene is a very important aspect of the treatment of cuts. Any infection must be prevented. A small wound must be sterilized with iodine and then covered with gauze or sticking bandaid. Longer and deeper cuts must be treated by a doctor. There are two reasons for this. Firstly, they need to be inspected to determine whether underlying blood vessels, nerves and muscle tendons have been damaged. Secondly, such cuts, and especially facial cuts, have to be stitched carefully.

13.3.5 Bruises

A bruise is an extravasation of blood into the skin or underlying tissues due to tissue damage. Such damage is caused by the violent impact of an object against the body. Examples of such impacts are a knee against the thigh, or a kick against the shin. The symptoms of a superficial bruise are:

- in most cases, brief localized pain;
- loss of function, which, depending on the position and strength of the violent impact, can range from mild to considerable;
- swelling as a result of extravasation of blood;
- a subsequent black and blue discoloration.

The swelling and the discoloration are only visible if the deeper-lying muscles are bruised. Bruises must be given the RICE treatment (see page 321). A minor swelling begins to recede after 48 hours. Recovery must then be stimulated with a hot shower, light massage, or gentle exercise below the pain limit. Extensive massage is out of the question during the first 24 to 36 hours, because this would damage the recovering tissues again. A doctor or a physiotherapist is the most suitable person to determine the severity of the bruising of a muscle, and to determine how to handle it. Inexpert treatment of a bruised muscle can result in the deposition of calcium in the muscle tissue, causing permanent functional impairment. Bruises can be avoided in the same way as broken bones, by protecting the vulnerable parts of the body with specific equipment such as shinguards and padding.

13.3.6 Sprains

A sprain involves damage to the tissues in and around a joint, usually the ligaments of the joint and their connections to the bone. Sometimes the surrounding muscles are also damaged and, in serious sprains, the joint capsule. Depending on the severity of the sprain, the ligaments may be torn or ruptured. A sprain is a consequence of an abnormal movement. The joint that is most frequently sprained in soccer is the ankle. In addition, goalkeepers often sprain their wrists and fingers. The symptoms of a sprain can vary from:

- mild, short-lived pain;
- no or minimal swelling;
- no or slight impairment of function;
- slight tenderness to the touch;

to:

- extreme, persistent pain;
- major swelling due to extravasation of blood in and around the joint immediately after the injury is sustained;
- complete loss of function;
- a cracking noise or sensation.

A mild sprain should be treated by cooling it and applying a pressure bandage. Sporting activity can then be resumed. Sport must not be carried out if:

- the joint becomes more painful;
- swelling occurs;
- the player's movements clearly indicate a functional impairment.

A player who suffers a serious sprain must be immediately withdrawn from the training session or match. It is advisable to consult a doctor or visit a hospital within 24 hours.

Knee and ankle sprains, which are very prevalent in soccer, can be avoided to some extent by providing the joints with more support. Research has shown that 75% of soccer ankle sprains are sustained by players who have previously had such a sprain. Soccer players who have 'slack' ankle ligaments also have a higher risk of suffering sprains. This group of players should have their ankles taped during training sessions and games. It takes 6 to 9 months to recover completely from a serious sprain. During this period, it is advisable to tape the ankle. It is also a good idea to strengthen the muscles. This must be done by means of specific exercises for the muscles that have a supporting function in the injured joint.

A player with a serious sprain must immediately stop playing or training.

13.3.7 Dislocations

A dislocation is the most serious type of sprain. When a dislocation occurs, there is no longer any contact between the articulating bones that form the joint. This results in serious damage to the joint capsule and ligaments. Soccer players often dislocate a shoulder when they fall awkwardly. Goalkeepers regularly suffer finger dislocations when they catch the ball incorrectly. Ankle, knee and hip dislocations also occur. The symptoms of a dislocation are:

- extreme pain when at rest and in motion;
- swelling due to extravasation of blood;
- abnormal shape and position of the joint (this can be seen by comparing the right and left sides);

- loss of function due to complete inability to move the injured joint.

The joint must be returned to its correct position as soon as possible. A doctor should therefore be called in immediately. Unqualified persons should never try to put a dislocated joint back into place themselves. The only thing that an unqualified bystander can do is immobilize the joint. It is also advisable to cool the joint, so that the swelling will decrease. Under no circumstances should anyone with a dislocated joint continue playing. Dislocations are caused, in particular, by the considerable range of movement and the less efficient development of the ligament system and the corset of muscles around the joint. Good recuperation is vital after a dislocation. Incomplete recovery can result in recurrence of the dislocation. For this reason, players who suffer sprains must concentrate on strengthening and coordination exercises. If the muscles attached to the affected joint are strengthened, they can help to prevent a subsequent recurrence of the dislocation. Joints that have already been dislocated in the past should also be protected by a supporting brace, bandage or tape during training sessions and matches.

RICE treatment

It is advisable to treat minor injuries by cooling the damaged tissues, so that the blood vessels in the affected part of the body contract. This reduces the flow of blood to the injury zone, thus ensuring that the degree of swelling is less than it would otherwise be. Cooling also reduces pain. Cooling can be carried out in a variety of ways, including application of a plastic bag that contains ice cubes, running cold water over the affected area, application of a cold pack (a pack containing a gel), and the use of a cooling spray. More serious injuries require more than just cooling. In such cases, RICE treatment is called for. RICE stands for rest (R), immobilization (I), compression (C) and elevation (E). Obviously, a player who suffered a serious injury must stop any sporting activity and rest the injured body part. Only in this way can the bleeding be brought under control. The next step is immobilization of the injured body part. This means that - for, example, in the case of a sprained ankle - the player must not walk at all, or, if he does, he must use crutches. Another way of stopping the bleeding is compression. A pressure bandage must be applied immediately. Ideally this will be done at the same time as the affected body part is being cooled. An elastic bandage is preferable, although it must not be applied too tightly. When the period of cooling is over, the cool pack must be removed and the pressure bandage must be wrapped around the injury again. The final step is elevation of the injured body part so that it is higher than the heart. This reduces the flow of blood to the part and increases the flow of blood away from it, thus minimizing the probability that any extravasation of blood will occur, and helping to reduce swelling.

13.3.8 Bursal damage

Bursae can be compared to cushions filled with fluid. These small cushions are located between skin and bone and between tendon and bone. Bursae are found at sites where there is a lot of friction, or where a lot of pressure is exerted. The most familiar bursae are above the kneecap and behind the lowest part of the Achilles tendon or the knee tendon. Bursae have a protective function. They protect the underlying tissues against violent impacts, such as those that regularly occur when a goalkeeper lands on his hip or elbow. Acute bursal damage is associated with the presence of blood in the bursa. The blood can cause inflammation. Longterm irritation can also result in inflammation in and around a bursa. Acute damage is characterized by symptoms such as:

> *For years, Diego Maradona has had back problems, a ruined ankle, and such a tendency to put on weight that, after his suspension, he is probably not yet fit enough to hold a fishing rod.*
>
> **Ben de Graaf**

- rapid swelling;
- pain, together with reddening of, or damage to, the skin.

Persistent irritation is usually associated with the following symptoms:

- gradual swelling;
- local heat and reddening;
- painful movement, which becomes worse during sporting activity.

Bursal damage should initially be treated by rest, avoidance of any painful movements, keeping the site cool for 48 hours, and application of a pressure bandage. A doctor should then be consulted. A doctor can prick the bursa, remove blood or fluid and, if necessary, prescribe inflammation-inhibiting drugs. A physiotherapist can treat the bursal damage so that the inflammation process is brought to a stop more quickly. Sometimes the inflammation recurs, even if protective material is worn. The doctor in charge must decide whether an operation is necessary.

13.3.9 Muscle cramp

Every soccer player has suffered a muscle cramp at some time or other. When muscle cramp occurs, the muscle tenses and contracts of its own accord, which results in a very unpleasant feeling. Muscle cramp is usually experienced at the end of a very tiring match or training session. Soccer players suffer most from cramp in the calf muscles. It is treated by active stretching (pointing the toes towards the nose as far as possible, and stretching the affected leg). Passive stretching by a teammate or a bystander must be carried out very carefully, to ensure that no tearing of the muscle fibers occurs. Another possibility is to grab hold of the muscle with one or both hands, and to stretch it diagonally while gently squeezing. Sporting activity must be resumed carefully, and must be stopped immediately if the cramp returns. Although this phenomenon is far from fully understood, there are a number of possible causes of muscle cramp:

- a slight muscle tear;
- excessive loss of fluid or salt;

- sudden cooling;
- disturbances of the blood circulation;
- lack of muscle fitness or general physical fitness.

Muscle cramp can best be treated by tensing the group of muscles whose action opposes that of the affected muscles. This causes a movement in the opposite direction (biceps/triceps, hamstring/quadriceps). Muscle cramp can be avoided by:

- maintaining a good level of physical fitness;
- wearing the correct (non-pinching) clothing;
- checking bandages, etc. during warming-up, to ensure that they do not pinch;
- drinking regularly if the weather is hot.

13.3.10 Torn muscles

There are all sorts of conceivable situations in which a player can tear a muscle. Usually an uncontrolled movement is the cause. A torn muscle often occurs immediately after the start of a match or a training session. This is usually attributable to insufficient warming-up. At the end of a match or an intensive training session, muscles are often tired and the players feel generally fatigued. Common actions such as kicking, sprinting and jumping frequently cause a muscle to tear. Unlike muscle bruising, which is always the result of external violence, torn muscles have an internal cause. The symptoms of a torn muscle vary from:

- a relatively slight but often sharp, penetrating pain, especially when the affected muscle is stretched to the utmost;
- minor functional impairment and less strength, so that maximum performance is lower;
- slight swelling (in some cases);
- a certain degree of muscle contraction;
- the muscle feels hard (a sort of muscle cramp);
- the affected part of the muscle is tender to the touch; to:
- extreme pain, similar to a whiplash;
- a snapping feeling, followed immediately by loss of function;
- extravasation of blood;
- swelling (fluid);
- muscle contractions (spasms).

Torn muscles can vary in severity from a strain to a partial tear or a complete rupture. A torn muscle must first be given the RICE treatment (see page 302). In more serious cases, a doctor must be consulted and physiotherapy is necessary. Torn muscles can be prevented by planning training sessions properly, by always carrying out warming-up routines, and by performing stretching exercises. Complete recovery is essential, because muscle tears can easily reappear at the same place. Local tenderness to the touch and stretching pains must disappear and the muscle must be restored to its initial strength and size before sporting activities can be carried out again at maximal capacity.

13.3.11 Tendinitis

Tendinitis is an inflammation of the tendon and the surrounding tissue. Fluid associated with the inflammation penetrates between the tendon itself and the sheath around it. Such inflammation usually occurs at a point where the tendon connects to a bone. Tendinitis can be regarded as a typical over-use injury. The major causes of tendinitis in sport are a too rapid increase in workload, repetitive one-sided movement, and repetitive one-sided work. In soccer, the tendons most frequently affected by this complaint are the hamstring tendons, the patellar tendon and the Achilles tendon. The commonest cause of this latter injury is a hard or a very heavy pitch. Not only top sportsmen suffer from tendinitis - recreational players are also at risk. The term 'over-use' is not very well understood. Players often do not know when the body's limit has been reached, or what to do in such a case. A sportsman who finds it difficult to run on the morning after participating in his sport must take a break. Most people underestimate the problem, because the pain disappears after the first few strides. Many sportsmen continue to participate in their sport when they are in this condition. In doing so, they are risking a chronic over-use injury, which is often very difficult to overcome. Any sportsman who is in pain while participating in his sport, or feels pain when at rest, should consult a doctor. A painful tendon can be helped by placing a piece of foam rubber in the heel of the shoe. Thick socks and a soft insole can help, too. It is advisable to wear shoes with a thick insole or a shock-absorbent heel. Sports shoes should be thrown away when they start to wear or lose shape. In addition, training sessions should preferably be held on a soft surface such as grass. The healing process can be stimulated by an ice massage of the affected area. Massaging and stretching the affected muscles also helps. When the discomfort has disappeared, the muscles must be strengthened to prevent any recurrence of the injury. Good physical fitness is, of course, a necessity.

13.3.12 Fractures

A bone may be fractured in one or more places, and may even be splintered at the site of the break. Fractures occur regularly in contact sports such as soccer. Fractures may be closed or open. If the skin at the fracture site is intact, then the fracture is said to be closed (or simple). An open fracture involves not only a broken bone but also an open wound. This means that the site of the fracture is exposed to the air. Sometimes a piece of bone may project from the wound. The most common symptoms of a fracture are:

- extreme pain;
- in many cases the bone or part of the body assumes an abnormal position;
- absolute inability to move or take any strain on the bone;
- swelling due to bleeding (closed fracture), or visible loss of blood (open fracture);
- a feeling that something has broken.

A fracture can resemble a bruise, strain or dislocation in all respects. It is sometimes very difficult to make the right diagnosis.

A player who has sustained a fracture must be transported under expert supervision.

The symptoms may be so slight that a player carries on playing until the end of the game, even though he is later found to have a cracked bone. If there is the slightest suspicion of a fracture, therefore, it must be assumed that there is one. Playing on is out of the question. The injury must be immobilized, and the injured player must remain lying down if he is in great pain. The player must be transported to hospital under expert supervision. An open fracture must be covered with sterile gauze to prevent infection. X-rays must be taken at a hospital to determine whether the player has really suffered a fracture. Fractures can be avoided by general preventive measures such as maintaining a good level of physical fitness, wearing protective equipment such as shinguards, and fair play.

> *Anyone who takes part in sport at the top, and ends up without any form of abnormality, can count themselves lucky.*
>
> **Hans van Swol**

13.3.13 Cartilage injuries

Soccer players regularly have problems with damage to the cartilage in the joints, with zones of irritation or wear being formed on the cartilage. Such injuries usually occur behind the kneecap. Excessive pressure builds up between the kneecap and the bottom of the femur. This pressure can be caused by unsuitable footwear, excessively strenuous conditioning, or insufficient muscle strength (through lack of fitness or during the growth phase). A cartilage injury is accompanied by symptoms such as pain around and/or behind the kneecap. This pain becomes more severe during sporting activity. Sitting for long periods with bent knees also gives rise to such complaints. Periods of more or less pain alternate. One way of preventing cartilage injuries is to cut down on the movements that cause the injury. Conditioning programs must be specially adapted for soccer players who have cartilage problems, as should their footwear. Drills that increase the strength of the muscles of the upper leg are crucial to the treatment of these problems.

13.3.14 Meniscus injuries

If the body turns and the lower leg is blocked, the lateral or medial meniscus may be jammed. This often happens in soccer, and fortunately there are usually no ill effects. Sometimes, however, the applied forces are so great that the meniscus tears. Detectable symptoms are:

- acute pain on the medial or lateral side of the knee;
- bending and stretching are only possible to a limited extent (sometimes the whole knee is locked);
- the knee swells rapidly;
- the pain extends to the back of the knee and/or the front of the knee;
- within a few weeks the upper leg becomes thinner.

The meniscus can also suffer chronic damage by being continuously jammed during rapid turns and changes of direction, and again a tear may occur. Here, too, there are also a number of characteristic symptoms:

- slowly worsening complaints;
- pain in the knee;
- slight restriction of bending and stretching;

- pain extends to the back of the knee or to the front, when a full bend or stretch is made;
- slight swelling of the knee.

Such patterns of complaints are indicative of meniscus damage. The player should consult a doctor, to prevent any further damage to ligaments and/or cartilage. An exploratory operation or radiograph enables a diagnosis to be made and, in most cases, the necessary treatment can also be carried out.

13.3.15 Various injuries
A fresh bruise under the nail must be pricked with a drill or the hot end of a paper clip.. The blood must then be drawn off, the wound treated with iodine, and a pressure bandage applied with tape or bandaid. Otherwise the nail will be lost due to the extravasation of blood. A blood blister under the skin or under a callous layer must be treated very carefully to avoid any infection. If necessary (for example, if an awkwardly situated blister is causing pain), a blister must be opened, emptied and disinfected. A broken collarbone is almost always clearly visible on an X-ray. Naturally the player must go to hospital for examination and treatment. There is a danger that the top of the lung may be pricked. Players who suffer eye injuries and/or a possible fracture of the orbit or cheekbone must always go to hospital for examination and treatment. It is possible to recover quickly from such injuries. During the preparations for the European Championship in 1988, Marco van Basten arrived from Italy with a fractured cheekbone on the Friday, underwent an operation, and took part in a training session on the following Wednesday. He scored his first goal in a practice match on Friday, just two days later.

13.4 THE TASK OF A DOCTOR IN THE LOCKER ROOM AND ON THE PITCH
A doctor should have very little involvement in the final preparations for a match. During and after the final training session, decisions must be taken on who is and is not fit to play. At that time it is also clear who will need a painkilling tablet or injection. The physiotherapist or masseur should be aware of any residual effects of old injuries that still require attention. Naturally it is known which players need what bandages and tapes. Symptoms of illness may appear in the period between the final training session and the match. A decision must be taken on whether the sick player can take part in the match. Gastrointestinal problems and influenza are notorious. The responsible doctor must be available in the vicinity of the locker room, so that he can answer questions, carry out any minor treatment (for example, nose drops) or advise the coach. The doctor should also observe everything that happens and how the players behave. The doctor must also be available during the warming-up session. He must check that the players drink enough.
During the half-time break he must look into complaints and possible injuries. In consultation with the physiotherapist, he decides on and implements the necessary first-aid measures. Cooling is one of the few therapy treatments that can be carried out during the break. The others include applying new or additional bandages, giving a painkiller, and tending to a wound. The coach must be informed about any (still) slightly injured player on the substitutes bench, who may have to come on in the second half.
During the match it is, above all, the physiotherapist or masseur who examines and treats complaints and injuries on the pitch. The responsible doctor has to reach clear agreements about this. If there is any doubt, checks must be carried out on or near the pitch,

so that a correct decision can be reached on whether the player can continue or not. A gaping cut may have to be stitched as neatly as possible. There are very few acute situations that require immediate treatment. These include acute concussion, serious fractures and a 'swallowed tongue.' Fortunately this occurs only rarely. If a player receives a blow to the head that renders him unconscious for a very short period, but there are no initial indications that he should not play on, he must be watched very closely during the subsequent play. The same applies to trauma caused by a blow to the stomach (from, for example, another player's knee). When this occurs there is always a danger of damage to the liver, spleen or kidneys.

A player with a head injury must be watched closely during the subsequent play.

After the match, complaints and injuries must again be examined and treated. If necessary, arrangements must be made for players to be transported to hospital for further examination. The coach must be informed of the prognoses concerning any injuries. Naturally attendance rotas must be drawn up for each week and for the whole season. If necessary, additional examinations must be arranged during the course of an injury or illness. All of these medical tasks also apply for the opposing team, if its own doctor is not present. Strict rules apply if no doctor is present at a match at the amateur level. In the absence of a responsible doctor, and if no clear diagnosis can be made, a player may not continue playing if he:

- has suffered a blow to the head, followed by a period of unconsciousness (even if it was of short duration);
- feels residual pain after a blow to the stomach;
- has a possible fracture;
- has a serious joint or muscle injury.

Clubs have a responsibility for ensuring that rapid medical assistance can be provided on the pitch, if necessary.

The club must have clear procedures for calling on medical assistance. The ambulance service, hospital and a (club) doctor must be accessible (telephone number!).

*This chapter makes use of the guidelines contained in the book 'sportblessures buitenspel' (F.J.C. Backx, B. Coumans and E. Karnebeek; Teleac/De Tijdstroom, 1994).

SUMMARY

- If a player sustains an injury, bystanders must observe a number of rules.

- The most common soccer injuries are: a nosebleed; scrapes; blisters; cuts; bruises, sprains; dislocations; bursal damage; muscle cramp; torn muscles; tendinitis; fractures; cartilage problems; and meniscus injuries.

- Before a match starts, the responsible doctor should be in or near the locker room, so that he is available to answer questions, carry out any minor treatment that may be needed, and advise the coach if necessary. He must also observe what happens and how the players behave.

- During the half-time break he must examine complaints and possible injuries. In consultation with the physiotherapist, he must decide on and implement the necessary first-aid measures.

- During a match, it is usually the physiotherapist or masseur who examines and treats complaints and injuries on the pitch. In cases of doubt, the doctor must carry out an examination on or near the pitch.

- After a match, complaints and injuries must again be examined and treated. If necessary, arrangements must be made for players to be transported to hospital for further examination.

FIVE PRACTICAL QUESTIONS

1. Especially in youth soccer, there are usually no medical personnel in attendance. Should those in charge of youth teams have to be in possession of a first-aid qualification?

A first-aid qualification is very useful, and it should be linked with a resuscitation course. Youth soccer coaches should also have a knowledge of young people's problems. It is especially important to have an insight into when a player can and cannot continue playing.

2. Trainers regularly use a cooling spray. Is this advisable?

If it is used properly, cooling sprays present no problems. If such a spray is applied for too long, freezing can occur. The consequences of this (chilblains) can cause persistent and serious infections. Cooling sprays should only be used to treat acute pain.

3. In view of the danger of AIDS, how should injuries involving loss of blood be treated?

The person who treats the injury should wear gloves. The chance of infection is extremely small. It is pointless, for example, to wear shinguards to limit the chance of AIDS infection.

4. Is it possible to overcome a chronic injury and to continue carrying out sporting activity?

Certainly it is possible, but only in combination with treatment activities. There are a lot of examples of this. Tendinitis is almost always an over-use injury. This form of over-use is a consequence of a deterioration in strength/fitness (in the calf muscle, with consequent inflammation of the Achilles tendon), posture problems (inflammation of the tibia, as a consequence of weak ankles), poor technique (tennis elbow due to a poor throwing action or using a racket that is too large), or pure stress (general complaints due to long workdays, evening classes and training sessions). In all of these cases a reduced workload, muscle massage, stretching, and better footwear are necessary. Sometimes complete rest is required, together with physiotherapy.

5. Under what ground and weather conditions should youth players be excused attendance at training sessions?

Frozen pitches, a covering of snow, and heavy rain are usually good reasons for canceling a training session. Training sessions can be held on very flat, frozen pitches, provided the correct footwear is worn. Outdoor sporting activities should not usually be carried out in winter weather at below-zero temperatures (except for skating, of course).

INTERVIEW WITH DR. CEES-REIN VAN DE HOOGENBAND (club doctor of PSV Eindhoven)

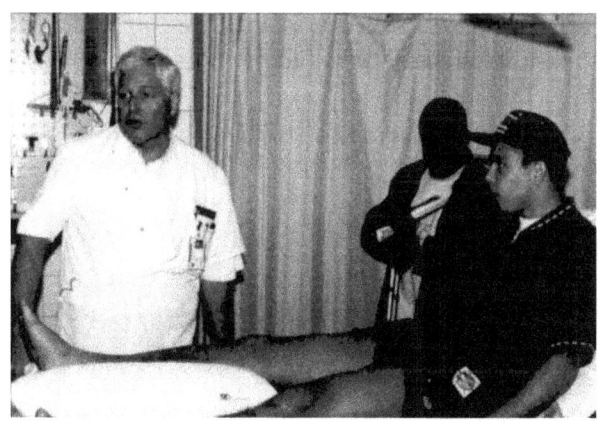

How did you, as a doctor, come into contact with PSV?
I was always very active in sport. At one time I was the coach of PSV's water polo team. When I was studying in Maastricht to become a specialist, I followed the basic sports medicine course in the evenings. In the meantime I had become the club doctor of MW Maastricht and advisor to Roda JC Kerkrade, and vice versa, so I entered the soccer world at quite an early stage. When I qualified as a surgeon, I was asked by Dr. van de Brekel, who was PSV's club doctor at that time, to join his team and relieve him of some of his work for PSV. When he retired, I became his successor. Moreover, I used to play for PSV at the youth level, so I already knew a lot of people at the club.

Are you on PSV's payroll?
No. As far as that is concerned, I take the same view as Dr. van Brekel. The relationship with PSV must be 'clean.' We are paid our expenses, but matters such as treatment are handled through the normal insurance procedures. This arrangement also means that the players know where they are. Up to a certain level, you have an independent relationship with them. In addition, I have a sort of gentlemen's agreement with PSV that I, as unpaid head of the medical section, ensure that the club's medical support systems function properly.

What is the structure of PSV's medical section?
I, as surgeon and traumatologist, am head of this section. We have a network of specialists. My deputy is Dr. Weber, who is also attached to the St. Anna hospital in Geldrop. Then we have an internist, Dr. Wolff, and Dr. Koster, who deals with the general practice side of matters. As a team of specialists, we work closely with Luc van Agt, the exercise physiologist. Three physiotherapists from the hospital also work for PSV on a part-time basis. Mart van Heuvel works full time for the first eleven as masseur. Ad Smits fulfills the same function for the second team, but on a part-time basis. PSV also has the services of three part-time physiotherapists for its youth section.

How often do you go to PSV, and is it possible to combine this with your work in the hospital?
I try to be present at the 'de Herdgang' training complex on two or three afternoons each week to check how players under treatment are progressing. I see all the other cases during my consulting hours at the hospital. We have also agreed that either I or my deputy will be present at every one of PSV's home and away games. That applies to league matches, tournaments, European Cup games and training camps, whether in the

Netherlands or abroad. Because there is a 'sport culture' within my team at the hospital, everyone cooperates fully in helping me to carry out my tasks for PSV.

What are your match-related tasks?
At home games, I see the players about 90 minutes before the game. I check how players under treatment are progressing, but otherwise I do not have a lot to do. Most of the work is carried out by the physiotherapist and the masseur. However, I always have to be available. The coach regularly asks about the condition of certain players. During the match, I sit on the bench. The Dutch Soccer Association has now made this mandatory. The doctor's most important task is to examine injuries and determine whether or not a player can carry on. In serious cases it is necessary to arrange transport to hospital, X-ray sessions, etc. After the game, I look at any injuries the players may have picked up, and, if necessary, in consultation with the physiotherapist and the masseur, I make appointments for the following day.

How do you determine whether a player is match fit?
That is always done in consultation. There is clearly a division of responsibility. We look at all the available information on any swellings, the severity of the injury and the work performed in the training sessions during the last week. Together with Luc van Agt, we then assess what a player can do, and submit our advice to the coach. A coach may look at factors such as the importance of the match, and the psychological effect of having a player in the squad again, even if he only sits on the bench. It is a very complex procedure, and each individual has his own input and responsibilities.

Have you ever been confronted with serious injuries on the pitch?
I have never been faced with a life-threatening situation. But serious injuries do sometimes occur. Think of the blow suffered by our goalkeeper, Waterreus, in the European Cup game against the German team, Werder Bremen. At moments like that, it is up to me to say whether a player can continue. Fractures also occur now and then, of course. In such cases you can often tell that a player cannot carry on simply by looking at him.

How does it feel to sit on the bench as a club doctor?
I always try to act as professionally as possible, but I regularly find myself slipping into the role of a PSV supporter. I always share the players' feelings, whether of joy or sadness. I am definitely involved, but I think I can maintain a proper perspective. It is very important to get a good view of the moment when an injury is sustained. This can often provide a lot of information on which to base a diagnosis. It is therefore crucial to follow the game closely, despite all your emotions.

How is the bond of trust with the players?
This is something that has to grow. After a while, players come to you of their own accord, but as a club doctor you have to appreciate that new players may have a bond with the doctor of their previous club. You have to respect this. In my opinion, a doctor always gets the patients he deserves. At the start of the season, I always talk to the squad of players, and explain the medical package that is available at PSV. At the same time, I tell them that they are free to choose their own medical support. The only condition is that we have to be kept informed if someone from outside PSV is consulted. If a player goes to another

doctor for a second opinion, for example, we always ensure that he is accompanied by someone from PSV. In this way you can stop things taking on a life of their own. One big problem is that players are regularly approached by outsiders. Some of them have good intentions, but there are also a lot of quacks, who are out to make money, and who find it interesting to treat PSV's players. The medical staff must demonstrate that they have confidence in their own abilities, so that players are not tempted to turn to this type of person.

Do you have any contacts with other club doctors?
A number of years ago, the club doctors of FC Twente, Ajax Amsterdam, Feyenoord Rotterdam and PSV met to discuss whether we could cooperate in some way. After all, we have a lot in common. At that time we set up the Club for Club Doctors and Consultants. This is now a flourishing organization, which meets twice each year, and whose members maintain close contacts. The questions it discusses are concerned with, for example, insurances and the specific injury or treatment problems that we are confronted with in our field of work. Because the club doctors now know each other much better, they are more careful with their statements and are less ready to criticize each other.

In your opinion, is the injury situation now worse than it used to be?
Soccer has become much faster and the players are much fitter. As a result, more confrontational situations now occur. When I look at the injuries that I have seen in recent years, it is my opinion that they have become more serious. This tendency can be seen in both professional and amateur soccer. It seems as though the players have a lot less respect for each other's limbs. This is reflected in the way that players now talk without any shame about committing 'professional' fouls. It has become perfectly normal.

Have the changes in the rules had an influence?
The heavier punishments now given for tackles from behind have clearly resulted in cleaner play. In my view you have to take the toughest possible line with such tackles. The fact that some referees only show a red card if there is actual physical contact is still a problem. A dangerous tackle that misses its target is too often ignored. The usual comment is, "But there was no contact!" I think that you should punish on the basis of intent rather than consequences. Referees should whistle preventively.

How can the injury situation be approached more effectively at the amateur level?
In amateur soccer, this is a very difficult problem. So many factors play a role. One of these is that soccer players at this level become fatigued more quickly, because they are not fit enough. As a result, uncontrolled situations arise, in which not only the player but also his opponent might be injured. In addition, there are a lot of recurrent injuries in amateur soccer. The most important consideration, perhaps, is that players should not start playing again until their injury is completely healed. Secondary rehabilitation also plays a large role here. This means that, when a player is fit again, he must work through a suitable program aimed at strengthening a weak point in a muscle or a joint. This is very difficult for amateurs.

Do you think that our general level of health has deteriorated, and that this results in more soccer injuries?
I do not know if that is true in general, but what strikes me when I see youngsters, in particular, is that the disappearance of physical education lessons in our schools has had a very negative effect on the development of children. In my opinion, a healthy body is one of the most important things in life, and the basis for this is established in our younger years. I therefore think that physical education should be reintroduced in our schools. When you see the players in our youth section, some of them cannot even do a forward roll. You know from the very start that these 'wooden' characters will stumble from one injury into another, and will never make it into professional soccer.

More and more money is coming into professional soccer. Will some of this be used to improve the medical facilities of the professional clubs?
PSV invests a lot of money in its medical section. My requests for facilities are always listened to. Many clubs now realize that, if they want their players to remain fit, they will have to invest in good medical facilities. The medical staff at PSV could no longer function without an exercise physiologist such as Luc van Agt. Professional clubs with less financial resources clearly have a problem. However, the medical section of the Dutch Soccer Association is a good alternative. The clubs can now send their players there for rehabilitation.

Do the increased sporting and financial pressures in soccer also result in more pressure on the medical staff?
The pressure has indeed increased, but I do not have any difficulty with this. For me, it is something of a challenge to ensure that a player has the best possible medical care, so that he will quickly return to full fitness. If the players had all the time in the world to recover, life might become boring. The players themselves want to play again as soon as possible, otherwise they will lose their regular place in the team. You are, therefore, working with highly motivated individuals, and this has a positive effect on the recovery process. You can gain a lot of time by making a good, quick diagnosis after an injury has occurred. At PSV, we take a forceful approach to diagnosis. This is not to say that we then proceed quickly to treatment and rehabilitation, but it is reassuring for the player and the coach. This, too, accelerates the recovery process. The only problem you sometimes confront is that people try to pin us down to a prognosis. I am optimistic by nature and I sometimes tended to give too positive a prognosis. If you do that, and you are then proved wrong, difficulties arise. This is why I am now more careful. If you give a longer estimate, the player will experience a positive impulse if he recovers faster than expected.

LITERATURE

1. F.H.B.O. bij Sport.
ISBN: 90-238-2213-7.

2. Handbook Buitensport E.H.B.O.
H. Palsma.
ISBN: 90-5189-448-1.

3. Preventie Voetbalblessures.
H. Inklaar.
KNVB.

4. Blessures-praktijik voor sporters, coaches, trainers en verzorgers.
V. Blum.
ISBN: 90-215-1351.

5. Het Sportmedisch Formularium.
Erasmus Publishing.

6. Sportblessures.
Uitgeverij Elsevier.

7. Sportgezondheidszorg.
Uitgeverij Stafleu.

8. Sports injuries prevention and treatment.
L. Persson and P. Renstrom.

9. Vaktijdschriften geneeskunde en Sport (artsen en fysiotherapeuten) en Sportmassage.

CHAPTER 14

PHYSIOTHERAPY IN SOCCER

Rob Ouderland

14.1 INTRODUCTION

The role of the physiotherapist is growing in significance within organized soccer in the Netherlands. However, his function is not always properly understood. Physiotherapists initially became involved in amateur soccer, because soccer is a sport in which a lot of injuries occur. More and more clubs called in a colleague for consultation, and eventually this became a matter of course. Every self-respecting amateur club can now call on a physiotherapist. In practice, he is often also a club supporter, who gives his services to 'his' club free of charge in his spare time. Physiotherapy in soccer therefore started off as a hobby. In parallel to this development, physiotherapists also acquired a permanent place in professional soccer. Currently all 36 Dutch professional clubs employ a full-time or part-time physiotherapist. They formed the Dutch Association of Physiotherapists in Professional Soccer. The part played by the physiotherapist within a soccer organization can vary.

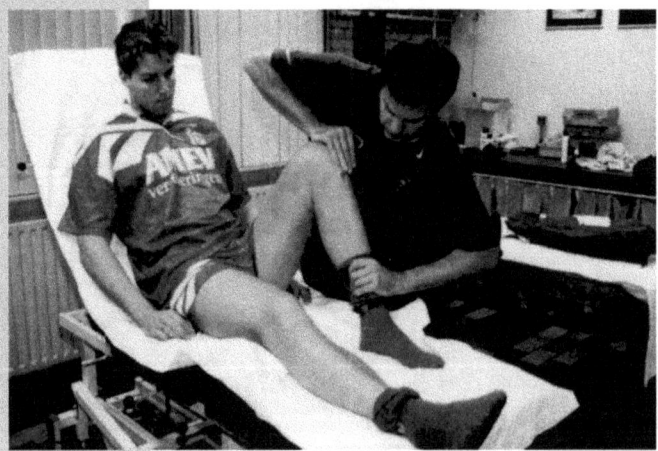

Treating injuries is just one of a physiotherapist's tasks.

Treating injuries

A physiotherapist must be aware of the various forms of treatment and the physiological healing process of damaged tissue. In practice, he has to decide whether an injured player has recovered sufficiently to be able to resume training. On the basis of an anamnesis (an intake interview with the patient) and an examination, he must be able to make a differential diagnosis, identifying the most likely form of injury. In addition, the recovery phase of the injured tissue must be registered, also its stress tolerance. Using this information, he can prepare a plan of treatment and indicate the expected progress of the injury.

Preparing preventive guidelines/measures and providing advice on training programs

A physiotherapist can provide advice on drawing up training programs for individual players and the first team during each phase of the season (preparation, competition, winter and summer break). An injured player obviously needs an individual (rehabilitation) training program. The main group of players must train in line with other criteria.

Cooperation with the coach(es), club doctor, masseur and players

This is a very important aspect of a physiotherapist's work. Good cooperation and sporting success depend on respect and confidence between the various disciplines (coach, doctor, physiotherapist, masseur and players). Team spirit is also essential. It is important that each individual is aware of the responsibilities of the others. Constructive discussion and clarity are crucial.

14.2 TASKS OF THE PHYSIOTHERAPIST BEFORE, DURING AND AFTER MATCHES AND TRAINING SESSIONS

There are a number of tasks that require close cooperation between the club doctor, physiotherapist, masseur and other medical helpers. This medical team is responsible for ensuring the availability of the resources needed during matches and training sessions. The physiotherapist often plays a focal part in the organization of medical care in soccer, mainly because he is the person who is closest to the players and coach. Due to the close relationship the physiotherapist builds up with a player (1 on 1 relationship), the mental aspect should not be an underestimated role in treatment. In addition to providing medical treatment, the physiotherapist often acts as a confidant. At difficult moments during the recovery process, he is someone to whom the player has direct access.

14.2.1 Specific tasks before matches and training sessions

Bandaging and taping ankles is a common preventive measure in soccer, especially at the highest levels. The physiotherapist or masseur often applies these preventive bandages. Opinions differ on the utility of bandages and tape. A fit, stable ankle without a bandage or tape is always preferable. However, bandaging and taping are often done to give a previously injured player the idea that his ankle is receiving additional support, thus raising his confidence. We must respect this. Due to the pressures of daily soccer, recurrent ankle injuries are a regular occurrence in top level soccer. Bandages and tape are then the easiest option. Sometimes players need treatment on the day of a match to ensure they are fit to start. Sometimes a player will be just on the verge of match fitness. A decision has to be taken as to whether or not it would be irresponsible to let him play. The physiotherapist is involved in making this decision. A fitness test may be carried out, either individually or in a group, to gauge whether or not a player can take part in a match. Ultimately, the player himself always decides whether he is 100% match fit. In practice, a player might wait until just prior to, or during, the warming-up stage before indicating that he does not feel fit enough to play. Soccer players often suffer from physical complaints. These can be arthrogenous (bones), ligamentous (joint ligaments), capsular (joint capsule) or muscular. The physiotherapist can indicate whether or not a player is fit to play. Finally, he needs to keep a watchful eye on the players while they warm up. The intensity and content of the warming-up period are significant. A player has 20 to 25 minutes to prepare himself mentally and physically for the match. Any doubtful cases are closely monitored with regard to the skills needed to be able to play well (running technique; sprinting, turning, and changing direction; kicking and heading technique; controlling the ball and passing).

14.2.2 Specific tasks during matches and training sessions

Often it is the task of the physiotherapist to do his fieldwork during a match. He must keep a watchful eye out for injuries occurring, so that he has an initial impression of the severity of an injury. If help is needed, it is his task to make a diagnosis as quickly as possible (analyzing the location, type and severity of the injury). This is not always easy. Serious injury must be excluded. He must be particularly careful with head injuries and must decide, together with the doctor, whether or not to allow the player to play on. In many cases, first aid can be provided. It is then important to reassure the player that the injury is not severe. In professional soccer, it is no longer possible to attend to injuries on the field during play. In terms of not slowing down the game, this is a good thing. However, referees should interpret this rule rather more freely than they currently do. The stretcher-bearers should never touch an injured player without the physiotherapist's permission. The physiotherapist is and remains responsible for the initial treatment, and neither the referee nor the first-aid teams should ever forget this. If necessary, the physiotherapist also treats players with complaints and injuries during training sessions.

14.2.3 Specific tasks after matches and training sessions

The most important task is to take stock and check out (minor) injuries suffered by the players, and to provide first aid and advice when it is needed. This often involves treating light abrasions or minor bruising of muscles and bones. Disinfection, cooling, and a prescribed period of rest (and possibly bandaging) often have the desired effect. The injuries are examined together with the doctor. If he is unavailable, the physiotherapist makes an initial diagnosis and refers the player to a doctor (general practitioner, or a specialist at a hospital). In addition, he packs up his materials neatly, ready for the following activity. Injuries must be discussed with the players concerned and the coach, so that they can decide how to proceed (code of behavior, recommended treatment and training program).

14.3 THE ROLE OF THE PHYSIOTHERAPIST DURING THE REHABILITATION PROCESS

The physiotherapist has another important task in addition to treating minor injuries before, during and after training sessions and matches. It is his job to help players with long-term injuries to get back to their original level, so that they can start to train again with the team and, eventually, regain match fitness. A physiotherapist is therefore also a rehabilitation coach. His training has prepared him to be a remedial therapist. In the field of sport physiotherapy, on the other hand, he often functions as a conditioning coach. It is, therefore, absolutely essential that he is fully conversant with not only the rules that apply to the healing of connective tissue, but also the physiological principles of the science of conditioning. These rules are easy to observe in practice during a normal physiological recovery period. The physiotherapist can then prescribe the best exercises and the appropriate intensity (duration and frequency) at the right time. It is known that minor skin damage should heal within 4 to 10 days, unless there are complications.

Muscular damage can take between 2 and 3 weeks. Broken bones generally take 6 to 8 weeks to heal, under normal circumstances. A damaged tendon may need 200 to 500 days before it recovers its tensile strength. Cartilage damage can take even longer to heal, and sometimes does not heal at all. More problems occur if persistent complaints develop. In practice, this happens regularly. Why does a player fail to recover from an injury within the 'normal' time? The physiotherapist and doctor have to investigate the background to such an injury. In short, good recovery depends on good investigation, combined with the right diagnosis. Before rehabilitation can begin, it is essential to have a clear picture of the location, type and severity of the injury. There is a procedure to achieve this picture: anamnesis, inspection and functional examination.

14.3.1 Anamnesis
An anamnesis is the initial consultation between a physiotherapist and the patient. A number of specific questions have to be asked during this consultation, so that a picture can be formed of the problem facing the patient. A good anamnesis consists of several steps.

The complaint
First of all the patient must describe the complaint in detail. Does he feel pain? Is there any functional impairment? A range of questions is used to chart the patient's symptoms. The physiotherapist needs to know the location of the injury, the type of injury and how serious it is. These factors largely determine the treatment and rehabilitation program. He also needs to know exactly how the injury occurred. The situation in which the player was injured must be analyzed. If the injury is the result of a fall (trauma), he must determine: how the patient fell;
- whether or not he could walk immediately after the fall;
- whether swelling occurred immediately or after several hours;
- whether the patient heard or felt anything snap or tear;
- where the pain was first experienced.

History
Once the symptoms of the complaint have been recorded, the physiotherapist needs to know the history of the complaint. Sometimes a complaint occurred recently, without any similar symptoms having appeared in the past. In this case it has a short history. It is essential for a physiotherapist to gather as much information as possible. In many cases he will be confronted with recurring complaints. It is important to be aware of the history of the injury. This involves knowledge of the following:
- How long ago did the injury occur?
- How serious was the injury at that time?
- Which medical personnel were consulted at that time?
- What therapy was prescribed?
- What was the effect of the therapy?

Course

The course of the complaint must be recorded. The physiotherapist must know whether pain has been continuous since the complaint first occurred. The pain may have decreased or increased, remained the same or fluctuated after a time. Sometimes pain is only felt at certain moments, such as when the player gets up in the morning, and it then disappears after a while. Physical exercise can also cause the pain to recur. Is pain felt only at the start of sporting activity or is it constant? Perhaps pain is only felt after sporting activity. If the physiotherapist is to get an accurate picture of the type of injury, he needs to know exactly when the pain increases (provocation) or fades (reduction). Every injury goes through a natural healing process. It is known, for example, that a muscle tear closes within 2 to 3 weeks. If a muscular injury is still causing trouble after two months, the physiotherapist will know that something is wrong, and that the normal healing process has not occurred. Information on the course of an injury can provide the necessary clarity.

> *Halfway through my active career as an athlete, I had my first massage. It took me a week to recover from it.*
>
> **Daly Thompson**

Stress and stress tolerance

During the first talk with the patient, it is important to acquire a good insight into his stress tolerance and the amount of stress (the load) to which he is subjected during his daily life and sporting activities. Figure 14.1 shows an overview of the factors that determine a player's stress and stress tolerance. An imbalance between the two could possibly be at the root of the occurrence and the course of the complaint. The balance between stress and stress tolerance can be disrupted in two ways. In the first case, it happens gradually. The load remains constant, but the player's capacity for coping with it slowly decreases. This is not a case of trauma but of chronic overstrain (microtrauma). This could be the result of medication, or the fact that the patient has recently been ill or undergone surgery. Stress at work can also lead to a decrease in stress tolerance. It is therefore advisable to get to the bottom of this. Another possibility is acute tissue overload. For example, this could be a torn muscle (see case study) that occurred when the patient started a sprint from an unusual posture. The muscle is not accustomed to having to supply so much power in this situation. Such cases of trauma often occur without any prior medical history. The player's stress tolerance has not changed, but the load has suddenly increased. This often happens in soccer.

The current status

Finally the patient's current situation must be clarified. How does the patient feel, and how is he functioning in daily life or in sport situations? Has the situation improved since the injury occurred (regressive complaint pattern), remained the same, or worsened (progressive complaint pattern)?

14.3.2 The examination

The examination can be subdivided into a general and a local part. The general examination includes observation of the patient's walking pattern. The way in which a patient enters the consulting room can sometimes provide a great deal of information. Does he exhibit an asymmetrical walking pattern? Is he using crutches? The muscle contours are

General stress:
- Work and pressure of work
- Sport
- Smoking
- Alcohol consumption
- Medicines
- Psycho-social context

Local/regional (functional unit) stress:
- Soccer load: number of hours
  level of performance
  circumstances
  position in team

- Hobby
- Sudden, major changes in posture and motion
- Long-term, one-sided postures and movements

General stress tolerance:
- Increased susceptibility to viral infections
- Soon tired
- Involuntary weight loss
- A specific arousal: difficulty in getting to sleep
  restless sleep
  concentration difficulties
  bloated feeling
  unspecific actions
  easily irritated
  harassed feeling

Regional /segmental ability to handle stress:
- Previous trauma or surgery in the affected area, which could impair circulation and lymph drainage.
- Anomalies in the affected area.
- Previous complaints of pains in the organs (viscera and musculoskeletal system) in the same areas, or neuro-anatomically connected areas

Figure 14.1: *Overview of the factors that determine the stress and stress-tolerance of a soccer player.*

also observed, as well as the individual body parts, and the changes in these contours during movement. Special points to look out for are posture, symmetry and an (antalgic) walking pattern. During the local examination, the site of the injury is viewed. The physiotherapist touches nothing. Simply by looking, he tries to collect information. Color is important, as well as any local swelling. A blue discoloration can indicate bruising, and a red one can indicate inflammation. When the findings of the examination are recorded, mention must only be made of, for example, redness and not of inflammation. Such a conclusion may only be drawn when all of the information has been collected and the diagnosis can be made. Finally, the severity of any swelling, the position of a joint and the temperature of the injury site can provide important information on the status of the complaint.

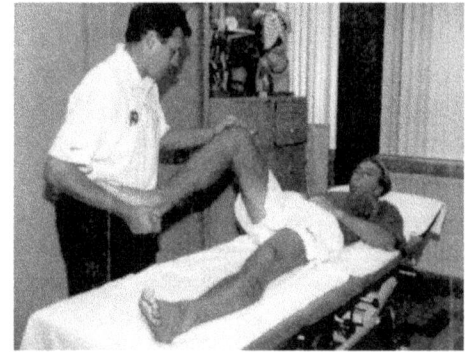
Active movement examination.

14.3.3 Examination of physical function

As a final step the physiotherapist will use a number of tests to find out which parts of the musculoskeletal system (muscles, tendons, capsule, ligaments and bones) are giving rise to complaints in specific situations and in various joint positions. He tries to trace the link between his diagnosis and the patient's symptoms. First of all, he evaluates the patient's general pattern of movement. He determines which tasks the patient can carry out independently/with a little help/only with help. By asking the patient to walk, he can gather information. For example he must observe how the patient moves. If the patient is limping, this could be the result of pain and/or shortening of the leg. The active movement examination follows. The patient carries out a number of movements prescribed by the physiotherapist, who looks at the range of movement, the pain experienced, the willingness to carry out each movement, and the patient's movement coordination. In the passive movement examination, the movements are carried out by the physiotherapist, who notes the range of movement and the sensation at the end of the movement. For example, if it turns out that, during the passive examination, the knee can be bent much further than in the active examination, this means that the patient, for some reason or other, is unwilling to carry out this movement. One reason for this could be pain. Depending on the type and location of the injury, a number of other tests and examination procedures can be applied: palpation, length tests, a stability test, meniscus tests and resistance tests. In these latter tests, the patient must exert strength against a specific resistance. The course of the movement and the patient's sensation at the end of it provide useful information for the physiotherapist. A person can exert much greater strength against a specific resistance if he has a minor pulled muscle than if he has a torn muscle.

14.3.4 Making a diagnosis

When the physiotherapist has completed the anamnesis and carried out an examination and a physical function examination, he can draw up his findings. In doing so, he can make use of additional medical data obtained from a general prac-titioner or specialist. The physiotherapist now has a good picture of the injury. His first task to remedy it. Every (connective) tissue structure needs functional exercise to help it recover. Recovery nearly always has the same aim - to regain the pre-injury level of soccer fitness. The diagnosis restricts the physiotherapist in his choice of exercises and their intensity.

14.4 VARIOUS PHASES OF CONNECTIVE TISSUE RECOVERY

The recovery process starts virtually at the moment the injury occurs. The quality of the initial first aid often influences the

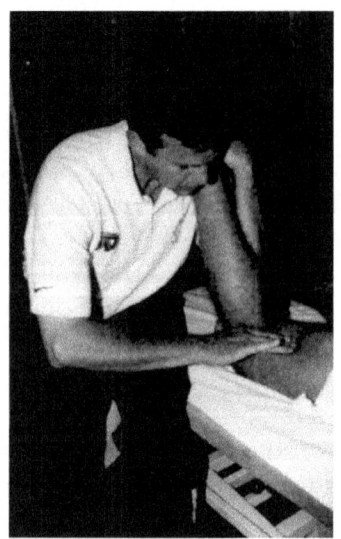
Palpation

subsequent course of the recovery process. Correct first aid can ensure that damage is restricted, so that recovery can proceed more quickly. A recovery process can be divided into a number of phases. A physiotherapist must be able to identify the current stage of the injury recovery process, and be competent in the specific treatment and conditioning methods appropriate to each phase.

14.4.1 The inflammation phase

As soon as the injury occurs, the body takes immediate measures to initiate recovery. The nervous system uses various stimuli (e.g. pain and/or bleeding) to set the necessary processes in motion. Any bleeding will stop within a few minutes unless it is arterial. The purpose of the subsequent inflammation is to cleanse the damaged area,

> There is no such thing as soccer without a sponge and water.
>
> **Theo Reitsma**

so that it can heal properly. The length of the inflammation phase can vary, depending on factors such as severity, location and any infection. This phase usually takes 48 hours, but it can last for up to 7 or 8 days from the moment when the injury occurs. Naturally this depends on the recovery capacity (health) of the patient. During this first phase, the physiotherapist must follow the recovery process without doing too much to stimulate it. The body has enough to do with handling the damage (lesion). RICE treatment (see page 302) can be given locally during this phase. The use of ice is not popular with all theraplsts. One of the main reasons for using ice is to kill pain. In a case of trauma, the initial pain can be severe. It is helpful if something can be done about this immediately. The use of a pressure bandage prevents the loss of too much body fluid through the damaged blood vessels. It can also have a painkilling effect. During the inflammation phase, the greatest possible attention must be paid to general aspects of fitness, as long as this does not endanger the natural progress of this phase. In this way a player can be kept fit, and this is valuable for the subsequent progress of his recovery. Less time needs to be spent on building up basic fitness, and an earlier start can be made on functional conditioning. The damaged area must be allowed adequate rest, but other bodily functions need to be kept up to the mark.

14.4.2 The proliferation phase (3 days to 3 weeks)

This phase is characterized by the repair of the damage to tissue. This repair is the result of the formation of new tissue cells, and starts from the third day, continuing until 3 weeks after the moment of injury (post-trauma). A number of general rules must be followed for therapy during the proliferation phase.

Mobilization depending on the damaged tissue

In the case of a pulled muscle, the patient will generally be allowed to walk (sedately). The injury is only bandaged. In the case of a torn muscle, absolute rest is essential during the first days after the injury. The degree of permitted mobilization depends largely on the severity of the Injury. The Injured body part may generally be subjected to partial load (for example, 50%). This is referred to as partial immobilization. A good example of this situation is a torn hamstring. A pressure bandage is applied to the upper leg, and the leg may not be used for walking or standing. The patient can be allowed to use crutches, so that he can walk without having to support his body weight on the injured leg.

Remedial therapy aimed at improving aerobic capacity
An injury often prevents a player from participating in training sessions. In order to prevent his basic fitness level from deteriorating too much, a great deal of attention must be paid to general fitness conditioning during the first phase of recovery. For example, if a player is not yet able to run, aquajogging can be used to maintain aerobic fitness. Obviously this conditioning must never have a negative impact on the recovery process.

Proprioceptive training
When tissue is damaged, a whole range of sensors (nerve endings) are destroyed. These structures need time to recover. The process can be favorably influenced by proprioceptive or coordination conditioning. This involves prompting the muscular reactions that are associated with the various exercises. In this form of conditioning, the body (including the muscular system) is prompted to react in ways that improve the neuro-muscular reflex associated with the required action. As a result, these sensors recover. This is a precondition for recovery of proper function. By using plenty of variety in the conditioning program, the nervous system is stimulated in many ways, prompting full sensor recovery. Immobilization always causes reduced sensor activity. For example, when a leg is put in plaster, the various muscle sensors (motor units) in that part of the body become inactive, because they no longer experience any stimulation. When the plaster is removed, a great deal of attention has to be paid to the reactivation of these sensors by means of proprioceptive training.

The therapeutic measures referred to above must be carried out within the pain-free mobility range.

14.4.3 The remodeling phase (3 weeks to 3 months)
This phase links with the proliferation phase. "Modeling" takes place at the site of the lesion. Newly formed tissue cells are functionally 'modeled' through specific stimuli. Naturally this occurs as quickly as possible by means of functional tasks. By carrying out soccer-specific movements immediately, the regenerating tissue becomes accustomed to the type of load it will be confronted with when the patient can resume all of his soccer activities. The tissue is specifically formed for its function. This phase begins 3 weeks after the trauma, and ends at the functional phase when full training recommences. Here again are a number of basic therapeutic rules apply:
- mobilization using the maximum range of movement (both passive and active);
- always compare the patient's recovery process with the normal recovery pattern for the injury in question;
- very varied proprioceptive conditioning, with   the emphasis on functional exercises;
- very varied coordination conditioning;
- very varied stability conditioning;
- functional conditioning (conditioning the fitness parameters that are of importance for the sportsman).

Variety, in the context of the above mentioned conditioning exercises, refers especially to the speed and frequency with which the exercises are carried out. In addition, stability conditioning can be carried out with the eyes alternately open and shut. When the eyes are shut, the emphasis is entirely on the "feeling of movement."

14.4.4 The functional phase

This phase is a logical follow-up to the remodeling phase. In fact the two phases merge. The start of the functional phase depends on the damaged connective tissue. All connective tissues have their own recovery times. The functional phase generally starts earlier after a muscle tear than after a tendon is torn. The functional phase is the phase in which the adaption capacity of the damaged tissue is called upon. The tissue models itself to meet the demands made upon it (soccer strength and coordination). This takes place under the influence of specific exercises and conditioning. Normal conditioning principles apply during this phase of recovery. Obviously the type of injury, the diagnosis and medical history of the player determine the selected conditioning exercises and intensity. The patient's personal experience of the situation also influences the conditioning. Experience and feeling (intuition) are important qualities in a physiotherapist during this phase of recovery. Obviously this phase

Proprioceptive exercises: teeter board.

is concerned with soccer-specific conditioning. The treatment and exercise targets are to improve flexibility, strength, coordination, stability and running. This is done through soccer conditioning. At the same time, the various aspects of fitness that a soccer player needs are conditioned. The physiotherapist has to know which energy systems the player is using. If a player has been injured for months, all his energy systems will be called on during the con-ditioning buildup. The buildup starts with long-distance running, followed by a long-distance run based on the Fartlek principle, and ends with interval training (especially anaerobic lactic). This has to be done with and without the ball. If a player has just recently been injured and the season is halfway through, soccer-specific conditioning can be picked up more quickly, with the emphasis on the (lactic) anaerobic system. The player's basic level of fitness will still be fairly good. If conditioning is focused on a specific energy system, this system must be given adequate rest to permit 'supercompensation' to occur. If these physiological recovery times (see Fig. 14.2) are insufficient, or are not respected, the conditioning buildup will be less than optimal. The risk of injury will increase, because there will be an imbalance in the equilibrium between buildup (anabolic) and breakdown (catabolic) in the body. This can result in damage to muscles, tendons, ligaments and cartilage (see Fig. 14.3).

Functional drills.

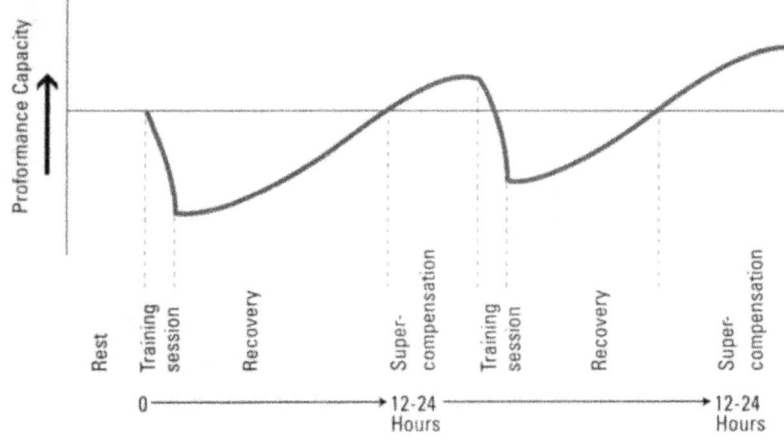

Figure 14.2: *The time needed for super-compensation in the various physiological systems (van Wingerden, 1996). Super-compensation for aerobic endurance needs a recovery time of 12 to 24 hours.*

Aerobic endurance	between 12 and 24 hours
Anaerobic lactic endurance	between 36 and 48 hours
Anaerobic lactic endurance	between 48 and 72 hours
Strength endurance	between 36 and 48 hours
Maximum Strength	between 48 and 47 hours
Fast Strength	72 hours.

14.4.5 Central points of attention during the recovery process

1. Giving the patient information and tasks to eliminate negative influences wherever possible, and to provide the stimulus needed for recovery. Therapy, behavior and rules for everyday living must be taken into consideration here. Sometimes it is impossible to avoid negative influences on other connective tissue structures during recovery. For example, it may be necessary to immobilize fractures in plaster for a long period of time, resulting in loss of muscle bulk (atrophy).

2. At the stage of the recovery process when a player can cope with a certain load, it is essential to start to rebuild soccer fitness. The first step is to develop good basic fitness. It is important to opt for varied loads, so that all basic motor characteristics can be restored to a normal level. Once basic fitness has been achieved, a more soccer-specific fitness buildup can be chosen. The exercises described in the case study at the end of this chapter can be used for this purpose.

3. In summary, it can be stated that a recovery schedule for an injured soccer player is largely determined by the physiological recovery mechanisms that are already present in rough outline. The treatment plan takes account of the diagnosis and a number of personal

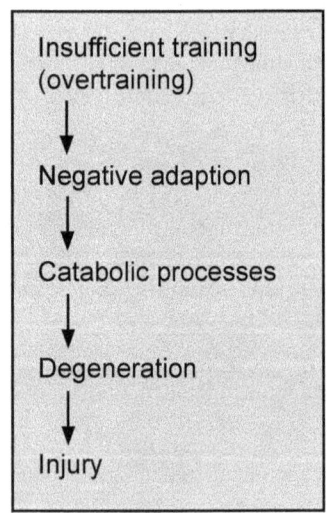

Figure 14.3: *Overview of the process that takes place if physiological recovery times are not respected, leading to injuries. There will be impairment of the balance between build-up (anabolic) and breakdown (catabolic) of various connective tissues (including muscles and tendons).*

details extracted from the anamnesis. Considerable skill is needed to take maximum advantage of the possibilities for recovery in the case of a soccer player with a long-term injury. Once a soccer player's history has been minutely analyzed, it is clear why someone fails to recover fully, or at all, and is unable to return to the game at his previous level.

CASE STUDY:

Profession: professional soccer player, right-footed, attacking midfielder
Age: 26
Sporting level: 8 years as full professional

> *Injuries arrive at the gallop and depart at walking pace.*
>
> **Gerard Nijboer**

THE ANAMNESIS SHOWS:

The complaint:

The player is referred to the physiotherapist by his general practitioner because he has a hamstring injury. He indicates that he feels pain at the back of his right thigh, close to the knee (distal). The injury occurred in the 30th minute of a match that was played on the preceding day. There was no physical contact. It happened at the moment when the player was sprinting at full speed. He suddenly felt a cutting pain at the described location. As a result of the injury, he could not play on. The patient states that he is able to walk, but each time he puts his weight on to his right leg he feels a sharp pain at the described location.

History

It becomes clear during the talk that the patient has not previously been confronted with an injury of this nature. There is therefore no question of a recurring injury.

Course

Since the moment the injury occurred, there has been no change in the situation. The situation described above has persisted for the past 24 hours. It is possible to walk, but painful and difficult. Immediately after the occurrence of the injury, a 15-minute ice treatment was applied, followed by a compression bandage. This bandage is still in place.

Stress and stress tolerance

The player takes part in 8 or 9 training sessions each week and plays in 1 or 2 matches. He tends to rest during his leisure time. He plays a round of golf once or twice a week. He is a non smoker, drinks very little alcohol, and only stays up late occasionally, on the evening after a match. There are no sleeping problems or signs of fatigue. He has taken no medicines in recent months and has not undergone surgery. His last injury was a head injury, nine months ago. The player emphasizes that his recent form has been very good and that he has felt no stress, because he has a regular place in a successful team. He still feels that he is at peak strength.

Current status

As already mentioned, the patient suffers from sharp pains in the back of his right thigh when he walks. There are no symptoms when he rests. Otherwise the patient feels fine and exhibits no other symptoms.

THE EXAMINATION HAS SHOWN:
The patient points out the site of the injury to the physiotherapist. It is immediately obvious that the site shows blue discoloration. There is no other visible difference between the right and left legs. When the patient is asked to walk backwards and forwards, an antalgic walking pattern becomes obvious. He supports his weight only momentarily on his right leg, and the heel-to-toe sequence when the foot is placed on the ground is incomplete.

THE FUNCTION EXAMINATION SHOWS:
- Blockage of right sacro-iliac joint (SIJ)
- Provocation tests ligament ilio-lumbar right + ligament sacro-tuberal right +
- Reduced contours M. triceps surae right +
- Muscle length test M. biceps femoris right + M. triceps surae right +
- Resistance test M. biceps femoris right +
- Palpation: dell (muscle defect) palpable at muscle tendon transition caput longum M. biceps femoris.

After consultation with the doctor who referred the patient, injury treatment and rehabilitation are started one day after the post trauma.

THE DIAGNOSIS
Rupture of the distal part of the caput longum M. biceps femoris right, tenomuscular transition with blockage of right SIj. The treatment plan takes account of the phases of injury recovery, combined with the clinical findings and the final aim - to play soccer at the highest level.

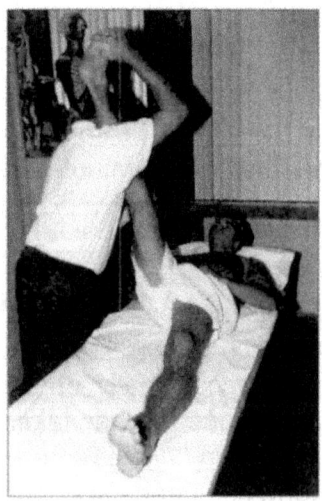
Muscle length test - biceps femoris/triceps surae.

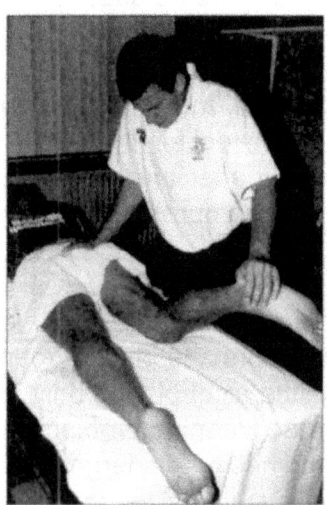
Resistance test - biceps femoris.

Palpation - palpable dell.

RECOVERY

Phase 1 = inflammation phase

Therapy during the first 48 hours:
- Partial immobilization with compression bandage.
- Ice application for 15 minutes, twice daily.
- Walk with crutches plus 15 kg load. The weight must be supported on the right, with a full movement of the right foot without pain. This is fine and is practiced several times daily for a few minutes at a time. The main purpose is to keep addressing the coordination of the hamstrings during functioning (walking).
- Mobilization of the metatarsophalangeal joint (MTP 1) via traction/lateral motion and roll and glide techniques.
- Mobilization of right SIJ by means of manipulation.

Phase 2 = proliferation phase

Therapy day 3 to day 21 post trauma

Purpose:
- To optimize the muscle length of the hamstrings and quadriceps femoris.
- Recovery of the balance of strength between quadriceps femoris and hamstring group.
- To optimize the metabolism.
- Stimulation of strength endurance with an aerobic, fitness character.
- Coordination conditioning.
- To optimize the walking pattern.

Methods used during days 3 to 10 post trauma (p.t.):
- Stimulating massage M. triceps surae.
- Day 3 to day 5 p.t.: 6 minutes cycling, 50 Watt, pedal frequency 70.
- From day 6 p.t.: 10 minutes cycling, 75 Watt, pedal frequency 70.
- Stretching hamstrings with the aid of hold-relax technique and various starting positions, both over the hip and over the knee, with active stretching impulse from the antagonist (m. quadriceps femoris).

	Repetitions	Sets	Resistance (lbs.)	Break (sec.)
Day 3 p.t.	25	4		60
Day 4 p.t.	25	4	2	60
Day 5 p.t.	30	4	2	60
Day 6 p.t.	35	4	2	60
Day 7 p.t.	40	4	2	60
Day 8 p.t.	30	4	4	60
Day 9 p.t.	35	4	4	60
Day 10 p.t.	40	4	4	60

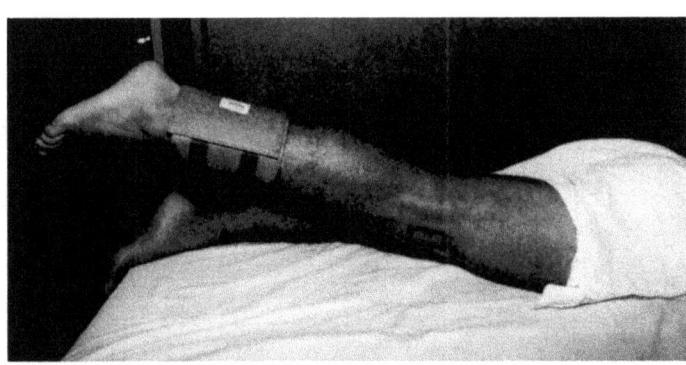

Conditioning the hamstrings in an open chain - dynamically over the hip.

Leg curls lying face down possible from day 5 p.t.:

	Repetitions	Sets	Resistance (lbs.)	Break (sec.)
Day 5 p.t.	25	4		60
Day 6 p.t.	25	4	1	60
Day 7 p.t.	25	4	2	60
Day 8 p.t.	30	4	2	60

Conditioning the **hamstrings** in an open chain, dynamically, over the hip (extension) and isometrically over the knee:
From day 9 p.t., the hamstring curl is carried out sitting up, also with the emphasis on strength endurance. A repetition maximum (RM) is determined via the left leg: RM = 100 lbs.

	Repetitions	Sets	Resistance (lbs.)	Break (sec.)
Day 9 p.t.	20	4	30	60
Day 10 p.t.	25	4	30	60

The muscle length test indicates that the SLR (straight leg raise) no longer provokes pain in the hamstrings. This is a precondition for conditioning the hamstrings while sitting:

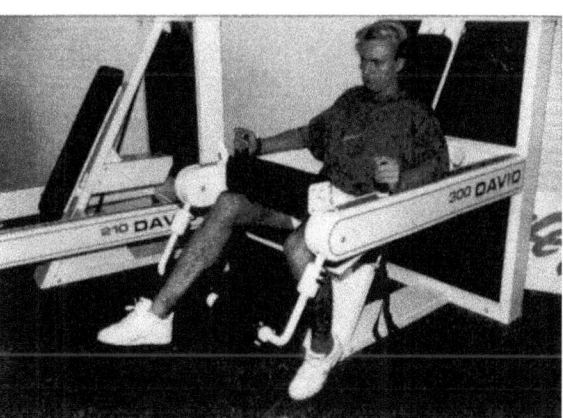

It is typical in this phase that strength endurance is addressed by means of numerous repetitions with relatively light resistance (20 to 40 repetitions at 20 to 40% of 1 RM). In connection with the transfer to functional exercises, conditioning is also carried out in closed chains as well as in the open chain described above. After the hamstring curl, the patient walks for 2 minutes before progressing to the following items. Pain-free walking is possible from day 6 p.t.

Leg press: RM left =160 lbs.

	Repetitions	Sets	Resistance (lbs.)	Break (sec.)
Day 3 p.t.	25	4	40	60
Day 4 p.t.	25	4	40	60
Day 5 p.t.	30	4	40	60
Day 6 p.t.	35	4	40	60
Day 7 p.t.	40	4	50	60
Day 8 p.t.	30	4	50	60
Day 9 p.t.	35	4	50	60
Day 10 p.t.	40	4	50	60

Calf raises (strength training for calf muscle) using 50% of the body weight (=70 lbs.)

	Repetitions	Sets	Resistance (lbs.)	Break (sec.)
Day 6 p.t.	20	4	70	60
Day 7 p.t.	20	4	70	60
Day 8 p.t.	25	4	70	60
Day 9 p.t.	25	4	70	60
Day 10 p.t.	25	4	70	60

After the specific strength training, walking is practiced **on the treadmill**. It is essential that the patient can walk symmetrically. The swing of the stride leg and the heel-to-toe placement of the foot are the same on the right and left at walking pace.

	Distance (m)	Speed (km/h)
Day 6 p.t.	500	4
Day 7 p.t.	750	4
Day 8 p.t.	1000	4
Day 9 p.t.	1000	4
Day 10 p.t.	1500	4

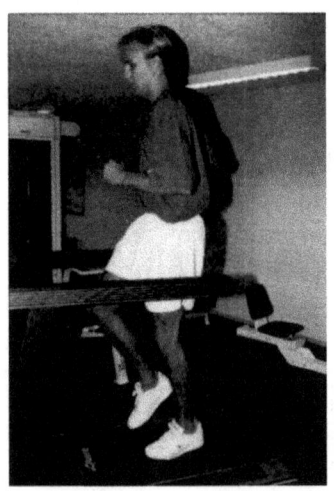

Subsequently the treatment is completed by stretching the hamstrings and the M. triceps. From day 10 to 14 p.t., the injury in the hamstrings has closed up completely. This means that sufficient new muscle fibers (fibroblasts) have been formed. The third week p.t. sees the introduction of aquajogging, walking exercises and steps. All of these are remedial exercises, with the initial focus on the coordination of the various parts. **Aquajogging** is carried out in a calm tempo, with good conscious control of the walking action. Later in the week the fitness (aerobic) aspect is addressed during this exercise. Walking practice is carried out in a 1.2 meter deep pool over a length of 20 meters. The following sequence has been chosen:

	Exercise time (min.)	Heart rate (beats/min.)
Day 16 p.t.	10	160
Day 17 p.t.	12	160
Day 18 p.t.	14	160
Day 19 p.t.	16	160
Day 20 p.t.	18	160
Day 21 p.t.	20	160

Aquajogging over lengths of 25 meters. Depending on the purpose of the exercise, a given heart rate can be selected if a heart monitor is worn.

From day 11 p.t., **isokinetic strength training** is carried out in the mornings to provide a specific conditioning stimulus to the damaged hamstring group. Initially the exercises are carried out at submaximal intensity for familiarization (raising confidence) with the hamstring action (knee flexion).
The protocol for day 11 p.t. was as follows:

Cybex setup for concentric hamstring strength exercises.

Repetitions	Resistance (°/sec.)	Break (sec.)
15	270	45
12	240	45
10	210	45
8	180	45
5	150	45

This exercise is prescribed on alternate days and is increased in the 3rd week p.t. to loads of between 300° (/second (20 repetitions) up to 90° (/sec (3 repetitions). Conditioning is carried out in pyramid form:

90°/sec --- 3 Reps.
120°/sec ----- 5 Reps.
150°/sec --------- 8 Reps.
180°/sec ------------- 10 Reps.
210°/sec ---------------- 12 Reps.
240°/sec ------------------- 15 Reps.
270°/sec ------------------------ 18 Reps.
300°/sec ------------------------------ 20 Reps.

This form of conditioning is always followed by functional exercises: aquajogging, walking on the treadmill or steps. This is in connection with the transfer that has to be made. This is important both for the nerve/muscle control (=proprioception) and for straightening (stretching/contracting) the 'new' (repaired) muscle tissue.

Phase 3 = remodeling phase/functional phase

Therapy during week 3 p.t. to week 8 p.t.
In view of the fact that, from day 21 p.t., this patient can carry out conditioning at full strength (90°/second), this quality is also introduced into the other strength conditioning exercises. The criterion is that there should be no pain when stretching and no resistance pain during isokinetic training (Cybex). After three weeks p.t., the hamstring injury has enough tractive strength to warrant increasing the exercise load. The hamstrings and the quadriceps are tested in both thighs, using the Cybex 6000, to get a picture of the various strength components (maximum strength, fast strength and strength endurance). An imbalance (20%) is found in the quadriceps of the right leg. This is why an adapted regime is then followed.

Taking account of the recovery time that applies to maximum strength conditioning (see figure 14.2), the schedule was as follows:

Repetitions	Resistance (lbs.)	Break (sec.)
15	100	90
12	110	90
10	120	90
8	130	90
5	140	90

Day 23 p.t.: **leg press**

Step-ups.

Step-ups: with 40 lbs. dumbbell weights.

Height	Repetitions	Resistance (lbs.)	Break (sec.)
Small Bench	10 (left and right)	40	90
Medium Bench	8 (left and right)	40	90
Highest Bench	5 (left and right)	40	90

This is repeated on day 25 p.t. On day 27 p.t. (= 4th week post trauma), all weights must be increased by 10 lbs.. The same load on day 29 p.t..

Naturally, running exercises are introduced as soon as jogging causes no pain. Work on the treadmill therefore began after day 21 p.t. at 1500 meters and a speed of 9 km. Running is practiced daily and the distance is increased by 20 meters per day. On day 27 p.t., indoor strength conditioning is combined with outdoor running exercises:
- 6 minutes warming up across the width of the pitch;
- 5 minutes stretching for hamstrings/quadriceps/triceps;
- 10 minutes of various types of running: coordination exercises over a distance of 15 meters;
    heel-toeing forwards/backwards;
    skipping forwards/backwards;
    'walking' forwards/backwards, always placing the heel of one foot to the toe of the other pacing sideways/diagonally forwards/diagonally/backwards, always placing the second foot beside the first before taking the next pace; cross-leg steps;
    Zigzag runs forwards/backwards;
    knee-raise jumps.

Heel-toeing

Skipping

Sideward step

Cross-leg step

Knee-raise jumps

Fitness/functional exercises:

Exercise A
- 3 tempo runs over 3/4 of the football pitch in 45 seconds with a break of 90 seconds;
- 3-minute break after the sets, with relative rest: juggling on the spot.

Exercise B
Dribbling with the ball in a 10 x 10 meter space, making longitudinal and transverse runs (see Fig. 14.4). A good speed must be maintained for dribbling. Each series comprises 3 x 45 seconds of work and 90 seconds of active rest.

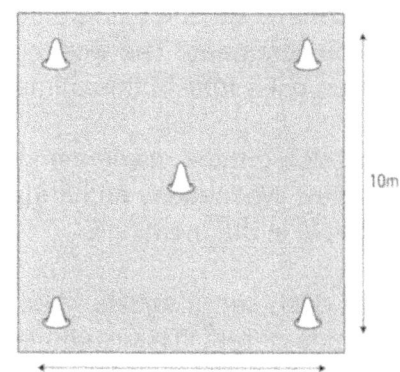

Figure 14.4: *Dribbling is practiced in a 10 by 10 meter square during the functional phase.*

Dribbling in a square measuring 10 x 10 meters.

Finally, 20 minutes of various soccer exercises without running, such as passing and shooting and controlling the ball. Work must be carried out alternately with the right and left leg and the kicking distance must be varied (5/10/15 meters). The purpose of these exercises is to regain feeling (= proprioception).

Finally, run the length of the pitch twice at a steady pace and stretch the hamstrings / quadriceps / calf muscles / adductors. The training session takes a total of 50 minutes. This training load is applied on alternate days in week 4 p.t., reaching a total duration of 60 minutes by the end of the week. Exercise B is adjusted (exercise C) in the final training session of this week.

Exercise C
Work is carried out in a square and in the same directions. The physiotherapist/coach stands at the intersection of the diagonals as a lay-off player. He can also be viewed as a

Repetitions	Resistance (lbs.)	Break (sec.)
12	60	90
10	70	90
8	80	90
6	90	90
4	100	90
3	110	90
1	120	90

fifth cone. A second ball is outside the square. The player must continue with this second ball on command. The work rhythm is again 45 seconds with 90 seconds of rest. This is carried out a total of three times.

In week 5 p.t. the maximum strength of the hamstrings and quadriceps is addressed on Monday, Wednesday and Friday. Squats are done with a bar and weights on the pyramid principle in the mornings.

After each set of squats, there are 10 seconds of dribbling on the spot followed by 90 seconds of rest. This is carried out twice. In the afternoon (3 hours later), a session of ply-ometric exercises is held outdoors. The purpose is to rapidly alternate eccentric and concentric muscle work and to condition maximum strength. This principle is repeated in all the exercises.

The introduction to the afternoon training session has already been described in week 3 p.t. Subsequently the following exercises have to be completed:

Exercise A
5 jumps off a bench. A total of 3 sets of 5 jumps have to be completed, with 90 seconds of active rest (juggling with the ball) after each series. Exercise A is followed by 3 minutes of active rest: the physiotherapist/coach passes the ball to the player from a distance of 5 to 10 meters. The player keeps the ball in the air 3 times and passes it back immediately. In this way a large number of ball contacts are completed on the spot.

Jump-down from a bench.

Exercise B
Each jump-down is immediately followed by a jump-up (= eccentric/concentric action in hamstrings and quadriceps) with a short moment of contact, followed by an acceleration of 2 to 3 meters. A total of 3 series of 5 jumps/accelerations are made. Between each set, juggling with the ball takes place for 90 seconds. Exercise B is followed by 3 minutes of active rest: passing/shooting over a distance of 10 meters. The focus is on controlling and passing the ball at speed.

Exercise C
After each jump-up/jump-down, there is an acceleration of 2 to 3 meters forwards, 2 to 3 meters backwards and another 6 meters forwards. This is done 5 times per set.

A jump-down followed by a jump-up.

Here, too, the ball is juggled between the series. After exercise C the player must stand on the spot and kick the ball back and forth with the physiotherapist/coach.

Exercise D
Speed run (fast strength) at 90/100%: 8 to 10 seconds with a flying start. This is done 3 times with an interval of 60 seconds of active rest (dribbling).

The total training session lasts 55 minutes. The session must be completed as described in week 3 p.t.

As already mentioned, this conditioning is repeated on alternate days this week (Mon., Wed., Fri.), whereby the third session before the weekend (which is a rest period) is completed with more emphasis on converting maximum strength to explosive and fast strength. One way to do this, for example, is by carrying out the accelerations described in exercise C in a zigzag formation:
- 2 to 3 meters left, diagonally forward;
- 2 to 3 meters backward;
- 4 to 5 meters right, diagonally forward;
- 4 to 5 meters backward;
- 6 meters right, forward;
- 6 meters backward.

Active recovery is always necessary between successive series.

Exercise D is as follows:
5 jump-ups with the left leg from a standing start, followed by a maximal sprint of 10 to 12 seconds in a zigzag pattern.

Conditioning on Monday, Wednesday and Friday is anaerobic lactic with the focus on converting maximum strength to explosive and fast strength. On the other two days of conditioning (Tuesday and Thursday), exercises are carried out as described in week 3 p.t.

The Cybex-test is repeated on the Monday of week 6 p.t. It is obvious that the strength imbalance in maximum strength has almost vanished (4%). The functional (= soccer) strength is intensified this week during outdoor conditioning, with the aim of being able to join in group training sessions from week 7.

On Monday, Tuesday and Friday, the training sessions are increased to 75 minutes. The exercises C and D as described in week 6 p.t. are adjusted.

Exercise C
The ball must be headed during each jump-up. The focus is on the height in the backward direction. The coach throws the ball behind the player. This action is followed by the familiar running pattern (see week 6 p.t.).

Exercise D
As in week 6 p.t., the sprint is in zigzag form. However, this is preceded by 5 headers and completed by shooting at goal. This is done 3 times per set. There are 90 seconds of active rest (juggling with the ball) between each set.
The anaerobic lactic conditioning exercises (see week 4 p.t.) are carried out on Tuesday and Thursday. The load times are increased to 1 minute. There are still 90-second rests. Finally, strength in the challenge is conditioned in 1 against 1 situations on a 10 x 10 meters pitch with small goals. This drill ensures constant pressure on the player (lots of actions) in the small area. One minute of work must always be succeeded by 2 minutes of rest. Total number of repetitions: 5.

In week 7 p.t., the player can train fully with the group. It is advisable to do this initially for 1 week. At the end of the week, he can progress to 45-minute match time in the second eleven or in a friendly match with the first eleven. After two weeks of group training sessions, he should be fully fit and able to handle a full match (competition). All in all, the player will be ready to return to group training sessions and competition 6 to 8 weeks after the injury occurred.

The exercises in the functional phase are very soccer specific.

SUMMARY

- The physiotherapist has a number of functions in soccer: treating injuries, setting up preventive rules/measures, and advising on conditioning as well as cooperating with the coach, club doctor, masseur and the group of players.

- The physiotherapist has to do a lot of taping and bandaging prior to a match or training session. In addition, he provides minor treatment to make sure that players are fit to play. It is also important to observe players during warming up.

- During a match or training session, the physiotherapist must observe the play carefully. In this way he can see how injuries occur. This helps him get an initial impression of the type, severity and location of the injury.

- After a match or training session, all complaints and injuries must be recorded and checked. This may be done in cooperation with the doctor.

- If players are to be supported through a period of rehabilitation, the physiotherapist not only needs to be familiar with the laws governing the recovery of connective tissue, but must also be familiar with the physiological principles of the science of conditioning. In addition, he needs to know all about the loads imposed on a soccer player during a match.

- Before rehabilitation can commence, he must have a clear picture of the site, type and severity of the injury. This can be achieved by means of an anamnesis, followed by an examination and a function test.

- The anamnesis is the first interview that the physiotherapist has with the patient. The purpose is to use specific questioning to find out as much as possible about the complaint, the player's medical history and the course of the complaint, the stress to which the player is exposed, his stress tolerance, and his current status.

- During the examination the injury site is viewed but not touched.

- Finally, during the physical function examination, a number of specific tests are used to discover which physical structures are actually causing complaints in specific situations.

- A diagnosis is made on the basis of all this information, and a treatment and rehabilitation plan is subsequently developed.

- The recovery process of connective tissue consists of four phases: the inflammation phase, the proliferation phase, the remodeling phase and the functional phase.

- In general, the inflammation phase is present during the first 48 to 72 hours after the trauma. Inflammation occurs at the site of the injury, for the purpose of 'cleansing' the damaged area to facilitate a good recovery.

- The proliferation phase is the period of 3 days to 3 weeks after the occurrence of the injury. This is the phase in which the damaged tissue is repaired. New tissue cells are produced.

- The remodeling phase starts after around 3 weeks, and slowly merges into the functional phase. In this third phase, the new tissue is organized. The tissue cells are all aligned in the right direction, so that the strength of the total tissue is optimal.

- The functional phase starts when the remodeling phase is complete. The switchover point is difficult to determine, because there is a slow merging of the two phases. During this final phase, the patient can be subjected to functional loads. In the case of soccer players, this means that more use is made of soccer drills, so that the body will slowly start to become reaccustomed to soccer stresses.

INTERVIEW WITH MARC OVERMARS (Arsenal)

Why did you choose to turn to the Dutch Soccer Association for help in recovering from your injury?

The medical section of the Dutch Soccer Association has every facility. It has weight training equipment, a gym and a pool. One of the main reasons is probably the restful atmosphere there. It is often busy and hectic at Ajax and this is not pleasant when you need to recover. In addition, I have often worked with Rob Ouderland in connection with the Dutch national team.

When did you start the rehabilitation process?

My meniscus was repaired in the first week after I was injured. It was discovered that the cruciate ligament was torn. The cruciate ligament operation was not carried out until four weeks later. They waited until the inflammation in my knee had disappeared, and the knee had recovered from the first operation. In this way it was possible to operate on a relatively normal knee. The period of 4 weeks between operations meant that the rehabilitation process only started then.

What exactly did you do in the period between the occurrence of the injury and the operation?

I spent three weeks with the Dutch Soccer Association in Zeist, keeping my general level of fitness up to scratch, so that I would be optimally prepared for surgery. Aquajogging was ideal for me. You can work out without having to put any strain on the injured joint. Obviously it was important that the strength of the muscles around the joint, and the mobility of the joint itself, should be maintained as far as possible. It was also important to keep the knee free of fluid.

Did you start your rehabilitation in Zeist immediately after the second operation?

During the first five weeks, I spent about three hours a day, seven days a week on rehabilitation exercises. Helped by Rob Ouderland, I worked on my recovery on Saturdays and Sundays, too. The first thing on the agenda was a detailed explanation of the short and long-term consequences of my injury, and what I could expect during the coming months. You are made aware of the fact that your own attitude and behavior are of major influence on the progress of your recovery. You need to do a great deal of work on your own, so self-discipline is essential. It was a really difficult period, because I had to walk with crutches and wear a brace on my knee. For example, I was not allowed to drive, and I was very dependent on others.

What exactly did the first phase consist of?

I had to do all manner of strength exercises, such as tensioning my thigh while seated with legs stretched and then lifting my leg. I had to do this face down and on my side, as well. While seated on a bench, I had to press my heel against the bench and draw it towards me before stretching again. This is called 'heel sliding'. I not only had to do strength exercises, but also exercises to keep the joint supple. I had to keep my leg relaxed, while the 'kine-tec' machine bent and stretched the knee. Every two or three hours, I had to apply ice to my knee for 15 minutes. The Cryocraft was often used during this time. This is a cushion filled with water and ice, which is wrapped around the joint. The ice water circulates around the joint, thus cooling it.

Did you have to exercise at home in addition to the program at Zeist?

A schedule was prepared with the aid of Cor van der Hart. I was given an exercise regime describing a block of exercises. This block took two to three hours, and after I had completed it, I had to start again. I completed 4 to 5 blocks a day. The only time I rested was when I was asleep. The rest of the day I was continuously occupied. Although the exercises were simple, they had to be carried out with commitment. I had to spend my every waking hour usefully.

Can you give us an idea of the various phases you went through?

From week 6, I spent five days a week in Zeist, working on my recovery for 5 hours each day. The second phase involved a great deal of cycling, squatting, walking on the treadmill, and light workouts, including work on the Cybex machine. A whole range of stability exercises was included in the program, on the trampoline and the teeter board. I did aquajogging in the deep part of the pool, and I used the shallow part for all manner of walking and running exercises. After 10 weeks, I was allowed to run on the treadmill for the first time. When that was seen to be going well, I headed for the woods where I could practice running on an uneven surface. The third and final phase began after week 14. At that time you are out on the pitch, practicing all sorts of running exercises, but without sudden turns. From week 16, I was allowed to practice with the ball. That is the moment you look forward to. A great deal of work is then carried out involving turns and changes of direction.

How long was your total recovery time in Zeist?

I was in Zeist for a total of six months. When I was able to resume group training in July, I returned to Ajax. This is when things really start - the second phase of recovery. You discover that you are far from being match fit. My first match was against AC Milan on the occasion of the opening of the Amsterdam Arena. During my recovery period, this was the match I had been working towards.

How would you describe the approach and the method of rehabilitation in Zeist?

The strong point of the medical section in Zeist is that you always work under supervision. This means that you get a lot of support. Obviously, you have to do a lot yourself, but there is always a watchful eye, so you are immediately corrected if necessary. You could call it a 'one on one' relationship. In addition, it is quite obvious that they have a great deal of experience in getting soccer players back to the top level. What I liked was the fact that I was allowed to work with the ball at the earliest possible moment.

What were the most difficult times during your recovery period?

There were no really difficult moments, because I knew what had to be done to regain my fitness. When your hobby is your work, you can concentrate fully on regaining fitness. The only thing I disliked was sitting in the bleachers watching Ajax play. That was definitely not for me, so I went to very few matches.

How important was it to be among other soccer players during your rehabilitation period?
Although everyone works individually on his own recovery, it is much nicer to work with a group than alone. You all have something in common - the will to get back to the top level. It is good when you meet each other in league matches later, and see that all the hard work was not in vain.

LITERATURE

1. Sports endued inflammation.
W.B.L. Leadbetter.
ISBN: 0-89203-0372.

2. Connective tissue in rehabilitation
B. van Wingerden.
ISBN: 3-907822-00-5.
Scipro-Verlag.

3. Fysiologie voor Lichamelijke Opvoeding, Sport en Revalidatie.
E.L. Fox en D.K. Mathews.
ISBN: 90-352-1406-4.
De Tijdstroom.

THE AUTHORS

Foppe de Haan (b. 1943) studied at the Dutch Academy of Physical Education, where he qualified as a professional soccer coach. From 1976 to 1996 he was a lecturer at the Dutch National Sports Training Institute, where he taught soccer, general games and the science of conditioning. He also gave coaching courses for the Dutch Soccer Association. From 1971 he coached a number of amateur clubs, and he has worked as youth coach and first-team coach of the Dutch professional club, Heerenveen, since 1985.

Luc van Agt studied at the Dutch Academy of Physical Education in Tilburg, before working for two years as a physical education lecturer. He then studied movement sciences at the Free University of Amsterdam and gained his doctorate in 1987, having specialized in exercise physiology. Since 1989 he has worked for PSV Eindhoven as exercise physiologist and conditioning and rehabilitation coach. As such, he is involved in the planning, content and implementation of training sessions during the preseason preparation period. He also works as an exercise physiologist at the St. Anna hospital in Celdrop, where he has the specific task of coordinating the medical sport center. Before he came to soccer, he was an athletics coach in the fields of sprinting, hurdling and the decathlon. He worked with athletes at the international level.

Dr. Gerard van der Poel (b. 1961) studied movement science at the Free University of Amsterdam in 1989, graduating in exercise physiology. Since then he has worked as an independent advisor. He gives courses, and writes articles on sport, movement and health. Since 1987 he has specialized in the subject of stretching.

Dr. Han Inklaar (b. 1948) was born in Deventer (Netherlands) He studied medicine at the University of Amsterdam. In 1973 he qualified as a doctor. In 1975 he began studying to become a cardiologist. On August 1, 1978, he joined the Dutch Soccer Assoclation at Zeist, where he is still active. In 1987 he joined the medical physiology and sports medicine group at the University of Utrecht as an unpaid scientific researcher. In 1995 he gained his doctorate in medicine. His thesis was entitled The epidemiology of soccer injuries in a new perspective.'

Bert van Lingen (b. 1945) played soccer for the Dutch clubs, Concordia and DHC. After studying at the Dutch National Sports Training Institute, he became assistant to Jan Zwartkruis, the coach of the Dutch military eleven. He worked for Holland Sport, FC Groningen, De Graafschap and NSF, then joined the Dutch Soccer Association in 1979. He was coach to the various national youth teams and was present as assistant coach at the youth World Championship in 1983, the European Championships of 1988, 1992 and 1996, and the World Championships of 1990 and 1994. He has specialized in improving the quality and coaching of youth soccer players. He is also a 'FIFA Instructor.'

Doctor Frits Kessel (b. 1937) studied medicine in Amsterdam and has been employed by the Dutch Soccer Association since July 1968. One year later he was appointed head of the medical section of the Dutch Soccer Association. In his function as a doctor, he accompanied the Dutch national team at the European Championships of 1976, 1980, 1988, 1992 and 1996, and at the World Championships of 1974, 1978, 1990 and 1994.

Rob Ouderland (b. 1958) played professional soccer for four years with F.C. Amsterdam. He also played 1 7 times for the Dutch national amateur eleven, and is still active as a player. While he was with F.C. Amsterdam, Rob Ouderland studied physiotherapy. He graduated in 1980 and then worked for 10 years in a private practice in Amsterdam, where he gained a lot of experience with sport injuries. He specialized in acupuncture and manual therapy. He has worked for the Dutch Soccer Association since September 1, 1989. As the Dutch national team's physiotherapist, he was present at the World Championships of 1990 and 1994 and the European Championships of 1992 and 1996. He is also a part-time lecturer at the Dutch Manual Therapy Education Foundation and has an administrative function in the Dutch Association of Professional Soccer Physiotherapists.

Vera Pauw studied at the Dutch National Sports Training Institute and the Dutch Academy of Physical Education. She is also a qualified coach. She is the captain of the Dutch national women's team, for which she has played since 1983, gaining 81 caps. She has worked for the Dutch Soccer Association since 1986, and has focussed in particular on improving the quality of youth soccer coaching. She has documented the position of girls in youth soccer for the FIFA 'Futuro' project.

Frans Hoek (b. 1956) was born in Hoorn, he studied at the Dutch National Sports Training Institute, qualified as a physical education teacher, and also acquired the Dutch Soccer Association's coaching certificates. A goalkeeper, he played for the Dutch professional team, Volendam, from 1973 to 1985, and was picked for a large number of representative elevens. He also worked as a physical education teacher in the education sector from 1975 to 1989. From 1986 to 1997 he was Ajax Amsterdam's goalkeeping coach, and worked under coaches such as Johan Cruyff, Leo Beenhakker and Louis van Gaal. In this period Ajax won a number of national league championships, Dutch Soccer Association cups, the three European cups, the World Cup and various super cups. Frans Hoek is the author of three books on goalkeeping and has produced an intructional video series for goalkeepers "The Soccer Goalkeeper". He has been a lecturer for the Dutch Soccer Association since 1980, organizing goalkeeping promotion days, clinics and seminars over the whole world. In 1995 he became an instructor for UEFA as well as FIFA. At the moment he is the goalkeeping coach of FC Barcelona (Spain).

Dr. Raymond Verjheijen (b. 1971) graduated as a movement scientist in 1995. During his studies, he specialized in exercise physiology in relation to soccer. As his doctoral project he studied the physical workload of soccer players in the English Premier League. During his 18-month stay in Liverpool, he also acquired his Diploma in Science and Football. He currently works for the Dutch Soccer Association in Zeist as a researcher, and in the faculty of movement sciences of the Free University of Amsterdam. He also arranges lectures and seminars on soccer fitness, writes articles and carries out contract research in the field of soccer. He is editor of the 'Soccer and Science' column in the Dutch periodical 'De Voetbaltrainer.'

NOTES

NOTES

NOTES

NOTES

www.ingramcontent.com/pod-product-compliance
Lightning Source LLC
Chambersburg PA
CBHW080528170426
43195CB00016B/2501